Inside the Drama-House

Inside the Drama-House

Rāma Stories and Shadow Puppets in South India

Stuart Blackburn

UNIVERSITY OF CALIFORNIA PRESS

Berkeley / Los Angeles / London

University of California Press
Berkeley and Los Angeles, California

University of California Press, Ltd.
London, England

Parts of this book were published in earlier versions.
Parts of chapter 4: "Descent into Performance: Rāma Avatār in a Folk Tradition of Kerala," in *Rāmāyaṇa and Rāmāyaṇas*, ed. Monika Thiel-Horstmann (Wiesbaden: Otto Harrassowitz Verlag, 1991), pp. 69–83. Reproduced by permission of Otto Harrassowitz Verlag. "Hanging in the Balance: Rāma in the Shadow Puppet Theater of Kerala," in *Gender, Genre, and Power in South Asian Expressive Traditions*, ed. Arjun Appadurai, Frank J. Korom, and Margaret A. Mills (Philadelphia: University of Pennsylvania Press, 1991), pp. 379–94. Reproduced by permission of the University of Pennsylvania Press.
Parts of chapter 6: "Epic Transmission and Adaptation," in *Boundaries of the Text: Epic Performances in South and Southeast Asia*, ed. Joyce Burkhalter Flueckiger and Laurie J. Sears (Ann Arbor: Center for South and Southeast Asian Studies, University of Michigan, 1991), pp. 105–26. Reproduced by permission of the University of Michigan. "Epic Transmission and Adaptation: A Folk Rāmāyaṇa in South India," in *Heroic Process: Form, Function, and Fantasy in Folk Epic*, ed. Bo Almqvist, Seámas Ó Catháin, and Pádraig Ó Héalaí (Dublin: Glendale Press, 1987), pp. 569–90.
Chapter 7: "Creating Conversations: The Rāma Story as Puppet Play in Kerala," in *Many Rāmāyaṇas: The Diversity of a Narrative Tradition in South Asia*, ed. Paula Richman (Berkeley: University of California Press, 1991), pp. 156–72.

Library of Congress Cataloging-in-Publication Data

Blackburn, Stuart H.
Inside the drama-house : Rāma stories and shadow puppets in South India / Stuart Blackburn.
p. cm.
Includes bibliographical references and index.
ISBN 0-520-20205-8 (alk. paper). — ISBN 0-520-20206-6 (pbk. : alk. paper)
1. Shadow shows—India—Kerala. 2. Shadow puppets—India—Kerala. 3. Rāma (Hindu deity) in literature. 4. Kampar, 9th century. Rāmāyaṇam. I. Title.
PN1979.S5B48 1996
791.5'3'095483—dc20 95-10678

Printed in the United States of America

9 8 7 6 5 4 3 2 1

The paper used in this publication meets the minimum requirements of American National Standard for Information Sciences—Permanence of Paper for Printed Library Materials, ANSI Z39.48-1984. ♾

I know people say these stories are only imagination, but I say they never deceive. They tell truths—one only has to know what is story and what is true.

Natesan Pillai, in performance

Contents

LIST OF ILLUSTRATIONS ix

ACKNOWLEDGMENTS xi

A NOTE ON TRANSLITERATION xiii

MAPS xv

Chapter 1
An Absent Audience 1

Chapter 2
Rāma Stories and Puppet Plays 22

Chapter 3
Ambivalent Accommodations: Bhakti and Folk Hinduism 39

Chapter 4
The Death of Sambukumāraṉ: Kāma and Its Defense 59

Chapter 5
Killing Vāli: Rāma's Confession 79

Chapter 6
Rāvaṇa's First Defeat: The Puppeteers' Oral Commentary 95

Chapter 7
The Death of Indrajit: Creating Conversations 134

Chapter 8
Rāma's Coronation: The Limits of Restoration 194

APPENDIX A: THREE SAMPLES OF THE PUPPETEERS' COMMENTARY IN TRANSLITERATION 241

APPENDIX B: SAMPLE COMMENTARY IN TAMIL SCRIPT 243

APPENDIX C: MAIN CHARACTERS IN THE PUPPETEERS' RĀMA STORY 244

NOTES 247

GLOSSARY 267

BIBLIOGRAPHY 271

INDEX 287

Illustrations

Maps

Following page xiv

1. India: Region of the Kerala shadow puppet play
2. Sites of the shadow puppet play in Kerala

Photographs

Following page 54

1. Natesan Pillai, senior puppeteer, at home in 1989.
2. The drama-house at Mannur in 1989.
3. Krishnan Kutty and his troupe performing the Śūrpaṇakhā episode, 1986, Cherpalachery.
4. Lakṣmaṇa and Śūrpaṇakhā face each other, 1986, Cherpalachery.
5. Rāma, Lakṣmaṇa, and Sītā march toward the Godavari River, 1986, Cherpalachery.
6. Krishnan Kutty's son holds up a puppet, 1986, Cherpalachery.

Acknowledgments

In 1986 I received a grant from the Fulbright-Hayes Program and spent six months in Kerala, India, recording performances on audiocassette and interviewing puppeteers. Another six months of recording in 1989 completed my fieldwork, although brief trips in 1988 and 1990 enabled me to track down missing information. A generous grant from the Translation Program at the National Endowment for the Humanities supported the translation work and library research from 1986 to 1989. Preparation of the final manuscript was assisted by a grant from the School of Oriental and African Studies, University of London, where the maps were prepared. For the support of these organizations I am grateful.

Some material in this book has appeared in another form in *Heroic Process: Form, Function and Fantasy in Folk Epic*, ed. Bo Almqvist et al. (Glendale Press, 1987), in *Gender, Genre and Power in South Asian Expressive Traditions*, ed. A. Appadurai et al. (University of Pennsylvania Press, 1991), and in *Many Rāmāyaṇas: The Diversity of a Narrative Tradition in South Asia*, ed. Paula Richman (University of California Press, 1991). I thank the publishers for permission to use this material in a revised form.

During the long years of working on this book, I benefited from the insights and encouragement of many friends and colleagues. In particular, David Shulman and Kirin Narayan carefully read drafts of this book and offered numerous, detailed suggestions for its improvement; Kausalya Hart also patiently answered questions about thorny passages in Kampaṉ. Many, many people helped me during my work in Kerala.

Among the local scholars who assisted me, I owe special thanks to A. K. Nambiar for leading me through difficult passages in Malayalam and to M. G. Sashibooshan for guiding me to isolated Rāma temples in Palghat District. Among the puppeteers, I especially want to thank Natesan Pillai, Annamalai Pulavar, Krishnan Kutty Pulavar, and the brothers Gangakaran and Prabakaran; to dozens of others who allowed me to tape-record their performances and pester them about their puppets, families, and texts, I am also grateful. To those puppeteers and to their Rāma story inside the drama-house this book is dedicated.

Berkeley and London, 1994

A Note on Transliteration

Transliterations of words from Indian languages, primarily Tamil and Malayalam, follow scholarly conventions for those languages. Indic terms familiar to English readers appear in their Anglicized form (such as dharma, karma). Place names (Palghat) and names of some persons (Krishnan Kutty) appear without diacritical marks. Names of some story characters appear in an approximate phonetic rendering of the puppeteers' speech ("Jāmbuvāṉ" instead of "Cāmpavāṉ," for example).

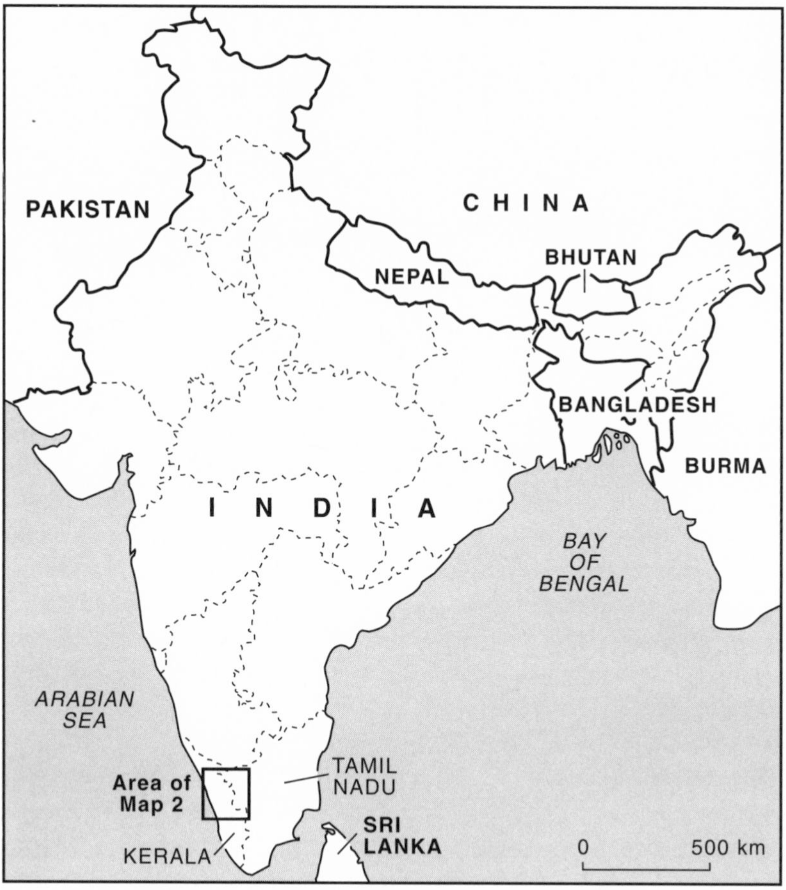

Map 1. India: Region of the Kerala shadow puppet play

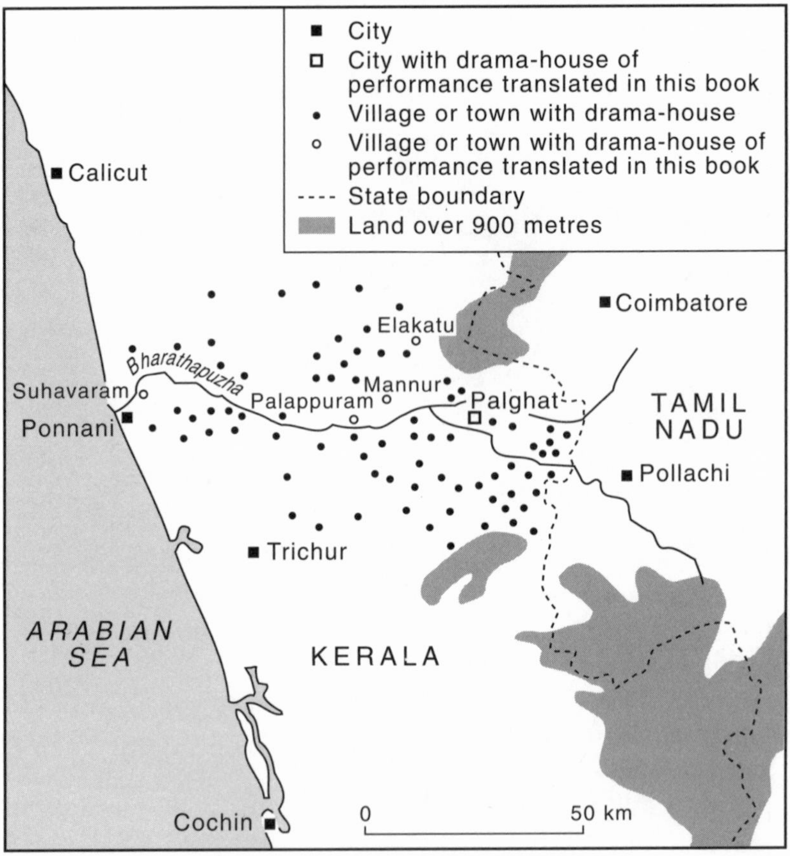

Map 2. Sites of the shadow puppet play in Kerala

CHAPTER I

An Absent Audience

This book describes the performance of a medieval text as shadow puppet play in a small corner of south India. The text is the *Kamparāmāyaṇam*, a Rāma story composed in Tamil by Kampaṉ, at the Chola court of Tanjore, probably in the twelfth century.[1] The puppet play is today performed in the Palghat region of Kerala primarily by Tamil-speaking puppeteers in temple festivals dedicated to the goddess Bhagavati. The recontextualization of this epic text, eight centuries after its composition, into a new medium, in a rural, ritual setting and a new linguistic context, is the central theme of this book. Although I will emphasize the Kerala puppeteers' particular telling of the Rāma story, especially through translations of their performances, I will also take up the wider issues of audience interaction, the interpretive role of oral commentary, and the intertextuality of Rāma stories. In this initial chapter, I begin with audiences and then provide an introduction to Kampaṉ's Rāma story in Kerala. Imagine that (a medieval) Shakespeare was thought to exist only in libraries, until a performance tradition with local commentary was discovered somewhere in Wales; then add that the players perform for an absent audience; and you have the Kerala shadow puppet play.

Even if it had no relation to the medieval Tamil epic, the Kerala tradition is important because Indian shadow puppetry is little known both inside and outside the subcontinent. Like Buddhism, the art was thought to have vanished from its Indian birthplace as it migrated and flourished elsewhere in Asia. But Indologists debated whether references in old Sanskrit texts proved the existence of an ancient shadow puppet play; if such a tradition had existed, where was it now?[2] The answer came in 1935 when a German scholar saw a performance in Karnataka and, in an uncanny coincidence, an American journalist stumbled on another in Kerala. The vanishing act had been an illusion, and we know that Indian shadow puppetry is performed in Kerala, Karnataka, Tamil Nadu, and Andhra Pradesh, and until recently, in Maharashtra and Orissa. The Kerala tradition was known to the outside world only by a handful of essays until 1986, when Dr. F. Seltmann published his excellent monograph.

Known as *tōl pāva kūttu* ("leather puppet play"), the shadow puppet theater in Kerala is never performed for one night, or for anything less than eight nights in succession. Night after night, for ten or twenty or even sixty consecutive nights, two or three men sit inside a small building and manipulate painted, perforated leather puppets, throwing shadows on a white cloth screen, chanting Kampaṉ's verses and explicating them in a rambling commentary that is generated both by convention and the predilections of individual puppeteers. How these various pieces of the tradition—shadow puppetry, epic story, commentary, and festival—come together in this performance of a Tamil text in Kerala took me many years to understand, for the Rāma story is multiple, the Kampaṉ text vast, and the series of overnight performances monumental. Any single book intending to cover all these topics fully would fail (a translation of the performance sequence itself would exceed a thousand printed pages). The puppeteers claim it takes ten years to acquire the knowledge necessary for a skillful performance, warning that attempting to explain a verse "without first studying the old books is like a man trying to bind a wild elephant with a wet lotus stalk."[3] A few lotus stalks have surely slithered through my hands in the past decade, but I believe that enough of the elephant has been bound for me to write this book about a text and its new audiences.

Nothing, however, had prepared me for my first full shadow-puppet-play performance, in January 1984, and had someone told me that I would spend the next ten years attempting to understand it, I might not have made the trip. As I hurtled along narrow, dark roads toward the village of Suhavaram in central Kerala in a taxi with five puppeteers who were to perform there that night, my thoughts ran on a single track—"How much sleep will I lose? When will I return in the morning? I said I'd be back around midnight, but they've now told me that it will be daybreak before we even leave this place I've yet to see." The puppeteers were asleep in the rumbling auto—Krishnan Kutty, the senior puppeteer; his two sons, aged sixteen and eighteen; and two assistants, Sankara Nayar and Narayana Nayar.

I met Krishnan Kutty in 1978 when I wandered into a large auditorium in Bangalore, the computer capital of modern India, during a national festival of shadow puppetry; I was supposed to be attending a Fulbright Conference for grantees, but shadow puppets seemed more interesting. Stumbling onto his spirited performance in that artificial setting, I was intrigued, for it seemed that the story had something to do with Rāma—in Tamil, in Kerala. Tamil I knew, from my first trip to India in 1970–72 as a Peace Corps volunteer (when I had to learn the language well enough to speak it faster than my friends spoke English), from later research trips, and from graduate school at Berkeley. Kerala, too, was familiar to me since I had done field work on its border with Tamil Nadu for an earlier book, but the Malayali temple festivals, food, and language were unfamiliar. Of the Rāma story, I knew only the barest outline—his exile, the loss of his wife, her recapture from Rāvaṇa in Lanka, and something about Hanumān, the monkey who aided Rāma. More than this, all those other names and episodes, which everyone else seemed to know, blurred into a jumble of sounds and kinship relations. But shadow puppetry in Kerala—wasn't that the premier performing art of Java and Bali? This intrigued me, so I scribbled down a few notes and returned to the Fulbright meeting, full of questions that I failed to pursue until, six years later, my wife and I visited her son, who was training as a Kathakaḷi dancer in central Kerala. Michael casually mentioned that some puppeteers lived nearby; the next day I found Krishnan Kutty's home, and he immediately invited me to the performance that very night at Suhavaram.

The taxi, puppeteers still snoring, reached Suhavaram about ten o'clock. Suhavaram is a small village of Tiyar agricultural workers and a few Nambutiri Brahmins in the far western reaches of the puppet-play region, on the banks of the Ponani River, not far from the town of the same name, where the river flows into the Arabian Sea. When we arrived, it was pitch-dark and chilly, but the large area in front of the temple was buzzing with activity, hissing with bright kerosene lamps, and booming with loud temple music. Climbing out of the taxi, I was drawn to a performance of Ōṭṭaṉ Tuḷḷal, in which a dancer recites mythic stories in Malayalam, but my companions showed no interest: "Sure, have a look," they said begrudgingly and then lifted the huge woven basket containing their puppets from the trunk of the taxi and lugged it toward the drama-house (*kūttu māṭam*).

Standing off to the side, at an angle to the Bhagavati temple, the small drama-house did not catch my attention at first; from a distance, anyone might mistake its red-tiled roof, wooden rafters, and white-washed walls for a modest home or shop. Only the long, open front, where the white cloth screen hangs down at night, marks this oblong structure as a stage for the shadow puppet play. Raised on a platform and reached by a few steps, its three walls stand six feet high at the perimeter and fifteen feet high in the center where the rafters peak. Platform, steps, walls, and floor are all made of hard-baked mud covered with lime paste and sometimes decorated with red vertical stripes, like a Viṣṇu temple. In front, the screen hangs down to the floor, which extends a few feet beyond the screen. Puppets appear on the screen only during the annual festival, which is held sometime between January and May, but the drama-house is seldom idle even when no performances are held—in the months of summer rain, in the autumn, and in the brief winter. With the cloth screen rolled up, a bamboo wicker screen wedged in front to keep out birds, and the puppet-play paraphernalia stored in the dry rafters above, the drama-house becomes a place where men gather to smoke and talk and sleep. A few drama-houses serve as public libraries during the off-season.

That night at Suhavaram, I watched from outside the drama-house as Krishnan Kutty and his assistants stepped up inside the small building. One of his sons sat off to the side of the stage with a tiny kerosene lamp and a battered school notebook while a steady trickle of people approached, gave their names, mentioned problems they wished to have alleviated, and pledged donations (invariably one rupee each), which information the young many duly entered in neat writing in the notebook. Later, sometime during the performance, the puppeteers would interrupt their narration to read every one of those names and sing a verse for each one-rupee patron, invoking the blessings of goddess Bhagavati and Śrī Rāma on their behalf.[4] That night the book held over one hundred names (one person may enter many names), and several hundred is not unusual; once, on the night of Indrajit's death, which signals the fall of Lanka, I saw a book with more than three thousand names.

About 11:00 P.M., when the Ōṭṭaṉ Tuḷḷal performance was completed and most of the crowd had gone home to sleep, preparations for the puppet play began in earnest. Krishnan Kutty, the *pulavar* (poet-scholar), was summoned to the temple, where the oracle-priest (*veḷic-*

cappāṭu) offered him a new white cloth and two brass vessels of raw rice; wearing only his clean white *vēsti*[5] and a towel across his shoulders, the senior puppeteer walked three times around these gifts, picked them up, and returned to the drama-house, where the cloth (*ayya puṭavai*) was fastened to the roof with rope, rolled down, and secured to the floor of the drama-house with heavy stones while the vessels were set in place for the Gaṇeśa *pūjā* to follow. Inside the now fully enclosed and windowless drama-house, I felt claustrophobic (my thoughts raced back to the baseball dugouts and underground forts I had inhabited as a boy). Awkwardly stepping over and around the five puppeteers, I found a corner from which to watch them prepare the "stage." They lowered a long plank of jackwood from the rafters, positioned it to hang by ropes very close to the cloth screen, and placed on it twenty-one half-shells of coconut; then they filled the shells with coconut oil and slipped in wicks, which they had just made by rolling bits of cotton thread into thin strips. At first the coconut-shell lamps remained unlit while experienced hands swiftly selected the Gaṇeśa puppet and a pair of Brahmin puppets from among dozens lying tangled in the enormous woven basket. Narayana Nayar fastened these puppets onto the screen with thick thorns and chuckled while I fumbled around trying to hang my microphone from the rafters so that it dangled directly in front of the wooden bench on which the puppeteers would sit during performance. When the puppets that would appear later that opening night—Rāma, Lakṣmaṇa, Sītā, Śūrpaṇakhā, a few nameless demons—were extracted from the basket and stacked to one side, everything was ready. A tray of glasses was poked through a corner of the cloth screen and passed around; slowly we sipped the milky, sweet tea, until, without warning, the puppeteers lay down on mats and fell asleep. I looked around the dark drama-house, realizing that, over the course of the weeks that the puppeteers perform, this would be their nighttime home and, if their village is farther than an hour's bus ride from the festival, their home during the day as well. This small space, soon to be alive with lights and puppets and epic events, is the world of the Kerala puppeteers.

From inside, the puppeteers look out on an open area and, off to one side, the Bhagavati temple, whose separation from the drama-house is more than physical. Although the puppet play is performed as a ritual for the goddess in her festival, it is kept at a distance, like the secular dramas performed on a wooden stage erected in another corner of the open space; events of higher ritual status, however, such as Kathakaḷi, Ōṭṭaṉ Tuḷḷal, or Cākkyār Kūthu, are performed inside the temple compound. The puppet play is also slighted in billing, for it begins only after the other performances (modern dramas as well as classical arts) have been completed, often at midnight or one o'clock in the morning. Watching from their perch on the stage, the puppeteers comment on these rival performances with jealous contempt—"They pander to the public, they require no intellect"—but no one inside the drama-house would complain if the puppet performance also commanded thousands of spectators. Kathakaḷi, whose elaborately costumed dancers are fast becoming an internationally recognized icon of Indian culture, receives most of the puppeteers' scorn: "Stamp your feet—bham! wham!—and you're off to Paris!" In truth, the numerous trips made by Kathakaḷi troupes to culture festivals all over the world have wounded the puppeteers' pride, for only one puppet troupe has ever traveled beyond Kerala. The drama-houses, permanent yet separate, stand as a monument to the ambivalent status of the puppet play, of Kampaṉ's courtly text in a Kerala village festival.

That first night at Suhavaram I did not feel at home in that dark, cramped space, where everyone but me was asleep. "When will the performance begin?" I wanted to know. Frustrated, and with little else to do, I double-checked my batteries and wrote more "context" notes in my black binder. Then, suddenly, everyone stirred, awakened by the *ceṇḍa* drums played in a procession advancing from the temple. Leading this nightly assemblage of musicians, temple-lamp bearer, officials, and patrons, the oracle-priest marched with measured steps that shook the bells on his ankles, on his belt, and on his curved sword held high above his head. His bright red skirt and ice-white hair shining in the kerosene lamps held high by servants, he became possessed by Bhagavati, but his prophetic shrieks were barely audible over the big-barrel drums booming behind him. Three times the procession wheeled in a great circle in front of the drama-house, and then the oracle-priest halted, executed a short, jerky dance, and spoke for the goddess to the small crowd gathered for this minor manifestation of divinity. Still shaking and uttering cries, he showered them with rice and shouted a blessing for tonight's sponsors and anyone who came forth with a problem.[6] Peering out from under the white cloth screen, we watched him make a final offering of rice to Krishnan Kutty, who then received the heavy brass temple lamp (*tūkku viḷakku*) and ducked back under the screen. When that lamp was hung inside the drama-house to mark the ritual transfer from temple to puppet play, the procession dispersed, leaving only the sponsors and a few hangers-on.

Inside the drama-house, Krishnan Kutty conducted a small *pūjā* for the Gaṇeśa puppet pinned on the screen. Placing the rice, flowers, incense, and a coconut on a banana leaf on the floor, he quickly chanted a verse, lit the incense, and waved it around the static puppet while the other puppeteers prostrated themselves in front of it. Each man then touched the feet of the puppeteers senior to him, as a sign of respect, until, finally, Krishnan Kutty touched the Gaṇeśa puppet.[7] After a puppeteer unhooked the temple lamp and lit the cotton wicks in the shell-lamps, I saw the puppets clearly for the first time in their bold colors, casting filigree shadows on the screen.[8] Now the performance began, as on every night, with a little uninspired drumming to which the puppeteers added a barely audible chant that gradually expanded into a series of devotional songs sung by the two Brahmin puppets flanking Gaṇeśa on the cloth screen.[9] These Brahmin puppets, the masters of ceremonies for this introduction ("Song of the Drama-House"), danced jerkily around the god and rang bells in imitation of the oracle-priest. Abruptly, one quoted a proverbial verse to the other:

"A great person should forgive
  the mistakes of little ones;
If he forgives not,
  he is no longer great."

"Right. And there are so many errors one can make in reciting these dense verses: errors in speaking, errors in meaning, errors in meter, errors in the story, and errors when reading and copying manuscripts."

"We ask that we be forgiven if we commit any of these mistakes."

"And now, Muttuppattar, let us begin our story."

"But first, there is a little delay."

"Delay? What for? Some scandal?"

"Hardly. The cause for the delay is us."

"Us?"

"Yes, we must thank the sponsors of tonight's performance for all the food they have given us."

"Ah, that's the puppeteer tradition—to acknowledge our patrons. As they say, 'Poets who get rice should give praise.'"

"Tonight we want to thank Kuncu Kuttan of Talaipurumpil since every year his family sponsors the first night of the puppet show."

"And again this year he sent a messenger to bring us here to Kunnumpuli Kavu. When our bus pulled up, he was there to greet us and then escort us to his home, where we ate a big breakfast and received every kind of honor. We slept on comfortable pillows, drank hot coffee and ate rice-cakes in the afternoon, and ate a huge meal this evening. Then he invited us to worship Bhagavati in the temple here. Afterwards, as we left for the drama-house, he supplied us with a large plate of betel nut and betel leaves."

"We ask that Bhagavati protect Kuncu Kuttan, his family and relations from every kind of disease and misfortune. By the power of Rāma's name and Bhagavati's compassion, may his family prosper for a thousand years."

As the twenty-odd tiny flames rose and brightened, the drama-house emerged from its darkness and the performance took shape within. After an hour, the puppeteers sang the first narrative verse, followed by some commentary, then more verses and more commentary, hour after hour, while the handful of an audience fell asleep and the outside world receded into a black wall of night. Inside, however, in the now dimmer but steadier glow of the little lamps, the puppeteers continued to sing and chant in an uninterrupted stream of words until early morning. Precisely at five o'clock, just as the final devotional song was sung, the coconut shells (with the "meat" still inside) were brought to the lead puppeteer, who quickly apportioned them according to seniority—a stack of three or four for his assistants, two or three for the drummers, the rest for himself.[10] Then the puppeteers stepped down from the drama-house and headed for home in the heatless air of early morning; and as we sat in the roadside tea stall waiting for a bus, I took stock of what I had witnessed. These five men, really three men and two teenagers, whom I barely knew and who appeared unremarkable in their slightly soiled *vēstis* and rumpled shirts, had just completed an extraordinary exhibition of verbal art. Yet something was missing. Sipping the weak tea and looking around, I realized that they were alone—no one had congratulated them after they put down the puppets; no one had even greeted them. What had been invisible during the marathon inside the drama-house was inescapable in the daylight outside: these men had performed for themselves.

Searching for an Audience

This realization was the starting point of my research on the puppet play—not the Rāma story, not the puppets, not even Kampan̲'s text, although it did intrigue me, but this curious aspect of the puppet-play performance, the absent audience, for which I was entirely unprepared. Performances had always fascinated me, even before I read what folklorists and anthropologists had to say about them. During my first stay in India (1970–72), I had delighted in the irreverent open-air dramas staged by the Tamil Rationalist movement, watched high-stakes *kabadi* games, observed my share of weddings and funerals, and stared at fire-walkers.[11] Returning a few years later to document a Tamil tradition of ritual singing and spirit possession, I began to think and write about performance as a cultural category. That research became a book in which I proposed that oral performance be studied as a conjunction of text and event, but I completely overlooked the equally important aspect of audience.[12]

We all know that tales require listeners, yet audiences seldom appear in folk narrative research, which has moved through a succession of emphases, from tales to tellers to tellings. Even in the study of oral performance, with its eye trained on the exchange between performers and listeners, the audience rarely appears as more than a passive receptor, or in Jakobson's famous words, "those to whom the message is addressed."[13] As if pulled by the hereditary instinct of its literary origins, the mainstream study of oral performance has moved back toward textual structure, textual composition, and other elements that constitute a new textual orthodoxy, or what might be called an "oral literary formalism." Audience was never entirely neglected, of course, and new studies, in India and elsewhere, suggest that we might yet fulfill the promise of early performance studies and recognize audiences for who they are—critics, consumers, and coperformers of the event.[14]

Fortified with this theoretical weaponry and zeal, I confidently took to the field in Kerala to study the shadow puppet play. Arriving that night in Suhavaram, my goals were unclear, but since the modern anthropological study of performance practically began in India, with Milton Singer's observations of events in Madras, my ambitions were high. By morning, however, before I had had time even to listen to my tapes, I was wrestling with the problem of audience in an unforeseen form: there was none. In the months and years that followed, despite my hope that the Suhavaram debut in an isolated spot on a cold night might have been an aberration, audiences refused to emerge. Unlike other, proper performances, the Kerala puppet plays have no ordinary audience. After the sponsoring family leaves (and they rarely stay after the first half hour of a performance, when their praises are sung), the large, open space in front of the puppet stage is virtually deserted. A few stragglers with nowhere else to sleep might camp outside the drama-house, and occasionally a handful of devotees or a rare connoisseur of the art might watch for a few hours and then go home, but no one stays awake and listens throughout the night.

At first, this absent audience troubled me simply because, as I now realize, I could not accept the plain fact that the shadow puppet plays are not public performances and that the puppeteers have no direct contact with the world on the other side. I chose to ignore this fact because it threatened to dismantle the conceptual model I had carried into the field—performance as an interactive event between tellers and listeners. I might have scrapped that assumption, except that I had no idea what would replace it. How could I analyze oral performance without an audience? The whole canon of performance studies—analyses of "verbal art," of tale-telling in Tuscany, of "talking sweet" in the West Indies—all turned on the role of the audience. My lodestone had always been Dell Hymes's definition of performance as an "event for which the doer assumes responsibility to be evaluated as a bearer of tradition," but I could see no such accountability in Kerala.[15]

Groping for new ground, I wondered if these temple-sponsored performances were "rituals," not storytelling events, and therefore did not require audiences. This is partially true, as we shall see. One form of Balinese shadow puppetry, for example, is performed as temple ritual without a human audience, but *wayang lemah* is a brief performance during the day, with neither screen nor light, and does not involve the complicated storytelling and explication of the Kerala puppeteers.[16] Likewise, in Java "[t]he vast majority of dhalangs [head puppeteers] keep very few people watching beyond halfway through the performance," but only in Kerala do the puppeteers present a full narrative performance for a truly absent audience.[17] It also occurred to me that the medium of shadow puppetry, with its ventriloquism, shadows, and invisible performers, so completely severed the link with an audience that these plays were not performances at all. This, too, is only a partial explanation because other studies demonstrate that shadow puppet plays in India and southeast Asia entertain large audiences.[18] Whatever explanatory escape hatch I sought, the nagging question remained: Where was that indispensable interaction between performers and audience in the listener-less puppet plays of Kerala?[19]

The absent audience sidetracked my original research goals in yet another way. Folklorists and anthropologists are interested in how performance constructs and reflects cultural meaning, and I set out to discover what the Kerala puppet play would reveal about the lived-in world around it. Drawing again on my earlier fieldwork, I assumed that the behavior of performers with their audience held as much explanatory power as does behavior in other normative, public events, such as marriages or soccer matches. This idea became fixed when I read Ward Keeler's book, *Javanese Shadow Plays, Javanese Selves,* in which he describes puppet plays in Java as a "series of relationships that can be compared with other (i.e., social and political) relations."[20] Keeler convincingly argues that the puppet-play performances in Java are iconic with other local arenas of authority, that the interaction between the dhalang and his audience and patrons is analogous to that between other senior males (fathers, kings, ritual specialists) and their dependents. Like those powerful men, the dhalang is a "dissembled center" who seeks to resolve the paradox of having power and wanting to be seen not to exercise it; fascinated by the shadows and the dhalang's perceived power, audiences wish to limit his power and, at the same time, to ignore it in order to maintain self-control. Given the popularity of the Rāma story, I anticipated that a study of the puppet play in Kerala would yield a rich harvest of similar insights.

The need for a different analytic model became unavoidable when I understood the full distance between the Kerala puppeteers and any potential audience. Performers are separated from audiences in all forms of puppetry, but especially in shadow puppet performances, which begin, not when the curtain comes up, but when it goes down! Among the shadow puppeteers of India, moreover, none are as isolated as those in Kerala. Only there, for instance, is the stage a permanent building; elsewhere it is a temporary shed erected for the night. This is an important point, for the men in the *kūttu māṭam* are not just invisible but are effectively cut off from any contact on the other side of the white cloth screen. Rereading Keeler's book more carefully, I found that in the Javanese shadow puppet play the puppeteer is seen; he is, in fact, on view, for although by convention invited guests may sit on the shadow side of the screen, most people "preferred to watch the puppet side, so that they could see the dhalang."[21] In this respect, the Javanese performance exemplifies what Don Handelman calls a "mirror event," which displays public behavior (as a pageant or march) without the intention (as in rites of reversal) to alter it.[22] Shadow puppet performance in Kerala, however, is not susceptible to this kind of sociological approach, and especially not to its visual metaphors. Eventually, I learned to think about the puppet play as verbal and interior, as a series of conversations within the drama-house. This is not to say that the *tōl pāva kūttu* is completely divorced from society—one of the main arguments in this book is that the Rāma story told by the puppeteers is shaped by a local worldview. In the absence of visible interaction between performers and audience, however, to read performance as social behavior would be misleading.

Having reoriented my perspective to look inward, I then realized on my second field trip that the term "absent audience" is not entirely accurate either. Goddess Bhagavati, as host of the temple, is considered the ritual audience for performance (as in the legend of the puppet play's origin). Likewise, village committees, even if not physically present during performance, do monitor its quality in order to make decisions about whom to invite to sing at next year's festival. Nightly sponsors, whom the puppeteers salute as in the exchange translated above, are also important to please. These audiences do assess, at least obliquely, the puppeteers' display of competence, but a more immediate, interactive audience continued to elude me until I turned my full attention away from public patronage to the puppeteers inside the drama-house. On the morning after that first performance, while waiting for a bus at the tea stall, I understood that they perform for themselves, and after sitting in the small space night after night, I discovered that they create their own listeners within their telling of the Rāma story. These experiences led me to the audience that I had originally set out to find—though in an unexpected place—inside performance.

This publicly absent, internalized audience of the Kerala puppet play sheds new light on oral performance in India. A convenient counterpart to this south Indian recitation of a medieval Tamil Rāmāyaṇa, for example, is the north Indian recitation of a sixteenth-century Rāmāyaṇa, the *Rāmcaritmānas* by Tulsīdās. This influential Hindi text is performed in several genres, of which the most spectacular is the Rām Līlā drama, although the most comparable to the puppet play is known as *kathā*.[23] Like the puppet play in Kerala, *kathā* is performed by male professional singers (*vyās*) who present the most important Rāma text of their region, a bhakti Rāmāyaṇa, in a combination of memorized verses and oral commentary. But the differences are also striking. First, unlike the Hindi recitation, the Kerala puppet play is rooted and continues to be transmitted in villages and small towns where it is performed and supported by non-Brahmins. Second, the Kerala performances move further from the source text than do the Hindi performances and even contradict Kampaṉ in key episodes, as chapters 4 and 5 will illustrate. The critical difference, however, lies in the interaction between performer and audience. Many readers will have seen Rām Līlā performances, especially the burning of Rāvaṇa's towering effigy, which draw hundreds of thousands of onlookers, and even the *kathā* recitations of Tulsīdās' epic poem by Brahmin expounders command large gatherings:

> Rāmāyaṇ expounders . . . frequently pause to solicit affirmation and approbation. . . . Almost invariably a *vyās* [expounder] . . . cultivates a special rapport with an appreciative and responsive individual in the audience. An expounder will often single out such listeners for special attention, developing a dialogue with them by glances and gestures and making them surrogates for the wider audience. This kind of behavior . . . reflects the interactive milieu essential to good performance in the Indian context and is also a reminder of the archaic sense of *kathā* as "conversation." (Lutgendorf 1991: 188–89)

This "interactive milieu," absent in Kerala, is characteristic of one kind of oral performance in India. Rām Līlā, *kathā*, and similar performances, particularly of epics, represent this type of performance, which is male, public, and professional. These performances attract both local and scholarly attention because they are important public displays of cultural knowledge and susceptible to the analytic models of visual behavior that I rejected as inappropriate for the puppet play. A second major type of performance in India, by contrast, is private (or semiprivate), non- (or semi-) professional, and largely female. Typically, in this kind of event, women tell tales and sing songs, usually in or around the home, often with little distinction between performer and audience. An example would be the women's group singing of the Rāma story in Chattisgargh, as described by Joyce Flueckiger: in neighborhoods and temples, older women gather, sometimes with a literate leader, and sing verses from Tulsīdās, but this time with a woman's slant, which introduces female characters (a wife for Guha the boatman, for example) not found in the Hindi text.[24] Similarly, in a Telugu tradition reported by V. Narayana Rao, Rāma's sister, Śāntā, is prominent and Sītā is tricked into drawing Rāvaṇa's big toe that later springs to life.[25] Public yet intimate, the Kerala puppet play combines elements of both the smaller, domestic events of women and the larger, open performances of men. Amid the scholarly debate on public and private spheres in Indian culture, the anomalous puppet play cautions that public performance is not always a behavioral display and may include the in-group communication of a domestic event.

The puppet play's internal dialogue leads to two final observations on audiences and performances in India. First, the puppet play resembles traditional Indian texts composed as conversations to be overheard by the reader, and Rāma stories provide prime examples. Tulsīdās's text and the Sanskrit *Adhyātma Rāmāyaṇa* and *Tattvasaṃgraharāmāyaṇa*, for instance, are all narrated by Śiva to Pārvatī, not to mention Vālmīki's text, in which Nārada recounts Rāma's history to the poet. Likewise, two popular folk Rāmāyaṇas in Tamil (*Catakaṇṭarāvaṇaṉ Katai* and *Mayilirāvaṇaṉ Katai*) are told by Nārada to another sage, Gautama. Within these dialogic frames, textualized audiences are created whenever a character summarizes the plot to another character, as when Rāma tells his story to Hanumān, who then narrates Sugrīva's story to Rāma, and so forth. Remembering these examples, I understood why listening to performances inside the drama-house sometimes felt more like reading a book than seeing a live performance. On the other hand, the persistence of the dialogic frame in literary forms of the Rāma story might be further evidence of its oral origin and transmission. In either case, we are reminded that all texts, written or spoken, have audiences who play a part in the storytelling.

Equally important, an internal audience need not be passive in performance and is capable of playing the creative role of ordinary listeners. This aspect of the internal audience in oral narrative performance is explored, although in different terms, by John Miles Foley in his recent book on Serbo-Croatian epics.[26] Drawing on reader reception theory, Foley introduces the notion of "traditional referentiality" in order to show that this epic tradition is sustained and recreated by the ability of audience members to understand the extratextual associations in performances. In fact, this is how the famous oral formulaic technique of composition works: when the *guslar* (singer) sings a line with a conventional allusion to the hero Marko, for instance, audience members

(Foley argues) recall other attributes and exploits of Marko, thereby filling in the story. Performances of the Rāma story in India assume a similar knowledge and stimulate a similar internal (and often external) participation on the part of audiences; writing on the Rām Līlā in north India, Anuradha Kapur put it succinctly: "The ability to see a performance is as culturally bound as the performance itself."[27] I hope to show that something like a shared referentiality exists among the puppeteers in Kerala and that it is essential to telling their Rāma story in the drama-house.

Patronage

Although an absent audience might suggest that the puppet play lacks popular support, its patronage system is firmly rooted in local society. The puppeteers earn money from two sources. The first (described above) is the one-rupee gift, given prior to performance, that earns a blessing from Bhagavati during a *nāṭakam* performed in the middle of the night. An unpredictable amount determined by individual needs, whims, and factors beyond the control of the temple, it can reach several hundred, and sometimes several thousand, rupees that are then divided, usually half-and-half, between the troupe and the temple.[28] Whatever the puppeteers earn from these one-rupee donations is "extra" money, however, because they are also paid for their labor through a second patronage system, which is administered by the temple. Between 1984 and 1989, my notes record that expenses for a night's performance ranged from 350 to 500 rupees. Of this total, each of the two or three puppeteers received anywhere from thirty to fifty rupees, and the accompanying drummers considerably less; remaining funds purchased ingredients for temple *pūjā,* food for the performers, eleven coconuts for the twenty-one shells, and the nearly one gallon of coconut oil necessary to keep the wicks burning all night. These expenses for a night's performance are often borne by a family, and sponsorship is so popular that families take out subscriptions long before the temple festival begins, even booking certain nights years in advance. If, for example, a child was cured of malaria after her family sponsored the night when Kumbhakarṇa is killed, that family might pledge to underwrite the performance of that episode every year for ten years. In return for this patronage, during the "Song of the Drama-House" (*māṭa cintu*) the puppeteers praise the family (dutifully waiting outside to hear these words) in the mock-serious tones of the passage quoted earlier. They describe in detail the gracious hospitality and sumptuous meals they enjoyed in the family's home (instead of the local tea shop where, in fact, they ate very plain food at the sponsor's expense) and then ask Bhagavati to shower the family with blessings.

If not a family, an entire village (*dēsam*) or an organization (police group, school) might pay the few hundred rupees necessary to sponsor a performance.[29] At Palappuram, for instance (see chapter 8), seven of the seventeen nights are supported by villages lying within a few miles of the drama-house. During the weeks before the festival, each of these villages is scoured by enthusiastic young men brandishing ticket books at tea shops and bus stops in an attempt to waylay potential contributors. A considerably larger amount (approximately ten thousand to twelve thousand rupees) is also collected from families in each village in order to pay for a procession from the local temple to the temple at Palappuram on the last day of the festival. No other day matches this finale for pageantry, exhilaration, and sheer fun; after an elaborate *pūjā* in the local temple, several elephants, musical ensembles, and hundreds of people carrying embroidered cloth parasols and an enormous papier-mâché horse advance in procession from each of the satellite villages toward the Palappuram temple. When the seven village processions converge on the temple grounds in the evening, the horse effigies are carried back and forth in mock battles before a massive crowd. And that night, with a large pool of potential donors milling around on the temple grounds, the puppeteers perform the final episode of the puppet play, the coronation of Rāma.

At some sites the puppet play is also indirectly supported by temple patronage in the form of donations of paddy from landowners, some of whom hold temple lands on lease. Some weeks before the festival, a large brass vessel, a *para̱*, is sent around to each wealthy household to be filled with about five kilograms of rice as an offering to Bhagavati. From the tons of paddy thus collected and deposited at the temple, the temple musicians, oracle-priest, and lampbearer each receive a fixed amount (nearly three hundred kilograms in 1986) as annual payment for services; the rice given by the oracle to the lead puppeteer on the first night of performance also comes from this store. Since the 1970s, however, when Kerala's Communist (CPI) government redistributed the lands of large landowners and temple estates to the tenants, this source of patronage for the puppet play has dwindled. In areas where land had belonged mainly to these estates, temple festivals and puppet plays have ceased after generations of performance, and to a puppeteer who performs at only five or ten temples annually, the loss of one site delivers a hard financial blow. On the other hand, where smaller family and village patronage had supported performances, the puppet play has not suffered badly from this transfer of land ownership. During five years of research, I observed isolated signs of growth: puppeteers began to perform at four more temples and for more nights at two others.

As a field researcher, I, too, was both patron and audience, although I pretended that this was not so. Other ethnographies of performance in South Asia had demonstrated the interpretive rewards of a self-reflexive perspective, especially Kirin Narayan's study of a swami's tales in India[30] and Margaret Mills' analysis of tales in Afghanistan,[31] but I preferred to consider myself absent from the performances I recorded. If sessions with the swami and the Afghan tellers were private, almost personal, and open-ended, shadow puppet plays in Kerala, I convinced myself, were different because they are more impersonal and formal. In fact, I chose to study this tradition in the first place because I wished to document an "authentic" performance event that reflected local culture unaffected by foreigners. If the previous sentence reads like a primer from the pre-postmodern age of enthnographic innocence, I did believe that my pretended non-presence would enhance the credibility of the event and, hence, my account of it. Retrograde thinking dies hard, and I am not yet convinced that the new convention of honest presence avoids any more deception than does the old fiction of feigned absence. But I now realize that my naive concept of authenticity was a shield behind which I could retreat into the role of detached observer and avoid the awkward duties of patron with its messy money transactions.

Without a large public audience on the other side, however, the shield hid little. Sitting on the mats night after night inside the drama-house with the puppeteers, I was often sleepy and sometimes bored but could not avoid becoming part of their internal audience. Still, I tried hard to escape the role of host. My rule in previous research projects had been to pay performers only if I had asked them to perform (the "induced performance"); recording a public, scheduled performance, in my code, required permission of performers and organizers but no payment. During my first extended trip to Kerala, in fact, I did not pay performers, with the result, I believe, that one particular troupe became uncooperative and eventually prevented me from recording an important episode at a major temple site; others, apparently, did not consider lack of payment a breach of any kind. A small number of scholars who preceded me in working with the puppeteers had certainly raised expectations for hefty payments. According to the sketchy details given by the puppeteers, a French woman once showed up with a video team, requested a special performance (outside the drama-house), and handed over thousands of rupees before leaving the following day. Other foreigners who stayed for a few weeks also paid handsome sums for puppets. I could not compete with that procedure, although on my second trip I mended fences with the uncooperative group and began to pay a small amount (Rs 50–100) to all performers whom I taped inside the drama-house. In the end, of course, my presence did affect what was said, but only (as far as I can detect) on occasion. A humorous aside about patrons who do not pay performers before they sing, for example, was a veiled criticism of me, and one puppeteer prematurely inserted the story of how Kampa<u>n</u> composed his epic, explaining later: "I don't usually tell the story here, but I thought you would like to hear it tonight."

All this does not mean that I did not form personal relationships with the puppeteers, but I did attempt to downplay them during performances. Most people viewed my work with the half-bothered, half-fascinated eye cocked toward the inexplicable mannerisms of foreigners. My ability to speak Tamil, the mother tongue of most of the puppeteers, went some distance toward making friends, although only Natesan Pillai seemed to understand what I was doing and why. Other puppeteers were mildly pleased at my presence in the drama-house, though rarely impressed, and often nonplussed; most slept while I worked. My presence did not greatly affect performance, but it affected me, my experience of the puppet play, and the way I have written this book.

This Book

Following this initial chapter and its discussion of audience, the next chapter introduces the Kampa<u>n</u> text and places it within the history of Palghat and the shadow puppet play. The puppet play's accommodation of Kampa<u>n</u>'s devotional Hinduism with folk Hinduism is introduced in chapter 3 and illustrated by the two subsequent chapters. Chapter 4 describes the highly controversial meeting between

Śūrpaṇakhā and Rāma on the banks of the Godavari River and analyzes the significance of an added episode in which Lakṣmaṇa kills Śūrpaṇakhā's son. Chapter 5 discusses the puppeteers' treatment of another contentious episode, Vāli's death, especially Rāma's unusual admission of wrongdoing. This first half of the book demonstrates the general point that the puppet play complicates Kampa<u>n</u>'s text, placing the moral relations between Rāma and his enemies on a new footing, without a substantial revision of its content.

The analysis in the second half of the book (chapters 6–8) shifts from narrative content to the puppeteers' commentary and conversations. My argument in these chapters will be that these techniques enable the puppeteers to gain control over Kampa<u>n</u>'s text in performance. Chapter 6 describes the oral commentary, which spins auxiliary stories and quotations around the text in order to place it within a wider frame of reference: Kampa<u>n</u>'s individual verses, I will suggest, become stepping stones to that wider world of Rāma stories, from which his text derives. Chapter 7 details the conversations in performance and argues that this dialogism further weakens the poet's voice and permits the puppeteers to tell a Rāma story in their own terms. The final chapter brings together the earlier analysis of narrative with the later analysis of conversation in a discussion of countervailing voices that challenge the bhakti ideals of Kampa<u>n</u>'s text: specifically, I discuss Sītā's anger and Jāmbuvā<u>n</u>'s cynicism as expressions of the puppet play's skepticism toward the bhakti text's attempts at restoration, especially Rāma's coronation.

Beginning with chapter 3, these points are made with reference to performances in translation, which represent the puppeteers' Rāma story as I recorded it inside the drama-house. I have worked directly from cassette recordings and not from an intermediary transcription because I believe that by continually rehearing (as opposed to rereading) a performance, one maintains close contact with the original voice; the puppeteers' voice, of course, cannot be fully captured in English, and others must judge the success of my efforts. Certainly any reader familiar with the Rāma tale will soon realize that the translations in this book do not tell the whole story; no single Rāma story does, but I have made decisions that severely abbreviate the plot of the puppet play. First, I decided not to include the entire series of overnight performances of more than one hundred hours and instead chose the most dramatic nights of performance: Rāma's meeting with Śūrpaṇakhā (chapter 4); Rāma's killing of Vāli (chapter 5); Rāvaṇa's first defeat (chapter 6); the death of Indrajit (chapter 7); Rāvaṇa's death and Rāma's coronation (chapter 8). Second, although each night of performance is preceded by the same introduction ("The Song of the Drama-House"), it is translated only once, in chapter 3. Third, I begin the puppeteers' narration of the story with the Śūrpaṇakhā episode (chapter 4) in the middle of the Forest Book because this is the point from which the puppeteers usually begin their story, and for good reason as we shall see. As a result, large portions of the subsequent books are omitted, although much of the long and important War Book is presented.

Omissions and abridgements have also been made within these selected performances. I have at times abbreviated the rambling and ponderous verbal marathon of the commentary (and indicated these omissions in notes), although I have retained some repetitions and digressions because they take the reader inside the experience of the puppet play. I have also omitted verse lines regularly repeated during the commentary as a mnemonic device, and I have summarized transitions between scenes, just as the puppeteers do in their prose summary (*avatārikai*), by placing them within brackets. Nor have I translated all the verses sung in performance. Because my aim is to analyze the puppet play as an adaptation of Kampaṉ's Rāmāyaṇa, most folk verses are translated, whereas Kampaṉ's verses are translated only when they are necessary for a comprehension of the commentary. Omitting the Kampaṉ verses does not seriously affect an understanding of the story, however, because their content is recounted in the commentary, which carries the narrative burden in the puppet play. Finally, I sometimes use English terms for certain Indic words ("old legends" for *purāṇa*; "old books" for *śāstra*, and so forth) because those original words, even when "translated" in a glossary, remain lifeless. "Demon," admittedly, is not a happy choice for *rākṣasa*, but it is an advance over its predecessor, "ogre," and I have provided a gloss in a footnote at its first usage. Although something is lost by each of these decisions, I have come to accept that something greater will be gained if they enable readers to enjoy the Rāma story as told by the puppeteers in Kerala.

What we read in this book, then, is not the entire series of twenty or thirty nights of performance, whose length, repetitions, and sometimes uninspired commentary were never intended to be read, let alone printed in English. We read instead a selection of performances, whose narrative and interpretive innovations teach us that text and audience are never quite what or where we think they are. These are the lessons learned after that first night at Suhavaram undid my original research plans. An absent audience meant that I could not investigate performance as cultural behavior, and so I reset my sights within the dramahouse, where I discovered that the Kampan̲ text was less important than the puppeteers' oral commentary. From this vantage point, I also saw that the puppeteers tell their own Rāma story, faithful to Kampan̲'s yet slanted to a local morality, and that they tell it to themselves.

CHAPTER 2

Rāma Stories and Puppet Plays

There are many Rāmāyaṇas—three hundred in one reckoning, though three thousand is more likely. However many, these multiple tellings are not an illustration of "The One and the Many," that shopworn slogan for Hinduism, because there is no single source. Although Vālmīki's Sanskrit poem is often regarded as the original Rāmāyaṇa, and although it is an early and influential text, it is more a cultural measuring stick than the origin of these many Rāma stories. Regional patterns and popular scenes exist, but there is no *the* Rāmāyaṇa, not even a standard text with numerous "versions," only a true ocean of stories in which Rāma marries Sītā, chases the golden deer, conquers Rāvaṇa, regains his wife, and ascends the throne in Ayodhya. These events are sung and danced, printed in comic books and paraded on television, performed with shadow puppets and told in the nearly fifty thousand lines of Kampaṉ as well as the three words of a Telugu proverb: "Built [the causeway], beat [Rāvaṇa], brought [Sītā]."[1] Each of these tellings is partial, incomplete, and any assumption that a particular motif, say Rāma's killing of Rāvaṇa, is indispensable to the plot is probably wrong; Jain texts, for instance, prefer that Lakṣmaṇa, not the evolved soul Rāma, incur the sin of violently killing Rāvaṇa. We are beginning to chart these many Rāmāyaṇas and their narrative variations, but their transmission and reception are more difficult to record. However, as the notion of a unitary text, tidily authored and passively received, gives way to the recognition of a historicized and composite telling, these processes of borrowing and accommodation become both more visible and more instructive.

The Rāma story itself was not the starting point of my interest, as I said earlier, partly because I knew so little of it, and I remember how my ignorance shocked Krishnan Kutty. One night, as he was pinning puppets on the screen, I asked him who they were. Glancing at me for a moment, he pointed to them one by one: "Gaṇeśa, *paṭṭa pāva* [Brahmin narrators], Rāma, Lakṣmaṇa, and Śūrpaṇakhā." "Sur . . ." I stumbled, and he shot back, "Śūrpaṇakhā! Rāvaṇa's sister." I didn't know the sister but I did know Rāvaṇa from my first stay in India, near Madurai, Tamil Nadu. In those days, I often went with my friends, faithful members of the local Rationalist League, to see the outdoor dramas staged by the anti-Brahmin movement; and when Rāvaṇa, the majestic and wronged Dravidian hero, defeated whiny Rāma from the north, the crowds cheered. Crude propaganda, perhaps, but far more compelling than the insipid "Marriage of Rāma and Sītā" that graced school plays and greeting cards. Still, the propaganda passed me by, and I thought of the Rāmāyaṇa as flowery Sanskrit literature, a litany of one-dimensional role models, whereas I was looking for gritty, subversive, oral stuff, preferably in low-caste villages.

After watching Śūrpaṇakhā meet Rāma that night in Suhavaram, however, I began to study the story and to appreciate its complexity. I read it first in English translations and then in Kampaṉ's Tamil, although not all of the twelve thousand verses (but then very few people read all of Kampaṉ). I also learned something from the reactions of young students to whom I taught R. K. Narayan's abridged translation of Kampaṉ in a high school in San Francisco. Its lovable fantasy never failed: "Ten heads!" fourteen-year-old Kate shouted and screwed up her lips in agony when she read about Rāvaṇa. "What headaches he must have!" Those anti-Brahmin dramas I had seen would have touched a cord in these comfortable American kids, one of whom wrote: "Is Rāma really a god? He was unfaithful, stupid, and lacked common sense. Why do Hindus worship him?" Weeks after we had finished the book, I overheard a student summarize the story to a visitor: "Well, Sītā marries Rāma, but she gets captured and then drops her jewelry so that Rāma can find her, and . . . he did." That was her telling, and it taught me as forcefully as any published writing that there really is no *the* Rāmāyaṇa.

When I returned to Kerala in 1986, and again in 1989, to work extensively with the puppeteers, I knew most of the episodes fairly well, and I had my favorites. The first book, the Birth Book, recounting Rāma's birth and marriage to Sītā, was not among them, but the palace intrigues of Rāma's exile in the second book, the Ayodhya Book, fascinated me. Aged Daśaratha, king of Ayodhya, finally begets sons—Rāma by Kausalyā, Bharata by Kaikeyī, Lakṣmaṇa and Śatrughna by Sumitrā—and then sets in motion the coronation of Rāma, his oldest and best-loved son. The plot begins when a servant stirs up trouble. Long ago Daśaratha had been saved by his young wife Kaikeyī and offered her two boons, but the promises lay unused until Rāma is about to ascend the throne. At this point, Kaikeyī's servant convinces her that if Rāma becomes king, she will become an ex-queen of an ex-king and a maidservant to Rāma's mother while her own son, Bharata, will be banished by Rāma. Gullible Kaikeyī forces Daśaratha to grant her two wishes: she demands that he exile Rāma and place Bharata on the throne. Daśaratha is stricken speechless, but righteous Rāma leaves for fourteen years in the forest with Lakṣmaṇa and Sītā, thereby upholding his father's word to Kaikeyī; Daśaratha cannot bear to lose his son and dies. ("Rāma faces a dilemma," one boy said in my high-school class. "He can either keep his father's word or keep him alive.") Still no other outcome seems possible since Daśaratha had been cursed to die grieving the loss of his son because he had accidentally killed another man's son. Besides, in order to gain permission to marry Kaikeyī, Daśaratha promised her father that her son would inherit the throne.

So Rāma, Lakṣmaṇa, and Sītā leave Ayodhya and enter the forest, where their adventures with sages and demons constitute the third book, the Forest Book. The interminable names, relations, and auxiliary stories in this section made little sense until I began to watch the puppeteers at work and learned to track the psychological and moral conflicts of this book, which set the direction for the remainder of the epic. It all begins with Śūrpaṇakhā, sister of Rāvaṇa, who attempts to seduce Rāma on a riverbank (the scene I saw at Suhavaram); Rāma rejects her, Lakṣmaṇa disfigures her, and she runs to Rāvaṇa, who falls in love with Sītā after listening to his bleeding sister's account of Rāma's wife. Rāvaṇa's plan to capture Sītā is brilliant: his uncle assumes the form of a golden deer which Sītā insists Rāma catch for her; after Rāma chases the deer, the uncle, in an imitation of Rāma's voice, calls out to Lakṣmaṇa for help; when Lakṣmaṇa reluctantly leaves Sītā all alone, Rāvaṇa approaches disguised as a Brahmin and takes her away to his palace in Lanka. Mistaken identifications, suspicions, love, and poor judgement have thus cost Rāma his wife and name. Because Rāma's meeting with Śūrpaṇakhā is pivotal to the plot, because it is an extremely controversial episode, and because it is the starting point of the puppet play, we, too, begin the story with that encounter (in chapter 4).

Events from the abduction of Sītā up to the battle with Rāvaṇa fill the fourth and fifth books (the Kiṣkindha Book and the Beautiful Book) and introduce the third group of characters in the epic, the monkeys. Here we meet Vāli and his brother, Sugrīva, and his son, Aṅgada, and the loyal Hanumān: Rāma befriends Hanumān and Sugrīva and then kills Vāli, who entrusts Aṅgada to him. Following Vāli's death, Sugrīva and Hanumān assemble a huge army of monkeys and bears, led by old Jāmbuvāṉ, and set out to find Sītā. They've almost given up, when the dying eagle, Śampāti, tells them that Rāvaṇa took her to Lanka, and it is left to Hanumān to leap across the ocean to the island kingdom. (I remembered this part well because a friend once pointed to a sharp cone of rock at the tail end of the Western Ghats, a few miles from the sea near Nagercoil, and said, "That's Mahendra-giri where Hanumān leapt to Lanka.") Discovering Sītā, captive but unharmed, Hanumān returns with the good news to Rāma, who orders the monkeys and bears to build a causeway to Lanka. Most of this middle section of the epic, from Vāli's death to Hanumān's discovery of Sītā, is omitted in my translations which skip to the beginning of the War Book.

The War Book is the sixth and last book in Kampaṉ and the puppet play and is the puppeteers' favorite. Rāma's army has laid siege to Rāvaṇa's fort and the demon-king convenes a war council, where we watch his brothers and ministers argue military and moral alternatives. Rāvaṇa's younger brother, Vibhīṣaṇa, dares to oppose his plan to fight Rāma, is dismissed, and joins Rāma, although we are left to wonder about the loyalty of one who has turned against his own brother. Giant Kumbhakarṇa, the older brother, also has reservations about Rāvaṇa's actions but will not desert him in this hour of need. Finally, after Rāvaṇa rejects the proposal of peace brought to him by Aṅgada, the long War Book unfolds in a series of battles between Rāma's army and Rāvaṇa's inexhaustible horde of warriors. In the first battle, Rāma defeats Rāvaṇa but allows him to return to his palace in humiliation. When mighty Kumbhakarṇa and then Atikāyaṉ, Rāvaṇa's son, are killed, Lanka seems doomed until the most powerful of Rāvaṇa's sons, Indrajit, enters the field of battle. Master of *māyā*, Indrajit twice uses magic weapons to defeat Rāma, and twice Rāma is revived: once, when Viṣṇu's eagle-mount, Garuḍa, destroys the snake-weapon; and again, when Rāma and his army lie unconscious on the field and Hanumān undertakes his famous mission to the Medicine Mountain, obtains herbs, and revives the fallen soldiers. Lakṣmaṇa finally kills Indrajit, but only because Vibhīṣaṇa divulges a secret. Now, without sons and brothers, only

Rāvaṇa remains until Rāma, also relying on secret advice, kills him. Soon Vibhīṣaṇa is crowned king of Lanka, Rāma is reunited with Sītā, and they return to Ayodhya for his delayed coronation, which is the closing scene of Kampan̲'s text, the puppet play, and this book.

Kampan̲'s Rāmāyaṇa

If this is only an outline of the Rāma story and if there are many Rāmāyaṇas, what kind of Rāma story do the puppeteers in Kerala tell? Since my book is a long answer to that question, I here provide a general historical background for its three related elements: Kampan̲'s Rāmāyaṇa, the Palghat region as context, and the puppet-play tradition. As to the first, I begin with a short passage from the introduction ("Song of the Drama-House") because it contains the puppet play's own view of its history. One of the Brahmin puppets speaks to the other:

> "Still, even assisted by all the gods we know, singing the Rāma story is an extraordinary task. There are the 100,000 verses of the *Campū Rāmāyaṇa*, the 60,000 of the *Mahānāṭaka*, the 24,000 of Vālmīki, and the 12,026 from Kampan̲, of which we use approximately 1,200. To complete these long hours of singing, we need extra determination."
>
> "Definitely!"
>
> "But we also need the blessings of our gurus and our patrons. There's a saying for that: 'Like a woodcock trying to imitate a peacock's dance.'"
>
> "Yes, learning these Kampan̲ verses is like a foolish woodcock imitating a lovely, dark peacock. A peacock dances almost without knowing it—whirling and whirling—but when the woodcock watches and tries to dance, well . . . it has no crown and no fan of feathers. It might be a 'dance,' but no one would mistake it for anything a peacock does. Kampan̲'s verses have a peacock's beauty—a crown and a fan—but we . . . we are unlettered woodcocks."

This internal list of textual sources for the puppet play is revealing rather than definitive. The *Campū Rāmāyaṇa* is probably the fifthteenth-century, heavily Sanskritized, Malayalam text attributed to Pūnam; the *Mahānāṭaka* is an earlier, elusive Sanskrit text, thought by some to be a libretto for a shadow puppet play, a hypothesis confirmed by the fact that the puppet play and that text share episodes not commonly found in Rāma literature.[2] Vālmīki is invoked (though not as a single source), and in a few details, the Kerala tradition follows his Sanskrit Rāma story more closely than it does Kampan̠.[3] Not mentioned in this list are the early bhakti (*āḻvār*) poems and the Tamil *Kantapurāṇam*, to which Kampan̠ owes a heavy debt as well. The many, many other sources of the puppeteers' Rāma story—unrecorded texts, songs, proverbs, quotations—may never be identified (unless a motif index of Rāma literature is published), although I did find two north Indian instances of the curious conversation between Rāma's two arms when he draws back his bow to kill Rāvaṇa.[4] For the present, it is enough to say that the puppeteers' Rāma story is hybrid, constructed out of bits of Sanskrit, Tamil, and Malayalam literary traditions, folk Rāmāyaṇas, songs, tales, and oral traditions as yet unrecorded.

From this medley of sources, the puppet play does draw heavily on the Rāma story composed in Tamil by Kampan̠, probably in the twelfth century A.D. This is significant because the *Kamparāmāyaṇam* is considered one of the great achievements in twenty centuries of Tamil literature; received wisdom that "while the Tamil have gone on attempting *Mahābhāratas*, no man has dared to attempt the Rāmāyaṇa after Kampan̠" is only a slight hyperbole.[5] As the first full-blown bhakti Rāmāyaṇa, which influenced other Rāma stories not only in India but also in Southeast Asia, Kampan̠'s epic was known outside the Tamil context as well.[6] If the *guslar* singers in the Balkans have preserved a technique of oral composition, the puppeteers in Kerala have orally transmitted an important text of Indian literature.

But Kampan̠'s composition is more than a text. It is an epic, a genre with a notorious tendency to turn up when linguistic or ethnic groups seek to establish a nation, extend political power, or recover a lost heroic past, as in Persia following Islamic conquest, the Balkans following Turkish rule, Scotland in the late eighteenth century, Finland in the early nineteenth, and so on. To this list, we may add the Tamil country in the twelfth century, when Kampan̠ composed his poem during the reign of the largest and most powerful Tamil kingdom, the imperial Cholas. Under the umbrella of that expanding empire, which claimed victories from the Ganga to Sumatra, Rāma shrines were built, extensive sets of Rāmāyaṇa reliefs were carved along the base of several temples, and temples supported recitations of the Rāma story.[7] Chola monarchs also bore Rāma's name in their imperial titles, and apparently one raja perceived parallels between his conquest and Rāma's when he erected icons to the epic hero to celebrate a victory over the Sinhala kings of Lanka.[8] One temple inscription goes so far as to suggest the story of Rāma (specifically, his pursuit of the golden deer) as an origin myth for the Cholas, which was a solar dynasty like Rāma's.[9] During this medieval period, then, Rāma stood as a paradigm of political power and a model of kingship (and not, a point to which I return shortly, an object of devotion). Still, what is an empire, a Golden Age, without an epic? So a Chola king, as the puppeteers tell it, commissioned Kampaṉ, and his rival, Oṭṭakkūttaṉ, to compose a "Rāmāyaṇa in the southern tongue."

The Chola period notwithstanding, Kampaṉ never served the Tamil language more valiantly than during the twentieth century. Nineteenth-century editions of the *Kamparāmāyaṇam* proclaim his poetic genius, but the boom in Kampaṉ scholarship came in the early decades of the twentieth century when south Indians set out to claim a new identity.[10] Left out of the neo-Hindu movements in the north, which pursued a return to "pure" Sanskrit texts, and reeling from the Christian reforms in the south, which rejected Hinduism and its "devil worship," non-Brahmin Tamils, especially high-caste landowners and merchants, sought an identity that was Hindu but not Aryan.[11] In Kampaṉ, many found what they needed: a Dravidian Vālmīki and an epic in the ancestral tongue of the land.[12] This promotion of Kampaṉ was the culmination of a series of Tamil self-discoveries from the mid-nineteenth century to the early twentieth. In 1856 came the definitive proclamation of Dravidian as a separate family of languages (they had been known as "Deccan vernaculars"), followed a few decades later by the recovery of ancient Tamil literature (the Sangam poems). Then, in the 1920s, excavations in the Indus Valley revealed an ancient civilization that predated the Aryans and, many concluded, was Dravidian.[13] The final touch on this new portrait of Tamil antiquity was Kampaṉ's Rāmāyaṇa, the ancient tale told in "the southern tongue." For the advocates of a Tamil-speaking state in the soon-to-be-independent India, here was the necessary link between land and language.[14]

Kampaṉ nonetheless presented a dilemma for the Dravidian movement because, although a great Tamil poet, he was a purveyor of the discredited Rāma story. Condemning the Rāma story as an immoral Aryan tale that introduced caste and other evils into a Dravidian eden, many politicians and intellectuals sought other texts in which to ground the new Tamil self-image. The earlier the better, and so popular candidates for "pure" Tamil unpolluted by northern beliefs were the Sangam poems, the moral maxims of the *Tirukkuṟaḷ* (c. 500 A.D.), and the Śaiva bhakti poems (600–900 A.D.), although some preferred the mystic verses of a nineteenth-century reformer, Ramalinga Swami. By championing these Tamil texts and castigating Vālmīki's by name, much of the Dravidianist attack on the Rāma story circumvented the problematic Kampaṉ text; even the defiant, flamboyant E. V. Ramaswami Naicker (1879–1973), who publicly beat Rāma's picture with his leather sandals, reserved his ire for the deluded Tamil Brahmins who translated Vālmīki's text into Tamil because they exalted the Sanskrit text over Kampaṉ's.[15] Likewise, M. S. Purnalingam Pillai (1866–1947), a founding father of the Dravidian movement, critic of the Rāma story as Aryan propaganda, and author of *Ravana, Great King of Lanka,* drew a protective circle around Kampaṉ's poem: the story may be derived from Sanskrit, he conceded, but its "morality" is Tamil, as evidenced by Rāvaṇa's "no-touch" abduction of Sītā that preserved her chastity and his chivalry.[16]

To the virulent anti-Brahmin wing of the Tamil movement, however, a Rāma story was a Rāma story, and Kampaṉ could not be spared, especially since, as they pointed out, his plot differs little from Vālmīki's.[17] One writer, for instance, took Kampaṉ to task for following Aryan models in his hyperbolic description of Rāma's arrow which "pierced the chest of Thadakai and in its flight and speed passed through a mountain, a tree and finally even the very earth!"[18] Later ideological descendants of the pure Tamil movement, such as C. N. Annaturai, criticized Kampaṉ for an unseemly mixture of erotic and religious sentiments.[19] But these writers were a minority whom other scholars directly challenged. When E. V. Ramaswami Naicker burned copies of the Rāmāyaṇa, a poet responded with this verse: "Palm-leaf will burn, paper will burn, but a poem written from the heart, and chanted day and night, will it burn in fire?"[20]

What Kampaṉ originally composed almost a thousand years ago in the Chola court at Tanjore will never be known because the extant *Kamparāmāyaṇam* is a composite text reconstructed from dozens of variant palm-leaf manuscripts, themselves the result of borrowings, interpolations, and inspirations from other Rāma texts, both folk and classical, primarily in Tamil and Sanskrit, including Vālmīki and its southern recensions. This is not to diminish the genius of Kampaṉ's poem or the considerable scholarship that produced its critical edition but to acknowledge that notions of a solitary author and unitary text owe more to a need for order and a respect for individual creativity than to history. Regarding the transmission of Kampan̲'s poem, we know very little except that it changed as a result of both oral recitation at temples and manuscript emendation at Vaiṣṇava centers: two eleventh-century Chola inscriptions and one thirteenth-century Pandiya inscription record endowments for the study of a Rāmāyaṇa (whether Kampan̲ or Vālmīki is unclear), while a fourteenth-century Kannada inscription mentions the reciter of a "Kamba Rāmāyaṇa."[21] The earliest known manuscript of the *Kamparāmāyaṇam* is dated 1578, after which the poem is thought to have been heavily influenced by Velli Tampiran, a Śaiva scholar from the Tanjore region, who added his own verses, now referred to as "Velli-verses."[22] Even more decisive steps were taken in the mid-eighteenth century in Alvar Tirunakari, a Vaiṣṇava center in the southern Tamil country, where a Tiruvenkatam Tacar worked from various manuscripts to compile an authoritative version that later formed the basis of the first (partial) printing in 1843 and subsequent modern editions.[23] A full edition appeared in 1914, although debates about authenticity and interpolations continued in Tamil scholarly circles even as the authoritative editions were issued in subsequent decades.[24] The four major editions available today range from ten thousand to twelve thousand verses, a measure of the text's uncertain history.[25] But the final irony in the political career of the *Kamparāmāyaṇam* must be the large statue of the poet standing with other cultural heroes on the seafront near the University of Madras, while his poem, the pride of Tamil literature, is recited by unknown puppeteers in Kerala.

Palghat and the Puppet Play

How and when the *Kamparāmāyaṇam* entered Kerala and the puppet play is also unknown. Neither the text nor the puppet play appears in records left by the early Portuguese and Dutch, or later English merchants who built factories and competed for the spice trade on the Kerala coast; even the usually zealous Christian missionaries entered this interior tract only in the nineteenth century, after British military rule had been established. Still, and although clues picked up along the years do not yet form a conclusive answer, enough is known to suggest what happened to Kampan̲'s text in Palghat.

Tracing this transmission of Kampan̲ into Kerala will take us through mountain passes and along trade routes, so I begin with geography. To cross from the Tamil country into Kerala, one must traverse the Western Ghats, a mountain range that runs down the spine of southern India and whose peaks reach well over eight thousand feet (see maps, pages xv and xvi). Pilgrims and local people are known to climb over the low hills, but most travelers enter Kerala through two mountain passes, the Shencottah Gap in the south and the Palghat Gap in the central range. Coming through the Palghat Gap by train or bus or car, one is struck by the abrupt shift from the rocky, cotton-growing soil on the Tamil side to the soft patchwork of rice fields on the Kerala side. This is the Palghat region, a broad fertile plain watered by heavy monsoon rains and several rivers, where two crops a year are frequent and three are not uncommon. Monsoon months are muggy and muddy, but there is palpable relief from the dry and dusty days on the other side of the mountains, a contrast that may have prompted a nineteenth-century British official to describe the Palghat region as the "most beautiful that I have ever seen."[26] Here, and only here, in this green swath of central Kerala through which the Bharatapuzha River flows—an area fifty miles from mountains to sea and about half that distance from north to south—the shadow puppet play is performed.

Fertile Palghat is a hinterland wedged between the Malayali kingdoms to the west and the Tamil kingdoms to the east, which explains much of its history and culture.[27] Although an outlying district of the ancient Cera kingdom, and later a minor principality of Venganadu, Palghat's natural riches and location attracted the evil eye of its powerful neighbors. Lying on the main trade route through the mountains, Palghat links the weaving centers in the Tamil country to the west-coast ports of Cochin, Ponani, and Calicut, and to Persia and the Arab world. Vying to control this valuable trade, the Zamorin of Calicut, the Raja of Cochin, and the Tamil Kongu kings turned Palghat into a battlefield in the medieval period. The Tamils invaded but never annexed Palghat, and political control swung back and forth between Calicut and the Cochin, eventually cutting the region in half: lands south of the Bharatapuzha River, containing the most productive rice fields and prosperous weaving centers, were ceded to Cochin and ruled by the Nambiti kings from a small palace in Kollengode;[28] lands north of the river, including those belonging to the rajas (Achans) of Palghat, remained attached to Calicut. Whatever independence these two ruling houses of the region managed to achieve was not long-lived. As the power of the Zamorin grew throughout the thirteenth and fourteenth centuries, the Palghat rajas courted favor with Cochin as a counterweight. South of the river, the Nambitis adopted the same strategy whenever threatened by Cochin and stood in alliance with the Zamorin. This cat-and-mouse game continued until the invasions from Mysore in the mid-eighteenth century pushed Palghat into one of the infamous stories of the British conquest of south India: the war against the Muslim rulers of Mysore—Hyder Ali and his son, Tipu Sultan.

Fearing such an invasion from Mysore, the Zamorin of Calicut occupied Palghat in 1746, but his forces were soon overrun by Hyder Ali, to whom the Palghat rajas had appealed for aid. In order to protect the valuable spice trade that traveled from the Kerala coast through the Palghat Gap to his landlocked capital at Seringapattinam, Hyder fortified Palghat town by building a massive stone garrison there in 1765. Commanding a plateau and surrounded by a deep moat, this imposing fortress became an obsession for British forces seeking to oust the Mysoreans; eventually, Colonel Fullarton led the victorious assault in 1783 (taking time to marvel that Palghat "is a fertile and extensive district and the adjacent forest abound in the finest Teek [sic] in India").[29] When Tipu Sultan was eventually driven back to Mysore in 1792, Palghat came under British rule administered from Bombay; and after Tipu was finally defeated in 1799, the line that had been drawn in the medieval period reappeared: lands north of the Bharatapuzha River, including Palghat town but excluding Chittur, became part of British-ruled Malabar; those south of the river, plus Chittur, were retained by the princely state of Cochin-Travancore. Finally, in 1956, for the first time in a thousand years, a united Palghat emerged as a district in the newly created state of Kerala. Today the Achan Rajas of Palghat retain their title and royal accessories, but little else;[30] during the annual coronation of the Raja, in 1989, I noticed that caparisoned elephants outnumbered spectators.

Politically divided, Palghat is culturally hybrid as well, and to some, it is a no-man's land—unorthodox, even dangerous. Suspicions of caste impurity are not an uncommon theme in India, but they cut deeply into the legends of both local royal houses. The Kollengode Nambitis, who ruled the southern Palghat region, are said to be descendants of a Brahmin mysteriously brought up as a blacksmith, while tales of pollution among the ruling family of Palghat appear in history books to explain why Tamil Brahmins (Pattars) and not Malayali Brahmins (Nambudiris) dominate the region.[31] The following version, told to me by an elderly Tamil Brahmin man in Palghat, is representative:

> Sometime in the 1500s when Palghat was a small principality under the Cochin Raja, only Nambudiris [Kerala Brahmins] lived here. Then a young prince of the Palghat ruling family, I think he was named Sekhari Varma, fell in love with a tribal girl. The Cochin Raja opposed this marriage, but the prince refused to budge and married the girl. Suddenly all the Nambudiris left and the prince sent to Tamil Nadu for Brahmins to conduct temple rites. These Pattars [Tamil Brahmins] had been coming to an annual Vedic scholars convention at Tirunavaya [near Pattambi] and so they knew the area. So they decided to settle in Palghat. Then the tribal queen turned all the Bhagavatis into tribal goddesses—Emur Bhagavati, Min Bhagavati, Manapully Bhagavati. The Pattars came from Tanjore, Madurai, and Kancipuram, and even now you can see this history in the names of their agraharams [settlements], for instance Cokanathapuram, after Śiva's name at Madurai.[32]

Another legend traces the marginality of Palghat to confusion of a different category: the first ruler was a Tamil, a Pandiya king named Subangi, who was actually a woman disguised as a man.[33] This stigma of crossed categories attaches even to Tamil Brahmins in Palghat, whose local name (*pattar*) is almost a synonym for miscegenation. Palghat's hybrid culture is evident today in the several castes who are both Tamil and Malayalam, worshiping at Bhagavati temples while wearing clothes (*vēsti*) and jewelry (double nose pin) the Tamil way and speaking Tamil words with Malayalam forms and sounds.

Languages are also intermingled in borderland Palghat and its puppet play. Tamil was the literary language of the west coast until perhaps the thirteenth or fourteenth century, when Malayalam began to emerge as a separate literature, in part as a consequence of Sanskrit influence. Predictably, Rāma texts illustrate this mottled linguistic history in Kerala. Although the first Rāma text on the west coast was probably the Sanskrit *Āścaryacūḍāmaṇi*, the more popular Rāmāyaṇas (*Rāmacaritam* and *Rāma Katha Pāṭṭu*), which date from around 1400 A.D., are an admixture of Tamil meters and usage with Malayalam vocabulary; the narrative in both these texts, however, follows Vālmīki.[34] Sanskrit eventually allied with Malayalam to form another hybrid (*maṇi-pravāḷam*) that eclipsed the Tamil stream of literature and produced the most famous Kerala Rāmāyaṇa, that by E<u>l</u>uttacca<u>n</u>, about 1600 A.D. (Some puppeteers claim that Malayalam is derived from Sanskrit and argued fiercely with me on this point in the drama-house.) Beneath this literary surface, Tamil and some kind of Tamil-Malayalam patois continued to be spoken in border areas, such as Palghat, where contact with the language on the other side of the mountains remained unbroken or was renewed by migration. By the early twentieth century, census reports show about one-third of the people of the Palghat region spoke Tamil as their mother tongue.[35] Nowhere is this polyglot more audible than in the drama-houses, where Tamils and Malayalis chant verses in literary Tamil and comment upon them in a Tamil-Malayalam patois (plus an occasional Sanskrit *śloka*) for their Malayalam-speaking patrons.[36] Small wonder, then, that local people say the puppeteers speak *ceṭṭi bāsai,* a mildly derisive term for "trader speech."

The term is not wholly inaccurate, either, since the Tamil-speaking puppeteers belong to the same groups of merchants, traders, and weavers (Mutaliyar, Chettiyar, Mannatiyar) who for centuries traveled to Kerala through the Palghat Gap, along the trade route linking Tamil commercial centers with the west-coast ports.[37] Upon entering Kerala, these merchants reached the town of Palghat, whence goods were transported down the Bharatapuzha River to Ponani and then by sea to Cochin or by an overland route northwest to the port of Calicut. Modern performance sites form a string of dots along these routes, from the Tamil centers to Palghat town, along the Bharatapuzha River, and along the road to Calicut. This trading must have been ongoing for centuries, but inscriptions show an increase around 1500, after a major Tamil temple was built at Kalpathy, near Palghat.[38] One family of puppeteers claimed that their ancestors migrated from Madurai "three hundred years ago," and another dated their migration from Pollachi about 1650. Whenever they came, they brought with them rice, textiles, jewelry, chilies, and, I believe, Kampaṉ's text.

One reason to believe that Kampaṉ's text was brought to Kerala by these Tamil weavers and merchants is their historical relationship with the Rāma cult in the region and with Kampaṉ scholarship generally. One might assume, for instance, that Kampaṉ manuscripts were brought into Palghat by Tamil Brahmins, who also began to settle there around 1500, but preservation and recitation of the *Kamparāmāyaṇam* is not and has never been a brahminical tradition.[39] Beginning with Kampaṉ himself, who was born in a caste of temple servants and musicians, and extending to the editors and commentators of his text, non-Brahmins have dominated the field. I was struck by the fact that Brahmins are insignificant in the shadow puppet play and that the few local Rāma temples in their control have no connection to Kampaṉ's epic;[40] Tamil Brahmins in Palghat, for example, celebrate Rāma's birthday in association with Vālmīki's Sanskrit epic or Eḻuttaccaṉ's Malayalam text but not Kampaṉ's. On the other hand, several small Rāma shrines in the countryside are visited by Tamil merchants traveling from Madurai via Pollachi and Palghat to Calicut along the old trade routes. I heard one legend explaining that a rice merchant dedicated a statue to Rāma on the spot where he recovered a cartload of lost merchandise, a spot that now has a stone temple with an image of Rāma and Lakṣmaṇa and a shrine to Hanumān.

Mutaliyars, in particular, have played a prominent role in Kampaṉ legend and scholarship.[41] According to most accounts, both Kampaṉ's patron, Caṭaiyappaṉ, and Kampaṉ's rival, Oṭṭakkūttaṉ, were Mutaliyars, as were most scholars who are acknowledged to have transmitted the *Kamparāmāyaṇam*.[42] We know that the commentary to both the first (partial) printing of Kampaṉ, in 1843, and the first full edition, in 1914, were edited by Mutaliyars. And they are the leading puppeteers in Kerala today.[43]

If Tamil weavers and traders brought Kampaṉ's text to Kerala and now perform as puppeteers, what about the art of shadow puppetry in Kerala, the third side of this historical triangle? Temple records indicate that in the early twentieth century the tradition was well established and spreading, new drama-houses built, and many puppeteers employed.[44] However, the only pre-twentieth-century evidence I located is the inclusion of "leather puppet play" in a list of performing arts and amusements in a mid-eighteenth-century poem by Kuncan Nambiyar, who was born and lived for some time in a village on the Bharatapuzha River where puppeteers still perform.[45] More clues, but only a few more, are provided from epigraphical and literary sources for the other traditions of shadow puppetry in India, especially in Andhra Pradesh, Karnataka, and Tamil Nadu.[46] Dating from the sixth century onward, the Tamil references are both the earliest and the most intriguing since the Kerala tradition is largely Tamil in textual origin; yet one wonders about the reliability of this literary evidence because it is so sparse, often ambiguous, and lacks corroboration from inscriptions. My own conclusion is that the modern shadow puppet plays in Andhra Pradesh, Karnataka, and Tamil Nadu developed only in the seventeenth century and derive from southern Maharashtra.

I make the case for Maratha derivation by culling information from several publications, especially Victor Mair's study of visual storytelling traditions in India (and elsewhere in Asia).[47] Mair demonstrates that painted scrolls, pictures, hand puppets, leather puppets, and other media are related and often used in a single performance. Other writers suggest that these arts of visual narration followed a southerly path of migration—from Rajasthan, into the Maratha country, across the Deccan, and into the Tamil country.[48] The itinerant performers of southern Maharashtra and the northern Deccan, for example, who performed with both painted pictures and leather puppets, trace their origins to Rajasthan and Gujarat, where painted-scroll and various (but not leather) puppet traditions have been documented.[49] Families of these Marathi-speaking picturemen probably migrated south with the Maratha armies moving across the Deccan in the 1600s, which would explain why the shadow puppets in Karnataka and Andhra Pradesh resemble the folk (Paithan) paintings and storytelling pictures in Maharashtra. Eventually, the Maratha armies entered the Tamil country in the late seventeenth century and established their court at Tanjore, where the modern Tamil shadow puppet play almost certainly evolved and where, much earlier, Kampaṉ lived. As Jonathan GoldbergBelle has shown, the Maratha court at Tanjore influenced several performing arts, such as Yakṣagāṇa, which in turn influenced the life-size leather-puppet tradition (*doḍḍa tōgalu gombeyāṭa*) of the northern Deccan and the storytelling art of Harikathā.[50] The most conclusive evidence of a trans-Deccan migration of shadow puppetry to south India, however, is that puppeteers in Tamil Nadu, Karnataka, and Andhra Pradesh speak Marathi as their mother tongue.

The puppeteers in Kerala, however, do not speak Marathi, and the *tōl pāva kūttu* appears to be a distant cousin of these other traditions. Still, despite its geographical cul-de-sac, the Kerala tradition cannot have been entirely uninfluenced by the others; the secret of Rāvaṇa's death, for example, the pot of ambrosia hidden in his chest, is a motif found both in Kerala and in many southern tellings of the Rāma story. In nearly every performative aspect, however, the contemporary Kerala tradition differs from the Maratha-influenced puppet plays. First, puppeteers in the other south Indian traditions are itinerant or semi-itinerant and perform as families, including the women, whereas in Kerala puppeteers live permanently in villages or towns and perform in exclusively male troupes. Second, puppets in Andhra Pradesh, Karnataka, and Tamil Nadu are translucent, but in Kerala (as in Orissa and most of Southeast Asia), they are opaque and perforated so that they cast shadows in black-and-white filigree silhouettes. Third, the puppets in Kerala are considerably smaller than those in Andhra Pradesh and Karnataka (but larger than those in Orissa and similar to those in Tamil Nadu). Fourth, although performances in other states have all but lost their ritual role, in Kerala they remain part of a temple festival and do not include the scatological scenes so prominent elsewhere. Fifth, as already mentioned, only in Kerala are performances held not in a temporary shed but in a permanent building (*kūttu māṭam*) built solely for the puppet play.[51] Finally, and more than any other factor, language separates the Kerala puppet play from the other Indian traditions; if elsewhere the puppeteers speak Marathi as their mother tongue, in Kerala they speak Tamil (or Malayalam).

Drawing all this evidence together, I believe that Marathi-speaking puppeteers came to Tanjore in the late seventeenth century, where they passed the art of shadow puppetry to Tamils, who then carried it into Kerala, where Kuncan Nambiyar described the puppet play around 1750 and where the Kampaṉ text had already been brought by Tamil traders.

Puppet Play and Kampaṉ: Overview

I close this chapter with four important points about the puppeteers' adaptation of Kampaṉ's epic in order to set the stage for reading the first translation in the next chapter. First, although this book highlights folk adaptations, I wish to stress that the senior puppeteers know the Kampaṉ text intimately. Any doubt on that score vanished during my early work with Krishnan Kutty: when I asked about the date of Kampaṉ's epic, he answered by going into his house and returning with a battered edition of the text in which he quickly found and read the one verse containing that information.[52] Not all puppeteers possess printed editions of Kampaṉ, and palm-leaf manuscripts are now rare, so most rely on painstakingly handwritten verses in flimsy notebooks that are copied again and again and handed down from teacher (*pulavar*) to student. These handwritten texts are especially valuable because they contain the actual verses sung by the puppeteers and marginal notes about emphasis and explication. Through long hours of practice these verses are memorized, and the first word of each verse is written down in tiny, cramped letters on a piece of cardboard, which beginners take into the drama-house for prompting. This memorization probably accounts for the standardization among the several troupes of puppeteers who perform at different sites but, with only minor variation, sing the same verses with the same words in the same sequence.[53]

A second point is that the puppeteers do not memorize or sing all of the ten thousand to twelve thousand verses in Kampaṉ. In fact, they never sing more than two thousand, and that many only in the few temples where they perform the entire story, beginning with the birth of Rāma. More commonly, they sing about twelve hundred verses when they begin their story at Rāma's meeting with Śūrpaṇakhā, or about eight hundred when they begin with the War Book.

Third, the puppeteers chant most of Kampaṉ's verses verbatim with their printed sources. Comparing my recordings with the printed editions, I found that 70 percent of the sung verses match the printed verses word for word or varied by no more than two words; another 10 percent varied by no more than one line (of the four-line verse). The remaining 20 percent of the sung verses had no basis in any of the major editions of Kampaṉ's poem, not even among the so-called dubious verses.[54] Parallels are known for very few of these verses, and I assume that most derive either from a textual source, unknown or excised in the editing process of the early twentieth century, or from an unrecorded oral telling.[55] I call these verses "folk verses," not because their language is less sophisticated than Kampaṉ's (though that is often true) but because they are not accepted in the official editions of Kampaṉ yet are sung in the puppet play, especially in controversial episodes.

A final observation is that, after the initial selection of some two thousand verses, the basic principle of adaptation in the puppet play is additive; that is, the puppeteers insert words, lines, characters, and episodes, all of which amplify rather than replace Kampaṉ's epic. This principle of accommodation is the main theme in the first half of this book. The next chapter, for example, analyzes the "Song of the Drama-House," which first reveals the tension between the theology of Kampaṉ's text and the folk religion that predates it.

CHAPTER 3

Ambivalent Accommodations: Bhakti and Folk Hinduism

Desired wealth, wisdom, fame, and
Lakṣmī's blessing, she of the sweet lotus who leads the way to liberation—
These are granted to those who sing of Rāma's strong shoulders
When he destroyed the *rākṣasa* armies and wore the *vākai* victory flower on his bow.

This folk verse, sung at the outset of every performance, is the signature of the puppet play and the motif of this chapter. I will return to it in more detail later, but for now notice that Rāma is described as a warrior with his bow and not as a god or an avatar and that Lakṣmī, not Rāma, leads one to liberation. This is a good starting point for an analysis of accommodation in the puppet play: a Rāma story is not the same as Rāma worship.

Without this distinction, history presents a paradox: although the Rāma story appeared in Tamil poetry centuries before Kampaṉ lived, Rāma bhakti never took root in the folk religion of south India.[1] References to episodes of the Rāma story are scattered throughout classical Tamil poetry (100 A.D.–300 A.D.); the notion of the Rāma-avatar appears in the *Cilappatikāram* (c. 600 A.D.); and Rāma bhakti is heard in the songs of the Āḻvārs (600–900 A.D.). Kampaṉ soon followed, but the pervasive and powerful Rāma bhakti in north India, evident in the popular theater of Rām Līlā and recitations of *Rāmcaritmānas*, has no equivalent in the south. As one general example, if the Daśara festival in north India and the Deccan usually celebrates Rāma's conquest of Rāvaṇa, in Tamil Nadu and Kerala it typically commemorates the Goddess's killing of Mahiṣa/Dāruka.[2] As I write this sentence, Hindus are again converging on the disputed mosque/temple site at Ayodhya in Uttar Pradesh (with certain loss of life), a controversy very unlikely in the far south, where Hindus also battle for religious causes but not for Rāma temples (which are hard to find). On the other hand, the quest of the exiled prince to rescue his abducted bride from the demon-king, the dilemmas of fraternal loyalties, and the terrible war against Lanka have been popular in south India at least since the earliest Tamil poems. In short, I agree with the Princeton translators of the Vālmīki text that the avatar concept in the Rāma story "cannot be the principal reason for its early spread and popularity."[3]

Not until the Chola period, in fact, nearly a thousand years after Rāma episodes first appeared in Tamil literature, do images of Rāma appear with any frequency in Tamil art.[4] Even so, the extent and religious content of this Rāma cult, supposedly rising like a tidal wave during the Chola period, has been exaggerated. For example, the medieval images of Rāma are far less common than contemporaneous images of Śiva. Similarly, it is well known that six Chola temples have sets of Rāmāyaṇa reliefs, but it is less well known that those temples are not Rāma temples; they are Śiva temples.[5] Regarding the Rāma story, as stated in the previous chapter, the entire corpus of south Indian inscriptions contains only four references to any Rāmāyaṇa recitation, and the extensive Chola records contain not a single mention of the *Kamparāmāyaṇam*.[6] It is also important to note that, almost without exception before and during the Chola period, Rāma appears as a human figure with two arms and a bow, as in the verse above;[7] in Kampa<u>n</u>, too, the most common epithet for Rāma is not "god" but "hero."[8] All this evidence confirms an emerging consensus that in pre-modern times, Rāma in story and stone was primarily a model for kingship, not an object of worship. Although the Rāma avatar did not much affect folk religion in south India, which is rooted in the worship of Śiva, the Goddess, and deified heroes, the Rāma story proved irrepressible and here and there achieved reconciliation with local religion, for instance, in the puppet play performed in central Kerala.

Accommodations appear first, and frequently, in the "Song of the Drama-House." More than any other segment in the long series of performances, this introduction is a creation of the puppet play; a song or two are borrowed from Kampa<u>n</u>, but everything else—the use of Brahmin narrators (*paṭṭa pāva*), homage to past puppeteers, history of the performance text, expression of gratitude to the sponsor, invocations to local deities, and (absent on this first night) summary of the previous night's action—are local innovations that give the first glimpse of how the puppet play has adapted Kampa<u>n</u>'s medieval epic to the drama-house. When the lamps are lit inside the drama-house and the two Brahmin puppets dance jerkily around the Gaṇeśa puppet in the center of the white cloth screen, the puppeteers sing songs to Viṣṇu-Rāma, Sarasvatī, Muruka<u>n</u>, and various goddesses, culminating with a verse to the presiding Bhagavati of the village. Then they launch into salutations and interpretations, as in the following segment of an introduction performed in Kunnumpuli:

"We pray to Kunnumpuli Kavu Bhagavati, to Chatran Kavu Bhagavati, to Kundalcheri Amman, to Valliya Kavu Amman, to Maceru Kavu Bhagavati, to all the Bhagavatis we know and do not know, we call on them all.

"Now let us praise our gurus, whom we honor not as Brahmins or Sudras but as *pulavars*, as poets and scholars. We praise those poets who sang in pure Tamil, those puppeteers who preceded us. We praise Sanku Pulavar, Meynanam Pulavar, Tamil Pulavar, and all their gurus—be they Sudras or Brahmins—we sing of them all. We sing of Cinna Tampi Pulavar,[9] who mastered the Vedas and *purāṇas*, of Cuntarar and Appar,[10] who sang the purest Tamil and corrected errors and taught songs by word of mouth from generation to generation."

"We bow at the feet of our own gurus, who taught us the eighteen *purāṇas*, the fifty-one letters,[11] the sixty-four sciences and arts, and this learned Rāmāyaṇa of Kampa<u>n</u>. We bow to those who taught us to sing and to sing correctly this story in sweet Tamil. We bow our heads to Krishnan Navalar, Cankai Pulavar, Laksmana Pulavar,[12] Ceruti Pulavar, Chandrasekhara Nayar, Narayana Nayar, Ramaswami Pulavar, Velayutha Pulavar, Gopalan Nayar, Kuncu Nayar.[13] Praise be to all the gurus, to those we know and those we do not know."

"Look, rajas mounted on elephants are arriving for the performance."

"Kings born in the line of the Guruvayur Raja, of Raghu, of Marttanda, and of Harishchandra, the great donor."[14]

"They have all come, from the north, the south, the east, and the west. The fifty-six rajas have arrived with their ministers, priests, and poets."

"No matter what story we might tell, no matter what knowledge we might possess, we are but small children playing at the feet of great men learned in the old texts, and so we ask their blessings and those of the gods:[15]

> We praise you, Sarasvatī, bright shining jewel,
> Dispensing boons to singers and musicians,
> And to your supplicants,
> who surround you with flowers and dance to your name;
> The poet's four gifts you grant to us:
> sweet voice and wise wit, correct words and creativity.[16]
> Radiant Sarasvatī, wearing white sari and pearls!
> Sarasvatī on a white lotus,
> Be the lamp that burns
> in the temple of our hearts."

"We praise the great sages of the past—Vyāsa, who arranged the Vedas, Kalaikottu Muni, and Agastya, who recited the Vedas, who traveled to the eight directions with his wife, Lopamudra, and who conferred boons on Rāma and knowledge on us all."

"Now we honor Rāma's name:

> Desired wealth, wisdom, fame, and
> Lakṣmī's blessings, she of the sweet lotus who leads the way to liberation—
> These are granted to those who sing of Rāma's strong shoulders
> When he destroyed the *rākṣasa* armies and wore the *vākai* victory flower on his bow."

"Those who tell of Rāma's strong arms and his annihilation of the demons—oh, they will gain their every desire. To say 'the *rākṣasa* armies were destroyed,' we must understand that the discus-bearing bowman, Rāma, strung his hard bow, fitted many arrows, and poured them down like a torrential rain on Rāvaṇa and his *rākṣasas*, all those cruel beings and all their armies. To those who sing of Rāma's magnanimous victory, of his strong shoulders, of the compassion of this All-Knowing God, and to those who hear it sung, to them all wishes will be granted. As the verse says . . . [*first line of verse repeated*]."[17]

"But what does this verse mean?"

"Everyone in this world, from the tiniest insect to the biggest raja, cries out for wealth: 'I want this, and I want that.' But more important than wealth is what we call *kalvi-celvam*, or 'wealth of learning.' Here 'learning' refers to intelligence, knowledge, the power to understand, and 'wealth' means enjoying family, wife, children, home, good food. Without these two gifts, which encompass all others, life is not worth living. Now if you want to gain this wealth of learning and enjoy the sixteen rewards it brings, listen . . . [*second line sung*].

"Here the verse speaks of 'liberation' [*vīṭu*], which means freedom, yet the question arises: Freedom from what? What to embrace? What of the four great aims in life? What of dharma [*aṟam*], wealth [*poruḷ*], pleasure [*iṉpam*], and liberation [*vīṭu*]? *Aṟam* is dharma, everyone knows that. But what is dharma? To whom should you do dharma? And to whom should you refuse it? Without studying the old books, one cannot hope to understand these subtleties. Most of us think that dharma brings religious merit—that's the popular idea—but the sages say that dharma can also produce suffering. There's a story my teacher told:

> Once a man wanted to practice dharma. Now at that time, money was divided into quarter annas, half annas, and whole annas. Our friend saw a diseased man and thought, 'Right, I'll do a quarter-anna dharma to him.' And so he took out the little coin and gave it to him. The second man then took the money and thought, 'If I take this penny and buy some line and a hook, I can fish. And if I can catch a lot of fish, I might become rich!' This is just what he did. He caught lots of fish, sold them, and became a rich man. When karma led him to the end of his life, he was brought to Yama (you know, the same person who tried to catch Mārkaṇḍeya and failed); and then it was time for Cittiraputra to work. He's the accountant who keeps that enormous ledger in which everyone's deeds are recorded; he knows just what each person did on every day and whether they should go to heaven or hell. When Cittiraputra finished this rich man's accounts, he turned to Yama and said, 'This fellow has killed thousands of lives, thousands of fish, and must go to such and such hell so that he will experience there the same pain he gave to those fish.'
>
> But Yama thought this over. 'There are three kinds of sins: of the mind, of speech, and of the body. Yet this man has committed none of these. No, the person who gave him that quarter-anna is the cause of this suffering.' Then he spoke to his henchmen: 'Send this man to heaven and bring the other man here.' Now, when Yama's assistants brought the first man to the realm of the dead, he felt confident

> about his next life because he had practiced dharma in mind, speech, and body. But there's something he had forgotten, that proverb: 'Give alms according to the recipient, give brides according to the horoscope book.'[18] And so he was sent to hell.

"When you do dharma, you must think of the person who receives it. What will he do with it? Will he use it wisely? Or waste it? We should do dharma where it produces good because otherwise dharma causes suffering.

"That's *aṟam,* the first of the four goals. The second is *poruḷ*—wealth, money, cash. It's certainly true that you can do nothing without it and there's that verse: 'A poor man is a nuisance to everyone, to his children, his father, his wife, even to the gods.' So we need money, but you must earn it without harming others—that's the main point—you can't just see a rich fellow and decide to kill him and take his money. The old books do not condone that kind of money—they call it 'money gained by taking life.' Money must not mean suffering. That's the point.

"Now the third goal is *iṉpam*, pleasure, of which there are two kinds: minor and major pleasure. The minor pleasures are growing up, arranging a marriage with a good family, going with your relatives to the bride's house, performing the rite to finalize the marriage contract [pouring water over hands], raising a family, settling into a home, and enjoying married life.

"Of course, it's not quite that simple. Again, there's a saying, 'True happiness occurs when two lovers are united in thought and mutual support.'[19] It won't work if the husband is a good man and the wife is a stupid woman, or if the wife is a good woman and the husband is a rotten man, for they must learn to pull through life together, especially when times are tough. If troubles arise, you can't just sink into despair and sigh, 'Well, it's my karma; nothing for me to do.' No! You've got to be even-minded and keep going and help your partner. Or suppose you come into a lot of money, it's stupid to go and spend it on this and that. You should realize that your turn has come and again be even-minded. Spend it to enjoy your life.

"After you have known dharma, wealth, and pleasure, life falls away by itself! That's the last goal—release [*vīṭu*]—and it comes unbidden, you can never measure it. But knowing all this requires wisdom, gained by studying the *śāstras* and by singing and hearing of Rāma's strong arms. Without study, you won't know a thing about dharma or pleasure or about the 'wealth of learning' or about the blessings of lotus Lakṣmī, in the verse I just sang."

Ambivalent Accommodations

I chose to quote this segment of the "Song of the Drama-House" because it includes not only the signature verse and its interpretation but also homage to the past. In the previous chapter I quoted a verse in which the puppet play claims mixed textual parentage, and here, the puppeteers acknowledge those who came before, the *pulavars* (poet-scholars), who "taught [them] to sing, and to sing correctly this story in sweet Tamil." Saluting this long list of predecessors, including their fathers and grandfathers, their teachers and their fathers' and grandfathers' teachers, the puppeteers reach back to the origin of the puppet play when the Kampaṉ text was first adapted to the drama-house. Such genealogies are part of every puppeteer's knowledge, as I quickly learned when, in response to a casual question, one man rattled off a list of fifty-five names stretching over seven generations. Most puppeteers know fifteen or twenty names, covering three or four generations, but all know the name of the legendary first puppeteer. With that man's story, the puppet play constructs its own past and reveals the ambivalence with which these folk-scholars regard high-caste patronage.

That legendary first puppeteer is "Cinna Tampi Pulavar, who mastered the Vedas and Purāṇas." A group of Tamil Chettiyars based in a village near Palghat claims eight generations of descent from Cinna Tampi, placing him in the late 1700s (a claim not inconsistent with the history proposed in the previous chapter). When I interviewed the last surviving puppeteer of this lineage in 1986, he was eighty-four and frail, lying in a sickbed and hardly able to raise his head to hear what was said. Yet, at my question about Cinna Tampi, he suddenly sat up and clearly sang three verses—one celebrating Kampaṉ as a saint (*āḻvār*) and two praising Cinna Tampi's poems, which "melt the heart so that even the deaf hear."[20] These verses, he explained, were once sung in the "Song of the Drama-House" but had long been forgotten. Cinna Tampi, the old man continued, came from a village near Pollachi in Tamil Nadu and settled outside Palghat, "Right here, in this village." He was a dull student who wandered from school and one day stuck his head inside a temple hall where he heard the Vālmīki Rāmāyaṇa recited by Brahmins—"by those Aiyars [Tamil Brahmins] over there in Ramanathapuram," the old man shouted, pointing toward the next settlement. Knowing he was a Chettiyar, a non-Brahmin, the Aiyars mocked Cinna Tampi and drove him away. His anger blazed until he undertook a pilgrimage to a famous temple (Mukampika) near Udipi in coastal Karnataka where he gained wisdom from the Goddess that enabled him to write the *Kamparāmāyaṇam* as shadow puppet play. At this point in the old man's narration, another member of the family interrupted and said that Cinna Tampi received this wisdom from the wind that blew Vedic chants as he passed Brahmins on the road; that was also true, confirmed the storyteller. Returning to Palghat, Cinna Tampi began to perform the Rāma story with shadow puppets, and as long as he lived (the old man completed his story with a soft smile), Cinna Tampi refused Brahmins entrance to the drama-house.

By its own account, then, the shadow puppet play was born of anger, humiliation, and caste prejudice. But the self-image is doubled, a combination of folk and high-status identity: Does Cinna Tampi's inspiration, and the tradition itself, derive from a popular goddess or from the Vedic winds? When I asked the old puppeteer to clarify this, he explained Cinna Tampi's relation to the Brahmins by likening him to the sage Nārada, who was homeless and hungry before the gods adopted him as one of their own. "Cinna Tampi," he said, "was like an adopted child or a servant to the Brahmins." Not born of Brahmins, the legendary puppeteer is adopted by Brahmins, but one wonders who adopted whom. In the previous chapter, I said that Brahmins in Palghat have little if any connection to either the *Kamparāmāyaṇam* or the Rāma cult in the area, and I can add here that few (if any) Brahmins ever patronized or performed the puppet play in Kerala.[21] Nevertheless, and although Cinna Tampi excluded them from his drama-house, the puppeteers are reluctant to exclude Brahmins entirely from their history of the puppet play. They honor their gurus "not as Brahmins or as Sudras," but whenever I asked about high castes, they found a way to assure me that "at one time" Brahmins were patrons and famous puppeteers. "Many were Aiyars," they insisted, and when I pointed out that "Aiyar" is a title and that even Cinna Tampi, whom they identify as a Chettiyar, is often given that title, they rejected that example as atypical.

Vedic winds blow in performance, too. If not as patrons or performers, Brahmins do appear as puppets, the *paṭṭa pāva* ([Tamil] Brahmin puppets), who sing the "Song of the Drama-House." As the first puppets on the screen every night, flanking Gaṇeśa in the center, they establish a brahminical frame for the puppet play; as one young puppeteer explained, "We use the Brahmin puppets because the play is really spoken by them; we are their mouthpiece." This pair of Brahmin narrators, an innovation by the Kerala puppeteers without counterpart in Kampaṉ or the other shadow puppet plays in India, is ironic since they have been given names (Muttu-pattar, Gangaiyati-pattar) identifying them with the Tamil Brahmins who, the puppeteers believe, humiliated Cinna Tampi long ago. Even as puppets, however, the Brahmin presence is unconvincing; they may confer legitimacy on performances, yet more than any other character on the screen they are stock figures that are manipulated to effect. For the whole of the "Song of the Drama-House" they dance and sing, but after the final verse of the introduction, they are removed from the screen and never appear in the Rāma story itself. Such vacillating attitudes toward high castes, evident in both the Cinna Tampi story and the role of the Brahmin puppets, arise from an ambiguity that defines the Kerala tradition on all sides: the drama-house separated from the temple yet linked to it by a ritual transfer of lamplight, the "trader-language" of the plays, a Tamil courtly epic performed in a rural Kerala festival, and the ambivalent cultural identity of the Palghat region as a whole.

But this uncertain social status may derive from yet another source—from legends about Kampaṉ and his text, told both in printed sources and by the puppeteers.[22] More than one Kampaṉ emerges from these stories. There is the poet-saint (*āḻvār*) who sings his poem at Srirangam and receives the blessings of Śrī Vaiṣṇava orthodoxy. But there is also the folk poet, a clever man of words and quite different from the figure favored by theologians and politicians; one wonders, in fact, who would marry their daughter to this poet who was continually poor, often deceptive, frequented courtesans, and slept a lot. This folk Kampaṉ has humble origins, as the etymologies for his name emphasize: he is a foundling discovered at the base of a post (*kampam*); or he is abandoned by his widowed (sometimes adultress) mother and lives a lowly life as a cowherd boy with a staff (*kampu*). He avoids school and takes up with an unmarried woman whom he met in a Śaiva monastery. Later, however, he finds his patron, Caṭaiyappaṉ, and rises to court poet.

This legendary Kampaṉ is more complex than a humble youth, however. On the one hand, he is a poet of the common man. In one story, an illiterate woodcutter, who fancies himself a poet, saunters into the assembly of poets and scholars at the Chola court. When he recites his coarse lines, the pompous poets scorn his presumptions until Kampaṉ laughs at their own pretensions by ingeniously breaking up the woodcutter's words to reveal a polished poem. In another story, wandering penniless after one of his many exiles from the Chola court, Kampaṉ meets a woman whose house wall will not stand; each time it is built, a *rākṣasa* tears it down. After listening to her story, the poet grabs a shovel, builds the wall, and then sings a verse that scares off the demon; when the woman asks who is he, Kampaṉ simply says, "A coolie. Give me my pay," and leaves.

More than simply a do-gooder, this Kampaṉ is also a clever poet-jester who plays tricks on everyone. A sample of his verbal powers is found in a long story that begins after his abandonment and discovery by his patron. Once in Caṭaiyappaṉ's care, little Kampaṉ is sent by his schoolmaster to watch over a field of millet, but he falls asleep in a Kālī temple and awakes to see a large horse destroying the precious grain. When his attempts to drive off the horse fail, leaving him to face a beating from the teacher, Kālī appears and supplies him with a special verse, which he duly sings, killing the horse. But then the teacher arrives on the scene and threatens to beat Kampaṉ because the dead horse belongs to a rich man who will beat the teacher. Clever little Kampaṉ then modifies the verse that killed the horse (substituting *mīḷa koṇṭu vā* [arise and come] for *māḷa koṇṭu pō* [go and die]) and everything is put right. Just as his youthful songs frighten demons and revive a dead horse, his later Rāmāyaṇa verses resuscitate a boy lying dead from a snakebite.

Always the artful dodger, Kampaṉ constantly uses his verbal chicanery to weave in and out of courtly intrigues. A favorite at court, he is often exiled by an insulted king only to be coaxed back because the raja misses his sweet poetry. On one occasion, he storms out of the Chola raja's court and takes himself to Kerala, where he enters the Cera court in the guise of a cook, Kampaṉ's cook, as he explains. Under this cloak, he presumes to explain the meaning of the Rāma story to the king and his court, but the jealous court poets plot to discredit him by claiming that he is a low-caste barber, even hiring a barber to feign kinship with the upstart outsider. Kampaṉ is equal to their tricks, however, and swiftly produces a priceless gold anklet, which, he explains, is one of a pair divided between him and his barber "brother." When this barber is unable to produce the missing anklet, his alleged kinship with Kampaṉ is exposed as false and he is forced to name the plotters, who are punished by the king.

The consummate display of Kampan̲'s linguistic deceptions must be the even longer story, told both in the printed sources and the drama-house, of how he came to compose his Rāmāyaṇa.[23] Briefly, when Kampan̲ and Oṭṭakkūttan̲ are summoned by the Chola raja and ordered to compose a "Rāmāyaṇa in the southern tongue," they set to work. Oṭṭakkūttan̲, at least, diligently writes day and night, while Kampan̲ sleeps and visits courtesans. Called to court to give a progress report on their Rāmāyaṇas, Oṭṭakkūttan̲ sings the story from Rāma's birth to the building of the causeway to Lanka; Kampan̲ then claims that he, too, has composed that much plus one more verse, which he recites for the raja. Listening to Kampan̲'s extemporized verse and knowing well that his rival has done absolutely no work, Oṭṭakkūttan̲ questions the use of a particular word, *tumi* (water drops). Quickened by this challenge, Kampan̲ wastes no time in asserting the correctness of his diction, and once again, turns to Kālī; with the goddess's help, his critics overhear an ordinary woman speaking the disputed word, which proves that Kampan̲'s verse is valid. None of this would have been necessary, however, if Kampan̲, the imperial poet, had not told a lie.

Several parallels between this folk Kampan̲ and the legendary first puppeteer, Cinna Tampi, are identifiable. Most accounts agree, for instance, that Kampan̲, like Cinna Tampi, was not a Brahmin; he was instead an Uvaccan, a temple servant who rang a bell in Kālī's temple. Still, both biographies contain the ambiguous relationship with Brahmins that I discussed above with reference to the puppet play generally. One legend claims a Brahmin birth for Kampan̲, who was abandoned by his mother after she was driven out of their village and then raised by an Uvaccan; in one version of this story, his mother is a Brahmin adultress.[24] We might remember that Cinna Tampi, too, in the old man's second version, was adopted by Brahmins.[25] At the same time, medieval poet and first puppeteer alike faced opposition from Brahmins and both composed a Rāma story in Tamil to replace Vālmīki's in Sanskrit. Caught between Brahminical and Tamil traditions, both men trod a thin line between high-status patronage and popular appeal, especially to the Goddess, and this mutual connection to the Goddess is perhaps the most important continuity between the Kampan̲ legends and the puppet play.

A humble poet of the people, a word wizard, the legendary Kampan̲ is also a devotee of Kālī. Not Rāma, and not Viṣṇu, it is the Goddess who appears everywhere in these legends, rescuing the lying poet or the sleepy boy from his self-created problems. She inspires his poetic gifts, saves him from social humiliation, and even holds a torch above his head so that he is able to compose his lines at night.[26] Goddess Bhagavati is also the source of Cinna Tampi's creativity (although Vedic winds do blow), and it is she, and Śiva her consort, who dominate performances of his Rāma story in the drama-house. Rāma's birth is sung in a series of devotional verses at the end of this first night's performance, but the presiding deity is the Goddess. The final song of the introduction, for instance, is addressed not to Rāma or Viṣṇu, as one might expect for a telling of their story, but to the local goddess:

> Bhagavati of Kunnumpuli Kavu
>   dancing wildly with Śiva
> Protect us as we sing Rāma's story.

No wonder that the puppet play is locally known as "a drama for Bhagavati."[27]

The prominence of the Goddess and Śiva in the puppet play exposes the thin layer of Rāma bhakti in south India. In popular culture, Rāma himself is a bhakta of Śiva; in major texts of the Rāma story, including Kampa<u>n</u> and the puppet play, the Viṣṇu-avatar installs and worships a Śiva lingam at the most famous pilgrimage site in south India, the Śiva temple at Ramesvaram (Rāma's Lord).[28] Here Rāma worships Śiva, while according to the legend of the puppet play's origin, Kampa<u>n</u> is Śiva:

> The goddess who guarded the gates to Brahmā's treasury grew proud and was cursed to serve as guard to Rāvaṇa's treasury in the demon city of Lanka. For thousands of years she guarded Rāvaṇa's wealth until Rāma and his monkey armies attacked the city. When Hanumān attempted to enter and she blocked his path, the monkey slapped her with his tail, and she immediately gained *mokṣa*. But in Śiva's heaven, she complained: "For years and years I have suffered under Rāvaṇa and now, just as he is to be killed by Rāma, I am here and cannot see this special event." Śiva then gave her a boon: "You shall be born on earth as Bhagavati and I will be born as the poet Kampa<u>n</u>; I will write the story of Rāvaṇa's death and you may watch it every year in your temple."[29]

In summary, both the Chola poet and the first puppeteer were buffeted back and forth between popular appeal and high-status patronage; both sought legitimacy from Brahmins yet drew inspiration from the Goddess. These parallels between the legendary Kampa<u>n</u> and the legendary Cinna Tampi shrink the historical and spatial separation between the medieval poem and its performance in Kerala. They suggest, too, that the recontextualization of Kampaṉ in Kerala is not as one-dimensional as I had first imagined; although performing the epic in the Bhagavati festival alters its bhakti orientation, the puppet play also returns this Rāma story to the folk culture from which it arose. The ambivalent status and self-image of the puppet play is a legacy of Kampaṉ and the *Kamparāmāyaṇam* itself.

Return, however, is not a reversal, and consistent with its additive principle of adaptation, the puppet play accommodates rather than eliminates the bhakti ideals of Kampaṉ's poem. For a clear example of this reconciliation, I return to the signature verse:

> Desired wealth, wisdom, fame, and
> Lakṣmī's blessing, she of the sweet lotus who leads the way to liberation,
> These are granted to those who sing of Rāma's strong shoulders
> When he destroyed the *rākṣasa* armies and wore the *vākai* victory flower on his bow.

A convention in traditional Indian literature, and known in Tamil as "benefit of the text" (*nūl payaṉ*), this is the first verse learned by puppeteers; it is inscribed at the head of the palm-leaf and handwritten manuscripts used by them, and sometimes at the head of each narrative section (*paṭalam*) in those manuscripts, and it is the initial verse in many folk Rāmāyaṇas in Tamil. In performance, when the lead puppeteer intones its initial line, all his assistants stop whatever they are doing (pouring oil in the lamps, for example) and sing this verse in unison. Finally, and unlike any other verse sung in the "Song of the Drama-House," it always receives a commentary, often an extensive commentary, whose quality is a measure of a puppeteer's talent. Why has the puppet play selected this verse, considered spurious by several Kampaṉ scholars, as its epigraph?[30] Probably for the same reason that others have disregarded the opinion of the authoritative editions and included it in their versions of the *Kamparāmāyaṇam*—it announces the fruits of devotion, binding performance to the religious belief system, without which there is no puppet play. Notice, however, recalling the distinction made at the outset of this chapter, that the recitation of the Rāma *story*, and not the *worship* of Rāma, earns rewards.

An accommodation of bhakti themes with a folk worldview is more apparent in the puppeteers' commentary on this verse. Whereas the puppeteers' recitation of the verse follows Kampan̲ verbatim, their explication reveals an ethos very different from that of the printed commentaries. Those commentaries explain the verse as a description of a series of rewards and pleasures that culminate in final liberation (*mokṣa*); the most traditional of the commentaries, for example, forces the four rewards of the verse (desired wealth, wisdom, fame, and liberation) into an uneasy correspondence with the Four Goals (*puruṣartha*) of classical Hinduism and concludes by declaring that Viṣṇu's compassion will lift erring humans from their misery to final liberation.[31] The puppeteers' commentary, by contrast, mentions the Four Goals, but only as a loose framework within which to offer more practical advice: both husband and wife must "pull the chariot" of marriage; faced with adversity, one should not "sink into despair and sigh, 'Well, it's my karma.'" Karma, *mokṣa*, and other abstractions are not the operative concepts in this tradition or in much of Tamil folklore.[32] In their commentary on this verse, for example, the puppeteers dutifully list *mokṣa* as one of the Four Goals and they mention it in closing, but they otherwise ignore this distant reward. Similarly, "spiritual wisdom" (*jnāna*), although explicitly listed in the verse and discussed in the printed commentaries, is mentioned only once by the puppeteers.

What is emphasized in the puppet play is not mentioned in the verse and receives little attention in the printed commentaries: proper conduct in this world, dharma or *ar̲am*. The puppeteers consistently pursue practical matters by construing the initial phrase "desired wealth" (*nāṭiya poruḷ*) to mean "intelligence" and the "wealth of learning" (*kalvi celvam*) to mean family comforts, and by concluding with a concrete commendation of learning. The heart of their explication, however, is an ironic lesson on dharma, an instructive tale about the well-intentioned gift of a quarter-anna to a man who buys a fishhook and becomes rich. Giving and taking, the puppeteers warn us, may have unforeseen effects, as intimated by a proverb they quote: "Give alms according to the recipient, give brides according to the horoscope."[33] Spiritual liberation is not rejected as a final goal, but the puppeteers' wary outlook recommends, for the time being, attention to worldly knowledge, the skillful handling of human relations, and the wise exchange of money and brides.[34] In the end, the puppeteers tell us, spiritual liberation depends on giving a quarter-anna to the right person.

This key verse and its interpretation illustrate the puppet play's reconciliation between the two great streams of Hinduism: bhakti, or devotionalism, and folk religion. Bhakti and folk Hinduism are not singular; each contains various strains. Emotional bhakti, for example, shares behavioral features with folk religion, such as an intense, personal communication with gods and goddesses, including ecstatic song and possession.[35] Practices may thus converge, but theologies diverge, especially in scholastic bhakti, whose goals of perfection and isolation conflict with the ideals of balance and relation in folk Hinduism.

The bhakti movement, originating around 500 A.D. in the Tamil country, introduced a radical soteriology based on the avatar not only as a personal god but also as a new kind of ethics, a flawless grace, which cuts the knots of karma and allows, even favors, the salvation of sinners and demons. An older worldview, in both Vedic ritual and folk Hinduism, is centered on a balance of forces—human and divine, gods and demons, lust and asceticism. Demons (*rākṣasas*) are none other than the older, darker cousins of the gods, with whom they form an intimate opposition; Rāvaṇa and his family are descendants of Brahmā and are considered Brahmins, so much so that Rāma must expiate himself after killing Rāvaṇa. Bhakti disrupted this prior balance, in which, as Wendy Doniger put it, "demons are purposely left unredeemed, demonic, to maintain a force of evil and distinguish them from gods."[36] In other words, Rāma's mission to eradicate the demons from "the root up" thrust a moral purity into the struggle between gods and demons; an opposition once polarized and symmetrical became ethicized and asymmetrical. To be sure, Kampa̲n's Rāma is more than a mere salvific tool, just as Vālmīki's hero is more than a man, and Kampa̲n's poem probes the psychological dilemma of a fully "divine man," for instance, when Rāma forgets his mission and must be reminded by the gods.[37] It is also true that the *Kamparāmāyaṇam* contains elements of a pre-bhakti, heroic worldview from early Tamil literature.[38] In the end, however, Kampa̲n's Rāma remains superior to animals and demons and humans because, wittingly or not, he is the vehicle of their salvation.

The particular strand of bhakti that influenced Kampa̲n's epic is Śrī Vaiṣṇavism, a brahminical synthesis of "qualified non-dualism" and popular Viṣṇu worship that developed in the Tamil country in the medieval period. Central to Śrī Vaiṣṇava theology are the concepts of *aruḷ* (grace), *prapatti* (surrender to god), and the avatar. The Te̲nkalai, or "southern branch," of this movement is especially important because it appears to have preserved Kampa̲n's poem in manuscript form at Alvar Tirunakari, a famous matt near Tirunelveli, in the southern Tamil country. For this Southern School, god's grace is loving, capricious, unmerited, and the devotee must surrender to it unconditionally, like a kitten clinging to its mother. But both grace and surrender are realized only through the avatar, god's manifestation on earth, who is beyond earthly codes of justice and who offers salvation to anyone, human, beast, or demon who worships him. Enshrined in its title, *Irāmāvatāram* (The Avatār of Rāma), the Rāma-avatar is the conceptual center of Kampaṉ's poem. George Hart put it this way: "Kampaṉ makes his idea of dharma totally dependent on Rāma-Viṣṇu. It is through the agency of Rāma that dharma is established and maintained, and it has no meaning without the worship of Viṣṇu."[39] Although the eleventh- and twelfth-century founders of Śrī Vaiṣṇavism made little reference to the Rāma story, later commentators and teachers, especially in the Southern School, placed great emphasis on Tamil devotional literature, such as early Vaiṣṇava poetry and Kampaṉ's praise poem to Rāma.[40] In time, Kampaṉ's masterpiece was recognized as scripture, and its poet was elevated to the status of a poet-saint (*āḻvār*).

This bhakti theology did not survive the text's journey through the mountains into Kerala, however. Cut off from the courts and monasteries that had supported it in the Tamil country, the *Kamparāmāyaṇam* underwent considerable change when it entered hinterland Palghat. This famous Rāma text is sung as ritual, but it is sung at temples where Rāma is not worshiped, a fact that would be astounding unless we remember the distinction between Rāma story and Rāma worship. In rural Kerala, Kampaṉ's text did not find a Hinduism of grace and surrender to the avatar but a religion of balance and revenge and powerful forces, including the deified dead.[41] Nevertheless, because the accommodation achieved in the puppet play is additive, the joys of total surrender to god are not excluded from the puppet play.[42] Indeed, precisely because the puppet play is caught between these conflicting demands, between the isolated perfection of the avatar and the moral balance of folk Hinduism, the puppeteers tell a Rāma story more complicated than either a bhakti or a folk text alone could produce. One complexity, and the topic of the following two chapters, is that the puppet play blurs the moral boundaries between the avatar and his adversaries.

Plate 1. Natesan Pillai, senior puppeteer, at home in 1989; see his performance in chapter 6.

Plate 2. The drama-house at Mannur in 1989, where "Killing Vāli" (chapter 5) was performed.

Plate 3. Inside the drama-house with Krishnan Kutty and his troupe performing the Śūrpaṇakhā episode (see chapter 4), 1986, Cherpalachery.

Plate 4. Lakṣmaṇa (r.) and Śūrpaṇakhā (l.) face each other just before the young prince mutilates her, 1986, Cherpalachery.

Plate 5. Rāma, Lakṣmaṇa, and Sītā (from left to right) march toward the Godavari River, 1986, Cherpalachery.

Plate 6. Krishnan Kutty's youngest son holds up a soldier in Rāvaṇa's army from the puppet basket, 1986, Cherpalachery.

CHAPTER 4

The Death of Sambukumāra<u>n</u>: Kāma and Its Defense

Complications in the puppet play cluster around the controversies in the epic. These are the moral pressure points in the story that generate many versions in Kerala and elsewhere told this way and that in an attempt to resolve, avoid, or explain away questions that are probably insoluble but which reveal the distinctive mark of any particular telling. Three such flashpoints stand out across the spectrum of Rāma stories, including the puppet play: (1) Rāma's meeting with Śūrpaṇakhā; (2) his killing of Vāli; and (3) his rejection of Sītā. Leaving Vāli for the next chapter and Sītā for the final one, in this chapter I examine the puppeteers' treatment of Rāma's fateful encounter with Rāvaṇa's sister, Śūrpaṇakhā, the scene which baffled me that first night in Suhavaram. This meeting on the banks of the Godavari River is the traditional starting point for epic narration in the puppet play, and it is a curious choice. In order to begin at that point, the puppet play must leap over nearly a third of Kampa<u>n</u>'s text, including what we thought were indispensable events, such as Rāma's birth, his initiation with Viśvāmitra, his marriage to Sītā, and his departure from Ayodhya. Landing on the banks of the Godavari River is not entirely haphazard, however, since the puppet play's opening scene subtly recalls the fertility and harmony in Kampa<u>n</u>'s opening description of the Sarayu River flowing by Ayodhya. Still, in the forest, perfection is not what it seems; barely thirty minutes into performance, the puppeteers veer off into an episode not told in Kampa<u>n</u>, the death of Śūrpaṇakhā's son, Sambukumāra<u>n</u>, which fixes this Rāma story on a new moral axis.[1]

The translation below covers the second night of performance: Rāma is already in exile and the events from his birth to his departure from Ayodhya with Sītā and Lakṣmaṇa have been quickly summarized on the previous night. Soon Rāma will meet Śūrpaṇakhā, but the performance opens with a famous Kampan̲ verse in which Rāma, speaking to Lakṣmaṇa, likens the Godavari River to poetry.

The Death of Sambukumāran̲

"Look, brother, here is the Godavari,
  lying as a necklace on the world
Nourishing the rich soil
  rushing over waterfalls
Flowing through the five regions
  in clear, cool streams,
Like a good poet's verse.[2]

"Look, Lakṣmaṇa, look at this wonderful river, which we have reached after taking delicate Sītā over these rough jungle paths, through thickets of thorns, through ominous forests, past dangers and animals, unknown and hidden from us on our long journey.[3] And, finally, look at this river, the lovely Godavari! It must be the Godavari because the poets say that of all the rivers on this earth the Godavari is the most beautiful, even more beautiful than the Ganga. Now, in this verse, the word *puvi* refers to the Earth Goddess, who wears the river like an ornament, but the river is more than just a sparkling jewel. Like two hands cradling the land, its banks support pious Brahmins who recite the *Rāmāyaṇa*, the *Mahābhārata*, the *Bhāgavata Purāṇa*, and other sacred books that tell us when to marry, how to live the four stages of life, when and where to travel at auspicious moments, how to perform dharma and sacrifices with the correct mantras and oblations. And that is how the Godavari feeds this special place of five landscapes, called 'Panca-vati.'[4]

"The poet says that the Godavari lies like a necklace on the earth, but the river also flows, it moves, like a poem. The word 'verse' in these lines refers to the poetry in Vālmīki's epic, those lines so dense with meanings that you need one commentary to find the literal meaning of his words and another to tell you their hidden meaning.

The Godavari, you see, resembles poetry because it, too, has sound and beauty and motion.

"Do you know what is truly special about this river? When one newly arrives at a location, one must build a house, which requires consulting the house-*śāstras* for selecting a site, finding trees, bringing wood, conducting a sacrifice and then a *pūjā*. Most places have one or two flowering trees, but look around—there are flowers everywhere. And look at these forests—the very banks of the Godavari are hands that hold up forests and offer these flowers at our feet. Tell me, Lakṣmaṇa, have you ever seen anything so wonderful?

> See the trees rising high
> sandalwood and eaglewood, silk-cotton and pepper trees;
> See them rising high above us
> along the river banks;
> These forests are full of demons,
> but we will perform *tapas* here.

"Lakṣmaṇa, there are five kinds of trees here, just as there are five types of landscape. We know that the forests are infested with demons who steal, kill, drink, lie, and abuse Brahmins—the five heinous crimes—but don't worry, little brother. It is for that very reason that we must perform religious austerities [*tapas*] here. That's our purpose on earth—to root out evil and protect the good—isn't it? We'll fight anyone who opposes dharma.

"But what actually is dharma? They say it's the earthly embodiment of an unreachable god who stands in front shielding us, like a fence protecting a field. Dharma stands on four feet—truth, charity, meditation, and dharma itself—in the form of a cow, and it stands on two feet in the form of a Brahmin. Dharma has been attacked by demons since the beginning of time, especially here in Pancavati, so we must stay and destroy them. But, first, we must build a hut to sleep in. Go into the forest, Lakṣmaṇa, and cut down trees."

[*Lakṣmaṇa replies*:]

> "Merciful Lord who upholds Brahmā's many worlds,
> Great Lord who snapped Śiva's bow,
> Watch my hands work quickly for the hut will be built
> Not by me, but by your own *tapas*.

"Rāma, you support all these worlds created by Brahmā, and you cracked that bow at Janaka's palace. How can what I do be anything but your work? [*Moves to extreme right hand of screen*] Let's see, what tree shall I cut down?

Bears and tigers are everywhere they say;
Oh, I hear a lion! Better hide and shoot;
But, look, that's no lion—
Only cuckoo birds chattering away!

"Well, I shot the arrow anyway and drove away those dangerous birds. [*Sambukumāran̲ puppet placed in tree.*][5] Now, look, somehow a sword came into my hand, and it's perfect for cutting down trees. [*He swings the sword against the tree in which Sambukumāran̲ has been placed.*]

Alone in this forest
  with a sword from the gods;
I strike this tree
  and a body falls in a river of blood;
What evil this act will bring
I do not know.

"I wished only to build a hut and now I have killed! I don't understand, but I fear evil consequences. One thing is certain: I cannot use this blood-stained tree."

[*Moving to another part of the forest, Lakṣmaṇa cuts down other trees, sinks them into the ground, lashes thick branches on them, and builds the forest hut. Lakṣmaṇa moves back to Sītā and Rāma, who speaks*:]

"Lakṣmaṇa, is the hut ready?"

"Yes, but something terrible happened . . .

I cut down a demon when I cut down a tree,
Why I cannot say—who knows what the gods do?
But the hut is complete for you and Sītā to enter,
As I guard the south protecting you from evil.

"Rāma, what does this demon's death mean? Something is very wrong. But for now please enjoy the safety of this hut and rest assured that I will protect you both."

"Sītā, let us enter the hut." [*All three puppets move toward the hut.*]

"Oh, Rāma, look. The hut is perfect. Lakṣmaṇa is a genius.

Like the great Vedas which drive out confusion,
Like the pure Milk Ocean surrounding Viṣṇu's island,

My brother has built a shelter
As perfect as the Ganga itself!"[6]

"Sītā, this hut is incomparable, unparalleled, unprecedented! To what can I compare it? One may say that it resembles the Vedas: once the demons had shrouded the whole world in illusion, so the gods went to Viṣṇu, who told them to churn the Milk Ocean. Then—to make a long story short—when they churned, the Vedas emerged and the illusion was dispelled. What other images of perfection match this hut? The Milk Ocean is one, for Vaikunta lies like a jewel in the very center of its 3,200,000 leagues. White, pure white! In ancient times that island was called 'heaven-seen,' but our human mouths have turned those words to 'haven-scene.'[7] This simple hut is also equal to the Ganga, the most wonderful river on earth. In fact . . .

Lightning-thin girl, from heavy-forested Mithila,
My brother has built a hut that is flawless
And incomparable,
Like your flower feet.[8]

"So much can be said of Mithila—its fabulous palaces and rich temples—but it's all said by you, Sītā, by your beauty. 'Light-ning' is the right word for you since your body is a lustrous streak of light; your feet are as soft as water lilies and the red lotus flowers of Lakṣmī's throne. You possess every beauty that Lakṣmī does, but Lakṣmaṇa's actions surpass all beauty. Does anyone compare to him? Here, in this remote forest, he builds us a shelter like a palace!"

[*Sītā and Rāma enter hut, while Lakṣmaṇa stands as guardian outside; Śūrpaṇakhā enters from the left and speaks in a gruff voice*:]

"Hey, what's this I smell? Human flesh is it? Brahmā may create them, but these humans really smell! Haven't eaten any flesh since yesterday—I'm famished. Gobble them up in a second when I find these stinking humans, but first I better look for my son, Sambukumāra<u>n</u>, who went to do *tapas* weeks ago and hasn't returned. Maybe he's won a boon from Śiva by now. [*Moves toward center of screen*]

"This looks like the tree he did *tapas* in. Yes, this is it, but . . . some branches are broken . . . and . . . over there . . . there's a body. Oh, no! My son, my poor son, Sambukumāra<u>n</u>!

Is cruel death your reward for long *tapas* to the gods?
Wearing fresh flowers you came and you wear them now

Riding to Śiva's heaven in death's golden bier;
I've lost you forever, my son, Sambukumāran̲.

"It can't . . . I . . . but it is you, Sambukumāran̲, though it cannot be so. You came here to win liberation, yet you gained death. Is this everyone's fate who worships Śiva? Or just yours? And where are you now? Somewhere on the journey to Śiva's heaven. Ah, who can say?

Covered with turmeric and ash, I prayed for a son at Lord Śiva's feet;
Now your golden body lies in bloody pieces at my feet;
Who did this, Sambukumāran̲?
Who makes me collapse in grief?

"I chanted and meditated on Śiva's name for months, and finally you were born. But can this—can your death be Śiva's boon? Did my *tapas* win your death?

Yes, your killers are gone but not escaped;
It might be Indra, or Brahmā on his lotus,
Or even Viṣṇu with sweet basil leaves—
No matter who he is, I will follow his trail,
And drag him to Lanka surrounded by dark seas.

"Hah, let them try to escape! They can jump off the earth and I'll follow. Revenge will be mine. Even if Lakṣmī's Lord, Nārāyaṇa, did this evil deed, he will not escape. Doesn't matter if it's that flower-god, Brahmā, creator of the eighty thousand lakhs of beings in our worlds. Killer of my son, whoever you are, I will find you and imprison you in Lanka, and no one ever escapes from the hands of my brother Rāvaṇa. [*Moves toward the river*]

"I'll eat anyone who comes my way, child-killer or not. Huh, can't see much from here. Better climb a tree and look around. Ah, yes, that's better. [*Rāma leaves Sītā and approaches the river to bathe.*] Hmm . . . who's that over there by the river? A man, I think, and a nice-looking one, too!

Is that Kāma visiting this earth with his love-bow?[9]
Or Indra, king of gods? or some earthly raja?
Could he be Lakṣmī's consort, Viṣṇu? Śiva glistening with garlands?
Sūrya in his circling chariot?
 Who, O heart, who is this man?

"Who *is* this beautiful creature? Must be a god come to this sun-measured earth! You see, the sun does circle the earth—it rises in the east at Mt. Manasottara, continues south to Mt. Dharma Raja in the first quarter of the cycle, and enters the waxing half of the cycle at midday. From there it enters the northern path to Mt. Meru, bringing night in the third quarter of the cycle, and finally comes around again to Mt. Manasottara at dawn. This is Sūrya Dēva, the Sun, by whose power it is possible to discriminate between night and day on earth.[10]

"On earth, however, Kāma is supreme, for he makes love possible with his sugarcane bow and flower-arrows. Perhaps that is he, standing there by the river, in human form. If not, he might be the great lover, Indra, the most beautiful of gods; or he might be a mere earthly king come to the Godavari on a pleasure hunt. Or is he Lakṣmī's lover, that dark-skinned Viṣṇu? Or Chandra, god of the smooth moon? Or fiery Sūrya, who drives his shining chariot through the sky? Whoever he is, he is beautiful beyond words.

"But no, he bears no marks of those gods—not Brahmā's brass pot, not Viṣṇu's discus, conch, club, or lotus, not Kāma's sugar-bow. What he carries, I see, is a hunting bow and a tiger skin, as if he's an ascetic! Oh, I can't bear this any longer; I've got to go closer and see him. [*Moves toward Rāma, who remains motionless by the river*]

"Huh! This demon form is a disgrace! What would he think if he saw me like this? I've got to change into a beautiful woman—then I'll catch him for sure. Yes, I'll use that boon given to me years ago when I did *tapas* to Lakṣmī and she appeared before me and said, 'Whenever you wish to change your appearance, chant this mantra.' [*As Śūrpaṇakhā chants the Lakṣmī mantra, a new (Mōhini) puppet appears and the old puppet is removed.*] There, that's much better!"

[*Rāma*] "Who's coming toward the river bank. Well, well, who is this lovely creature? No woman on earth or in the netherworld is her equal. Not Mēnakī, not Urvaśī, not Tilōttomā, who dance in the heavens, none of them possesses this woman's beauty. Nowhere among the eighty thousand lakhs of beings in these worlds have I seen any woman so beautiful as she! No thing, no person, no other object in this universe, is as lovely! I must talk with her. [*Rāma moves toward Śūrpaṇakhā.*]

"May I ask your name, faultless beauty? You come just as I am finishing my holy bath, which makes me wonder: Did goddess Lakṣmī herself step off her red lotus throne and take form here on earth? But, then, what have I done to deserve this honor? Certainly my acts of dharma would not bring me such good fortune. There's so much

I want to ask you. Who are you? Where are you from? Speak to me, lovely peacock!"

"Handsome one, my family line begins with Brahmā, who rests on a lotus of a thousand petals. Tradition says he had ten daughters but only one son, born of his infinite wisdom, and he was Pulastiyan̲, who had a son named Vicaravasu, whose daughter I am."[11]

"But what is *your* name?"

"My father, Vicaravasu, married four women and his last wife, Kēkaci, bore me and gave me the name Kāmavaḷḷi.[12] But listen: I have two brothers. The older, Kubera, is strong as a mountain; that god riding on the powerful bull, that powerful Śiva, gave him boons for his *tapas,* and now he rules Alakapuri. But my other brother, the younger one, Rāvaṇa, is even more powerful.[13]

"Let me tell you a story. This world has eight directions: east, southeast, south, southwest, and so on to the northeast. Each is guarded by an elephant: Airavata, Pundarikam, Vamana, Kumutam, Ancanam, Putkakam, Savapavam, and . . . the others.[14] Each direction also has a special snake, like Ādiśeṣa, and a special god. This wide world, held up by those elephants and snakes, was the object of my brother's ambitions, and so he marched in every direction and conquered every raja until he came to those eight elephants and threatened them: 'Fight me or step aside!' But the animals did not move, and among themselves they thought, 'Instead of attacking one by one, better to fight him as a group of eight with our thirty-two tusks.' Charging hard, they pierced my brother's chest with their tusks, but he didn't show the tiniest scratch. Calmly, he drew his sword and proceeded to lop off the tusks, still stuck in his chest, and then cried out, 'Is that it? Have you no more strength?' The elephants were silent, and he ordered them back to their stations. That's my younger brother, that's Rāvaṇa.

"Not only that. Once this little brother challenged Lord Śiva. It's a very long story, but I'll just say that in the end he shook mighty Mt. Kailasa and ruled over the earth, heavens, and netherworlds, and was given the title 'King whose crown bows to no one.'[15] His name is Rāvaṇa and I am his sister, Kāmavaḷḷi."

"You say that your older brother received boons from Śiva and that your younger brother defeated the cosmic elephants and conquered the Three Worlds. But, then, where is your wealth? Your jewelry? Your silk dresses? Your armies? If your family is so exalted, why are you left alone in this forest?"

"Of course, of course. If a woman walks alone, some man will ask why and she must explain! Frankly, since you are probably a god, you ought to know these things anyway. I think you ask just to get an answer from me.

"And since you are so anxious to know, I will give you an answer. It's *kāma*, 'desire,' the first and worst of the thirteen dispositions that make up our bodies.[16] Desire, lust, is what it is, and it comes from that basic disposition called 'energy' [*rajas*]. As the *Bhagavad Gītā* says, 'Greed, lust, cruelty, fraud, cowardice, and desire all spring from "energy".' Call it *kāma*, call it lust, call it what you like—my heart is bursting with it! Before I ached with one question: 'Where? Where is he?' Then I saw you and thought you might satisfy my desires. Of course, women of high rank do not understand their *kāma*, and even if they did, they would not express it openly like this. I am only telling you, Rāma, because the pain is too great!

"And this *kāma* is eating me alive, destroying me life and limb, consuming my life force [*uyir*] inside. That force when heated by the fires of *kāma* swirls around and rises straight to the head and sometimes kills. My pain is great, Rāma, and if you don't do something, I will die, right here, in front of you!

"But don't think I am blameworthy. No, this is the work of god Kāma, whose five arrows are five flowers: the red lotus, the mango, the asoka, the jasmine, and the lily.[17] Each flower-arrow has a different quality and causes a different condition when it hits; those effects are part of a long, magnificent story, but for now I'll just say that the worst is the red lotus arrow. When it strikes, whatever is in the heart grows and grows, like a lotus stalk, until it bursts your brain! I'm sure Kāma has hit me with that red lotus arrow because my *kāma* is rising, higher and higher . . . and now you have come. Please help me, make love to me, marry me!"

[*Rāma*] "Shamelessly you roll your blazing red eyes at me! No decency, no pride! What kind of a woman would speak to me like this?"

"What you say may be true, sir. But remember that I have not come here of my own free will. No, Kāma's arrows have driven me. Understand, too, that this lust is not mine; it belongs to nature. You must know that proverb: '*Kāma* is the source of the whole world; it's impartial.' Realize that this energy, this passion, is everywhere, in every one of us, in every kind of being. If a man desires a woman and wants to marry her, that's *kāma*—it's a neutral force. Like the proverb says,

'*Kāma* is blind.'[18] But it takes intelligence and maturity to know how to act on *kāma*, and when. If it is not satisfied, it brings great pain, even death. Sure, the *śāstras* say that we must avoid this disease of *kāma*, but it's not that simple. Our bodies are a balance of three dispositions—purity, energy, darkness—and *kāma* is part of energy. Get rid of *kāma* and you lose the balance. Of course, when *kāma* swirls around inside in hot gusts of wind, it is dangerous, but it's not my doing, and you must do something to save me!"

"But . . . but I cannot possibly marry you! No matter what you say, you are a demon and I am a human. A demon–human marriage is not permitted, and that's the end of it."

"Yes, that's true. Whenever the serious business of marriage arises, questions of compatibility must be considered. As you probably know, there are ten primary ways in which the partners should be compatible, and the most important of these is disposition. If the boy and girl don't match in that, then they shouldn't marry even if the other areas are compatible. But if the two *are* matched in disposition, then all other issues are inconsequential. Remember, too, that there is more than one kind of marriage, eight to be exact. The first seven—Brahmin, divine, demon, human, and so on—are traditional marriages, but the eighth, Gandharva marriage, is entirely different. According to the *śāstras*, it's for a couple matched only in disposition, when questions of caste, money, and status do not apply. If two people are joined in love, that's enough. And you don't need to run away either, you can marry right then and there."

"But it's not proper."

"And don't think that this Gandharva marriage is just my idea. No, the Vedas have described it, in much detail, as you probably know. Besides, if you agree to this marriage, don't worry about getting permission from anyone else because my brothers will be pleased to know that their sister found such an eligible man. Rāma, they'll treat you like a brother-in-law and offer gifts to satisfy all that you desire—you'll rule the Three Worlds—that's the life I am offering you. How can you say no?"

"Yes, the law books do accept that kind of marriage, but I am already married. Besides, you're a fraud. You're not a human. You're a demon in disguise. And what do I want with the pleasures you offer. My home is Ayodhya, a heaven on earth, where Lakṣmī resides. I didn't leave it and come to the forest to enjoy demon pleasures with you. Go!"

"Rāma, how can I leave you? Please, you must relieve this *kāma* pain. Do not torment me."

[*Realizing that Rāma has not returned, Sītā approaches the river. Seeing Sītā, Śūrpaṇakhā cries out*:]

"Rāma, watch out! There's a dangerous woman behind you! She's a sorceress, who'll bewitch you. Wrapped in the veil of illusion, she's *māyā* herself. I can see right through her—she's one of those thieving demons and nothing more. Look, her every movement betrays her inferior birth. Tell her to leave, and then take care of me."

[*Rāma*] "I finally understand your hidden intentions. They say, 'The face mirrors the mind,' and now I see your thoughts in your words.[19] Listen, why not approach my brother? He might accept you."[20]

[*Sītā*] "Don't speak to her like that. It might seem like play, but we'll suffer later for your cruel humor. Besides, Lakṣmaṇa will be angry if he finds out. Let's go back to the ashram."[21]

[*Rāma and Sītā leave Śūrpaṇakhā, who speaks to herself*:]

"So, that woman tells him to go and he goes. Her black hair is beautiful and her body shines like gold—no wonder he follows her. Obviously, I'll have to destroy her first; and Rāma mentioned a brother . . . well, let that be for now, evening is coming and tomorrow is another day. But where to lie down for the night? These little jasmine flowers will make a nice, soft bed. There we are . . . but oh, this *kāma* pains me even at night. Ah, here comes the full moon rising in the sky, yet even its cool beams drive into me like iron spears!

> Waxing moon, I'll make a curry of you and then eat Rāma, too;
> But no, the mountain wind like harsh Death's spear
> Enters my seething breast.
> And now I will sleep.

"Moon God! Yours is no easy task for your beams must cool the earth scorched hot by the thousand-rayed sun, but even now, in the last and coolest hour of night, you burn me more than the noontime sun. I can't stand the pain! I'll . . . I'll rip you from the sky, cook you up like a curry and devour you! Then I'll grab that troublesome, lovemaker Kāma and eat him, too.

"What's this? Ah, that cool southern breeze, which cures disease when it touches the body.[22] The winds that blow into our body have no precise names, only the directions from which they come, like 'east wind,' 'south wind,' and so forth. Very few people understand the nature of these winds, although the *śāstras* tell us that winds from the east, south, and north can cause illness, whereas this southern wind—it brings health.

"Why the southern breeze? Well, it originates from Mt. Potikai in the south, where Agastya, the great Siddha adept lives with his wife in the full grace of Śiva. From the edge of his ashram the wind blows, descends into the hot, barren plains where it begins to heat up, then drops into deep pools of water and runs through the stalks of red lotus deep in the muddy bottom. Absorbing the lotus fragrance, the southern wind blows on, mixing with jasmine and lilies until it becomes as pure and clear as a mind that has seen into the inner meaning of an esoteric text. For this reason, the southern wind will cure diseases for which there is no cure.

"Of course, there's a special time when all of us can be cured, during the last seven days of Panguni and first fifteen days of Cittirai, during the Fire Asterism, when the sun burns with intense heat and Murukan̲ resides on his mountain at Palani. Anyone who journeys to Palani at this time will gain his blessings. Of course, you will receive Murukan̲'s blessings anytime you worship him, but if you go during the Fire Asterism and stand on top of Palani mountain, the southern wind will cure the most incurable disease.

"Bah, what good is this southern wind to me? It's blowing right now as I lie beneath this full moon, yet the moon's rays burn like a blast from a blacksmith's forge, like hot spears thrust into my chest! And what's this I'm sitting on? Burns like cinders, but they are soft flower petals. Damn them! I'll rip them up, everywhere, in every corner of this forest, and destroy the whole place. What's that? That noise? Oh, the love call of the red-headed nightingales. They are inseparable lovebirds, they say. If the male leaves to get food, he returns immediately when she calls him in their bird language. But if he doesn't, then she dies on the spot. But me? Their love song only makes me wince in pain."

[*Indra appears above and speaks*:]

"Gods, hear what happened on the following morning when Śūrpaṇakhā returned to Rāma's ashram. Rāma put Lakṣmaṇa in charge of Sītā and went off to bathe, but when Śūrpaṇakhā tried to grab Sītā, Lakṣmaṇa caught her and almost killed her. What an auspicious moment it was! The day that Śūrpaṇakhā's breasts, ear, and nose were cut off was the day that Rāvaṇa's crown began to fall. Nevertheless, we must consider the background—this didn't simply 'happen.' When Rāvaṇa conquered his brother Kubera, took his nine treasures, including his flower-chariot, and went on a victory march which took him to Kailasa, that was the beginning of his end, but Lakṣmaṇa's mutilation of his sister was the next step toward that final moment when his jeweled crown would fall."

Kāma and Its Defense

Reluctantly, I interrupt Indra's lecture on the force of fate, which lasts for more than an hour, so that we may consider the Sambukumāran̲ episode as an early and clear indication of how the puppet tradition recontextualizes Kampan̲'s bhakti poem. Rāma's meeting with Śūrpaṇakhā, into which this folk episode is inserted, is an explosive mixture of eroticism, mutilation, and deception that has stimulated multiple revisions in Rāma literature.[23] Compared to his Vālmīki model, for example, Kampan̲ complicated and amplified this encounter between Rāma and demon by softening the figure of Śūrpaṇakhā, and the Kerala puppet play moves further, much further, in the same direction. Adding the Sambukumāran̲ episode, in fact, does nothing less than shift the fulcrum of the epic plot, the conflict between ascetic avatar and demonic *kāma*. When Lakṣmaṇa kills Śūrpaṇakhā's son, the bhakti mission falters, and when Rāma and Śūrpaṇakhā meet shortly thereafter, its assumption of a moral separation between divine Rāma and lustful demons crumbles.

Despite this radical effect, the Sambukumāran̲ episode cannot be considered apocryphal (a concept inappropriate for a composite text such as the Rāma story) because it is found in a broad band of Rāma stories: the puppet plays of Andhra Pradesh, Karnataka, and Kerala; the *chitrakathi* tradition of southern Maharashtra; literary Rāmāyaṇas in Sanskrit, Prakrit (Jaina texts), Assamese, Telugu, Kannada, Thai, and Malay; an Oriya *Mahābhārata*; and surely other unreported texts, both folk and literary.[24] In these versions, Śūrpaṇakhā's son is known variously as Sambuka, Japasura, Darasinga, Vikkirasingan, Kumbhakash, Jambukumara, Sunkumara, Kulaivalarakkan, and Chakrabhubala, but we will call the boy "Sambukumāran̲," after the Kerala puppet play. The episode begins after Rāma, Lakṣmaṇa, and Sītā have reached Pancavati and Rāma sends Lakṣmaṇa to build a hut. Its core event is Lakṣmaṇa's accidental killing of Sambukumāran̲ with a sword that has miraculously fallen into his (Lakṣmaṇa's) hands while Sambukumāran̲ is engaged in religious austerities (*tapas*), although in some versions Sambukumāran̲ dies from Lakṣmaṇa's errant arrow aimed at a rhinoceros.[25]

To this core, several texts prefix another episode that provides motivation for Sambukumāran̲'s *tapas*: Śūrpaṇakhā's husband has been killed by Rāvaṇa during his victory march; Sambukumāran̲ then enters meditation in order to win a sword with which to avenge his father's death, but the weapon ends up in Lakṣmaṇa's hands. Among the numerous variations of this prefixed episode, my favorite is a Tamil folk story that traces the family tensions in Lanka back to Rāvaṇa's wife's (Maṇḍōdari's) refusal to give meat to her sister-in-law, Śūrpaṇakhā; things heat up when Śūrpaṇakhā's husband temporarily swallows Rāvaṇa, who later induces his sister to kill her husband in return for his promise that her son, Sambukumāran̲, will inherit the throne of Lanka. Śūrpaṇakhā does her part, but when Rāvaṇa reneges on his, she plots to kill her brother and sends Sambukumāran̲ into the forest to perform austerities in order to gain a sword fit for the task.[26] Some combination of these two events (the death of Śūrpaṇakhā's husband and the death of her son) is told in many south Indian Rāma texts. The Kerala puppeteers sing only of Sambukumāran̲'s death, but they do refer to his father's death in oral commentary, as do the Tamil Uttara Kāṇḍa (attributed to Oṭṭakkūttan̲) and Vālmīki's Uttara Kāṇḍa.[27] Kampan̲ mentions neither death.

For these reasons, rather than saying that the Sambukumāran̲ episode is "inserted" into Kampan̲'s epic, it might be more accurate to say that Kampan̲ omits it. This perspective allows us to view the episode within the broader framework of Rāma-story literature, which the puppet play borrows and reworks; certainly the death of a demon-boy engaged in *tapas* is not unique to the Sambukumāran̲ episode. I am thinking here of the controversial killing of Śambūka, as told in Vālmīki, the Tamil Uttara Kāṇḍa, and elsewhere: when Rāma learns that a Sudra is engaged in *tapas* in a tree, a violation of dharma that has caused the death of a young Brahmin boy, he kills the Sudra with a sword, gains a boon, and revives the Brahmin; later texts identify the Sudra victim as Śambūka. Initially I dismissed any connection between the Śambūka and the Sambukumāran̲ stories because the shared motifs of *tapas,* tree, and death by sword are commonplace in Hindu mythology; even the similarity in the victims' names proves little since Śūrpaṇakhā's son has many names. Motives are also dissimilar: Rāma kills Śambūka in order to maintain proper dharma, whereas Lakṣmaṇa kills Sambukumāran̲ unintentionally.[28]

After reading more versions of these stories, however, I believe that they are multiforms generated by a pattern with three elements: killing, innocent victim, and grief. By substitutions in these elements, a telling of one story can easily metamorphose into another. First, as frequently occurs in Rāma literature, Lakṣmaṇa takes Rāma's place, here as the killer of the Sudra.[29] Second, the Sudra is conflated with Sambukumāran̠; in one text, for example, Śambūka is cursed to be a tree and is released when Rāma cuts down the tree.[30] Third, the role of mother grieving for her dead son, the Brahmin wife in the Śambūka story, is assumed by Śūrpaṇakhā in the Sambukumāran̠ story. These three changes produce role reversals—innocent victim (Śambūka) becomes sympathetic hero (Sambukumāran̠/Śūrpaṇakhā); hero (Rāma/Lakṣmaṇa) becomes villain—just as we have in the puppet play, perhaps as an attempt to redress Śambūka's unjust death.

These speculations aside, the killing of Sambukumāran̠ in Kerala commands our attention because, as the opening episode in the puppeteers' narrative, it frames their telling of Rāma's story. Rāma has met and killed demons in the forest before, in the Birth Book and earlier in the Forest Book, but here at Pancavati he faces his adversary in the more intimate and pleasing shape of Rāvaṇa's sister, Śūrpaṇakhā. Although it appears to be accidental, their meeting is the pivot of the epic plot and joins the two halves—the events in Ayodhya and those in Lanka—which may have circulated as two separate tales.[31] No matter how the epic is told, later action is invariably a consequence of this early encounter: because Rāma rejects Śūrpaṇakhā, she tries to harm Sītā, for which Lakṣmaṇa mutilates her, which causes her to seek revenge by inciting Rāvaṇa's love for Sītā, whom he abducts, which leads Rāma and his armies to Lanka, where he kills Rāvaṇa. Or, as the puppeteers' Indra (following Kampan̠) says above, when Lakṣmaṇa cut off Śūrpaṇakhā's nose and breasts, Rāvaṇa's ten heads began to fall. Within this causal chain of events generated by the meeting at Pancavati, the moral positions of Kampan̠'s Rāma and Śūrpaṇakhā are uncomplicated. We may sympathize with Śūrpaṇakhā and believe her punishment was severe—she was, after all, smitten by love—but Kampan̠ reminds us that she is evil, "a congenital disease about to strike its victim."[32] Besides, Rāma showed restraint and followed dharma in not killing the demon-woman, who might have killed or injured Sītā. Mutilating poor Śūrpaṇakhā was unfortunate, but eradicating demons is Rāma's mission.

In folk tellings of the Rāma story, however, Śūrpaṇakhā acquires other emotions and motives. In one text reported by a missionary in Kerala, for example, she spies Rāma only after an exhaustive search through the

Three Worlds to locate a suitable husband, during which each of the major gods is interviewed and rejected—even Viṣṇu is too "dark."[33] Only Rāma, it seems, will do. The puppet play also supplies Śūrpaṇakhā (and later her brother) with another motive when it positions Sambukumāran̲'s death at the beginning of the epic plot. Retaliation drives Śūrpaṇakhā to "get even" in many folk tellings of the Rāma story, especially by instigating rumors in Ayodhya about Sītā's infidelity, but even then her earlier behavior at Pancavati remains little more than lust. In the puppet play, on the other hand, she enters the story looking to avenge her son's death. That event scrambles the roles that Rāma and Śūrpaṇakhā play in the epic and entangles them in a more complex net of motives: after the death of Sambukumāran̲, the puppet play seeks not simply victory over the demons but also revenge against Rāma.[34]

This shift in moral logic occurs very quickly in the puppet play. Although the opening scene at Pancavati presents an earthly realm that matches Rāma's righteousness, the third verse sung in performance reveals danger at its edge in the form of the demons whom Rāma must destroy. Hardly a half hour of narration has passed and already the puppet play has lined up the opposing forces in the central conflict of the epic—divine perfection threatened by demonic evil. To this point, the third verse, the puppet play follows Kampan̲, yet these battle lines are drawn so abruptly and unambiguously that one suspects they have been set up only in order to be tested by the subsequent string of thirteen folk verses which comprise the Sambukumāran̲ episode.

Cracks in the smooth surface of the avatar mission first appear when the intrepid Lakṣmaṇa, sent into the forest by Rāma, mistakes a cuckoo's chatter for wild animal noises and runs for cover. His next miscalculation, killing the pious Sambukumāran̲, is not so humorous since it sets in motion the sequence of events leading to Sītā's capture and near death. Fearful of the consequences of his terrible act, Lakṣmaṇa nevertheless returns to Rāma and builds the hut, which prompts Rāma to exclaim:

Like the great Vedas
  which drive out confusion
Like the pure Milk Ocean
  surrounding Viṣṇu's island
My brother has built a shelter
  as perfect as the Ganga itself.[35]

Despite the repeated metaphors of purity in this Kampan̲ verse, which recall the perfection at Pancavati in the initial verses, we know that the hut is stained with Sambukumāran̲'s blood. And with it, the very purpose of the avatar mission has been subverted—evil is let loose in the forest by those sent to remove it.

Moral distinctions between Rāma and the demons continue to narrow when Śūrpaṇakhā appears on the cloth screen. Whereas in Kampan̲ she enters the epic "inflamed with desire, the instrument of a cruel fate,"[36] in Kerala she is the victim of a cruel fate and cries out over the dead body of her son:

Is cruel death your reward, for long *tapas* to the gods?
Wearing fresh flowers you came, and you wear them now
Riding to Śiva's heaven in death's golden bier;
I've lost you forever, my son, Sambukumāran̲.

Covered with turmeric and ash, I prayed for a son at Śiva's feet;
Now your golden body lies in little pieces at my feet;
Who did this, Sambukumāran̲?
Who makes me collapse in grief?

At the emotional center of the folk episode, these verses are sung like Tamil funeral songs (*oppāri*): the puppeteer's voice cracks with pain and rises, halts, and falls spasmodically. This outcry against a breakdown in religious logic (Why death for "long *tapas* to the gods"?) signals the role reversal mentioned above and expresses the folk demand for moral balance. Śūrpaṇakhā's appeal for justice to an uncaring god is angry and mocking (and addressed to Śiva not Viṣṇu), but she is sympathetic, a mother who has lost her son, a woman who has been wronged, in short, another of the well-loved, pious demons in Hindu mythology.[37] Hungry to gobble up the human meat she smells ("Brahmā may create them, but these humans really stink!"), Rāvaṇa's sister is no angel, but neither is she an embodiment of evil and lust. Like her son and her brother, Śūrpaṇakhā is a devotee of Śiva.

Ethical barriers between demon and avatar, so hurriedly erected in the opening scene of the puppet play, are breached again when Rāma first speaks to Śūrpaṇakhā. Although Rāma's speech closes the folk episode and returns the puppet play to Kampan̲'s verses, the puppeteers continue to depart from the bhakti epic by altering verses and adding commentary. The angry Śūrpaṇakhā is suddenly transformed when she spies Rāma on the river bank, but first she must change her outer form to match this new emotion; her oversized arms and squat legs, missile-like breasts and bumpy nose clearly will not do, so she chants Lakṣmī's mantra and her demon puppet is replaced by a beautiful human puppet.

Both puppet play and epic text compare Śūrpaṇakhā to Lakṣmī (one of the many misidentifications that reveal truths in this scene), but in the drama-house, Rāma's speech rings with an excitement not found in Kampaṉ's restrained verses: "Well! Well!," he cries, "Who is this lovely creature?" Although his first words to her, in the following verse, differ only slightly from his words in the printed text, they alter his meaning entirely. Kampaṉ's verse turns on the incompatibility between Rāma as "source of the Vedas" (*vēta mutal*) and Śūrpaṇakhā as a "silly, young woman" (*pētai*); one printed commentary points out that she is a "silly, young woman" precisely because she is ignorant of Rāma as the "source of the Vedas."[38] In the puppet play, however, this defining distance between speakers is reduced when the puppeteers omit *vēta mutal* and alter *pētai* to an endearment by adding "peacock" ("lovely peacock!"). With these minor changes in the verse, Rāma now speaks to Śūrpaṇakhā as a man infatuated by a woman's beauty.[39]

The impropriety of union between omniscient god and deluded demon, the crux of Kampaṉ's scene, is again undercut in a later verse, this time by the alteration of a single letter.[40] Arguing with Śūrpaṇakhā that humans cannot marry demons, Rāma is forced to suppress a laugh at her stupidity (her *pētai*) because, as the printed commentary explains, "loud laughter would not be appropriate to his excellence [*mēṉmai*]." When the puppeteers chant the same verse, however, Rāma's "laughter" (*nakai*) becomes Śūrpaṇakhā's "beauty" (*vakai*), so that the verse is stood on its head: Rāma does not laugh at Śūrpaṇakhā; her beauty pulls at his heart. The difference between the two verses is this:

Kampaṉ

When the demon spoke, that
white-edged rain cloud,
Rāma laughed inside and
mocked her:
"Lady, it is not proper
For a human to marry
Within the easy demon clan, so
wise poets say."[41]

Puppet Play

"Oh, demon-lady, your beautiful
hair shining
Like a white-edged rain cloud
pulls at my heart!
But you are an easy demon-
woman and I am human;
We can never marry, so wise
poets say."

In Kampaṉ's poem, the silly (again, *pētai*) demoness may deserve Rāma's secret mockery, but in the drama-house, Rāma is far too infatuated with her to laugh. When Rāma does reject Śūrpaṇakhā's offer of marriage, we hear no derision in his words for he must suppress not his contempt but his desire for her. For her part, Śūrpaṇakhā is not unaware of Rāma's attraction to her. Consider her tart reply (in the commentary) to Rāma's sarcastic question about her lack of an escort in the forest:

"Frankly, since you are probably a god, you ought to know these things anyway. I think you ask just to get an answer from me." After accusing Rāma of attempting to chat her up, a somewhat disingenuous claim since she was love-struck at first sight, Śūrpaṇakhā does offer an explanation for her behavior: it is *kāma*, or sexual desire.

In Kampan̲, her defense of *kāma* is confined to one, moving verse ("It may not be proper for women of high rank to speak when *kāma* afflicts them, but what I feel is killing me. I have no one; what can I do? Please protect me from this work of god Kāma").[42] Her apology, in effect, is a confession that enables Rāma to see through her disguise and denounce her as "base" and "shameless." At one point, Śūrpaṇakhā attempts to convince Rāma that, even though she was born a demon, she has renounced evil and embraced the way of dharma, but when Rāma is unconvinced and does not speak, she again plays the silly (*pētai*) lover and imagines his silence as a sign of his desire for her. Kampan̲'s Śūrpaṇakhā, in sum, is a fool whose words and actions reveal what they are intended to conceal. In the puppet play, by contrast, she does not resort to wheedling deceit or pretence of virtue. After declaring her lust for Rāma (in the Kampan̲ verse quoted above), Śūrpaṇakhā launches into a robust defense: "realize that this energy, this passion, [*kāma*] is everywhere, in every one of us, in every kind of being." Love and lust are natural and necessary, she instructs Rāma, and should not, and probably can not, be eliminated.

Śūrpaṇakhā's impassioned defense of *kāma* as universal and morally neutral is an explicit challenge to the theology of many devotional texts. To Kampan̲'s Rāma, *kāma* is the lustful appetite that threatens his ascetic mission, but to the puppeteers' Śūrpaṇakhā, *kāma* ("Call it *kāma*, call it lust, call it what you like") is blind to distinctions and afflicts demon and avatar alike. Her mistaken identification of Rāma as Kāma (the god of love) thus contains a disturbing truth.

In this opening scene, then, in Rāma's confrontation with *kāma*, the puppet play enacts its interpretation of the core conflict in the Rāma story. Lurking like a dark shadow at the edge of perfection in Pancavati, Śūrpaṇakhā's love for Rāma is mirrored in (and causes) Rāvaṇa's love for Sītā, and both are outbreaks of the demonic force that Rāma must defeat. This is the true war in bhakti Rāmāyaṇas—a story of the good prince exiled to the forest where his asceticism is tested and his battles with lustful, violent women (and men) are moral victories.[43] Temptation of the ascetic is an old theme in Hindu mythology, which bhakti rewrote. Whereas in the early myths the sage is seduced and his loss of spiritual power produces a more balanced distribution of forces, in

Kampaṉ and other bhakti Rāmāyaṇas, the ascetic avatar must retain power in order to save those who would seduce or conquer him. Countering this claim that isolation produces moral power, the puppet play, like the early myths, exposes false ascetics and their inherently unstable seclusion. Rāma's war on *kāma* and Śūrpaṇakhā's defense of it exemplify the distance between the bhakti ideal of isolated perfection and the folk ideal of balanced relations.

Balance is the goal in many folk Rāmāyaṇas and in Tamil folklore, generally. For instance, Yama, the king of the dead and final arbitrator of future lives, is known as the Balancer (*cāmaṉ*) because he metes out punishments to those who cheat servants, mistreat women, or underpay tale-tellers; should he falter and favor the guilty, a huge mountain dangling by a hair in the sky will fall and crush him. Lack of impartiality also plagues husbands, such as the polygamous Murukaṉ, who is disqualified from arbitrating a dispute, and the moon, who is cursed to lose his power because he fails to treat his (thirty-two) wives equally. But balance is more than a metaphor in the huge ledger that Yama's accountant, Cittiraputra, pores over to determine what fate awaits each person at death, and even bodily health, the puppeteers instruct us, depends upon the correct ratio of inhalations to exhalations. Proper balance is thus required for cosmic order, social justice, and individual longevity.

In her defiant assertion that *kāma* is not unique to demons, Śūrpaṇakhā speaks in this idiom of equilibrium, the language of other folk texts in which Sītā harbors desire for her ten-headed captor, Lakṣmaṇa covets Sītā, and Śūrpaṇakhā, in her next birth, marries Lakṣmaṇa.[44] If, as Bob Goldman has suggested, the demons represent dark forces exiled from Rāma, the puppet play seeks to restore a prior balance.[45] Recoiling from this mixture of categories, bhakti theology maintains the separation of Rāma-Viṣṇu, an insularity which in many Rāma texts explains why the avatar descended in the first place.[46] The story goes that the earth has sunk under the weight of the demons' evil, a manifestation of a moral imbalance that must be rectified, and the problem grows worse when it turns out that all the great gods—Indra, Śiva, Brahmā—are ineligible for the task because each is somehow associated with the demons. Finally, Viṣṇu is pressed into service since he alone is untainted by that association. But when Viṣṇu truly descends and appears on the white cloth screen in Kerala, his isolation is short-lived because the puppet play knows more than the bhakti text can afford to admit. *Kāma* is blind, Śūrpaṇakhā said.

CHAPTER 5

Killing Vāli: Rāma's Confession

As Rāma moves further into the forest, his encounter at Pancavati is succeeded by a more dangerous entanglement with the natural world, an alliance with monkeys that leads the avatar to kill their king, Vāli. The killing of Vāli is perhaps the most contested episode in the whole of Rāmāyaṇa literature, for to the violence of the Śūrpaṇakhā episode it adds dilemmas of loyalty to friends, to brothers, and to god. Once again Rāma battles against passion, this time in the form of male aggression, lust, and competition, and once again the ascetic prince will conquer and reform this dangerous animality. Although the puppeteers alter Kampaṉ's Vāli episode less extensively than they do his Śūrpaṇakhā episode—no new characters or events are added—they nevertheless continue to undermine the bhakti text by narrowing the ethical distance between the avatar and his adversaries. Looking at the arrow in his chest, Vāli condemns Rāma in many texts (including Kampaṉ), but the puppet play takes a crucial second step and forces the man-god to admit his error and ask forgiveness from his victim. In telling this story of Vāli's death, the puppet play once again tempers a theology of separation with a moral reciprocity.

Skipping to the Vāli story, we leap over large portions of the plot (the second half of the Forest Book and the first section of the Kiṣkindha Book). But this is also the emphasis of the puppet play, which races through these intervening events with an uninspired commentary; and many of those events are covered here by a prose summary with which the puppeteers introduce the performance translated in this chapter.[1] Yet, this is a special night, and when the puppeteers approach the death of Vāli, the pace slows, special *pūjās* are conducted, and the barrel-shaped *ceṇḍa* drums resound across the temple grounds.[2]

The performance of the Vāli episode translated in this chapter was sung in 1989 by (appropriately enough) two brothers; they belong to the Mannatiyar caste and represent a Malayalam branch of the puppet-play tradition in Palghat. In the western reaches of the tradition, where Tamil is less well understood, Malayalis are the primary puppeteers, memorize Kampaṉ's verses from a Malayalam translation, and use mostly Malayalam in their commentary; in Palghat, however, the brothers appear to be the only Malayali performing troupe.[3] When I visited their ancestral house, a spacious but dilapidated building surrounding an inner courtyard, the older brother took me into a dusty room, empty except for a large wooden chest. He explained that he and his brother had learned the two-thousand-odd verses of the puppet play and some of its commentary (especially the *piramāṇam* quotations) from their father and their grandfather, who wrote out the verses in notebooks, in Malayalam, which the brothers memorized by reciting hour after hour. Opening the heavy lid of the chest, he pulled out those battered and torn notebooks, scraps of palm-leaf manuscripts, and books that they use for reference, including the *Kanta Purāṇam, Visarasāgaram* (a compendium of advice), and *Naṉṉūl* (an old Tamil treatise on grammar), all in Malayalam. Their father became ill and stopped performing in 1967, passing on his set of five performance sites to his sons. One site is Mannur, the location of the performance translated below, where the brothers sing the Rāma story for sixty consecutive nights.

Mannur is distinctive also for its two-storied drama-house, the brothers' home during their two-month stint. They sleep inside and leave only to go to the bathroom or to eat at the tea stall erected for their benefit at the side of the drama-house. High off the ground, with no electricity and thus no microphone, they are cut off from the outside world during those sixty performances, which attract virtually no viewers and are little known outside the village. When I first recorded them in 1986, the brothers were reserved, almost uninterested in the recordings, but their precise, measured style of delivery intrigued me, so I returned three years later determined to record more. I knew that they would be singing at the big drama-house during the Malayalam month of Kumbham (mid-February to mid-March), and I checked my earlier field notes to anticipate the night when they would sing the Vāli episode. I arranged for a taxi from Palghat and waited for nightfall. Riding in the taxi as it rumbled over country roads toward the temple, I began to reflect: "It's been three years since I've seen them, and I'm coming (as always) unannounced." Remembering that there was no electricity at this drama-house, I had brought extra batteries for my tape recorder, and that made me feel more confident. Still, personal pride, money haggling, reluctant temple officials, virtually anything, can and sometimes had prevented me from recording in the past. I was expectant but anxious.

After an hour, the car turned onto an unlit road then onto a narrow, rocky lane and soon bumped to a halt in front of the temple at about ten o'clock. Having determined that I could return to Palghat by bus the next morning, I paid the driver and watched the taxi disappear. It was dark and absolutely deserted, but I shouldered my recording equipment, climbed up the ladder of the drama-house, and peeked under the white cloth screen. In the dim light of a single kerosene lamp, I could make out their faces, which had not changed—a good sign, it seemed. Grinning hopefully, I greeted them and took a few steps forward, but no glimmer of recognition registered on their faces. Moving toward them in the near darkness, I spoke again, reminding them of the nights we had spent together in this same drama-house three years ago. They squinted at me impassively, and I began to panic: "They don't remember me; they won't let me record. But it's dark," I reassured myself, "and they can't see well. Besides they didn't show much enthusiasm on the first trip either." Sitting down on the mat opposite them, I repeated my name and rehearsed our past association, but still nothing moved in their faces. Then, I understood—of course they don't recognize me—my thick moustache and long hair of three years ago are gone! Confidence restored, I went on to chat with them about puppet plays and tonight's performance, which turned out, miracle of miracles, to be the Vāli episode. But suddenly, just when I thought I had established rapport and started to unpack my recording equipment, they stood up and my heart sunk ("They're not going to cooperate after all; a wasted trip!") until I realized that they were responding to the *ceṇḍa* music outside.[4] The procession from the temple had arrived; soon the lamps were lit and the performance began.

Inside the drama-house, the brothers took their usual positions: the large, chunky younger man sat bolt upright on the wooden bench, while the older man, very lean and bony, preferred the mats. In a corner, two musicians slept. An assistant, a slightly stunted man of undetermined age, acted as a support for both brothers, supplying the necessary "ahhhh" when they paused for breath during the commentary, tending the flames in the coconut shells, and, most important, fetching tea and cigarettes. As on other nights I had spent in this special drama-house, the brothers delivered a sparse exegesis of the verses, quite unlike the digressive, tale-telling commentaries of most puppeteers. After jointly reciting the four-line verse, one brother repeated the first line and the other explicated it; each of the three remaining lines they treated in the same manner, after which they chanted a new verse and began the pattern again. At all times, whether singing verses or declaiming commentary, their speech remained unpunctuated by any modulation of voice or shift of register, while their phrases issued forth like hard, solid blocks on a verbal assembly line. But what they lacked in texture, they made up for in concentration and precision. Throughout this long night of the Vāli episode, their smooth brown faces seldom moved and their eyes rarely opened, although occasionally they tightened their lips or squinted hard as if to gain control over a line or an idea. I remember very clearly their hands, thumb pressed to forefinger, inscribing word-images in the lamp-lit shadows.

The translation begins at the end of the "Song of the Drama-House" with the prose summary, which makes a transition from the previous night's performance.

Killing Vāli

"Where were we, Muttuppattar, in the story from last night?"

"Oh, great events, great events, Gangaiyati."

"Go on, tell us."

"Still searching for Sītā, who had been carried off to Lanka by the ten-headed Rāvaṇa, Rāma and Lakṣmaṇa were befriended by Hanumān, who introduced them to Sugrīva. Sugrīva then told them he was hiding from his brother, Vāli, and asked for their assistance in regaining his kingdom; Rāma pledged his aid and demonstrated his strength by shooting an arrow through seven trees. Later as Sugrīva, Hanumān, Rāma, and Lakṣmaṇa approached Kiṣkindha, Tārā warned her husband, Vāli, that trouble was near, and when Sugrīva challenged Vāli to fight, Tārā tried to stop him, saying that Sugrīva was not alone and had the support of Rāma. But Vāli declared her fears mistaken since Rāma, the embodiment of dharma itself, would never intervene in the affairs of brothers; then, calling on Rāma's very name, Vāli fought Sugrīva. As they fought, Rāma was unable to distinguish one monkey from the other and told Sugrīva to wear a scarf around his neck. Again the monkey brothers battled, and this time, hiding behind a banyan tree, Rāma shot an arrow that pierced Vāli's chest and knocked him to the ground. Confused, Vāli looked at the arrow and spoke."

"Whose arrow is this? Whose could it be? Nārāyaṇa's? No, he would never use deception to attack an enemy. Could it be Śiva's arrow? It doesn't look like a trident, and besides he wouldn't shoot his own devotee. Maybe it's Indra's weapon, but he's my father and no father shoots his own son. It might be Murukan̲'s spear, but he has nothing against me. Then, whose is it? [*Vāli rips the arrow from his chest and inspects it.*]

"Two letters I see: *rā* and *ma*. Rāma! Can his arrow be the mantra of my death? Rāma, come closer to me. [*Rāma puppet stands over fallen Vāli.*] You who support these many worlds with your compassion, you who are soft as a lotus, why did you shoot this arrow at me? There must be some reason, but I have never done anything against you. You are learned in the dharma of bowmanship, and this is not the first time you have used a bow, for you are the son of Daśaratha. Then, why did you attack without cause? Explain."

"The dharma of bowmanship, proper conduct, morality and such are matters unknown to you, animal. First, one must know *brahman* and that understanding is beyond you."

"Rāma, what you say may very well apply to the demons, especially to the one who ran off with your wife. But we are monkeys. Don't confuse the two categories."

"Such disrespect is not proper, monkey! After all, I know that story about you—when you hurled the dead water buffalo Dundhubi into the sage's ashram. Like Rāvaṇa, you have harassed Brahmins and so, like Rāvaṇa, you are my foe. Thus, I had every right to—"

"No. You erred by shooting an arrow at an innocent monkey. It was not me, but Rāvaṇa—that demon-raja luxuriating in his palace, in his countless halls of silver and gold and emerald, in his spacious rooms with high windows and ceilings and delicately carved pavilions—it was Rāvaṇa who abducted Sītā. This arrow belongs in his chest, not mine! Not only that, but you hid behind a tree and shot at me, like some low-caste hunter! From behind a tree! What courage! Tell me, Rāma, is your bow so weak that you must resort to deception?"

"Listen, monkey, I acted to protect dharma. I lost my kingdom and my wife; and so when Sugrīva told me he had lost them, too, I pledged to protect him. I had to fight you as I must fight all enemies of dharma."

"And who are you to speak to me of dharma? Your act is a black mark on the solar dynasty. A dark, dark stain, Rāma. Even the clear moon has a blemish in the center—everyone can see that—but you were born into the dynasty of the sun, that flawless sphere circling around Mt. Meru, Mt. Kailasa, Vaikunta, Brahmā's heaven, around the fifty million *yojanas* of the earth's circumference in a chariot ninety million *yojanas* wide and fifty-one million *yojanas* long. And, now, that perfect orb has been scarred by your arrow!"

"You speak wondrous words, Vāli, but you understand nothing of dharma. Besides, what of your own actions in the past?

> You told your brother to rule the kingdom
> Until you killed Māyavi and he waited for you;
> Yet in hot anger you returned, seized his wife and the throne!
> Tell me, Vāli, what wrong had he done to you?

"When you failed to return from the cave where you battled Māyavi, Sugrīva was saddened by your apparent death. Others tried to console him and urged him to accept the throne, which he did; and when you returned, victorious over Māyavi, Sugrīva fell at your feet and begged for forgiveness, but he received god's grace, not yours. Instead you drove him away, took his wealth and wife, showing neither wisdom nor generosity, yet you presume to advise me on my conduct."

"Rāma, you simply don't understand us . . .

> No marriage by those ancient customs
> None of that righteous conduct of kings
> Guides us who follow where our emotions lead,
> Oh, Rāma, whose weapon drips with ghee and flesh.[5]

"I see your point, Rāma—you shot at me because I took my brother's wife—but that reasoning only shows your ignorance. Sugrīva may have said that I committed wrongs against him and his wife, but among us monkeys there is no 'marriage' and no rule that we must 'marry' the women we sleep with. You are a human, a warrior, so you marry one woman, only one, whereas we wander in the forest looking for food, and if we want to, we have sex. That's all. What is right for you is not necessarily right for us."

"Vāli, dharma means—"

"Can't you see, Rāma, that there's no wrong in what I did? We monkeys are another, a lower type of being. Actually, I didn't sleep with Sugrīva's wife because she's my sister; but even if I had, there would be no wrong in it. Judge your own, not us, Rāma.

> Do our women have crescent-moon foreheads,
> Or possess grace and chastity, like yours?
> Is it wrong to make love deep in the forest as we hunt for fruit?
> Tell me, Protector of the Right Way, what is right for us?[6]

"Rāma, your women regard chastity as a virtue, while that just isn't so for us, even among royalty. Your people follow marriage rules, consult horoscopes and so forth, but we monkeys don't do anything like that. We make love when we feel like it—that's the essence of what I'm saying: we are different. Besides, as Viṣṇu, you should show compassion."

"Maybe all you say is true, Vāli, but you are not an ordinary monkey. A devotee of Śiva and son of Indra, you ought to follow the path of dharma, yet what you did with Sugrīva and his kingdom does not befit a person of your noble background. And remember, even animals may win liberation. There's the story of the elephant Gajendra who won *mokṣa,* so your 'animal defense' is not valid."[7]

"I'm not an elephant."

"Birds, too, may attain *mokṣa*. When Sītā was carried off by Rāvaṇa, the eagle Jaṭāyu heard her cries and knocked off Rāvaṇa's crown but lost his life because he told the truth while Rāvaṇa lied about the location of his life force.[8] In the end, however, he won liberation."[9]

"No matter what you say, Rāma, I did absolutely nothing to justify your cruel act."

"Listen, Vāli. Most important is knowing what is right and what is wrong, truth and untruth. Many beings in these worlds have this knowledge, and not all of them are humans; some are animals. And one more thing—evil may come from the gods, so don't think of yourself as an 'animal.' The law of karma is the same no matter what your birth: animal, Brahmin, Ksatriya, Vaisya, or Sudra. Good acts cause good, evil acts cause evil; and taking Sugrīva's wife produced evil. Think before you act, especially in fights between brothers, and especially when women are involved—that's the most dangerous issue of all. That is the reason for your death, not my arrow."

"Yes, but now explain your barbarous act, Rāma. You speak of many things, of right and wrong, that a Brahmin who does wrong is no better than an animal and that a righteous animal is equal to a Brahmin. Consider, then, your own actions. Born a prince, you were educated and became a wise person, a yogi; yet after studying all those *śāstras*, you hid behind a tree and killed me, like an ill-bred hunter shooting a bird. Why did you do it? Answer me!"

[*Lakṣmaṇa moves in front of Rāma and faces Vāli.*]

"I'll answer that, Vāli. Rāma hid to prevent you from seeking refuge with him. When Sugrīva fell at Rāma's feet and asked for protection, our lord pledged to kill anyone who was Sugrīva's enemy. If he had faced you directly, you also might have asked for refuge and then what could he do? He couldn't refuse you, but neither could he renege on his pledge to Sugrīva. Listen, Vāli, this is not the time to argue. It's the time of your death, time to worship Rāma."

"Rāma, your brother has shown me the way. You are the Lord of Dharma, while I . . . I'm an imperfect being, a monkey, who has spoken thoughtlessly. Now I ask for a boon: liberate me from this body. I realize that this life is full of sorrow from the moment a child is conceived, from the second the seed enters the egg and becomes an embryo; then it grows and grows, suffering all the time, until the last month comes and it is separated from its mother's body. What pain when the cord is cut! Who can comfort the baby? And we go on living, dying, born again to live and die, endlessly. Karma causes all this, and karma is caused by good and evil acts, and those acts are caused by mental impressions, and they are caused by desires, which come from ignorance, ignorance of you, the eternal cause, the imperishable essence of the universe."

"Vāli, I forgive your monkey words and grant you *mokṣa*, now, at your hour of death."

"Rāma, you are this, you are that, you are everything."

"Vāli, ask for another boon."

"Whatever wrong Sugrīva might commit, do not attack him. I drank sweet flower wine and lost my head, but if Sugrīva gets drunk and commits a misdeed, do not shoot at him for he cannot bear your strength. Your arrow would destroy him immediately; that is certain."

"Vāli, I will honor your wishes and never turn against Sugrīva."

"One thing more, Rāma. The coming battle with the demons . . . ah, how I could bind Rāvaṇa with my tail! Yes, hold him and cut off his ten heads with my own hands! But why speak of what I cannot do? I yield. Listen. Let Hanumān be my surrogate in the war against Lanka; let him be an arrow in your hand. And treat Sugrīva as a brother; rely on him as you rely on Lakṣmaṇa. With these two at your side, you will never falter. Never. You will cross the sea and you will kill Rāvaṇa."

"Vāli, you speak kind words."

"Sugrīva, my brother, listen to me. You know that we monkeys are apt to drink and act stupidly, not knowing right from wrong. Reform yourself and others and follow Rāma. Do not think he is a man, he is not. He is an avatar, he is Viṣṇu. If you ignore this fact and get lost in drink, everything will go wrong."

"I will follow him, Vāli."

"Rāma, send for my son, Aṅgada."

[*Aṅgada approaches his dying father and speaks*:]

"You lie dying, struck by Rāma's arrow, but what harm have you ever done to anyone, at any time, anywhere in this wide world? Neither by thought nor by deed have you wronged another, yet I see in your face that Yama is here to drag your body away. But who is here to drive off Yama? I see no one."

"Do not grieve at my death, Son, since birth and death run in endless cycles for everyone. Know only that Rāma is the highest existence; no thing is beyond him. Consider him your savior, not your enemy; if he is attacked by Rāvaṇa, you must shine as a jewel in his defense."

"Hard as it will be, Father, I will treat your killer as you command."[10]

"Rāma, look after my son, Aṅgada. This is my last request—no longer son of Vāli, he is son of Rāma!"[11]

"I will, Vāli, and as I listen to your words, I realize how wise you are. Now you must forgive me. You did nothing against me, absolutely nothing! My action was senseless.

I have wronged you, mighty Vāli!
By the power of my *tapas* I restore your life;
You and your brother again shall rule
Kiṣkindha kingdom and its citizens."[12]

"Rāma, I appreciate your words, but realize that although you may revive my life and my kingdom, you cannot revive my name.

Lord of the Five Elements, listen to me.
Shall the tongues that sang of 'Inimitable Vāli' speak of 'Wounded Vāli'?
I may escape your arrow and live but
I'll not escape cruel darts of speech.

Death I may avoid but not its undying stain.
Listen to me, Eternal Rāma.
 ruling this earth for thousands of years,
I bow at your feet and plead:
 take back your arrow and give me *mokṣa*."

"Granted, Vāli."[13]

Rāma's Confession

After Vāli is cremated, Sugrīva crowned, and plans laid for recovering Sītā when the rains cease, the epic and the puppet play move on. Notwithstanding this textual resolution of the Vāli episode, the moral questions raised by Rāma's action have never been put to rest and continue to provoke scholarly debate and public comment to the present day. For instance, one day several years ago in Madurai, I picked up a Tamil newspaper and read a letter to the editor titled "Rāma Vindicated," which argued that the god-man had every right to slay the monkey king. It is true that the princes of Ayodhya commit other acts of questionable virtue—Lakṣmaṇa kills Sambukumāraṉ and (with Rāma's consent) mutilates Śūrpaṇakhā, and after their long delayed reunion, Rāma cruelly rejects Sītā—but those actions are either inadvertent, not fatal, or cancelled by a change of heart. Rāma's attack on Vāli, on the other hand, is intentional, lethal, and unmitigated by misgiving. However, if "the Devil can quote scripture," the excesses of the avatar are also convertible to theological currency, and many bhakti texts and their commentators argue that, since Rāma transcends human understanding, the very injustice of his act is its justification.

In the Vālmīki text and other Rāmāyaṇas in which Rāma is not deified, murder committed by the ideal man was difficult enough to justify, but humans are fallible, especially in observing the niceties of dharma during battle (as the *Mahābhārata* so amply attests). One recension of Vālmīki's text, for example, puts forth the minimal defense that, as a warrior, Rāma had every right to hunt animals and to shoot them, in the back.[14] Later Rāmāyaṇas, however, faced a more intractable contradiction: How could Viṣṇu's avatar as the embodiment of dharma violate dharma? That question has generated an astonishing array of explanations, rationalizations, obfuscations, and ingenious dharmic disputations. So impenetrable did this ethical dilemma become that some Jain texts preferred to avoid the problem altogether: either Lakṣmaṇa (not Rāma) kills Vāli, or Vāli is removed from the action altogether and another monkey is killed.[15] More conventional responses in bhakti texts (including the *Kamparāmāyaṇam*) are that Rāma is obligated to honor his pledge to Sugrīva, that Vāli deserves to die because he acted reprehensibly toward Sugrīva and his wife, and that death by Rāma's arrow ensures *mokṣa* anyway.

But why did Rāma hide when he shot the arrow? To this nagging question, answers tend to be pragmatic: Rāma hid because Vāli had a boon that any enemy who faced him would forfeit half his power;[16] or he hid because (as Lakṣmaṇa argues in Kampa<u>n</u> and the puppet play) if he had faced Vāli directly, the monkey-king would have asked for his protection, and compassionate Rāma would surely have granted it, thus preventing him from fulfilling his promise to Sugrīva. The contrivance of this excuse has not escaped even Kampa<u>n</u> enthusiasts, one of whom conscientiously noted that the poet put "this irrelevant explanation" in the mouth of Lakṣmaṇa and thus "preserved the glory of Rāma."[17] More ingenious than Lakṣmaṇa's solution to the "Vāli problem" was one suggested to me by a puppeteer: if Rāma had not killed him, Vāli would have forced Rāvaṇa to release Sītā, rendering Rāma redundant and robbing Bhagavati of the spectacle of Rāvaṇa's death. In most bhakti texts, however, the decisive argument is the theological one, advanced in Kampa<u>n</u> and elsewhere: that Rāma breaks moral laws because he is beyond them and that questioning his actions, as Vāli does, only demonstrates limited understanding and imperfect piety.[18]

Such explanations and circumventions have not satisfied everyone, and condemnations of Rāma's action match the justifications in variety if not ingenuity. Severe censure is frequently leveled at the hypocrisy of Rāma, as god or man, who preaches one thing (dharma) yet practices another (violence); indeed, one of Vāli's early denunciations of Rāma sets a high standard: "I hold you to be naught else than a scoundrel covered by (the cloak of) virtue and I consider you like a well covered with grass, sin dressed in the garments of the righteous, like a fire covered by ashes."[19] Other texts deride Rāma as an abject failure, a puny man who lost his kingdom, then his wife, chased after a false deer, and only regained Sītā when some monkeys and bears aided his cause. Failed Rāma has proved embarrassing not only to recent Hindu nationalist campaigns that prefer to promote the victorious bowman but also to nineteenth-century intellectuals who sought an antidote to British imperialism: many ignored effeminate Rāma and turned to martial Rāvaṇa.[20] Nothing, however, matches the ferocity of the anti-Rāma campaign unleashed in the twentieth century by the Dravidian movement in the Tamil country, as noted earlier. Predictably, E. V. Ramaswami Naicker, the movement's colorful founder and (despite his name) lifelong critic of the Rāma story, aimed his most vehement attacks at Rāma's killing of Vāli; why do Brahmins (to him, north Indians), he asked, hold up a murderer as a role model?[21] Even a temperate scholar like Achyuta Menon, writing in the 1940s, was moved to liken Rāma's act to the barbarous events then unfolding in Europe.[22]

Vāli's death provokes outrage in the puppet play, too, but the Kerala folk tradition occupies a special place in the gallery of Rāma literature: not content with condemnation, it forces Rāma to make a startling admission of guilt. As we follow the twists and turns of the debate between Rāma and Vāli, I wish to emphasize not only this confession but also the method of the puppet play's radical solution to the Vāli question; exemplifying the additive principle described in chapter 3, it adds little "new" content to Kampaṉ and relies primarily on the commentary to express the rising anger of the monkey-king.

When Vāli first demands to know why Rāma shot an arrow at someone who has done him no wrong, Rāma counters that an animal cannot understand dharma and that Vāli himself has violated dharma (hurling a dead buffalo into a Brahmin ashram and taking Sugrīva's wife). Vāli suddenly interrupts Rāma in mid-sentence (creating a tension not possible in writing) and rebukes him as someone who "hid behind a tree and shot at [him], like some low-caste hunter." Rāma then claims he was bound by his prior pledge to Sugrīva, but Vāli turns Rāma's earlier relativist argument (that animals occupy a different moral plane) against him: "What is right for you [Rāma] is not necessarily right for us." At this point, a folk verse is chanted, not to advance a new accusation but to sharpen the anger in Vāli's voice; below we can compare that folk verse with its Kampa<u>n</u> counterpart (sung earlier):

Kampa<u>n</u>
No marriage by those ancient customs,
None of that righteous conduct of kings
Guides us who follow where our emotions lead,
Oh, Rāma, whose weapon drips with ghee and flesh.[23]

Puppet Play
Do our women have crescent-moon foreheads
Or possess grace and chastity, like yours?
Is it wrong to make love deep in the deep forest as we hunt for fruit?
Tell me, Protector of the "Right Way," what is right for us?

Although Vāli makes essentially the same point in both verses—that monkeys are less constrained than humans—his conciliatory voice in the Kampa<u>n</u> verse bears little resemblance to the sarcastic, almost insulting tone of the folk verse.

Having lost the relativist argument, Rāma changes tack and argues the universalist position that Vāli should understand dharma and that animals (such as the elephant Gajendra) are capable of liberation if they surrender to god. Rāma relentlessly pursues his theme of salvation, and Vāli maintains its irrelevance to monkeys and turns the argument against him once again: if bhakti is universal and dissolves all categories (human, animal), then Rāma, too, must be judged by standards of mercy and compassion. In the end, Vāli mocks him: "You speak of many things, of right and wrong. . . . Consider, then, your own actions . . . after studying all those *śāstras*, you hid behind a tree and killed me, like an ill-bred hunter shooting a bird. Why did you do it? Answer me!" When Rāma is silenced by the sheer logic of Vāli's arguments, Lakṣmaṇa steps forward to explain that his brother hid in order that Vāli would not be able to ask him for refuge, which Rāma, as the compassionate god, would not refuse.[24] Abruptly and inexplicably, in light of his vehement attacks, Vāli undergoes a change of heart, announces his acceptance of Rāma as the highest god, and places his son, Aṅgada, in Rāma's care.

Up to this point in the Vāli episode, the puppet play faithfully reproduces the events and arguments in the Kampa<u>n</u> text, but the cumulative force of Vāli's attacks on Rāma in the puppet play cannot be erased by his sudden conversion. Nor does he acquit the avatar. A departure from Kampa<u>n</u> is inevitable, and it comes when, after accepting Aṅgada from Vāli, Rāma admits his guilt and asks forgiveness from his victim. In this radical turn from the Kampa<u>n</u> text, the shadow puppet play subverts the religious lesson of the Vāli episode, and it does so with a single folk verse. Kampa<u>n</u>'s episode teaches the lesson of Job, for Vāli questions but eventually acknowledges Rāma's identity as the supreme god; his conversion is a function of his comprehension of Rāma's unconditional love. However unconvincing and abrupt his conversion may appear, from the bhakti perspective that is just the point: only by accepting Rāma's seemingly irrational and unjust action does the devotee break through petty categories and earthly existence to acquire a new vision of god. In the puppet play, on the other hand, it is Rāma who acquires a new understanding when Vāli's magnanimous gesture, entrusting his son to the person who wrongly slew him, moves the god-man to recognize his own meanness. Again, and with only minimal narrative changes, the puppet play has reversed Kampa<u>n</u> and established a new moral relationship between Rāma and his enemy: the avatar is taught compassion by a monkey.

This drive for ethical balance in the puppet play advances still further when, in a bid for full restitution, Rāma offers to restore Vāli's life. A similar offer is proffered in Tulsīdās's Hindi text, where Vāli rejects it on the theological basis that the body is meaningless, thereby showing himself to be a worthy recipient of Rāma's teachings.[25] In Kerala, however, Vāli's refusal is based on the pre-bhakti Tamil notion that death is dishonorable and that rebirth will not remove the "stain" of his death; speaking very much like a warrior in ancient Tamil war poetry, Vāli proudly refuses the gift of life: "Shall the tongues that sang of 'Inimitable Vāli' speak of 'Wounded Vāli'?"[26] Although this older attitude toward death disallows a bhakti resurrection in this life, it sanctions reparation in the next life, when victims of unjust and violent deaths exact revenge, and so Vāli is reborn as the hunter who shoots the fatal arrow into Kṛṣṇa's foot.[27] This is another example of the accommodation between bhakti and folk ideals achieved by the puppet play: Vāli accepts Rāma as god, but his unjust death must be avenged; Śūrpaṇakhā is punished, but retribution must be sought for her son's death. This pursuit of a moral balance pervades the puppet play and surfaces later in the Vāli episode when Rāma lectures Sugrīva on kingship; the verses in

Kampaṉ address abstract notions of dharma, whereas the folk verse sung by the puppeteers has this to say:

> A raja who punishes not those who deserve
> And punishes those who deserve not—
> That raja will suffer on this earth
> And be judged by the great judge, Yama!

Rāma's admission of guilt is absent in the *Kamparāmāyaṇam*, yet so powerful is the drive for moral restitution that certain Tamil scholars have read it back into Kampaṉ's poem. T. K. Chidambaram Mudaliar, one of the great Kampaṉ scholars of the twentieth century, reconstructed what he thought was the "original" text before sectarian interpolations had buried it. Apparently without any direct knowledge of the puppet play, he inferred that the unexpurgated text included Rāma's admission of guilt and that later Vaiṣṇava redactors removed it to fit their conception of Viṣṇu-Rāma as faultless and divine. Another scholar, M. Arunachalam, has adduced the puppet play as evidence that this reading is correct: "We have a corroboration of T. K. C.'s reconstruction in a puppet-shadow play of Kerala . . ."[28] According to Arunachalam, then, the puppet play is a return to Kampaṉ, not a reversal of it. Motives of these scholars who seek to insert Rāma's admission into an "original" text, however, are difficult to differentiate from those of scholars who, they allege, expunged it: if the early editors sought to remove any stain from Rāma's glory (a true god does not err), the later ones wish to restore his lost honor (a great hero admits his mistakes).[29] The correct text is a scholar's fool's gold.

Although retellings of the Rāma story encompass nearly every imaginable reversal and subversion, Rāma's confession appears to be rare: my search turned up examples only in the eclectic *Mahānāṭaka*, in an eighteenth-century Bengali text, and in two Tamil folk texts.[30] Even the legends of Kampaṉ in Tamil do not countenance this controversial admission; the *Vinōtaracamañcari*, for instance, presents a condensed version of the exchange between Rāma and Vāli, including most of the accusations made by Vāli in the puppet play, but not Rāma's admission of guilt.[31] We also know that Kampaṉ's text as presently compiled, and probably from as far back as the sixteenth century, has been transmitted without it. Rāma's confession in the puppet play must therefore be accounted as a radical departure from a text that the puppeteers otherwise follow either verbatim or in large measure. This fundamental ethical, but minor narrative, shift produces a pattern that underlies the puppet play: a breakdown in moral logic—Śūrpaṇakhā mutilated, Vāli murdered—prompts the puppet play to seek compensation by enlarging the victims and deflating Rāma. Whereas a bhakti text might react to these controversies by further separating the avatar from his enemies, thereby justifying their punishment or death, the puppet play moves in the opposite direction and closes the gap between them and Rāma. Considering the historical argument that Rāma was first a human hero later lifted into identity with Viṣṇu, we might be tempted to interpret the puppet play as a return to Rāma as ideal man, but this would distort the adaptation of Kampaṉ's epic in Kerala. Rāma's confession is not so much an exposure of clay feet as an accommodation between the claims of perfection in the bhakti text and the demand for balance in folk Hinduism.

CHAPTER 6

Rāvaṇa's First Defeat: The Puppeteers' Oral Commentary

The narrative changes described in the two preceding chapters are not the only means by which the Kerala shadow puppet play adapts the *Kamparāmāyaṇam* in performance; the alterations to the Śūrpaṇakhā and Vāli episodes are not insignificant, but taken as a whole the effect of such changes on the story told in the puppet play is limited. Instead the puppeteers press their interpretation of the Rāma story more forcefully and persistently through an oral commentary, which is the special provenance of the puppeteers—their own world of scholarship and storytelling that stretches beyond the received text and into the wider Rāma story tradition. As an explanation of Kampaṉ's verses, the commentary may appear to be a textual appendage, but my intention in this and succeeding chapters is to demonstrate that the commentary is the dominant voice in performance. While reading the translation below, the reader may want to keep in mind this distinction between verses and oral commentary in preparation for the discussion that follows.

This chapter leads us into the War Book, which we will follow until its final episodes of Rāma's victory over Rāvaṇa and his coronation in Ayodhya. Once again, in skipping from Vāli's death to the War Book, much has been omitted—the last section of the Kiṣkindha Book and the whole of the Beautiful Book. Despite these omissions, the War Book is our proper focus because it is the heart of the puppet play. At most temples, in fact, the War Book *is* the Rāma story. Having summarized the preceding five books on the first night, the puppeteers begin their narration of the epic on the second night with either the episode of "Rāvaṇa's War Council" (as in the performance translated here) or

"Building the Bridge" and then sing the War Book for the remaining nights of the festival.

The Kerala shadow puppet play is not alone in this preference for the War Book; many Rāma texts, both folk and literary, give disproportionate emphasis and space to its events, sometimes omitting everything but the final book.[1] For instance, the battles between Rāma and Rāvaṇa comprise nearly the whole of the earliest Rāmāyaṇa in Kerala, the *Rāmacaritam*, and half of the original Kathakaḷi plays on the Rāma story.[2] Kampaṉ did not slight the War Book either. Vai. Mu. Kōpālakiruṣṇamācāriyar, perhaps the most learned of Kampaṉ's editors, pointed out that his War Book possesses more poetic density and thematic complexity than his other five books combined. It stands on its own merits as a great work of literature, he wrote, because from it we learn the epic's essential teachings—Lord Rāma's saving grace, the establishment of dharma on earth, proper conduct in human affairs—all revealed as "clearly as a *nelli* fruit in our hand."[3] Certainly the War Book is the longest book in any edition of Kampaṉ, and, if textual variation is any indication of frequency of performance, it has been told more often than any other portion of the epic: the percentage of variant verses and suspected interpolations (*mikai pāṭal*) in the War Book is twice that in the Birth Book and nearly four times that in any other book. For example, several manuscripts of Kampaṉ's text contain two (brief) episodes usually considered interpolations: "The Revival of Vacantaṉ" (Vacantaṉ Uyir Varu Paṭalam or Iyama Paṭalam) and "The Pūjā" (Pūcai Paṭalam).[4] It is significant that both episodes are included in the puppet play (see chapter 8) because this anticipates the arguments developed later in this chapter: that the puppeteers' telling of the War Book belongs to a long history of elaboration of this popular section of the epic, and that the entire puppet play emerges from a narrative and commentarial tradition broader than the *Kamparāmāyaṇam*.

I understood none of this popularity and significance of the War Book when I began to study performances in Kerala. Its prominence first startled and then disappointed me. What had happened to the intricacies of the early books that (by reading) I had learned to love? How could the puppeteers bury those subtle dharmic dilemmas underneath the rubble of interminable battles and mysterious weapons that pile up in the War Book? For their part, the puppeteers were baffled by my preference for the Ayodhya Book, in which, as one man pointed out, "Rāvaṇa does not even appear, while the War Book has everything: love, death, humor, and grief, especially grief." A few nights in the drama-house taught me that the episodes in the War Book are inseparable from those in the earlier books. And this led me to realize that my conception of the epic as a sequence of narrative events was fundamentally at odds with the epic as performed in the puppet play: in the drama-house, the Rāma story in Kampaṉ's verses is subordinate to the commentary, through which the puppeteers are capable, at any point, of telling the entire epic or retelling, and complicating, any single event in it. In brief, the puppeteers tell their Rāma story as much by spinning their commentary as by singing Kampaṉ's verses.

The performance translated in this chapter was recorded from the drama-house where Cinna Tampi, the legendary composer of the puppet-play text, is said to have performed. In his time, the drama-house and its temple stood in the center of a village that today is a prosperous suburb separated from the concrete buildings of Palghat city by a small strip of rice field.[5] Beside an enormous banyan tree, this famous drama-house appears unremarkable, and no outsider passing by would suspect that it was other than an old building or know that behind it live several families of Chettiyars who claim descent from the famous Cinna Tampi. These families are no longer active performers, and the local temple committee hires an outside troupe to perform, but they retain the privilege of lighting the lamps inside the drama-house before each performance.[6] In recent years, the lamps have been lit by the local schoolmaster, whose house was easy to identify by the tumble of red bougainvillaea along the front gate and by the large, framed photograph hanging above the front door. Each time I entered his house, I saw in that photograph his father, a puppeteer in Cinna Tampi's line, holding a palm-leaf manuscript in one hand and a vina in the other, like Sarasvatī, goddess of learning. His son carries on the family tradition of learning, but he appeared wistful when I asked if he had ever sung in the drama-house. Perhaps the historic role of this drama-house also explains why performances here occasionally draw connoisseurs. One local man, a rotund, cheery engineer who works in Madras, spent most of one night inside the drama-house, relishing the recitation and playing one of the drums during battle scenes. Another man, who would not identify himself, watched several nights from outside, alone, and when I asked him why he showed such persistent interest, his only words were: "The Rāmāyaṇa is within you."

What follows is a performance sung in 1986 by three senior puppeteers, a measure of the importance of the drama-house, although nearly all the interesting commentary was produced by one man, the seventy-year-old Natesan Pillai. He had been performing since 1935, when he was twenty, yet he does not consider himself a "full-time" puppeteer and makes more money as an accountant in the off-season; like his father and other puppeteers, he is also a *vaittiyar*, a specialist in medicine and astrology. Four years of study with a local *vaittiyar* introduced Natesan Pillai to these fields of knowledge, which eventually led him into the mysteries of an esoteric Tamil religious-philosophical system (Saiva Siddhanta), then to the Rāma story, and finally to shadow puppetry, which he learned from a Malayali carpenter who also made leather puppets. Natesan Pillai once told me that a puppeteer must study Hindu mythology and philosophy for at least ten years in order to gain the knowledge necessary to explain the Rāma story through oral commentary. When I asked how he was able to complete that task, he laughed and explained that as a young man he "absorbed" the *Kanta Purāṇam* during nightshifts in a lumber mill because his supervisor couldn't stay awake and left him to read that old text in the cool night air.[7]

Despite his age, Natesan Pillai is a sturdy man with a broad face who perched cross-legged on the wooden bench in the drama-house. His stiff, white hair shining silver in the lamplight, he boomed out his commentary while rocking himself back and forth on the bench, one hand cupped to his ear like an Anglo-American ballad singer. And he is a superb storyteller; his characters laugh, they ponder, they agonize, and, what is all too rare, his monkeys sound like real monkeys. Whenever a story is told in the translation below, whether about the ill effects of rapid breathing while asleep or how Kampaṉ composed his poem, the voice belongs to Natesan Pillai. Unfortunately, a stomach ailment has put an end to his fifty years of performing in the drama-house, and he was bedridden on my last visit in 1989. But he was happy because he had just purchased a black-and-white television set. I asked him about the Rāmāyaṇa series that had enthralled viewers in India the year before and he replied, "Oh, the acting is very good. Sītā's perfect. The killing of Rāvaṇa was well done." When I disagreed, he seemed relieved and added, "You see, it's really not any particular Rāmāyaṇa. They take whatever they like from wherever they like and fit it in. Not like our puppet play."

The translation below opens in Lanka after Hanumān has found Sītā and returned to Rāma, leaving the city in flames. First the puppeteers recount these events in prose summary and then begin their formal narration of the War Book at the point where Rāvaṇa convenes his council of ministers and Vibhīṣaṇa instructs his brother concerning the true cause of Lanka's destruction. Very quickly the action moves to the building of the bridge, after which Aṅgada knocks off Rāvaṇa's crown, Rāvaṇa is humiliated by Rāma in battle, and the demon-king seeks counsel from his uncle, Māliyavā<u>n</u>.

Rāvaṇa's First Defeat

"Now, what happened last night, Muttuppattar?"

"Ah, that, the story. Eventually Hanumān found Sītā in the Ashoka grove and urged her to return with him to Rāma, but Sītā refused—'Although you are certainly the person to take me back, I will leave Lanka only after I see Rāma kill Rāvaṇa'—and gave Hanumān a jewel to show to Rāma on his return. As Hanumān left, he fought and killed many demons, including Rāvaṇa's youngest son, Akṣakumāra<u>n</u>. Hanumān was brought to Rāvaṇa, who interrogated his prisoner, and when he learned that Rāma had killed Vāli, he asked:

"Vāli dead? What power did Rāma use to kill him? And if Rāma killed Vāli, why does his son, Aṅgada, help Rāma search for Sītā?"

[*Hanumān*] "When Vāli was dying, he called Aṅgada and told him to serve Rāma as a son. He has obeyed his father's wishes."

"Then you serve a coward, who does the bidding of the man who killed his father. He should take revenge, and if he can't himself, he should get someone who can. This is a disgrace for your entire monkey race!"

"But Rāvaṇa—"

"Wait! Didn't you tell me that your king is Sugrīva, the one who killed his own brother by deceit? Then . . . you are the messenger of a traitor [Sugrīva] and a coward [Aṅgada]. Not only that—you have killed my own son, yet I have spared your life because you say you come as a messenger. Speak your messenger words and leave!"

[*Brahmin narrator*] "And that's where we stopped, right?"

"No, no. Eventually Hanumān's tail was wrapped in an oily cloth and set afire, but he broke loose, used his fiery tail to burn Lanka, doused it in the ocean, returned to Rāma, and issued his famous announcement: 'Sītā I have seen.' That's where we stopped."

"Yes, and before we sing tonight we have a duty to perform."

"As is true every year, Lakṣmī Amma has sponsored this performance and supplied us with excellent food cooked by Appa Nayar. For them and their families, for generations to come, we call on Bhagavati to bless them with good fortune."

"Now, as Rāma readied his armies, Rāvaṇa called his ministers to a war council in Lanka, and Vibhīṣaṇa was the first to speak."

"When your palace and your city were set ablaze
By the chastity of the Earth Goddess, Sītā,
Do you think it noble, my brother,
To say 'A monkey burned them'?[8]

"Rāvaṇa, do you actually believe that a monkey burned Lanka? This magnificent city of ours—its towers and sculpted palaces—has been burned to the ground not by that silly animal but by the fire of chastity, the chastity of Rāma's wife, Sītā. I think you know the reason for all this destruction. Remember when you won weapons from Brahmā and were called the 'Raja whose crown bows to no one'? On your victory march, surrounded by a host of horses, elephants, and soldiers, you circled the Three Worlds and defeated Indra, the Eight Cosmic Elephants, the fifty-six rajas, and then a curse befell you. Have you forgotten?"

"Curse? No, I remember—"

"While you enjoyed undisputed sway over the Three Worlds, your brother Kubera sent a message: 'Rāvaṇa, have you lost sight of your ancestry? We are the sons of Brahmā! Stop this cruelty toward Brahmins, ascetics, and women.' But you unsheathed your sword and split the messenger in two, and as his spirit rose to the skies, it hovered above and called out, 'Hey, Ten Heads! You may have studied the Sāma Veda, but you don't know the proverb: "Kill your mother, but never kill a messenger."[9] For this, I curse you, your lineage, and your city of Lanka to be destroyed by a messenger.' But this only inflamed your arrogance, so you sped your chariot toward Lanka to kill Kubera, when you saw Vedavatī, daughter of a sage, deep in meditation. Overcome with desire, you stopped the chariot, climbed down, and touched her. Suddenly, she cried out: 'For this destruction of my purity, I will take birth as another woman and destroy you and all you own.' With that, Vedavatī leapt into a fire and was reduced to ashes.

"You, however, simply continued on your way to Lanka, traveling at high speed, until your chariot smashed into a tall mountain. Perturbed, you climbed down and saw Nandi, Śiva's bull, who laughed at you: 'Rāvaṇa, this is Mt. Kailasa and no one passes without first bowing down to Śiva.' To which you responded: 'Listen here, Monkey Face, out of my way!' Yet, as you passed overhead, Nandi had the last word: 'For that insult, Rāvaṇa, you will be destroyed by a real monkey-face!'

"Later, Nārada passed the spot where Vedavatī had entered fire, scooped up her ashes and bones, stored them in his vina and walked on. Reaching the gates of Lanka, he learned that you had a fondness for the sankarabarana raga from the Sāma Veda, so he played it every day on his vina. One evening, after singing, he left his vina outside your chamber door, and in the morning a baby girl was found next to the instrument. You asked your ministers who she was and they replied: 'Dispose of her. If you keep her, Lanka will be destroyed; if you kill her, the Three Worlds will be destroyed.' Their advice you honored and placed the little girl in a golden box, which was put out to sea and reached Mithila, where the childless raja Janaka was sprinkling water on the ground as part of a sacrifice and saw a long tunnel made by ants. Following it, he found the golden box and the little girl inside. In the earth displaced by the ants, he saw the Sanskrit letters *S-i-t-a*, so that became her name. Her chastity, not that monkey, burned our beloved Lanka, Rāvaṇa."

"But if that is true, Vibhīṣaṇa, why did the city not burn when Sītā first came here nearly a year ago?"

"Sītā is the sun, Hanumān is the mirror. Together they destroy."

[*Angered by Vibhīṣaṇa's disloyalty, Rāvaṇa orders his brother to leave Lanka. Vibhīṣaṇa joins Rāma's forces and together they reach the ocean that separates them from Lanka. On the shoreline Rāma summons Varuṇa, god of the seas, by chanting his special mantra. Eventually Varuṇa appears and, although Rāma needs immediate help in building the causeway to Lanka, launches into a long discourse on the nature of god and truth, which concludes thus*:]

"Something else, Rāma. This verse refers to you as *curuti mūrtti,* the Truth of the Vedas, but Saiva Siddhanta takes the position that even the Vedas cannot explain truth.[10] You see, in one section of the Vedas you repeatedly hear 'No, no.' Negation is truth. But the counterargument is that god can be known, that at the very edge of ignorance is knowledge. Travel to the edge, repeating 'Not this. Not that,' and then you can reach knowledge. Even the word the Vedas use for the truth—*a<u>n</u>mai* [negation]—is important. It refers to something distant because it begins with *a*. If a word begins with *i*, it refers to something close; if with *u*, to something in between. It's more complex than this, but just take it that the Vedas use a distant word [*a<u>n</u>mai*] for truth because it is beyond words. And you, Rāma, you are that unknowable.

"Swami, this world is your plaything! In every era you assume forms to please us and to defeat our enemies. Master of Mystery, you once humbled mighty King Mahābali when you took birth as a dwarf Brahmin and approached Mahābali as he conducted a sacrifice. He offered you a boon, you asked for only three feet of land, and when he agreed, you expanded into Viṣṇu's cosmic form, covering the earth with the first step, the heavens with the second, and with the third you pushed Mahābali into the underworld. Long ago, a king was cursed by Agastya to become an elephant, which—"

"I know that story, Varuṇa."

"Good. The cursed elephant was unable to find water, wandered everywhere, and finally fell into a pool near the Three Peak Mountain in the middle of the Milk Ocean. The myths say a sage once bathed in this pool—I know people say these stories are only imagination, but I say they never deceive. They tell truths—one only has to know what is story and what is true. In any case, while the sage was bathing, a Gandharva named Huhu flew overhead and decided to have some fun, so he left his heavenly form and became an alligator in the pool. He caught the sage in his coils and began to squeeze with all his might until the sage cursed him: 'You want to be an alligator? Fine. You are one, forever!' Into that same pool the raja-turned-elephant fell and had his legs caught by the alligator, but he called out to Viṣṇu, who immediately left Vaikunta, sailed down on Garuḍa, and cut off the alligator's claws with his sharp-edged discus. And so the elephant, Gajendra, was granted the third state of liberation [*cārūpam*]."

"Yes, yes, Varuṇa, but it is I who have come to ask you for help. The whole world laughs at me because Rāvaṇa stole my wife and holds her in Lanka. I must free her, yet I can do nothing unless I cross this water, and if you, the King of the Seas, don't help, who will?"

"Forgive me, Rāma, I knew nothing of your plight. You must free Sītā since you, too, rule the waters, and that is why the verse calls you Sacred River.[11] You know the story, so I'll make it brief. When you went to Mahābali as the Brahmin dwarf and took your three steps, the egg-like shell of the earth split and the Heavenly Ganga threatened to drown us all. We shook with fear until Śiva agreed to break the force of the river with his long, thick hair. He did, and the water dribbled out into a stream at a place we now call Kumbakonam, where you reside in a little temple on the river bank. For this we call you Sacred River."

"That's a wonderful story, but I need a path to Lanka."

"Crossing this vast ocean is no easy task, Rāma."

"Then—?"

"Build a causeway of stone—no, then all the fish would die, and I cannot allow that. Listen. Rip up the mountains, throw them into the sea, and I will carry them all on my head to save the fish. My head will bear those stones until you and the monkey army cross over to Lanka."

[*As the monkeys set to work, Indra appears high on the cloth screen and addresses the other gods*:][12]

"Look at that monkey Kumutaṉ carrying those huge mountains! Nine of them, toward the sea . . ."

> Kumutaṉ threw a mountain into the sea
> Whose spinning, roaring waters [*tumi*]
> Reached the heavens where the gods danced
> Thinking the ambrosia would rise again.[13]

"This verse carries several meanings. It's said that it is the very first verse Kampaṉ wrote and that he wrote it to make a point. It also contains the story of how that point was demonstrated to the court poets. A long history lies behind this simple verse, but we can begin with what we all know—that the earth was ruled by the Chola, Pandiya, and Cera rajas. The Chola rajas ruled Tanjore, and in their palace lived sixty-four learned men: thirty-two poets and thirty-two scholars. At that time, a great man named Caṭaiyappaṉ also lived in Tanjore and had the reputation of helping everyone who brought him their troubles. Because he offered his support so liberally, he was given the title Great Benefactor.

"Generous Caṭaiyappaṉ was also a close friend of the raja and often visited his court, where one day he said, 'Raja, you have sixty-four poets and scholars in your court, but we have no Rāma story in the southern language, no Rāmāyaṇa in Tamil. Vālmīki's story is written in the northern language with all those meanings condensed into one line—who can understand it? If it were in Tamil, all of us would follow and enjoy the benefits that come from hearing that great story. Summon your best poets—Oṭṭakkūttaṉ and Kampaṉ—and command them to compose a Rāmāyaṇa in the southern tongue.' So the raja called the poets and made the request, and they agreed.

"From that day, Oṭṭakkūttaṉ began to write. He finished the Bāla, Ayodhyā, Araṇya, and Sundara Kāṇḍas, until he came to the beginning of the Yuddha Kāṇḍa, when Rāma, Lakṣmaṇa, and the monkey army travel for twelve days and reach the edge of the salt ocean.[14] When Oṭṭakkūttaṉ told the raja he had completed all this, Kampaṉ was embarrassed. 'I've not yet written a single verse,' he thought to himself. 'But if I admit that, the name of Kampaṉ, praised everywhere as a great poet, will become inferior to that Oṭṭakkūttaṉ. Certainly there are books that admonish us not to tell lies, but there are others that say we may lie. How do we know when to lie and when not to? Well, if we do lie, the most important thing is that it should not cause any trouble or evil. If you lie in order to accomplish a good deed, it's not wrong; in fact, it ceases to be a lie and becomes the truth. The old books say you may tell not just one of those lies, but two or three, a hundred, even hundreds of them, and all at the same time. There's a verse:

> To get a woman married or set a spy spying
> To produce good or teach the Three Essences
> To save an innocent man from certain death—
> To these ends, a hundred lies may be told.

"'This is what Hindu philosophy teaches us. In order to get a woman married and give her a good life, you might have to tell more than one lie. Certainly you can't get anyone married today without telling several lies, right? To do some good or avoid evil, lies are also useful. Likewise, if someone tries to kill an innocent man, you may tell lies to save him.' Kampaṉ thought about all this and convinced himself that the lie he was about to tell wouldn't have any evil consequences. Then he looked at the Chola raja and declared, 'I have composed the story up to the point where Rāma comes to the ocean, is unable to cross, does meditation, threatens to fire an arrow at Varuṇa, and waits for him. Varuṇa finally appears, places a garland on Rāma, worships him, asks forgiveness, and then tells him that he may cross to Lanka by throwing rocks into the ocean. The last verse I've written is this:

> Kumutaṉ threw a mountain into the sea
> Whose spinning, roaring waters [*tumi*]
> Reached the heavens where the gods danced
> Thinking the ambrosia would rise again.'[15]

"When Kampaṉ told the raja that he had written this verse, he lied, and Oṭṭakkūttaṉ knew it because he had seen Kampaṉ wandering about, not writing a single verse. Oṭṭakkūttaṉ also knew that the verse was ungrammatical and, hoping to expose him, issued a challenge: 'Kampaṉ, your verse may sound nice, but look at the line about the gods dancing when the water [*tumi*] reached the heavens. Does that word *tumi* have any grammatical basis? Does anyone use it in common speech?'

"Kampaṉ had to stop and think because at that time the word *tumi* was not commonly used. Quickly he retorted, 'Is that it? Even if it were grammatical, that's not enough? It must be used by the common people?' Oṭṭakkūttaṉ continued, 'No one uses that word; if it were correct, people would speak it, but they don't. And if they did, you could prove it.' To which Kampaṉ shot back, 'I will prove it. I'll prove it tomorrow.'

"Without taking any food, Kampaṉ went straight to the temple of Ampikai [Kālī] and called to her, 'Goddess, you have blessed me to be a poet in the raja's court, and he has ordered us to compose a Tamil Rāmāyaṇa, and I have told a lie about a verse. Now the other poets have challenged me to prove that a certain word is used in common speech. Of course, if you don't want to help, it's no loss to me.' With this plea, he fell into a half sleep. Soon Ampikai appeared and spoke. 'Kampaṉ, why worry like this? Tomorrow morning, before the night has gone, bring all the poets to the Shepherds Lane and I will show them that the word is used.' She vanished and Kampaṉ slept.

"Early next morning, after completing his bath, Kampaṉ went quickly to the raja who greeted him, 'Well, Kampaṉ, can you prove to us that *tumi* is grammatical?' 'I can,' he replied, 'but we must hurry now before the night is gone.' With the raja, Caṭaiyappaṉ, Oṭṭakkūttaṉ, and the other poets following him, Kampaṉ set off for the Shepherds Lane, where they saw two lines of houses, one on each side. Going down the lane, they looked into every house, but not a single door was open or a single lamp burning, until, at the very end of the lane, they saw light, in a tiny hut, where a woman and four children sat around a milk churn. As the woman churned, she turned to the nearest child and said, 'Stand back, don't let the *tumi* fall on you; watch out for the *tumi*.'

"The raja and the poets were astounded! Why, among all these houses, they wondered, why did this single house have a lamp? And who was that woman? They ran forward to look, but when they reached the house, there was no woman, no children, no lamp, not even a house—only a dark open space. They stopped for a moment, and then cried out, 'This is the work of Ampikai; it can be nothing else. If Kampaṉ has her powers, how can we debate with him? What goddess or god can we summon to prove our point?' Convinced of Kampaṉ's skill, they returned to the palace.

"Only at this point did Kampaṉ begin to compose his epic. With the aid of learned Tamil scholars and Sanskrit pundits, he composed seven hundred verses every day between sunrise and sunset; every evening, he took his manuscript to Ampikai's temple and placed it beside her as he worshiped. After his prayers, when he took up the manuscript, all his errors were corrected. This is how Kampaṉ composed his Rāmāyaṇa in 12,026 verses and six books.

"Oṭṭakkūttaṉ was despondent. Seeing that Kampaṉ had outwitted him in front of the raja and the assembly of poets, he decided to destroy all that he had written. One by one, he tore each palm leaf, from the Birth Book through the War Book, and threw them into the River Kaveri. Then, just as he was starting to tear up his Uttara Kāṇḍa, Kampaṉ grabbed his hand and spoke: 'You have suffered; you wrote this Rāmāyaṇa with great effort and skill. Why destroy it? Look, let the first six books go; we can't retrieve them. But save at least this last, the Uttara Kāṇḍa. Let us join it to my six books and then we shall have a complete Tamil Rāmāyaṇa.' Only a great poet would say that. Kampaṉ was willing to join his verses, with their hidden meanings, to another poet's verses. His only desire was that the world should have a full telling of the Rāma story in Tamil. And that is what we have.[16]

"Next Kampaṉ had to sing his poem in a debut. For that occasion, great scholars of many languages gather in an assembly, and the poet reads his new poem, explaining each verse, breaking up the words if necessary. He must be able to explain the grammar and meaning of any line or word disputed by the scholars. If he does so successfully, then the assembly will accept the composition and declare it worthy of public recitation. Kampaṉ was ready for his debut, but the raja asked him something else: 'Where's your *cāṟṟu kavi* [verse praising the poet]?' Today we pronounce it "certif-icate," but it's the same thing: proof that the poet is worthy. 'Kampaṉ,' the raja continued, 'we need to see your certificate. Go to Chidambaram, to the court of the Three Thousand [Brahmins], to those scholars and poets and win their approval; then we will arrange for your debut recitation.'

"Kampaṉ took his manuscript and left for the town of Chidambaram. Of course there were no motor vehicles then, so he walked for six days and finally reached the outskirts where he went to the first house and announced, 'I've composed a Rāmāyaṇa; where do I go to sing it?' 'Sing it? Oh, next door.' But this was the answer he received from every house he visited, and soon it grew dark and he was hungry. Finally he saw an Ampikai temple and he laid down his burden at her feet: 'I've finished the Rāmāyaṇa, but now I have to earn a certificate in order to be able to sing it. Can you help?' Ampikai, who was in deep meditation, shouted at him, 'Kampaṉ, if you complain like this, no one will give you any title. If you want to earn it, go to the Three Thousand in a single house and begin to sing. That's all; I'll do the rest.'

"'I don't understand.'

"'Listen, tomorrow morning, bring your poem and come this way. In a house a child will be dying of a snakebite; the Three Thousand will be there, too. Enter and announce that you have come to earn a certificate for composing a Rāmāyaṇa. They'll rebuke you: "This is no time to sing a Rāmāyaṇa! A child is dying. Go away!" Then you say, "Oh, a child? Let me see, please." They'll refuse, but you must keep on asking and finally someone will say, "Let him take a look. What's the harm?" Go slowly to the child's bed, find a comfortable seat, and take out your manuscript. Find the Snake-Snare [*nāka pācam*] section and sing the ten verses in praise of the gods; if you sing them well, the snake that bit the child will come back, draw out its own poison, crawl away, and then die.[17] The sleeping child will awake and sit up, fully alive! When they see this, the Three Thousand will grant you a certificate.'

"With these instructions, Ampikai disappeared. Kampaṉ did as he was told, the snake came back, the child was saved, and the Three Thousand put their signatures on the certificate. Kampaṉ then walked the six days back to Tanjore and gave the certificate to the raja. 'Not bad, not bad. But one cannot say that the Chidambaram Three Thousand are the only judges of poetry. Ampikāvati, your son, for instance, is also an excellent poet. Get his approval, too.'

"'I will do that, raja,' Kampaṉ said, thinking: 'My own son can't possibly refuse me a certificate.' He approached his son.

"'Welcome, Father, what brings you here?'

"'Nothing special. In order to have my debut, the raja says I must get a certificate from you.'

"Kampaṉ's son, who was quite young and playful, said, 'I'll give you a certificate, but first you must tell me something special about your Rāmāyaṇa.'

"Kampaṉ had to think for a moment before he responded, 'I've composed four very special verses, just to please you; four miracles.'

"'Tell me the four miracles, Father, and you'll have your certificate.'

"'First, there is the case of Kalaikottu Muni. When Daśaratha learned that he must bring that sage to perform the sacrifice for a son, Vasistha told him the long story about how Kalaikottu Muni brought rain and ended a famine. Enticed by dancing girls, he entered the Anga country and soon all the clouds drew close together making the sky as dark as Śiva's throat. Suddenly, after years and years of drought, the rain fell, "sala, sala, sala." Watching this miracle, everyone began to dance with joy. Here the special thing is that the sounds "sala, sala, sala," which refer to the rain, are play words with their own rhythm. A second miracle occurred when Rāma shot his fire-arrow into the Heavenly Ganga, causing Brahmā's water pot to boil over.' Then Kampaṉ described a third and fourth miracle and received from his son this certificate: 'The Rāma-Veda, sung and praised by the greatest poets, has now been written by Kampan̲: thus I, Ampikāvati, do declare.'[18]

"When Kampan̲ ran back to the raja and showed him the certificate, another condition emerged: 'Good. Now there is one more thing. In Tanjore there is a famous courtesan, who is also a respected poet. Get her approval.' When Kampan̲ found her, she did what he asked and said, 'You needn't have come yourself. If you had sent a messenger, I would have given you the certificate.' When the raja saw her certificate, he finally agreed to hold the debut.

"What year was that? There's a verse . . .

> In Venneynallur, where Caṭaiyan̲ lived,
> In Cakāttam eight hundred and seven, on Pankuni asterism
> Before Lord Viṣṇu at Srirangam
> Kampan̲ first sang his Rāma story.[19]

"Yes, it was Saka 807 when Kampan̲ first sang his poem. The word *cakāttam* here means the Saka Era. There are various ways of counting years, and I don't recall when that era began—you can look it up in different books—but it's approximately one hundred years after the Christian era. So Saka 807 is about 900 A.D., and the *Kamparāmāyaṇam* has been sung from that date—for the past eleven hundred years.[20] This famous verse also refers to Caṭaiyan̲, or Caṭaiyappan̲ Mutaliyār, Kampan̲'s patron, and to Venneynallur, the tiny village where Kampan̲ lived, and to Pankuni, a favorable lunar asterism when Kampan̲ first sang his epic before a statue of Nārāyaṇa as the Primal Source at Srirangam temple. To that temple, which was then in the Chola country, the poets were invited by the raja and there they heard Kampan̲ sing his Rāmāyaṇa for the very first time, from the very first verse to the very last. This is the history of Kampan̲'s Rāma story. I didn't have to recount it all, but Kampan̲'s explanation of the word *tumi* led me to it.

"*Tumi* came in that verse about the water. When the gods felt the water splash up from the ocean, they gurgled happily: 'Remember that day when we put Mt. Mandara in the Milk Ocean and churned up the ambrosia? That was only a single pot of ambrosia, and these monkeys have thrown thousands of boulders into the sea, so imagine how much ambrosia will arise!' With that thought, the gods danced in ecstasy and sang 'Let Rāvaṇa and his demons shake with fear when they hear of Rāma's bridge.'"

[*Drums rumble and the scene shifts as Rāma and his army cross the causeway and step onto the shore at Lanka, where Rāma commands Naḷa̱n to build a fort. When Rāvaṇa summons his ministers for another war council, his uncle, Māliyavā̱n, speaks first*:][21]

"Rāvaṇa, you are wise. Give up the folly of fighting against this Rāma-Viṣṇu."

"Me? Even if Śiva took the form of a monkey and fought me, he would never win. He may have swallowed the poison from the Milk Ocean long ago, but no one swallows my arrows. Uncle, you say this Rāma is an avatar of Viṣṇu, but his divine chest will split when my missiles strike, and his little brother Lakṣmaṇa doesn't scare me either. You are cautious only because you are frightened. You may leave now, and let me fight."

[*When Māliyavā̱n leaves, Rāvaṇa's generals stand forward and speak*:]

"We should attack now. Rāma has only foot soldiers; no chariots, elephants, or horses."

[*Meanwhile, Rāma calls Vibhīṣaṇa to his side*:]

"You have described Lanka to me, but I want to see it with my own eyes. Can we see it from here?"

[*Vibhīṣaṇa leads Rāma to the summit of Suvela mountain and points south toward Rāvaṇa's palace. At that very moment, when Rāvaṇa stood in his northern tower, dressed for battle, Rāma sees him and cries out, "He is as strong as Mt. Meru!" Later, Rāvaṇa looks down on Rāma's army of monkeys and insults them. Furious, Sugrīva flies up to the tower, dashes Rāvaṇa to the ground, grabs his crown, and escapes! Sugrīva moved so quickly that Rāma did not realize he had left his side, but when the monkey-king returns and places Rāvaṇa's crown at his feet, Rāma smiles*:]

"You are truly great, Sugrīva."

"Swami, I am not unusual. Jaṭāyu gave his life for you. What of Vāli, who was stronger than I? And, there is Hanumān."

"What is this you have brought back to me?"

"Ask Vibhīṣaṇa."

"Rāma! It's Rāvaṇa's crown—not even the Three Great Gods could do this!"

[*Rāma decides to attack and sends Sugrīva to collect food stores for the long siege. The monkeys gather around each of the four towers, ready for battle, but Rāvaṇa fails to engage them. They wait, but still no Rāvaṇa, so Rāma summons Vibhīṣaṇa* :]

"What shall we do, Vibhīṣaṇa? Rāvaṇa has failed to appear yet another day. Maybe he fears the seventy thousand troops surrounding his palace. I want to discuss a plan with you because you are a great *vaḷḷal,* a benefactor."

"I am ready to listen, Swami."

"You are called 'benefactor' in this verse for a reason. The word refers only to people with a big heart who give gladly, not just to earn a name. Of the three ranks of benefactors, you are a First-Rank Benefactor. Explaining the traits of each would consume much time, but in brief they are these. If someone comes and asks for something, you must be able to ascertain why he came and what he's thinking. He might have any number of reasons for asking. Impossible to know, you say? But it is possible. As the Vedas declare, 'Look closely at his face and you see inside his mind; whether anger, sincerity, or deceit, you can see its outer sign in the face.' A First-Rank Benefactor can do this, but a Second-Rank Benefactor gets rid of petitions by simply giving to everyone, even when it's not appropriate. Suppose a person comes and asks for something, you might think: 'If I say no, he'll just come back again; or maybe he won't even leave now.' To avoid that problem, the man gives whatever is requested. The Third-Rank Benefactor takes the opposite attitude: 'Let them ask for anything; I give nothing.'"

"Your words are kind, Rāma, but please tell me why you have called me."

"I have called you because devotees of the gods are greater than the gods and because you have a heart as pure as a lake. But, yes, I called you to ask advice about strategy. We have the palace under siege—no demon can get in or out—but how can we force Rāvaṇa to appear?"

"What is your plan, Rāma?"

"How can one measure your compassion, Vibhīṣaṇa? We might as well ask, How much water is in the sea? Your love is as unknowable as Śiva because when one learns the truth of Śiva, there is no 'Śiva.' The word *śiva*, as we know, denotes auspiciousness [*maṅkalam*]; however, if Śiva appears like us, with hands and feet, and labors through this world, can we say who he is or where he is? No. Śiva is not that kind of 'thing.' As a great poet wrote, 'He is without clan, without quality [*guṇa*], without limit; he has family, house, and wife, but he is not those things.'[22] We speak of eyes, nose, mouth, and through them we have sensations, but Śiva cannot be known by them because he is not them. He is formless."[23]

"Rāma—"

"Although this is what our Hindu philosophers have discovered, this is not what we practice. People make images out of clay, bronze, copper, gold, wood, out of anything! Sun god, Moon god—whatever image arises in their head, they make into a god. This is the long train of tradition, and it continues today: some worship a stone, some worship a wood statue, and so forth. If Śiva is not those forms, and he is not, why do people worship them? Because their ancestors did, and now there are books that justify that kind of worship, yet none of the *śāstras* encourages the worship of an image. No. Śiva is not found in an image of stone.[24]

"I say this to you, Vibhīṣaṇa, because you have placed god in the temple of your heart and chant his names there. And I say this in order to demonstrate my respect for you. You see, most people would counsel me this way: 'Why wait to attack that thief Rāvaṇa? Go, kill him now!' "

"But, Rāma, he *is* a thief, a bandit."

"Listen. My idea is to send a messenger who will deliver two messages: first, 'You stole Sītā from Pancavati; release her immediately.' If Rāvaṇa relents, it won't be necessary to say the second thing; but if he refuses to release Sītā, then the messenger must say, 'Dress for war with Rāma!' Rāvaṇa will then be forced to choose between the two alternatives. Now, what do you say?"

"Rāma, your plan is consistent with the practice of your ancestors and with the dharma of warriors. I have no objection."

"Lakṣmaṇa, now I want your opinion. Shall I send a messenger to Rāvaṇa to ask if he is willing to release Sītā?"

"What? Show civility to that enemy of dharma? Have you forgotten that he has imprisoned your wife?"

"That is true. Rāvaṇa has done evil, including eating people as meat. Such a person does not deserve the courtesy of a messenger, you say. However, you must remember that Rāvaṇa was born a demon and that compassion is something a demon never has. Their hearts are hard rocks, not only our Rāvaṇa's but the hearts of other demon-rulers, too. Besides, it's a demon's dharma to be cruel, and we cannot censure Rāvaṇa for his actions. A verse by the ancient poetess Auvaiyār explains: 'A lily according to water; knowledge according to the book; character according to birth.' Just as the nature of a flower depends on the water in which it grows, a person's mind is influenced by what he reads, and a person's character is shaped by his background. A man born in the Brahmin caste will not have the intelligence of a man born in the Sudra caste; only if a Sudra woman eats pure foods, like ghee and curds, and meditates on god, will her foetus absorb those qualities. Similarly, a person born in a Brahmin family will become wicked if the mother is a demon.[25]

"That's what happened with Rāvaṇa. His father was Vicaravasu, but his mother was Kēkaci whose evil character has been Rāvaṇa's from birth. He has not violated dharma and, therefore, I cannot accept your opinion that sending a messenger is in any way a violation of our dharma. Tell me, Lakṣmaṇa, what undesirable consequences will arise from this plan, and I will change my mind."

"What of your promise to Vibhīṣaṇa? When he came and asked for refuge, you accepted him with these words: 'Fear nothing. I will make you king of Lanka for as long as the world chants "Rāma, Rāma."' Now, if Rāvaṇa accepts your offer and releases Sītā, how will you give his crown to Vibhīṣaṇa? Remember also that in the forest you pledged to the sages that you would destroy Rāvaṇa. In view of these facts, I advise against sending a messenger."

"Lakṣmaṇa, you are both wise and kind. However, I have not forgotten my promises to Vibhīṣaṇa and to the sages, and neither will be compromised by sending a messenger. In the end, Lanka will be destroyed—that is certain—and sending a messenger before attacking is required by the law books composed by the greatest sages. If we simply ignore their laws and invent our own, *that* would be a violation of dharma. Lakṣmaṇa, a wise man gauges the strength and intelligence of his enemy before battle. He calculates not only his personal qualities but those of his assistants also. Who are his brothers? His generals? And so on. If, on balance, the enemy is stronger, then he should not go to war—death will be the end. I might be a powerful man, but I must also practice patience; only then will my full strength be realized. Strength without patience is a burden, not an asset.

"Most importantly, victory depends on dharma. Any step away from dharma is a retreat from victory. There's the saying: 'Without dharma, even the gods cannot gain victory.' But what is dharma? It includes four things, four instruments of statecraft: conciliation, confrontation, generosity, and punishment. What is conciliation? If a person is brought to you for a first offense, sometimes you must say, 'Don't do it again.' This person may think he can get away with the same crime again, and why not?—the raja let him off once. If he is caught and brought before you again, you must censure him. Use confrontation—the second instrument of dharma—to change his mind, but still not punishment. Then, if the same man is brought before you a third time, you must say, 'You're free. Go away.' This is generosity, a gift. Only when the man returns for the fourth time should you punish him. If this advice is wise, how can we attack Rāvaṇa without first sending a messenger to sue for peace?

"Understand also that Rāvaṇa will never release Sītā. If such were his character, he would not have abducted her in the first instance. Even if one of you rescued Sītā and returned her to me, Rāvaṇa would not ask for forgiveness. If, somehow, he did, I would honor my pledge to Vibhīṣaṇa and crown him king of Lanka, after which I would escort Rāvaṇa to Ayodhya and conduct his coronation there."

"Rāma, I agree that this plan is consistent with your promise to Vibhīṣaṇa, but the promise to the sages in the forest remains, does it not?"

"Yes, and it will stand forever. I promised the sages that I would protect their sacrifices. If Rāvaṇa releases Sītā and bows at my feet and I make him king of Ayodhya, then he will not harm the sages. So, you see, Lakṣmaṇa, my pledge to the sages also will not be compromised. Now, tell me again, do you retain an objection to sending a messenger?"

"No, you have convinced me."

[*Lakṣmaṇa is removed; Sugrīva takes his place.*]

"Sugrīva, whom shall we send?"

"Once before when we required a messenger, we sent that black-faced Hanumān. Again if you send him, you will not err."

"True. Hanumān has been to Lanka and knows the city well; he would be successful in this mission. However, if Hanumān goes a second time, what will Rāvaṇa conclude? That he is the only true warrior among our seventy thousand troops, and we cannot let Rāvaṇa think that he can win by defeating only me and Hanumān. No, we must frighten him by sending another warrior, and, Sugrīva, there is none better than your own adopted son, Aṅgada! Even if the demons attack, he has the strength to escape and return here unhurt. What do you say?"

"Your reasoning is correct. Call Aṅgada."

[*After receiving instruction from Rāma, Aṅgada leaps into Rāvaṇa's palace chanting Rāma's name, which angers Rāvaṇa and prompts an argument between the monkey emissary and the demon-king. Aṅgada, insulted that Rāvaṇa has not offered him a proper seat, coils his tail into a tall throne and sits upon it; Rāvaṇa speaks*:][26]

"Who are you, monkey?"

"I am the messenger of Rāma, whose armies are camped outside your gates and—"

"Forget about him. What is your name?"[27]

"I am Vāli's son, Aṅgada."

"Vāli's son? Son of my enemy's enemy? Why, you're almost family. No need to oppose me. Here, I'll give you a kingdom, many wives—"

"A kingdom received from you is a disgrace I will never suffer! I have already been promised a kingdom by Rāma."

[*At this, Rāvaṇa drew his sword and nearly cut him down, but his ministers held him back, pleading that Aṅgada be allowed to speak. When Aṅgada delivered Rāma's message, Rāvaṇa ordered his guards to seize the impudent monkey, but Aṅgada leapt high into Lanka's northern tower and called out, "Demons! You are doomed to die. Escape now before Rāma's armies annihilate you." Then Aṅgada leapt again, and landed at Rāma's feet.*

[*The First Battle was imminent, for Rāma, having heard what had happened, ordered his captains to advance. His armies formed outside the palace, the gates opened, and the demon armies moved against them. In the fierce fighting that ensued, Lakṣmaṇa fell unconscious on the field, and Rāma, riding Hanumān, came to his rescue. Eventually, when Rāma and Rāvaṇa faced each other, Rāvaṇa fell and lost his crown. Not wishing to kill an opponent who had fallen, Rāma declared, "Enough for today. Go home and return tomorrow." As Rā-*

vaṇa dragged himself back to the palace, the gods, who had assembled above to witness the spectacle of war, spoke among themselves:]

Mighty chest that conquered Cosmic Elephants,
Shoulders that shook Kailasa, tongue that outsang Nārada,
Ten jeweled crowns, sword from Śiva, and his bravery—
All these Rāvaṇa left on the battlefield and returned empty-handed.[28]

"Gods, look at what has happened on earth."

"Yes, Maharaja Indra. Who is that down there?"

"It's Rāvaṇa, defeated in battle. After dismissing Aṅgada, he dressed for battle, thinking 'I'll never be defeated.' But he has been defeated, and that is remarkable."

"Why?"

"Long ago, Rāvaṇa sat on the shore of Kuntalam in fierce penance to Brahmā and won invincibility in the Three Worlds. On his victory march, when he challenged the gods stationed at each of the eight directions, they all changed their forms and fled. Indra changed to a peacock, Varuṇa became a swan, Kubera a lizard, Yama a rook. Then, as if that were not enough, he battled with the Cosmic Elephants of the eight directions. Joining together, the elephants charged and planted their thirty-two tusks in Rāvaṇa's chest, but the Raja of Lanka felt nothing, unsheathed his sword, and cut them off, one by one. And today that mighty chest has been defeated by Rāma!"

"How did it happen, Indra?"

"When Rāma and his monkey armies attacked, Hanumān jumped ahead, scattered the demons, and advanced on Rāvaṇa. Rāvaṇa pounded Hanumān with his twenty fists, but Hanumān stood his ground; then he struck Rāvaṇa with his two fists and knocked him down.

"But Rāvaṇa lost more than a fist-duel. When Brahmā gave him boons, Rāvaṇa received the power to defeat his brother, Kubera, and seize his kingdom of Lanka. Seated on the throne of that island, Rāvaṇa proceeded to harass Brahmins and sages, which caused Kubera to dispatch a messenger to censure his brother and warn him to follow the path of dharma. But Rāvaṇa, furious that his brother should seek to instruct him, took out his sword and killed the messenger. Then Rāvaṇa flew in his magic chariot to challenge Kubera and suddenly rammed into Mt. Kailasa, where Nandi commanded Rāvaṇa to go around the mountain, but the demon responded by calling him a monkey-face, to which Nandi responded with a curse: 'You and your kingdom are doomed to be destroyed by a monkey-face.'

"Rāvaṇa roared in anger, got down from the chariot, made his twenty hands into one, and ripped up the entire mountain. On top, Śiva felt something shake, looked down, placed his big toe upon Rāvaṇa's head, and pinned him to the ground. Kailasa rocked back into place, driving the demon into the underworld. When the demon-raja did not return to Lanka, his lieutenants set out to search for him, and when they found their king trapped beneath Kailasa, they went to Śiva and asked how he might be freed. Śiva said that the Raja of Lanka should challenge him to a musical contest, so Rāvaṇa cut off one of his twenty hands and made of it a vina; his sinews became strings, and he began to sing from the Sāma Veda. He sang and he sang, some say for a thousand years, until Śiva was moved to release him, announcing, 'Because you are a *rāga-vaṇṇaṉ* [song-master], I name you Rāvaṇaṉ.' Rāvaṇa then asked for a boon of immortality, and Śiva granted him three and one-half million lives, and a special sword. When the gods learned of these gifts, they were frightened because they realized that they would face Rāvaṇa's evil forever. To Nārāyaṇa they pleaded, 'Śiva has given all these lives to Rāvaṇa. Do something!'

"Viṣṇu agreed and took the form of a Brahmin, placed a bush on his head, watered it with a cracked pot, and stood on the path where Rāvaṇa was returning from Śiva. Amazed at the sight, Rāvaṇa cried out, 'Foolish Brahmin! What's that plant growing from your head? And why do you water it with a cracked pot?' Viṣṇu [the Brahmin] replied: 'It's not me but you, Rāvaṇa, who are the fool! Who else would ask for three and a half million lives? One million, or two, or three, but three and a *half*? That's truly stupid.'"

"Puzzled, Rāvaṇa asked the Brahmin what he could do. 'Go back to Śiva,' he was told, 'and say this: "Besides the three and a half million lives, give me another half."' Rāvaṇa thought he would get a half million more, but the word 'besides' (*oḻiya*) also means 'cancel.' Thus, when Rāvaṇa went back to Śiva, he said, 'Cancel the three and one-half million lives, and give me one-half.' And Śiva did just that. He gave him half a life. And it is this Rāvaṇa, whose enormous shoulders once rocked Kailasa, who has now been defeated on the battlefield."[29]

"Tell me exactly how those shoulders were defeated."

"Well, when they fought, Rāvaṇa hurt Lakṣmaṇa badly; struck by the demon's spear, he fell to the ground, unconscious. Rāvaṇa came to his side and tried to lift him with his twenty arms but could not! The same shoulders that had once lifted Kailasa could not lift Lakṣmaṇa's body!"

"What else?"

"I said that Rāvaṇa became famous for singing a tune from the Sāma Veda, that he surpassed even Nārada in singing that tune, but his tongue, too, was useless, defeated. What do I mean? Toward the end of this first battle, after Rāma had destroyed Rāvaṇa's chariot, Rāma spoke to him of dharma, but Rāvaṇa did not answer. He could not answer. He who had once outsung Nārada had lost the power of speech!"

"Is that all he lost?"

"No. He had ten crowns, each made of precious jewels, but Rāma knocked all ten to the ground! Even the sword given him by Śiva was taken from his hand. The mighty demon-raja returned to his palace without his crowns, without his weapons, without his chariot, and without hope."

"When he retreated, how did Rāvaṇa feel?"

"Sad, very sad.

> Like the moon swallowed by Rāhu, like a frog swallowed by a snake,
> Rāvaṇa writhed in pain, defeated by Rāma's arrows;
> Like crops withered by a cruel sun, like a deserted, penniless debtor,
> The Raja of Lanka had lost all hope.

"The moon in this verse is the poisoned moon that Rāhu swallows once a year causing an eclipse. But think how the moon feels—that's how Rāvaṇa felt. Like a frog caught halfway inside a snake, he couldn't move or say a word. His defeat by Rāma also made him hopeless, like a man debt-ridden forever."

"I see, Indra. You mean that Rāvaṇa suffered like a debtor to Rāma. Had he borrowed money from him?"

"Well . . . he had taken Sītā from him. If he had given her back, his debt would have been cleared, but he kept her in the Ashoka grove, and he suffered for it."

"What happened when he entered the palace?"

"His head hung so low that Rāvaṇa saw only the earth. Normally Rāvaṇa looked at the door guards, but that day he did not. Nor did he look at any part of the palace or at his children, lined up to welcome their father as they did whenever he returned victorious from battle. He didn't even look at the faces of the women who greeted him. Looking neither right nor left, he saw only the woman we call 'earth,' Bhūmi Dēvi. With his ten heads hanging down and his twenty eyes trailing along the floor, he entered his chambers."

"Why was Bhūmi Dēvi the only woman he looked at?"

"Sītā was born of the earth, so she is a sister of Bhūmi Dēvi, and Rāvaṇa now realized that by stealing Sītā he had brought the disgrace of defeat upon himself. Ashamed, he could not face his wives."

"But tell me exactly how Rāma defeated Rāvaṇa."

"Rāvaṇa possessed extraordinary strength! He had defeated the once invincible gods, subdued the Three Worlds, and earned the title 'the raja whose crown bows to no one.' Nevertheless, with his hands hanging low, he entered the palace just as the sun set—"

"Did you say 'as the sun set'? Is there any special significance to that?"

"First realize that this twenty-armed Rāvaṇa was defeated by the two arms of Rāma."

"The right and left arms of Śrī Rāma, right?"

"We'll get to his arms in a minute. You asked something about the setting sun?"[30]

"Nothing really. Some might say that the setting sun was a symbol of Rāvaṇa's life. It's going down, I mean."

"No! No! Absolutely not! Understand that the demons have a habit: they fight only at night because you can't defeat them in the darkness. The point of this verse is that the initial battle took place during the day and not at night, and that's why Rāvaṇa lost. To say that Rāvaṇa's entering the palace when the sun set symbolizes the end of his life is sheer nonsense; it indicates the time of day and nothing more. Rāma's hands are a different matter, and there's a verse about them: listen to what the left hand asked the right hand:[31]

> 'O, right hand holding our *vaḷḷal*'s bow,
> do you fear to fight this Rāvaṇa?
> Having fed us all these years,
> do you now draw back in fear?'

'No. I only whispered in Rāma's ear:
"Those ten dancing heads,
Shall we cut them off all at once—
or sever them one by one?"'

"The important word here is the first: *vaḷḷal* or 'benefactor,' a generous person. Because Viṣṇu offered Rāma as his avatar, the poet has used this word in this spot, but what the verse actually describes is a conversation between Rāma's two hands in the heat of battle. When the right hand drew back on the bowstring, the left hand was shocked: 'You've cared for us from childhood and kept us from hunger, yet, now, when we face this demon in battle, you are scared!' To this the right hand responded, 'You needn't think that. When I drew back, it was no retreat; I went close to Rāma's ear because I wanted to ask a question, in secret: "How should we cut off this big oaf's heads?"' This is the meaning of this verse."

"I see, Indra. Is there any special rule about how to hold a bow?"

"Rule? The left holds the bow and the right draws the string. That's all. No one holds the bow in his right hand and draws with his left."

"I thought so. Now I think we should stop talking and look down to see what is going on in Rāvaṇa's palace."

[*Indra and the gods leave. After his defeat, Rāvaṇa again summons his uncle, Māliyavāṉ.*]

"Greetings, Rāvaṇa. But what is this? What's happened?"

"Uncle, come closer, up to the throne."

"You are kind and, though it is not right for me to assume the status of a king, I will sit with you because you wish it so. Besides, you are like a son to me and can do nothing wrong. Yesterday you were angry and sent me away from the Council of Ministers, but it pains me to see you like this—your once mighty shoulders sag with despair! Could you, whose very name scatters kings in fear, could you have lost a battle? What am I saying? That's impossible since you are fearless even before the gods. Still your twenty shoulders always rode erect like mountains, but now . . .

"Rāvaṇa, once you dug a fire pit by the Ganga, sat on a tiger skin, raised a fire high into the sky, and worshiped Brahmā for thousands of years. Each of your ten heads and twenty arms was blessed in that roaring fire, while Brahmā granted you spiritual wisdom. Rāvaṇa! Who can match your achievements? You are a raja, a warrior, a master of mantras. Why are you so shaken? Did some enemy violate a rule of conduct on the battlefield? What has happened? Tell me."

"That's why I have called you—to tell you what happened yesterday. It's true. I have been defeated on the field of battle. Ordinarily, I wouldn't care if the whole world learned about my defeat, but sometimes, like the present, circumstances are different."

"Tell me."

"You see . . .

Twenty eyes blazing with fire,
Ten noses flaring like roaring hot bellows,
Tongues too dry to taste sweet ambrosia,
I speak with a heavy heart.

"I entered the field thinking that I would defeat Rāma, Lakṣmaṇa, Hanumān, and their monkey armies, but now my heart, which races in anticipation whenever I join battle, is weighed down by despair. Look at my eyes! Once they shone like burning fires, but now they are so faded I can hardly see. And my noses—look at them breathing hard and fast."

"Rāvaṇa, an ancient text—'The Breathing *Śāstra*'—tells us that a healthy person breathes 360 times every twenty-four minutes.[32] One-third of those breaths, however, is unwanted air; it is simply exhaled and then used by grasses, bushes, and things like that. The remaining two-thirds of the inhalations is used by our body. Now, if we need 360 breaths every twenty-four minutes, a healthy person will take in 21,600 breaths each day, of which he uses about 14,400 and exhales the other 7,200. This kind of evenly balanced breathing makes us strong and protects us from illness.[33] But our rate of breathing changes with our activities: when we work, it tends to increase, and when we sleep, we need less and should not breathe heavily. Waking hours require those 360 breaths every twenty-four minutes, but in sleep only 120 are necessary. So this is the problem: if you breathe too fast, you'll also exhale too much—like a rutting elephant or a panting horse—which decreases your life span."

"That's just it, uncle! Look at my breathing! It's out of control, and that's not all. I couldn't taste the purest of pure sugar, even if it were put on my tongue. You know that sweet syrup boiled down from sugarcane juice, that white stuff so thick that you can't chew it or drink it—you have to lick it—even that I couldn't taste now because my tongue is as dry as a dead man's tongue."

"Rāvaṇa, what happened?"

"As I said, ordinarily I wouldn't care if the whole world knew about it, but . . . you see, I have been disgraced in the eyes of Sītā. Uncle, it might be true that my arms are hard as diamonds and that I have conquered the kings on earth and the gods in heaven. Let them all laugh at my defeat; I do not care. Why should I? I have humiliated them already. No, it is not for them that I am overcome with shame. It's for that one with the long, fish eyes, that red-mouthed Jāṉaki."

"The epithet 'fish-eyed' is noteworthy.[34] There are many things to which eyes may be compared—there's even a book that lists them: a flame, a lotus, a lily, a poem, the ocean, ambrosia, and much more. But you can't use just any comparison; each has its proper place, its context. Knowing that makes a great poet. In this case, the phrase 'fish-eyed' implies a carp [*keṇṭai*] because a carp's body is soft and pleasing like an eye. The fish-eyed one is known by many names: some call her Jāṉaki because she is the daughter of king Janaka; others call her Mithili because her family is from Mithila; and many know her by the name Sītā, or 'furrow,' because her father discovered her while ploughing the fields. The Tamil word for 'furrow' is *paṭaiccal*, but in this instance we follow the northern language and call her Sītā."

"Yes, her. It is Sītā's laugh that I fear. If she hears this news, she will consider me weak and unworthy of her love. That's why I am buried in grief."

"Rāvaṇa, what disgrace is there in defeat? You fought fairly on the field. Of course, I did warn you that your horoscope held no victory, but you ignored me and listened instead to the shouting of your armies. Now you say that only Sītā worries you, but what is she to you? Look, you are a great warrior! What is all this needless fear about?"

"If Sītā finds out, I would be disgraced—that's what. I thought I couldn't lose. I had elephants and horses, while Rāma had only monkeys—but what a horde of monkeys they were! From nowhere, Hanumān leapt up and challenged me to a duel without weapons. I made a huge fist and pounded his chest; he was stunned, but regained his balance. Then I bared my chest and Hanumān struck a blow I cannot describe; it reached the stubs of those thirty-two elephant tusks cut off in my chest, and I fell down. Even now I feel the pain.

"We had other enemies, too. The gods who had gathered to watch chanted mantras for Rāma and conducted sacrifices for his victory. Our soldiers fought, but they fell in heaps, losing their heads, arms, and legs on the field. With vultures picking at their bodies, suddenly I was all alone, facing Rāma; then the vultures, clutching bloody flesh in their beaks, flew off in a such a mass that for a moment the sun was blacked out! Suddenly my crown was drenched in blood and flesh from those vultures flying overhead, while the gods showered Rāma with a crown of flowers. The humiliation was unspeakable! Not only for me but for the entire demon race descended from Brahmā and Pulastiyaṉ. The world knows that Rāma attacked us because I stole Sītā, and now I look like a fool. I can't believe it—the greatest raja in the Three Worlds beaten by two men and a bunch of monkeys!"

"It all proves one thing, Rāvaṇa: no matter how strong one is, an alliance with others is indispensable for victory—not just any support, though, for it must also be timely. Like the husk that protects the grain: the husk may seem useless, but for a time it is essential. From your account of the battle, I'd say the error lay in your decision to face the enemy by yourself."

"I did have support, uncle. Mountainous armies of spear-carrying demons, a full two hundred divisions, advanced against Rāma. But they are no more; after Rāma's arrows flew, not one head remained on a horse, an elephant, or a soldier."

"Two hundred divisions annihilated by one man is highly unusual. And they all lost their heads? There's something strange here. It's not just a matter of strength, because you've got that. Is it Rāma and his arrows?"

"Yes. Everyone said, 'Don't worry. Rāma is a mortal man.' Well, he may be human, but his arrows are not."

"Tell me more about his arrows. Why could nothing stand against them?"

"Well [*laughs*], when the head is cut off, what can one do? And it's not just Rāma; there's his brother Lakṣmaṇa, too.

> Even if Śiva, wearing the waxing moon,
> and all the gods in these Three Worlds
> Stood firm with my armies,
> We would not defeat Lakṣmaṇa, brother of Rāma,
> Whose mighty bow showers arrows upon us.[35]

"This first line about the waxing moon alludes to a story. Śiva is usually called Moon Crown but Kampa<u>n</u> uses the words 'waxing moon' to remind us of the tale of Dakṣa Raja and his sixty daughters. Many daughters married, but twenty-seven remained with him until one day he asked the moon to marry them, and the moon agreed. However, as the moon was leading his wives away, Dakṣa warned him: 'Treat them all equally; if you show preference for one, I will punish you.' When they arrived in his country, the moon was fair to them all, but there's destiny, *ū<u>l</u>vi<u>n</u>ai*, which no man can control, not even ascetics or Brahmins. No one. As it turned out, the moon loved one wife deeply, and the other twenty-six complained to their father, who cursed the moon: 'Your strength will now decrease, and the sun's will increase.'

"From that day forward, the rays of the moon grew weaker and weaker, and the sun grew hotter and hotter. Finally, as the moon was about to fade out completely, people on earth sought relief from Nārāyaṇa, who went to the moon and said: 'Quick, before you have no power, go and ask Śiva for refuge.' To Śiva he went and was comforted by these words: 'I cannot change Dakṣa's curse, but I will give you the strength to regain your sixteen phases each time you lose them.' And that is the origin of the waxing and waning moons each month. But—and this is the point—even if that powerful Śiva and all the other gods joined me and stood against Lakṣmaṇa, we would meet defeat."

"What about Rāma?"

"Rāma? He needs nothing more than the arrows he holds in one hand. His arrows have yogic powers and they follow you everywhere—into the netherworlds or up into the heavens. Even the cosmic fires that destroy the world would be burned by his arrows, which obliterate everything, including any mouth that questions their powers and any mind that disregards their purpose."

"But, Rāvaṇa, you are a great warrior—"

"Listen, Uncle. When Rāma releases his arrows . . . I . . . I don't know how to describe them . . . he shoots so fast, such a flash, they blind even the gods. Straining my twenty eyes, I can't tell if he's lifting his bow, fitting an arrow, or shooting one! When he does shoot, the whole world becomes one enormous arrow. It's hopeless. He is no ordinary man. You know the power of Śiva's trident? Indra's thunderbolt? Viṣṇu's discus? Well, none have the strength of Rāma's little finger!"

"Tell me more, Rāvaṇa."

"I've already mentioned Lakṣmaṇa, Rāma's brother. Once, after battling with the gods, I considered red-eyed Viṣṇu the most powerful force in the Three Worlds. Then I met Arjuna and realized that he was the strongest, but now, after facing Lakṣmaṇa, I know that he is invincible. He's a yogi, a great yogi. How can I describe him? Only that the power of Viṣṇu and Arjuna are mere specks of dust on Lakṣmaṇa's feet."

"And Rāma?"

"The power of Rāma's arrows is beyond the power of my speech. He shoots not one or two, but ten, even hundreds, all at once, producing them like the creator god Brahmā. They are guided by Viṣṇu and never miss their mark; and when they strike, they destroy like Lord Śiva. But these are simply words and cannot measure the power of Rāma's arrows. There is nothing more to say."

"Are you saying that Rāma is equal to the Three Gods?—to Brahmā's creative power, Viṣṇu's protective power, and Śiva's destructive power? Is that right? Your similes are fine, but, Rāvaṇa, why are you chanting the name Rāma, Rāma with every sentence? Even when you call me Māma [uncle], it sounds like 'Rāma'! Why sing a song to that mortal? Tell me that."

"I'm still in shock from the battle. I see Rāma everywhere. Isn't that him, over there? No, I can't see straight. Did he advance from the west? Or the east? First I saw him on earth, then above in the sky—soon north became south, and left right. I look at you, and I see Rāma coming to attack again! It's this fear, as if the battle rages on, that makes me slip and say 'Rāma' instead of 'Māma.'"

"Don't shake so, Rāvaṇa. Probably some unfavorable constellation has caused your confusion, some inauspicious, unavoidable arrangement of the planets. No shame in that—just bad luck. But what about your great chariot? Didn't that give you an advantage?"

"At the beginning, yes. When I set out for battle in my flower-chariot, I felt confident because Rāma had no conveyance at all. As he fought, however, I realized that he was riding on something. But what was it? It was so powerful for a moment, I thought it might be that great eagle, Garuda. He moved so quickly, it might be Vāyu. So invincible, it might be Agni. Raining down death everywhere, it might even be Yama. But when he came closer, I saw it was that monkey who raided Lanka! Rāma was riding on Hanumān—that's why he was everywhere at once.

"Māma, my end has come. I am able to defeat Indra, the mountain god, and Śiva bearing his axe, and Brahmā on his lotus throne, but this new enemy, this Rāma, he will kill me and Lanka will be no more. What shall I do, Māma? Can I escape and save Lanka, too?"

"So, this is what happened. You lost a battle to Rāma."

"Oh, if that was all, I would not have called you. I cannot fight him again. The very name Rāma terrifies me."

"Why consult me? Ask your ministers, your generals."

"I did consult them before—and look at the result!"

"Defeats do happen; don't let it discourage you."

"I need your advice, Māma."

"Listen, Rāvaṇa, this is all your own doing."

"Look, I will make you Chief Minister; your word will rule Lanka."

"Hmmm . . . Chief Minister?"

"Yes. Even I will follow your advice; your every word will be my command."

"But I fear to give you advice. I know what to say, but I don't dare."

"No confidence? Don't worry; that will come in time."

"Rāvaṇa, when have you ever heeded a warning?"

"All I want is a little support, some advice."

"You asked for advice once before, from Mārīca when you planned to steal Sītā, and—"

"And what?"

"And what did Mārīca say? He said: 'Don't do it; stealing Sītā will bring dishonor and destruction.' And what did you do?"

"Well . . . I got annoyed."

"Annoyed? You drew your sword and threatened his life!"

"But—"

"Did you or didn't you?"

"I did."

"Then you went straight ahead, brought back that woman to Lanka, and that's exactly where we are now."

"Then what can I do? Is there no way to save Lanka?"

"Release Sītā."

The Puppeteers' Oral Commentary

In the introduction to this chapter, I said that the puppeteers are primarily commentators, that their role is to explicate the Rāma story as much as to tell it; and if we multiply by twenty or thirty nights what they did in the performance translated above, we may grasp the extent to which this is true. This is the point I want to expand upon, before picking up the story again, because this relation of the oral commentary to the Kampan̲ text is fundamental to the art of shadow puppetry in Kerala. Traditions such as this, in which a major literary text is orally performed, often fall prey to two opposite but equally misleading assumptions. On the one hand, it might be thought that the oral performers "make up" their version of the Rāma story, that the performance is very different from the text; we know, however, that the puppet play relies heavily on verses from the *Kamparāmāyaṇam* and other sources. On the other hand, oral performance might also be misunderstood as a mechanical reproduction of its source text, that performance is no different from the text; but this, too, given the narrative alterations discussed earlier, is misleading. Still, the full extent of puppeteers' creative retelling is apparent only from their commentary as described in this and subsequent chapters.

A distinction between narrated text and exegetical commentary is recognized in Tamil, and in Indian tradition generally, in much the same terms as in the West: written texts (*mūlam*, root) may have written or oral commentaries (*urai*, speech, utterance). In the Kerala puppet play and many Tamil traditions, the written text comprises verses (*kavi*, *pāṭṭu*), and the commentary (*vacaṇam*, speech) is an oral, largely improvisational, explication of those memorized verses and the events narrated within them. Ordinarily, the text/verses are thought to carry the narrative burden by presenting the events of the story, and the commentary adds explanation. In the puppet play, this separation of story and explication is also plainly marked by language since the verses are chanted in formal Tamil, whereas the commentary is spoken in various forms of hybrid Tamil-Malayalam. Nevertheless, any conventional distinction between narrative and exegesis does not accurately describe the division of labor in the puppet play, in which the epic verses amount to less than the full story and the oral commentary offers more than an explanation. A more accurate description is that the verses operate as a mnemonic trigger to the commentary, which has its own stories to tell.

Those stories are part of the puppet play's broader interpretive task, which is to build coherence for Kampaṉ's Rāma story. My understanding of the concept of building coherence owes much to John Miles Foley's discussion of "traditional referentiality," mentioned briefly in chapter 1. Extending his earlier analyses of the Yugoslav epic tradition from "structure to meaning," Foley first discusses the formulae (of the oral formulaic theory) and then explains that they "command fields of reference much larger than the single line, passage, or even text in which they occur" and "bear meanings as wide and deep as the tradition they encode."[36] This traditional referentiality is metonymic, Foley continues, because it evokes in an informed audience a set of historical and intertextual associations, which complete the story in Yugoslav epic singing. Foley may have overstated the referential power of epic language (all language is metonymic to an extent), but surely he is correct that oral epics call forth an immense field of associations. Something very much like this traditional referentiality operates as well in the commentary of the Kerala puppeteers. In fact, the puppet play is doubly referential: the puppeteers create meanings not only through the language of Kampaṉ's text but also through the tales, proverbs, and quotations in their commentary. In the text-world thus built by the puppeteers, no event is isolated, no act unexplained, no character adrift; each piece is attached to another piece, and so by picking up any one episode or verse, the skilled puppeteer may move to any other episode or verse. On a larger scale, single Rāma texts are also fragments that touch, extend, and overlap others in a mosaic that local traditions reassemble. Even Kampaṉ was aware of this wider referential frame, when, as the poet setting out to compose a Rāma story, he compared himself to a cat attempting to lick up the whole of the Milk Ocean. So, too, if we think of the puppeteers as storytellers recounting and revising the

Rāma story, we will not hear all that they say, but if we listen to them as commentators, they teach us what we already know—that there is no *the* Rāmāyaṇa, only Rāma stories, each incomplete and therefore inexplicable without reference to others.

The principal pathways to this wider narrative world in the dramahouse are fixed-phrase expressions and auxiliary tales. As is true of other oral performers, the puppeteers have a weakness for epithets ("benefactor"–Vibhīṣaṇa; "raja whose crown bows to no one"–Rāvaṇa; "Truth of the Vedas"–Rāma; "waxing moon"–Śiva), for etymologies (of *tumi*, of *aṉmai*), and for proverbs ("Kill your mother, but never kill a messenger")—all of which lead to episodes beyond the epic content of the verse under discussion. More unique is the puppeteers' use of another fixed form, the *piramāṇam* (explanation, rule), which are quotations from traditional Indian literature, mostly Tamil and occasionally Sanskrit, but rarely Malayalam.[37] Commonly in proverb form, *piramāṇam* are second only to the epic verses as a source of knowledge and a basis of textual authority. When Rāma wants to explain the meaning of the word "benefactor" to Vibhīṣaṇa, for instance, he quotes from a Tamil book of maxims (*Tirukkuṟaḷ*, misidentified in performance as the Vedas): "Look closely at his face and you see inside his mind; whether anger, sincerity, or deceit, you can see its outer sign in the face"; and to explain that birth determines personality, he quotes the Tamil poet Auvaiyār. Every skilled performer knows two or three hundred quotations, which he memorizes from old palm-leaf manuscripts or, more often, from the notebooks in which he has carefully copied them. Some *piramāṇam* are contained within an auxiliary tale and are quoted as a tag line for retrieving that tale, which is then told in order to explain the meaning of a verse (see below). In disputes between puppeteers, nothing silences an opponent more quickly than to throw a *piramāṇam* at him.

Auxiliary stories unconnected to these fixed-phrase expressions are also told by the puppeteers in their commentary. Folktales, pan-Indian myths, and Tamil temple myths, especially Śaiva myths, are often woven into the wandering discourse, but the richest repository of these explanatory stories is a group of tales inserted into the Birth Book or compiled in a sequel, the Uttara Kāṇḍa. These tales contain material which editors apparently could neither fit neatly into the narrative nor omit altogether and thus chose to insert at the beginning or at the end of the story. The tales in the Uttara Kāṇḍa, omitted in Kampaṉ but central to the puppet play, form a sort of "folk supplement" to the Rāma story.

This sequel, the Uttara Kāṇḍa, contains two general categories of stories: those describing Rāvaṇa's history prior to the beginning of the epic (the history of Lanka, his genealogy, his exploits, and so forth) and those that extend the plot beyond the return to Ayodhya (Sītā's banishment from Ayodhya, the birth of her two sons, Rāma's horse sacrifice, and the final separation of Rāma and Sītā). Since neither the early Rāvaṇa stories nor the later darker tales about Rāma suit bhakti intentions, the *Kamparāmāyaṇam* does not contain the Uttara Kāṇḍa. In fact, a clear line is drawn between it and Kampaṉ's composition: the Tamil Uttara Kāṇḍa is attributed to Oṭṭakkūttaṉ and is not usually printed with Kampaṉ's text.[38] This intertextual tension surfaces in the puppeteers' story of how Kampaṉ came to write his epic. After Oṭṭakkūttaṉ's defeat in the poetic competition with Kampaṉ, he despairs and destroys his Rāma story, but the victorious Kampaṉ intervenes in the nick of time to save the loser's Uttara Kāṇḍa and then persuades him to "join it to my six books . . . then we shall have a complete Tamil Rāmāyaṇa." A unified Rāma text, however, is exactly what we do not have, and the puppeteers' reliance on stories from the omitted Uttara Kāṇḍa in order to interpret Kampaṉ's text indicates how far the folk tradition reaches beyond its source text.

The puppeteers choose to tell stories from the Uttara Kāṇḍa about Rāvaṇa and not Rāma, and this selectivity reorients the epic. Although Kampaṉ alludes to events in Rāvaṇa's past, his narrative begins with and ends with Rāma; at the other extreme, some Rāma texts begin with the history of Lanka and tell the story from Rāvaṇa's perspective. Effecting a compromise, the puppet play formally adheres to Kampaṉ's sequence and its Rāma orientation but circumvents it in two primary ways. First the puppeteers actually begin the narrative either at Pancavati or with the War Book, and thus introduce Rāvaṇa and his family at the beginning of the story; second, throughout performance, the puppeteers use the commentary to tell Rāvaṇa's story (at Pancavati, we might remember, Śūrpaṇakhā narrates Rāvaṇa's past history in some detail). The stories told most frequently in the drama-house form a cycle that describes Rāvaṇa's exploits before he enters Kampaṉ's epic plot and thus creates a symmetry between what we know of Ayodhya and what we know of Lanka. From this "Rāvaṇāyaṇa" we learn, in the above performance alone, that Daśagrīva has Brahmin ancestry, is a fervent devotee of Śiva and Brahmā, received boons from both gods, defeated Indra and the Cosmic Elephants, molested Vedavatī, is a master of the vina, and is a megalomaniac.

This last quality is also the theme of a story that illustrates how the puppeteers' commentary reframes Kampa<u>n</u>'s text from Rāvaṇa's point of view. When, in the first scene of the above translation, Rāvaṇa wonders how a mere monkey was able to burn Lanka, Vibhīṣaṇa reminds him of his victory march after conquering the Three Worlds, during which his arrogance earned him three curses: from Kubera's messenger (that Rāvaṇa would be destroyed by another messenger); from Vedavatī (that, in a later birth as Sītā, she would destroy him); and from Nandi (that a real "monkey-face" would destroy him).[39] As a result, Vibhīṣaṇa informs his brother, the fire of Sītā's chastity, magnified by the mirror of the emissary Hanumān, has burned Lanka. Told as the very first scene in the puppet play (and not found in Kampa<u>n</u>), the story of the three curses reframes the entire epic around Rāvaṇa's flawed character: the king of Lanka is doomed by his own past—by an arrogance that engenders vengeance in proud monkeys and chaste women. What device more firmly links past and present, placing one Rāma story in relation to others, than a curse, especially three of them?[40] No wonder that the puppeteers often call their Rāma story "a tale of eighteen curses."[41]

Throughout the War Book, the puppeteers tell other stories from this Rāvaṇa cycle to explain other aspects of his character, and each story may be repeated to a different effect. Vibhīṣaṇa's version of Rāvaṇa's victory march, for example, emphasizes his pride and lust, whereas a second version of the story later, told by Indra to the gods, emphasizes his stupidity when he gives away many of the lives granted by Śiva. If a puppeteer wishes to praise Rāvaṇa's devotion, on the other hand, he may select the story of Rāvaṇa's encounter with Śiva, in which he received his name, or the story of his austerities to Brahmā on the shores of Lake Kuntalam, in which he received his weapons, his sword, chariot, and invincibility against gods and demons. Rāvaṇa's heroic endurance, as another example, is glorified by the story of the Cosmic Elephants, during the victory march, in which he conquers the Guardians of the Eight Directions by lopping off their thirty-two tusks stuck in his chest. Rāvaṇa himself alludes to those tusks in describing to Māliyavā<u>n</u> the pain he felt when Hanumān pounded his chest during the first humiliating battle. These episodes from the Uttara Kāṇḍa, many of which are not even mentioned in Kampa<u>n</u>'s verses, are essential to the puppeteers' retelling of the *Kamparāmāyaṇam*.

The puppeteers tell other stories, as well, especially of Śiva (the Mārkaṇḍeya story) and of Viṣṇu (Churning the Ocean, Gajendra *Mokṣa*,

Madhu and Kaitabha). The last story deserves mention here because it is told frequently (three or four times in the course of a festival and twice in our sample of performances) and because it illustrates the fact that the commentary tells stories to explain the actions of epic characters other than Rāvaṇa. Madhu and Kaitabha, as the puppeteers tell it, are two demons born from Viṣṇu's earwax (or feces) to humble Brahmā's pride because the creator god was prematurely drawing up plans for the next creation when he should have been fast asleep in Viṣṇu's stomach. Tricked by Viṣṇu into losing their invincibility in this life, the demons are given boons to fight the god again and are reborn as Kumbhakarṇa and Atikāyaṉ, who then face Rāma-Viṣṇu on the battlefield. From the same story, the puppeteers also derive Jāmbuvāṉ, born from Brahmā's nose water, which was loosened by his fear of the demons, rolled down his face, and settled in the cleft of his chin.

A final illustration of the commentary's power to create coherence is Natesan Pillai's account of how Kampaṉ came to compose his epic.[42] Narrated within the explication of a single verse word (*tumi*), this story demonstrates how completely the commentary subsumes the narrative function and enables the puppeteer to move from the part to the whole—from a verse in the *Kamparāmāyaṇam* to the history of its composition—within the mosaic of the Rāma story tradition. Looking closely at the performance, we see that the Kampaṉ verse serves as the door through which this senior puppeteer exits the epic text and moves to a different vantage point, where Indra and the gods speak as detached observers of the events on earth. By stepping outside the verses, Natesan Pillai is able to talk about Kampaṉ's epic, and when his tale of Kampaṉ's composition is completed, he reenters the epic narrative through that same "verse door." This and other auxiliary stories dominate the puppet play, exceeding in total performance time the narrative delivered in the verses.

I first suspected the limited role of the verses when I realized that the puppeteers do not chant all the verses that they know. After comparing several performances with Kampaṉ's text, a consistent pattern stood out: if Kampaṉ summarizes a story in a string of verses, the puppeteers sing only one of those verses and use the commentary to cover the material contained in the others. This selective use of the verses occurs in the scene already discussed, when Vibhīṣaṇa addresses Rāvaṇa in the war council: Although the puppeteers sing only one of the several Kampaṉ verses spoken by Vibhīṣaṇa to tell the story of Rāvaṇa's victory march, their commentary includes all the details of that story—the curses, the names of elephants, and so forth. The puppeteers do not chant all the verses they have memorized because they do not need them. Instead, the verses are mnemonic devices, like the *piramāṇam*, memorized to trigger narration in the oral commentary of episodes from the wider Rāma story tradition. To adapt Foley's idea of "traditional referentiality," Kampaṉ's verses are similar to other pieces that comprise the referential realm of the Rāma tradition, that field of meanings which every performance evokes and none can exhaust.

CHAPTER 7

The Death of Indrajit: Creating Conversations

In the previous chapter, I made the general point that the puppeteers adapt Kampan̲'s epic poem primarily through their oral commentary. The specific techniques by which the commentary subsumes the text and dominates performance are the subject of this chapter. In brief, my argument will be that the puppeteers gain control by creating conversations through which they speak in their own voice. For that reason, as with the previous chapter, readers may wish to pay special attention to the use of dialogue in the following translation, which takes us straight to the heart of the War Book.

Here, in the War Book, one might expect to find Rāvaṇa's death because it is both the narrative climax in Kampan̲ and the ritual center of the puppet play, which originated in order that Bhagavati could view the auspicious spectacle of the demon's final defeat. The Kerala tradition, however, seldom honors our expectations: it lives in performance but holds no interactive audience; it presents one of the most popular stories in Indian literature but is not primarily a narrative tradition; and the interminable, chaotic War Book, rather than one of the tightly plotted, earlier books, occupies center stage. Looking at the puppeteers' treatment of the War Book, we see once more that the puppet play has its own logic, sometimes in counterpoint to its textual source: the long series of overnight plays inside the drama-house reaches its dramatic climax not with Rāvaṇa's death but with that of his son, Indrajit.[1]

The puppeteers kill off Rāvaṇa matter of factly, almost as a prelude to the moving scene of Maṇḍōdari grieving over her husband's corpse.[2] Killing Indrajit, by contrast, consumes nearly three nights of performance and requires the most complicated manipulations of puppets in the entire sequence of performances; on the second night, for instance, a spectacular event occurs when a large, wooden Garuḍa swoops down on a wire leading from a tall pole to a corner of the drama-house and revives Rāma felled by Indrajit's snake-weapon. By no means is Rāvaṇa a minor character on the cloth screen, but he is less dangerous than his son, more vulnerable, more human, and continually misled, particularly by his love for Sītā. Indrajit, on the other hand, is ascetic and invincible, except against someone of equal self-denial—someone who has fasted in the forest for fourteen years, that is, against Lakṣmaṇa.[3] As is true of other heroes in Indian folklore, the tragedy of Indrajit is intensified by the very fact that he, unlike Rāvaṇa, is unmarried and therefore dies a premature death.[4] In this respect, father and son exemplify that complementarity between secular authority and spiritual power which is well known in Indian culture. King and renouncer are represented also by Rāma and Lakṣmaṇa, for example, which explains why the weak-willed Rāvaṇa is killed by his counterpart, Rāma, and the resolute Indrajit must be conquered by his equal, Lakṣmaṇa.[5] As the puppeteers themselves explain: "Rāvaṇa is the body of the demons, Indrajit their life. When the life is gone, the body will not live long." That Indrajit's death, not Rāvaṇa's, heralds Rāma's victory in the drama-houses of Kerala is a local innovation.

In the following translation, a eulogy to the majestic Indrajit is delivered by one of the senior puppeteers, K. L. Krishnan Kutty. After his performance, when I asked why Indrajit received three nights of performance and Rāvaṇa less than one, his eyes popped wide open and he said excitedly, "Because Indrajit is a great warrior! The greatest warrior!" He then went on to tell me in detail the story of Lakṣmaṇa's fasting in the forest for fourteen years, of his diet and his austerities, and of how they produced the power necessary to subdue the "greatest warrior." It is only right that Krishnan Kutty should deliver this tribute to Indrajit, for his enthusiasm is matched by his skill. I still remember my first visit to his home, in 1984, when I casually showed him a handwritten copy of a folk Rāmāyaṇa in Tamil, which he opened, read for a moment, winced, quickly corrected two spelling mistakes, and then rhythmically chanted the invocatory verses (which he had never seen before). His learning is bred from four generations of puppeteers in a Tamil family attached to the temple at Kavalapara, near Shoranur, one of only three places where the full Rāma story is performed, which is a source of great pride for his family. In the 1930s, his father,

Laksmana Pulavar received a commemorative medal (*vīraśrīṅgāla*) from the Raja of Kavalapara in recognition of his performances at that temple; fifty years later, Krishnan Kutty received a commemorative wooden plaque from the Sangeet Natak Akademi in New Delhi.

These shifting sands of patronage have shaped the professional life of Krishnan Kutty. Among his family possessions are many palm-leaf manuscripts, those crumbling packets that scholars invest with mystical status because they are now so rare. Puppeteers have always considered these manuscripts valuable for reference and useful for memorization and teaching, but since the arrival of foreign (and Indian) text hunters, they have become wampum in a new trading relationship. Responsive to these demands but unable to produce more manuscripts and with editorial help from local scholars, encouragement from a cultural organization in New Delhi, and money from a private donor in Sweden, Krishnan Kutty has published the shadow puppet text of the Ayodhya Book (in Tamil) and the Birth Book (in Malayalam).[6] Although very few copies have sold, all this activity has excited the jealousy of rival puppeteers, who speak eagerly of plans to publish their editions of the shadow puppet play. By the end of the 1980s, the shadow puppet tradition had completed its rite of passage to the printed page.

In the same decade, the tradition also made an uncertain entry into the international culture trade when the puppets were taken out of Kerala—first to New Delhi, then to Moscow, and eventually to Europe. In recognition of his learning and dedication, Krishnan Kutty was chosen to perform on these foreign tours; consequently, his modest ancestral house of two rooms and a storage space gained a new, concrete facade and a porch, where glass shelves display photo albums of his trips, the scarce palm-leaf manuscripts, rows of his edited books, and a stack of handsomely printed business cards. The new patronage supporting folk performing arts on the international festival circuit is difficult for anyone to ignore: "I make thirty rupees for an overnight performance here [in Kerala]," Krishnan Kutty confided, "but one thousand rupees for one hour in New Delhi." Still, he longs for the old days, when puppeteers were respected as learned men, like his father, and he worries about the steady decline of shadow puppetry in Kerala. New puppets are not made now—it is cheaper to repair the old ones—and few young men are taking up the art; although each of his four sons is a competent performer, only the two eldest say they want to make the puppet play their livelihood. Supported by his dutiful sons, a complete set of puppets, and a few lucrative performing sites inherited from his father,

Krishnan Kutty commands a large group of six puppeteers, but they are often thinly spread in order to cover two (even three) performances at different temples on the same night. As a result, he admits, the quality of the performances is declining. Sitting in a molded plastic chair on his new porch, he speaks of his travels, his successes, his books, but rarely the future.

Krishnan Kutty's own performances, fortunately, have lost none of their brilliance, as evinced in the following translation. It was recorded in Elakatu, a village not quite fifteen miles from Palghat on the old trading route northwest toward Calicut and the Arabian Sea. Local patronage here supports seventeen nights of puppet plays, and some nights fetch two or three thousand rupees (divided between performers and temple) in individual donations. Sitting directly opposite the Bhagavati temple on a hill that rises steeply away from the main road, the drama-house has a long front and a high ceiling. With such ample space and patronage, this is a popular site for puppeteers but not a favorable one for field research. On one occasion, a performer prevented me from recording (he was miffed, I later learned, that I had not given him any money for an interview the week before). On another day, temple officials, confident that I would sell my recordings abroad and become rich, forced me to cease tape-recording until I submitted a written request to the village council. When I returned with that request in 1989, the electrical power continually fluctuated between too much and too little current, so that my tapes were garbled beyond comprehension; when the power finally went out altogether, I fumbled with batteries and lost part of a valuable scene. I did learn something in the frustration of that power cut, however. All night about a dozen people were sleeping and lounging on the ground in front of the drama-house, but when the microphone and loudspeakers went silent, four men moved up to the entrance of the stage and sat on the steps, where they listened to the commentary for most of two hours. This handful of connoisseurs is hardly an audience (they, too, eventually went to sleep), but they reassured me that my appreciation of the puppeteers' art is not necessarily the self-serving enthusiasm of a field researcher.

The translation below picks up the story where we left it at the end of the previous chapter, after Rāvaṇa's humiliating first defeat, and covers four nights of performance from the War Book, including the deaths of Kumbhakarṇa, Atikāyan̲, and Indrajit. Other figures, unknown or silent in Kampan̲, such as the umbrella holder (*kuṭakkāran̲*), a comic pair of messengers, and the temple oracle (*veḷiccappāṭu*), also appear, but a discussion of their roles is deferred until the next chapter. The translation opens with an abridged prose summary of the previous night's narration and moves quickly to Kumbhakarṇa's appearance on the field of battle.

The Death of Indrajit

[*Indra*] "Gods, listen to what Māliyavāṉ told Rāvaṇa. He said that if the great demon-raja wanted to live in Lanka, he must release Sītā. Rāvaṇa accepted this plan, reluctantly, but was intercepted by Mahōdara, who sang his praises so loudly that Rāvaṇa once again grew confident. Sending messengers, Rāvaṇa summoned his brother Kumbhakarṇa, but when the giant demon entered the palace and saw the court in a war panic, he was shocked, bowed before his older brother, and asked what had happened. When Rāvaṇa explained the terrible loss in yesterday's battle and asked him to assume the responsibility of winning back the war, Kumbhakarṇa looked at Rāvaṇa and spoke: 'Brother, the only reason for this chaos is your foolish love for that man's wife. As long as she stays, the destruction of Lanka is certain. Release her and free us all from this shame.'

"But Rāvaṇa roared back, 'Quiet! It's not your place to advise me. She stays and Rāma dies, that is the end of this debate.' Kumbhakarṇa called that mere 'words,' but Rāvaṇa reminded him of their proud heritage, their descent from Brahmā: 'We are half-demon, half-Brahmin, and we do commit mistakes. If you are opposed to the idea of Sītā's captivity, you might at least consider attacking the enemy who has attacked us.' Kumbhakarṇa replied that Rāvaṇa should have fought Rāma first and then taken Sītā, which so infuriated Rāvaṇa that he ordered his brother to leave the court. In the end, Kumbhakarṇa said that he, by force of blood, would obey his brother and king and fight Rāma.

"And so with thirteen thousand soldiers, Kumbhakarṇa entered the field. Rāma saw the gigantic figure emerge in the distance and spoke to Vibhīṣaṇa, standing by his side:[7]

> "Mighty shoulders spreading so wide
> My eyes can not measure them in a day,
> Legs planted on the earth like mountains,
> It can't be a warrior, but what is it?[8]

"Vibhīṣaṇa, yesterday we defeated Rāvaṇa and his two hundred thousand demon soldiers; I felled him, knocking off his crown, and he can no longer hold any hope of victory. Only one question remained: 'Will he release Sītā and end this war? Or will he send more demons to be killed?' Yet, look! Over there! Another huge warrior has taken the field, and he is enormous! My eyes will require more than a day to move from his right shoulder to his left. He cannot be human-born—he looks like a mountain that emerged from the earth, like Mt. Meru, flanked by the cosmic elephants, with the nine planets circling his head. Who is this mountain-man?"

"Rāma, look closely. What do you see?"

"I cannot answer. Could it be Rāvaṇa in disguise—has he changed his twenty arms and ten heads for these two arms and single head? Is his *māyā* frightening us again? Tell me, tell me quickly."

"Rāma,

> Listen, noble one (*āriya*), he is younger brother to
> the Raja of Lanka on this earth (*aṭitalam*)
> And older brother to me;
> Wearing anklets of black death, wielding a cruel trident,
> He is Kumbhakarṇa, O, Lord of Victory.

"Notice, Rāma, that the poet calls you *āriya*, or 'noble one.' We also call you *pūjyaṉ*, which means both 'noble one' and 'nothingness,' a cipher.[9] Numbers are useful when we add, for instance, ten to twenty to find a sum, but more useful is this concept of nothingness and of everything at the same time. That's you, Rāma. Nameless, formless, you are the unknowable, the hidden essence, the self-generating reality.

"People often ask, 'Why worship this nothingness?' Our answer is that nothing, this *pūjyaṉ*, takes form to protect us. You, too, assume the eight dispositions, such as love and compassion, that we all have. So what separates you from us? Consider the Śaiva texts, which describe three layers of body: subtle, gross, and physical.[10] The physical body is that which is visible to the naked eye; inside is another, the gross body, which can be known by yoga and meditation; and inside it is a still more subtle body, which is known only by wisdom. Humans and gods alike have these three layers, but there is a difference. The outer bodies of all the beings in the world comprise the outer body of god, and the inner bodies of all the beings form the inner body of god; the innermost bodies are subsumed in god's innermost body. In short, god's body is this world. People debate the nature of god: some say he has name and form, some deny it, whereas the simple truth, Rāma, is that god takes bodily form to protect this world in times of crisis. Because you are an example of that compassion, we call you *pūjyan̲*."

"Yes, Vibhīṣaṇa, but who is that giant warrior bearing down on us?"

"Right, and look at the rest of the first line, in which 'foot place' (*aṭitalam*) refers to the earth because one walks on it. This is an example of a derived noun; the other category of nouns are those understood by conventional usage. Now, words in each of these two categories can be either a general noun or a special noun; thus, there are four classes of nouns. For instance, we use the word *paṅkam* to denote 'mud' [*cēr̲u*]. Other things that come from mud, like the word *paṅkayam* (lotus) are derived nouns, though many would consider this a noun by convention. On the other hand, people seldom use the word *paṅkayam* and prefer instead *centāmarai*, which is a special derived noun.

"Similarly, *mūkkaṇṇan̲*, or 'three-eyed,' is a derived noun when we use it to mean 'coconut.' But when we use it to mean 'Śiva,' it is a special derived noun. 'Foot place' is also a special derived noun because it arose for a special reason, which is Vāmana, the dwarf-avatar of Viṣṇu, who—"

"Vibhīṣaṇa, I appreciate your learned explanations, but first tell me, who is this ferocious warrior about to kill us?"

"That's what I am telling you, Rāma, by explaining this phrase 'foot place.' Long ago a raja and his son Mahābali built a magnificent city of Asurapati, whence the demons ruled the Three Worlds. Soon the gods and sages petitioned Brahmā for relief from the demons' violence, and Brahmā sent them to Nārāyaṇa, who assured them that he would end their troubles once and for all. 'First,' he said, 'we must churn the Milk Ocean to acquire ambrosia. Bring that huge Mandara mountain; the long snake named Vāsuki; the sixteen-phased moon, Candra; and finally that snake Karkottan. But, for this task, you gods also need the help of the demons, especially their king, Mahābali.'

"Then with the demons' help, the gods set up Mt. Mandara as the churning stick, using the moon as a latch and a horse as a pin to fasten the stick to the tortoise as its resting place. With Vāsuki wrapped around the stick, the gods held his tail and the demons his head, and they began to churn. They churned and churned until Vāsuki was unable to bear the pain and spat out his dangerous poison, which swelled into a huge ball and advanced toward the demons, who dropped the snake's head and fled. Nārāyaṇa stopped them by saying he would swallow the poison, which he did, but he could not hold it down, and it emerged again in a murderous mass. Knowing it would kill them all, the gods ran to Mt. Kailasa and pleaded with Śiva to assist them.

"'Do not fear, gods. Stay here,' advised Śiva, who then summoned a great ascetic and told him to bring the poison back to Kailasa. When the ascetic approached the black mass, it called out, 'Stay back or die!' But the ascetic simply said, 'I am Śiva's messenger. Come rest in my hands,' and the poison entered his palm—at least that's what the old legends say. The ascetic returned to Kailasa and put the poison in Śiva's hands, who pressed it into a ball, like soft rice, and tossed it in his mouth. There are two versions of what happened next. Some say that Pārvatī, fearing that Śiva would die if he swallowed the poison, squeezed his throat so that the poison went no further—it stayed right there in his throat. The other story is that Śiva himself halted the poison in his throat to protect those who sought his refuge. The old legends often differ like this, but no version fails to state that Śiva held the poison without swallowing it. That's why Śiva is called Dark Throat or Poison Throat.[11]

"Śiva then told the gods to return and churn again for the ambrosia. They did, and eventually the liquid emerged, but the demons and gods fought over it. In that battle, Indra, riding on his elephant Airavata, cut off Mahābali's head with his thunderbolt, while Śukra, Mahābali's guru, watched—"

"Vibhīṣaṇa, this is a fascinating tale about Mahābali's death, but what about this figure bearing down on us *right now*?"

"Swami, every story has details, which unfold as the story is told, and eventually we will return to the starting point. For now, just listen. Grieving over Mahābali's loss, Śukra tried to revive him. Carrying his head and body to the Milk Ocean, he fitted them together, chanted a secret mantra and . . . Mahābali arose as from a dream. Bowing at Śukra's feet, Mahābali said, 'Great guru, you have let me live again. When I battle Indra for the second time, is there a boon that will protect me from death?' 'Yes,' the guru replied, 'if you perform an esoteric sacrifice, you can defeat a thousand Indras.' And so

Śukra and Mahābali kindled a fire, made offerings of milk and fruit and ghee, and chanted mantras into the flames. Soon Brahmā emerged from the flames and gave Mahābali horses, arrows, bows, and a jewel-garland that made its owner invincible. Armed with these boons, Mahābali summoned his demon armies and again charged against the gods, who fell back in fear when they saw the once-dead king leading the charge. Bṛhaspati, guru to the gods, explained what had happened and said, 'Flee now while there is time; we can do nothing against this Mahābali.' "

"Yes, Vibhīṣaṇa, this is all very interesting, but who is this warrior? At least tell me his name before he slays me."

"I'm coming to that. So the gods fled and Mahābali occupied the heavens, entertained by celestial dancers and musicians. Indra was furious and prepared to attack Mahābali, but Brahmā intervened and bade him consult Viṣṇu, who promised Indra that he would destroy Mahābali. Meanwhile on earth, a son of Brahmā, sage Kaśyapa, married the thirteen daughters of the moon. With one wife, Aditi, he fathered the gods, and with another, Diti, he brought forth the demons. Aditi knew at once that Diti's demon-sons would overcome her god-sons, so she asked her husband, Kaśyapa, for another son to subdue the demons. Kaśyapa listened and spoke: 'Even barren women will conceive if they follow these instructions: for the twelve days after the new moon in Panguni, you must repeat the Five-Letter Mantra, the *Māyā* Mantra, and the Truth Mantra.'[12]

"For those twelve days, Aditi meditated on those mantras, and when the star rose early on the thirteenth morning, she cried out, 'Swami, you must take some form to defeat the demons.' 'So be it,' a voice responded. Ten months later, on Kṛṣṇa's birthday, Vāmana [Viṣṇu's dwarf-avatar] was born. The old stories provide a long description of his tiny body, but it can be summarized in one sentence: 'If you understand a banyan-tree seed, you understand Vāmana.' Meanwhile, Mahābali dug a deep pit, filled it with sandalwood, poured on ghee, and kindled a roaring fire. For days the sacrifice continued, as the demon-raja distributed gifts to anyone who came and asked. When Vāmana approached, Mahābali himself fell at the little Brahmin's holy feet and escorted him in a royal chariot to the guest house. After his esteemed guest had rested, Mahābali spoke. 'Sir, why have you come?'

"'I am a student of the Vedas; I need a small plot of land to live on while I complete my studies,' Vāmana politely replied.

"'Granted. How much land do you wish?'

"'Only as much as I can measure in three steps.'

"'Such a large request from such a little man,' Mahābali muttered and shook his head. 'If you had asked for three entire villages, I would not refuse you.'

"'Oh, no, sir. Only three steps of land, please.'

"Now in those days no deeds, surveyors, or documents were needed to transfer land. What's the point? Someone says you have the land—and it's yours. A person's word was sufficient. However, when Vāmana spoke with Mahābali, Śukra, his guru, was suspicious. Leaning toward his king, Śukra whispered, 'This is no child; he's Viṣṇu. Give him land and your life is finished.' But Mahābali rebuked him. 'Don't say such things. You know the saying: "Those who give even when they have nothing live forever; those who prevent a gift will struggle to earn saltless rice." That's what the old books say. Besides, if I say "I give," it means I gave.'

"As Śukra watched, Mahābali poured water through Vāmana's hands to seal the agreement and said, 'Take your three steps.' Suddenly, the dwarf expanded into a huge figure that covered the earth with one step and the heavens with his second. Mahābali then realized this was Viṣṇu and offered his own head as a resting place for the god's third step.

"This is the point, Rāma. When Viṣṇu took his dwarf-avatar and measured the earth with his steps, the phrase 'foot place' became a special derived noun for 'earth,' which brings me back to your original question about the giant warrior before us. The earth's loveliest city is Lanka, whose raja is the older brother of this warrior on the battlefield. Strong as Yama, wearing a special anklet that rings a warning to anyone on the field, wielding a spear in his right hand, surrounded by thousands of demons, that is no mountain before you, no *māyā* form of Rāvaṇa, that's Kumbhakarṇa![13]

> You who swallow the worlds,
> In his hand he holds
> A spear that swallows warriors' lives,
> Given by him who swallowed poison."[14]

"I see. This is Rāvaṇa's younger brother and your older brother, right? But, tell me why the spear is special."

"Rāma, permit this ignoramus to ask a question. Is it necessary to say that Kumbhakarṇa is both my older brother and Rāvaṇa's younger brother? Would not one relation be sufficient? Since you did not notice this apparent redundancy, let me explain. Both relations, in fact, are necessary to establish Kumbhakarṇa's identity because his father, Vicaravasu, married four women: Tevavaṉṉi, Putpa, Kalai, and Kēkaci. Thus, only if I say that Kumbhakarṇa is both my older brother and Rāvaṇa's younger brother can one know that his mother is our mother, Kēkaci.

"But there is another level of meaning in all this. When I said he comes 'after Rāvaṇa,' it means that he is junior not only in age but also in demonic disposition.[15] He's a *rākṣasa,* yes, but he has something of Śiva in him, too, and therefore commits fewer sins than Rāvaṇa. At the same time, he comes 'before me' and so is more demonic than I am. Is the meaning of this line clear now, Rāma?"

"It is, but please tell me about his spear before it pierces me."

"You are wise to single out that spear from among the hundreds of weapons he holds because it's Śiva's spear, as the verse explains. Notice that the poet uses the word 'swallow' in the first line to identify Viṣṇu as 'He who swallows the world,' which refers to you, Rāma. During the periodic dissolutions of the world, all living creatures return to Brahmā seated on the lotus stalk, which recedes back inside Viṣṇu, who then holds the earth's waters in himself. However, in the last line, 'swallowing poison' refers to Śiva's actions in the story I just told about churning the ocean. Also, the spear itself is said to 'swallow,' to consume the lives of enemies. Do you see how the verse works? It says: 'You who swallow the worlds, listen: this spear, which swallows warriors' lives, was given by him who swallowed the poison.'"

"Oh, it's Śiva's trident. But is this *the* trident of Śiva? Aren't there many such spears?"

"Good question. Particularly because in the *purāṇas,* Śiva appears to give weapons to nearly everyone! Suppose he gives a specific weapon to a person, who then gives it to another, is it still a 'weapon given by Śiva'? I think not. The weapon must be given directly by Śiva; otherwise it's not a 'Śiva-weapon.' When a great devotee meditates and asks Śiva for a weapon, the god fashions a special one for that person. Kumbhakarṇa is a case in point because he received his spear in return for devotion to Śiva, and, remember, Śiva doesn't give weapons to everyone who asks. If he did, he would do absolutely nothing but make weapons and give them away."

"Yes, yes, but how powerful is this spear?"

"Long ago, when Indra attacked the city of the gods, the white elephant Airāvata blocked his path. Rushing headlong, Indra grabbed its tusks, but the massive elephant flew up into the sky and tried to shake off the king of the gods. To avoid the disgrace of falling from heaven, Indra held on firmly to its tusks, swinging wildly as the elephant flew through the air. That's how Indra conquered Airāvata, yet that same Indra was conquered by Kumbhakarṇa, who is coming toward us now."

"What else can you tell me about Kumbhakarṇa?"

"Well, the trident indicates his hand strength, but there is also body strength and leg strength . . .

> Greater than he who is death to Death,
> Greater than he who ended the Ender with his foot,
> Kumbhakarṇa conquered Viṣṇu and
> Tied the *vākai* victory flower on his spear.[16]

"The verse begins with a reference to Śiva as 'death to Death,' which is a separate story and time—"

"You mean the story of Mārkaṇḍeya? Please tell it."

"Very briefly, then, in the city of Katakam a Brahmin named Kuccakan and his wife Ilava gave birth to a son, who grew up to be a scholar and one day left the house to meditate in the deep forest. Meditating on Śiva, he sat motionless as a stone while wild animals crept silently around him. Soon Viṣṇu appeared before the boy, who slowly withdrew from his meditation and bowed. Then the god spoke: 'Because you are motionless as a crane (*kocca*), I name you Kocciyaṉ.[17] Study well, and wait for Śiva's blessings.' Having completed his education, the boy returned home where his father explained that he must get married, but the young man refused: 'Married life is not for me. All life has problems, but at least they end, whereas the troubles of married life are endless. True pleasure comes with Śiva's grace and that requires asceticism.'

"His father was fed up with this philosophizing: 'You must marry; it's my command and you know very well that a son must never contradict his father's word. As the proverb says: "He who opposes his father or harms his mother or denies a sadhu's wishes will swallow balls of molten iron in hell."' And so the boy relented: 'As you wish, Father, but I impose these conditions: my bride should not come from a motherless family, a fatherless family, a family with disease, or a one-child family; she must not be named after any of the seven constellations, after a river, or a bird.[18] She must possess a healthy body, the balance of this earth, the wisdom of a sage, and the humility to serve others.[19] Find this woman, Father, and I am ready to marry.'

"His father then set out on a journey and eventually reached an ashram where a sage named Uccattiyan̲ had a daughter with all the qualities his son had demanded. Meanwhile—this is a complex story, hard to tell in a few words—Uccattiyan̲'s daughter was bathing with her friends in a pool when a rutting elephant suddenly appeared. The girls scattered in all directions, but the sage's daughter fell into a deep well. Uccattiyan̲ searched and searched and finally found her body lying at the bottom of the well; dragging it up, he laid it on the ground and collapsed in grief. At that moment, the Brahmin, Kuccakan̲, came along to ask the sage to accept his boy as a son-in-law, but when he saw the girl's corpse, he turned to Uccattiyan̲ and said, 'Why grieve about death? Take the body over to that temple, and protect it for now. Tomorrow I will revive your daughter.' Kuccakan̲ knew perfectly well that Yama had taken away the girl's life and that he would have to fight the God of Death to win it back. As soon as he left the scene, the elephant returned, went straight to the temple, lifted up the corpse, and ran off with it. When the girl awoke, she was stunned: 'An elephant? Carrying me in its trunk? Elephants trample and crush, so why is this one cradling me like a baby?'

"Then with her divine eye she saw into the elephant's past lives, and this is what she saw: Once there was a man named Devataccan̲ whose son, Dharmatattan̲, became an orphan. When the son began to spend his inheritance wildly, he met a Brahmin named Nēcamāhi, disguised as an alchemist. Hoping to trick the rich Dharmatattan̲, the alchemist said, 'Give me whatever coins you have, and I will turn them to gold. Bring me everything, and the gold you gain will not be contained within the walls of a house.' Crazed with greed, the young man sold all his possessions—cattle, cows, furniture, jewels—and then gave all the coins to the alchemist. Placing them in a box, the man chanted a mantra and poured ghee into the flames rising from the box. Soon the heavy smoke overwhelmed Dharmatattaṉ, who fell down unconscious while Nēcamāhi quickly snatched away the box of coins and replaced it with another that held old scraps of metal. When Dharmatattaṉ recovered, the alchemist spoke: 'I must go to perform a Kālī *pūjā*; on the third day I will return and then the gold will be yours. Watch over the box until I return.' The third day came, but not Nēcamāhi. Deciding that if he got no gold, he would at least recover his coins, Dharmatattaṉ cautiously put out the fire, opened the lid, and to his horror, saw only twisted pieces of brass and iron. With no means to support himself, Dharmatattaṉ committed suicide.

"For his suicide, Dharmatattaṉ was cursed to be reborn as an elephant, and for many years, in many previous lives as elephants, he performed good deeds. Only one more good deed was required in order to regain his human form; and so it happened: he, as an elephant, revived the sage's daughter and gained a new life as Dharmachatra, and the girl was married to Kuccakaṉ's reluctant son. The couple lived happily and had a son named Mirakaṇṭaṉ, who soon married Kuruvati, daughter of sage Bhradvasi. This couple had no children, even after repeated acts of charity, so Mirakaṇṭaṉ decided to set out to Benares to ask Śiva for a child. Arriving at the Ganga, he undertook fierce austerities in Śiva's name until, finally, the Great God appeared and asked him what he wanted.

"When he learned that Mirakaṇṭaṉ desired a son, Śiva offered him a choice: 'You may have a son who is evil and stupid but will live for a hundred years, or you may have a son who is virtuous and wise but will die at sixteen years. Which do you wish?' Immediately Mirakaṇṭaṉ answered, 'Give me the sixteen-year-old son. What good is a dolt even if he lives for a century?' In due course, the son was born and his parents named him Mārkaṇḍeya. As his sixteenth year approached, his parents watched him anxiously and when he asked why, his father replied, 'You were born by the grace of Śiva and were allotted only sixteen years of life. Soon you will die and we cannot bear it.' But the son consoled his father: 'Appa, do not worry. I will approach Śiva myself.'

"Young Mārkaṇḍeya went straight into the forest, selected a secluded spot, and sat down in deep meditation. There he sat, and when his sixteenth year arrived, Yama looked at his accountant and asked, 'Anyone due today?' The clerk leafed through his enormous ledger of lives and stopped at a line: 'Yes, here we are. A boy named Mārkaṇḍeya was due yesterday, in fact, and he's still in meditation in the forest.'

"'Did we simply overlook him, or is his meditation so powerful that it confused us?'

"'No matter. We must go get him now.'

"But when Yama's men arrived on the scene, they were paralyzed by the sheer force of Mārkaṇḍeya's devotion, and they returned empty-handed. Yama was furious and rose to go himself, but his minister, Kālaṉ, stopped him. 'Lord, please remain here. I will go and bring back that little boy.' Riding Yama's buffalo and swinging his noose, Kālaṉ charged toward the forest and only stopped within a few inches of the seated Mārkaṇḍeya, who neither moved nor spoke. Finally, Kālaṉ was forced to speak. 'Mārkaṇḍeya! You know that Śiva gave you only sixteen years, and now you've crossed over into the seventeenth. What gives you the authority to transgress Śiva's boon? Speak!' Mārkaṇḍeya said nothing, and again Kālaṉ screamed at him, 'Listen, this is no trifling matter. I am Kālaṉ, Yama's henchman. Even if Brahmā were slated to die, I'd take his life! You can delay death no longer.'

"Finally, the boy spoke: 'So, you are Kālaṉ. Come to take my life, have you? If my life is over, there's no need to take me to Yama. I will go directly to Śiva. Leave!' As they argued, Kālaṉ drew out his noose and flung it around Mārkaṇḍeya, but the boy threw himself around the Śiva lingam he was worshiping and cried, 'Śiva! Receive me, receive me!' Suddenly Śiva appeared in a form visible only to Mārkaṇḍeya and said to him, 'I grant you a long life.' Then Śiva kicked Kālaṉ's chest with his leg, driving him into the earth and killing him. All the gods gathered and requested Śiva to revive Kālaṉ, so that Death might resume its normal course. Śiva did that but also said to Kālaṉ, 'Do not go near my devotees again. Henceforth, I will receive my own worshipers.'

"This is the story contained in the phrase that describes Śiva as 'death to Death' (*kālaṉ* to *kālaṉ*). Notice also that Śiva killed Death with his foot (*kāl*), so the line reads: '*kālaṉ* to *kālaṉ* by *kāl*.' The underlying meaning, Rāma, is that Kumbhakarṇa is more powerful than Śiva, the Destroyer of Death."

"You've described Kumbhakarṇa's body strength, Vibhīṣaṇa, but tell me more about his trident."

"As the verse says, Kumbhakarṇa once decorated that weapon with the victory flower after he defeated Viṣṇu. That's the power of his spear, Rāma."

"What! Are you saying that he conquered Viṣṇu in battle?[20] Does this Kumbhakarṇa have no weaknesses?"

"No. He does. You know that story of his boon, I presume. When Rāvaṇa asked and received a boon of invincibility against the gods and demons, Kumbhakarṇa was about to ask for the same, but the gods realized that such a boon would be too dangerous, and so they asked Sarasvatī to help. The goddess of learning seated herself in Kumbhakarṇa's tongue, and when he opened his mouth to ask for a boon of immortality, she changed the words so that he gained deathlessness only for six months; during the other six months when he is vulnerable, he sleeps. We are fortunate, indeed, that this is the period of his sleep; in other words, if Rāvaṇa had waited a little longer until his giant brother awoke, Kumbhakarṇa would kill you."

"Here he comes, Vibhīṣaṇa, prepare for battle."

[*The battle is joined and, eventually, Rāma kills Kumbhakarṇa, who lies dead on the field. His funeral pyre roars and the news is brought to Rāvaṇa, who grieves for his brother until his son Atikāyaṉ steps to his side and vows revenge. When Atikāyaṉ enters the field of battle, Vibhīṣaṇa describes his history and powers to Rāma.*[21] *Lakṣmaṇa then battles Atikāyaṉ, matching the demon's arrows with his own, as wounded bodies on the battlefield are torn and eaten by vultures. Vibhīṣaṇa advises Lakṣmaṇa to withdraw from the field and asks Rāma to direct Hanumān against Atikāyaṉ, but the monkey is beaten back. Again Lakṣmaṇa engages Atikāyaṉ in fierce battle, smashes his weapons, and sends him to Yama. In his palace, Rāvaṇa is informed by his messengers and cries out*:]

"First that monkey burned our city, and then my palace is put under siege. I've lost a battle to Rāma, Kumbhakarṇa has been killed, and now I've lost my son!"

[*His wife Danyamālīṉi*:] "Kumbhakarṇa is gone, our beloved son is dead, and who is next? All this because you want to keep that Sītā as a concubine! [*To Indrajit*] Son, your brother is dead and now the fate of Lanka rests on your shoulders."

"Do not grieve, Mother. I will surely defeat our enemies. Father, send me to battle."

"Just seeing your strong hands, Son, gives me courage, but we have suffered another loss, a great loss."

"Now you tell me! Why did you send my little brother when I, conqueror of Indra, was here to fight? I humiliated that monkey Hanumān when he spied on us. Armed with special weapons, I leave for the battlefield this very minute."

"What weapons have you, Son?"

"Many. Śiva granted me the snake-weapon, the Brahmā-weapon, and the Nārāyaṇa-weapon, and many more. And they have not yet been used. Remember that I am your son and will enter the field chanting your name."

"Yes! Go! Go and kill them both, especially the younger one who has killed your brother."

"Lakṣmaṇa? I'll offer his head as a gift to the Earth Goddess."

"Go quickly, but not alone. Take these forty divisions and two generals, Dumrākṣa and Mahapārsha."

[*Surrounded by his huge armies, looming like black clouds on the horizon, Indrajit advances to the battlefield; seeing them, Lakṣmaṇa speaks to Vibhīṣaṇa*:]

"They are packed as thick as Śeṣa's coils, as massive as a herd of elephants, yet they move more swiftly than the wind. Who is that in front? Who could have given birth to such a monster?

> Like rolling thunder the war drums sound!
> Who is that, Vibhīṣaṇa?
> Who rides his gleaming chariot onto the field
> Like a mad elephant chased by Saturn?"[22]

"That is Rāvaṇa's son Indrajit, who never steps backward on a battlefield. Beware, oh, beware, Lakṣmaṇa!"

"Vibhīṣaṇa, what is this? You are performing a full-length prostration to him, whimpering with fear!"

"Yes, Lakṣmaṇa, because Indrajit is incomparable in battle. No one is stronger, and I fear for you. I thought that the death of Atikāyan̠ would deliver the last blow to Rāvaṇa, but now we must face this giant!"

"How formidable is he?"

"Swami, to recount his history would do violence to your ears! I will not speak without Rāma's permission."

[*Rama*] "You may speak!"

"Lakṣmaṇa,

> Listen, wide-shouldered Prince of Ayodhya.
> He was brought up by the demons as 'Rāvaṇi,'
> Until he learned mantra-magic, conquered Indra,
> And earned the title Indra-jit.

"I will attempt to tell his story briefly, yet even then it should be interesting, well enunciated, and its meter clear. The commentary should be learned, combining rules from the *śāstras*, logic from the philosophies, and myths from the *purānas*. Anyone who attempts to explain a verse like this without first studying these texts is like a man trying to bind a wild elephant with a wet lotus stalk. First, however, I need the blessings of Viṣṇu to erase the karma I will earn for uttering the harsh words in this story. As the saying goes: 'Viṣṇu is invoked even before the invocation.'"[23]

"Is Indrajit evil as well as invincible?"

"No, Lakṣmaṇa, he is not evil. Powerful, majestic, but not evil. He knows only integrity and nothing base. Listen now to his names."

"Names? More than one?"

"As you know, there are several namings: at birth, after ten days, one month, and six months, and this son of Rāvaṇa was named on each occasion, according to his nature."

"Are these naming days the same for all castes? And would the different nature of the castes mean different types of names?"

"Your guru is best qualified to answer such questions. All I can say is that each caste follows the custom of naming a child after his father; Rāma, for instance, is called Daśarati, after your father. Generally this applies to the first-born son, but not always since Paraśurāma, the fifth son of Jamadagni, was also named after his father. Now this Indrajit, Rāvaṇa's first son, roared so loudly at his birth that he was called Rāvaṇasiya-abutiya-kumāṇḍa-Rāvaṇi, or Rāvaṇi for short. His first name is thus an example of a derived noun, which I explained to you earlier, based on his father and his father's qualities. His second name is Meghanātha, or Cloud Lord, because his birth roar sounded like thunder clouds.

"His third name is Bastard because he was born of a woman not married to his father. You see, one day long ago Pārvatī went to take her bath, and Śiva made love to her maidservant, but when he released his seed, she begged him not to impregnate her. Śiva agreed and arrested his seed in her womb, saying that when she was married, she would conceive from his semen. Now when Pārvatī learned of all this, she was furious and cursed the woman: 'You who have the brains of a frog will give birth to a frog!' Meanwhile, a man begged Śiva for a child, and the god decided that the cursed maidservant should be his wife; thus, when she became pregnant, she gave birth to Maṇḍōdari, from *maṇḍūka* or 'frog.' Much later Rāvaṇa rode on his victory march and abducted Maṇḍōdari, along with much else, and eventually married her. In due course she gave birth to Indrajit, so he is called Bastard."

"Has he other names?"

"A fourth name referred to in this verse is Māyāvi because he is skilled in *māyā*."

"All the demons in Lanka are skilled in *māyā*. Why should Indrajit in particular be given that name?"

"True, but not all those demons have traveled to Mt. Kailasa and studied magic with Śiva. You see, Indrajit's mantras frighten even the gods in heaven because he has more yogic power than those sages who are immune to the charms of young breasts sparkling with jewels."

"I know that his last name is Conqueror of Indra [Indra-jit], but Rāvaṇa and Kumbhakarṇa also subdued Indra. Why has Rāvaṇa's son alone been given this name?"

"Excellent question—because there is an answer! Remember that he not only defeated Indra but also captured him and imprisoned him in Lanka. Having lost their king, the other gods then went to Brahmā, who pleaded with Rāvaṇa for Indra's release, but the demon-raja explained that his son, and not he, was responsible. When Brahmā heard this he burst out, 'Then that son of yours should be known as Conqueror of Indra.'"

"Now that I know his history, Vibhīṣaṇa, please tell me how to fight him. Remember, as a prince, I fight honorably."

"He, too, is a warrior of honor. But if honor fails, he will resort to magic. Let me explain.

> He leaps to the sky and you follow,
> Now he is on earth, now he is gone,

He is a mountain, a ghost, a demon;
He is here, there, everywhere!

"Indrajit is a master of what is known as The Reverse. That is, he does the opposite of what he says; he attacks when he says he is defending and defends when he says he is attacking. If he says 'front,' you'd better protect your back. He also knows *māyā* fighting, which is a little different: after battling him for a long time, suddenly he's not there! You see him in the heavens and speed there, but as you arrive, he jumps back to earth. He comes at you from the north, the south, all the eight directions! And he never, never retreats; he fights until his opponent lays down his bow and prostrates at his feet.

"He'll attack in the form of a huge mountain with feet and arms, and if he doesn't win, he'll metamorphose into myriad monstrous forms. Lakṣmaṇa, you must never forget that these forms are not real, they are *māyā*, and that in order to destroy those forms, you must shoot for the hands and legs. Still, Indrajit will fight on, for his power is immense. Even when you think you have destroyed him several times over, he will continue to attack, for days and days, without hunger or thirst.

His magic battle shapes are many:
A wild animal deep in a forest,
A Brahmin chanting your name, a blazing fire, or an avalanche of stones,
Even King of Lanka, broad-shouldered Rāvaṇa himself!

"He will come at you snarling like a lion, and you must destroy that illusion with your arrows. The next moment you will see a Brahmin chanting the holy Vedas, discoursing on dharma, and singing your praises; prostrate at this Brahmin's feet and he will bludgeon you to death. Fire or stones will rain down on you, but do not be afraid; stand your ground and attack. In the end, he may take the form of his own father, Rāvaṇa, and attack."

"Vibhīṣaṇa, is there more?"

"Listen. This magician will turn day into night, so do not be fooled if suddenly you see the moon and stars. Do not lay down your weapons and leave the battle. Count the hours as they pass during each day's battle so that you know when night should come. At all times, remember this: you must disregard what you think you see and instead destroy his *māyā* forms with your arrows."

"What am I to do? His strengths are endless and so, it seems, are his deceptions. How can I possibly defeat him?"

"He is cunning, Lakṣmaṇa, but no matter what form this Indrajit assumes, he is never invisible. Three marks identify him always: his chariot, his eyes, and his legs. His chariot moves to the right or left according to his whims; it knows none of these distinctions between earth, sky, and netherworlds. Up to the fiery sun, into the cool waters, around the highest peaks—it goes anywhere he wishes.

> He turns night to day, day to night
> Creates clouds that rain down blood,
> Appears as elephants, horses, chariots,
> Even as you, as Lakṣmaṇa!"

"Is there more?"

"More, much more. Whatever he wishes, he becomes. It's that simple. He will appear to you, for instance, as Lakṣmaṇa, or several Lakṣmaṇas. One will say, 'I'm Lakṣmaṇa,' and another, 'No, I am.' You must shoot an arrow at each Lakṣmaṇa and dispel its *māyā*. Then Rāma will appear from nowhere, walk up to you, and say, 'Brother, where have you been? After killing Atikāyaṉ, I called for you.' But if you fall down at his feet, this Rāma will cut your throat. Bharata might appear and say, 'Lakṣmaṇa, the fourteen years are finished.' Although the voice will be Bharata's, you must not be deceived. Without a moment's hesitation, shoot an arrow and kill that false Bharata. If not, in the second that you delay, this grand deceiver, this cunning Indrajit, will destroy everyone on the battlefield!"

"I understand, Vibhīṣaṇa. Is this all I must know?"[24]

"Listen, Indrajit may appear as me, as Vibhīṣaṇa!"

"As you? Then how do I know that you, right now, are not an illusion?"

"That is quite easy. No matter what form the demon assumes, his teeth will protrude, and his eyes will roll around and around. Then, of course, his feet will rest firmly on the ground."[25]

"Is there anything more I must know, Vibhīṣaṇa?"

"Oh, yes, something very essential.

> No one in this sun-encircled world can break his bow,
> No one except a man who has fasted in the forest

For fourteen years without food, water and sleep,
No one else can conquer this conqueror of Indra.[26]

"You understand what this means, Lakṣmaṇa? Having followed Rāma into the forest and lived as an ascetic for these fourteen years, you, and only you, are empowered to defeat this terrible colossus![27] Still, victory is not assured. Look! As we have been talking, Indrajit's armies have surrounded us. Our monkey armies are unable to break through, and we are cut off from Rāma resting in the battle house.[28] Take command, Lakṣmaṇa; your word I obey as Rāma's."

"Draw back, Vibhīṣaṇa. I will advance."

"Remember all that I told you."

[*Drums and shouts are heard, as Hanumān bravely leads the army. Quickly the monkeys are thrown into disarray; Sugrīva is felled by Indrajit's arrow. Hanumān rips up a tree and advances on Indrajit, who jeers at him*:]

"Monkey-face! Stop jumping around and talk with me like a man."

"I'm not—"

"Shut up, monkey, and listen to me. Is this some kind of game you're playing? Attacking me not with bow or spear but with trees and stones? Are you mad? Will that spindly branch ward off my missiles?"

"With this stone—"

"Speak up, animal, speak up!"

"You think words will defeat me? Quit babbling and fight. Why should I stop to talk? Does lightning wait before it strikes? Or a lion before it leaps? Advance, brave Indrajit, or are you afraid?"

[*More battle noises*]

"Take this, runt!"

"I'll rip out that tongue of yours!"

[*Hanumān hurls mountains, stones, and trees at Indrajit, who calmly reduces each to powder with his arrows.*]

"C'mon, monkey, pick up a bow and fight like a man."

"We pick up trees and rocks, but we never 'eat grass,' as you'll soon do."[29]

"Where is that pitiful one named Lakṣmaṇa? Has he fled, too? I want revenge for the death of my little brother, Atikāyaṉ."

"Where were you, Indrajit, when he was killed?"

"My brother was a mere boy, and he fought without deceit, yet Lakṣmaṇa would not spare his life. Where is he?"

"He's there, just—"

"First, see what you can do with my arrows."

[*After driving off Hanumān, Indrajit sees Lakṣmaṇa cut down row after row of demons and turns his arrows against the prince. Suddenly Indrajit disappears, and the monkeys think he has been killed, but Lakṣmaṇa hears a voice calling to him from above*:]

[*Śiva puppet*] "Lakṣmaṇa, I've come from Kailasa to see you. Have you no humility? Put down your bow and speak with me."

"Humility? No, only insight. Die, false Śiva."

[*An arrow pierces the Śiva puppet; Viṣṇu puppet appears.*]

"Lakṣmaṇa, I am Lord Viṣṇu. Will you show me no respect and bow at my feet?"

"Lord Viṣṇu? No. Die, *māyā*-man, Indrajit."

[*An arrow pierces the Viṣṇu puppet; similar scenes are repeated with Gaṇeśa and Rāma puppets.*]

[*Indra*] "Listen, gods, to what happened next. The sun set, night fell, and the moon and stars shone in the sky. The monkeys were about to turn back from the field when Lakṣmaṇa remembered Vibhīṣaṇa's warning and destroyed this *māyā*, too, with a hail of arrows. Then a ten-headed demon appeared and told Lakṣmaṇa that he no longer desired Sītā, that he was releasing her, and that the war was over. But Lakṣmaṇa realized again that this, too, was *māyā* and destroyed the mirage with his arrows. Finally, Indrajit attempted another trick: two celestial women tried to seduce Lakṣmaṇa, but he fended them off with words.[30] Then, Vibhīṣaṇa reappeared."

"Lakṣmaṇa, night will fall soon and then we are helpless against the demons' *māyā*."

"Let's return to camp and consult with Rāma, but first we must feed our armies before they die of exhaustion. Vibhīṣaṇa, go quickly into the forest and bring back fruits and nuts. I'll wait here. Aṅgada, hold my bow."

[*Indra*] "Gods, what happened was this: seeing that his enemies were now scattered and off guard, Indrajit climbed high in the sky and readied his most powerful weapon, the snake-missile with coils that bind and deceive. Praying first to Śiva, who granted him the weapon, and then to Rāvaṇa, he released the arrow, which immediately bound Lakṣmaṇa and the rest of the army lifeless on the field."

[*Enter the* kuṭakkāraṉ, *or umbrella holder, who approaches Indrajit and parodies the battle sounds made by the puppeteers*:]

"Bing-bang! Wham-bang! Bing-bang, who are you?"

"Me? I'm Indrajit—just shot the snake-weapon, the whole point of this performance!"

"Oh, and you came here by this chariot, I suppose."

"Right. How'd you come?"

"I'm the umbrella holder; I just grabbed onto the chariot and came along for the ride."

"And what do you want?"

"Problem is your snake-weapon didn't kill them; only knocked 'em out. I'll finish them off by stabbing them with the tip of my staff. We'll walk along the battlefield and inspect each body, and if my staff doesn't finish them off, you can shoot another arrow at them."

"All right."

"Who's this lying here?"

"God! It's all the monkey children, little kids whom I have killed!"

"Terrible, but they are the little monkeys who stole fruit from Lanka. Let's revive them with some water and shoo them away. Now, who's this?"

"It's Naḷaṉ, the one who built the causeway to Lanka by carrying all those stones on his head."

"A boss man, a contractor, huh?"

"Yes. Give him a good stab."

"Ugh! [*Stabs him*] And this one?"

"That's Nīlaṉ."

"Oh, I need some of that."

"Of what?"

"You see my wife hasn't washed her sari for a week and—"

"You wash your wife's saris?"

"If you saw them, you'd understand why no one else would touch them. Besides, who is low enough to be a washerman to me?"

"Forget it. Do you know what Nīlaṉ did?"

"No."

"When the monkeys entered Lanka, Rāma ordered a fort built of stones, and this monkey did it. He's a mason. Pierce him."

"Here's Sugrīva."

"Give him a double dose!"

"Why?"

"Might not be dead, might just be lying down because he's got a hangover."

"Sugrīva did like his drink, didn't he? Besides, remember what he did to your father? Knocked off his crown as he stood on his parapet looking down at Rāma."

"Let him have it.

"Here's Aṅgada."

"Vāli's son?"

"Yes, he's the one—"

"I haven't forgotten. He came as Rāma's messenger, demanded a throne from Rāvaṇa, and then spoke crudely: 'Release Sītā or fight!' Stab him through the heart."

"Done. And this is Jāmbuvāṉ."

"Who?"

"The smart one, with brains, but there's a story about that. There were four fishermen. It was four o'clock in the afternoon, when kids return from school, and the four walked along the edge of a pond, talking: 'No use fishing now; it's the wrong time. We'll return tomorrow at noon and catch whatever's in this pond.' They left, but a wise, old frog in the pond had heard them and gave a warning to a big fish:

" 'Tomorrow at noon four fishermen are coming here with their nets,' the frog said, 'so we'd better escape tonight and go to another pond.' But the big fish replied, 'I'm One Hundred Brains, and I'll use them to wiggle out of this problem. You are Poor Brains, so you must flee.'

"Then Poor Brains the frog went to a turtle and told him that the fishermen were coming, but the turtle shouted, 'I'm One Thousand Brains and you have none. Go on alone.'

"Then the frog saw a crab, with eight legs, and invited it to flee with him. 'I'm Eight Brains,' answered the crab, 'and I can escape, but you have no brains and must leave now.' 'All right,' thought Poor Brains the frog, 'if you can all escape, then I can, too.' So the frog decided to stay in the pond with the rest.

"On the next day, the fishermen cast their nets, and the first thing they caught was the big fish. They put it in their basket, and when the frog heard its cries, he laughed and sang, 'One Hundred Brains got the basket!' Next the turtle was caught, but they thought it might escape from the basket, so they trapped it under a stone. Again the frog laughed. 'One Thousand Brains got the stone!' When the crab was caught, they tore off its eight legs and tossed them away, and Poor Brains sang, 'Eight Brains got the earth!' Lastly they caught the frog, but they took pity on it and didn't kill it. They let it go, and thus Poor Brains survived because of compassion, not brains.

"But Jāmbuvān̲ has real brains, so we best kill him before he awakes." [*The umbrella holder stabs him several times.*]

"Look. It's Lakṣmaṇa."

"Ah, the Beautiful One. Blessed with the thirty-two marks of beauty, which even the gods do not possess. Because he's the one who killed your brother, you must drive your arrows deep into his chest."

"There! He's dead for sure. Next is Hanumān."

"He's not alive, is he? When he came to Lanka to find Sītā and leapt from house to house, I stuck my head out of a window, and he slapped it with his tail so hard it hurt for three days."

"Don't worry. He's dead."

"How do you know?"

"Put your finger in his nose—there's no breath. Anyway, it's too dark now to cut off their heads. We'll wait until tomorrow morning. Let's return to Rāvaṇa." [*They enter the palace.*] Rāvaṇa, good news. They're finished! All of them, killed by my snake-weapon."

"You bring me great happiness, Son, as I knew you would."

"Only Rāma and Vibhīṣaṇa escaped."

"That's nothing. Tomorrow we will finish them off, now that they're alone. To celebrate, we have a little treat for you, a little dance, and then you should sleep well. Summon the dancers from the heavens."[31]

[*Two celestial dancers are pinned up around Rāvaṇa and the* nāṭakam *is performed for ninety minutes, during which the puppeteers bless each one-rupee donor with a song*:]

"By the grace of Kunnumpuli Bhagavati, let Lela's grandmother survive her illness;
"By the grace of Kunnumpuli Bhagavati, let Murthy study well and pass his exams;
"By the compassion of Lord Rāma and Kunnumpuli Bhagavati, let Sashi's baby goats get well."

[*Meanwhile, Vibhīṣaṇa returns from gathering fruits for the army, sees his comrades fallen on the field, and fears that Rāma will suspect him of treachery because Indrajit is his nephew. When Rāma is led to the battlefield and sees his brother and his friends lying dead, he is shocked into disbelief. He calls out Lakṣmaṇa's name, imploring him to rise, but falls down on his body and wails*:]

"No more war for me, and no more fame!
My victory bow, my wife, my kingdom,
Even Śiva who gave me life—I renounce them all!
If you, Lakṣmaṇa, do not live.

"Father and mother we left; Ayodhya we left,
Yet, like the Vedas, we were inseparable, Lakṣmaṇa;
Now you've left me and earth is not my home;
Let my soul leave, too, if Yama will receive it."

[*Vibhīṣaṇa arrives and is reviled by Rāma but manages to convince him that Indrajit's weapon is to blame. Rāma speaks*:][32]

"I see. But what is this snake-weapon? How can we remove it?"

"There are two stories, Rāma, and one has a *piramāṇam*. Listen. Long, long ago, lost in the cycles of time, when Brahmās succeed Brahmās, when nothing is ever 'first' and creation is without beginning, a Brahmā with five heads emerged from Viṣṇu's navel. Immediately he kindled a great sacrificial fire and began to form the Fourteen Worlds from his lotus-throne, and from that fire came the snake-weapon, the Brahmā-weapon, and the Nārāyaṇa-weapon. Śiva did *tapas* to Brahmā, his father, who then conferred the weapons on him, because Śiva is a warrior god. Meanwhile, in Patala Loka, Indrajit was born to Rāvaṇa and began his long training under his guru, Śukra. At the end of twelve years, Śukra sent his student to Śiva to learn esoteric mantras and *māyā,* and from Śiva, Indrajit gained the most powerful weapon, the snake-weapon. This is one story."

"Forget the second. What can we do to revive the army?"

"We can do nothing, Rāma. No one can. Not the gods, not the sages, not even Brahmā, who created the weapon. Anyone who tries to neutralize it will lose his own life first. The snake-weapon can only be removed of its own accord."

"We can do nothing?"

[*As Rāma grieves over Lakṣmaṇa, Indra and the gods appear above.*][33]

"Gods, look at what has happened—Indrajit has knocked out Lakṣmaṇa and the monkey army, and Rāma has lost heart! What will happen to us now? We all went to Viṣṇu, sang his praises, and asked for help against Rāvaṇa. He agreed and was born as Rāma to destroy our enemies—you know the rest of the story—but now Rāma lies unconscious on his brother's body.[34] If nothing is done to revive Lakṣmaṇa, Rāma will remain inert; if Rāma remains inert, Rāvaṇa will continue to rule this world; and if Rāvaṇa continues to rule, what about us? Think hard: Is there any way to rescue Lakṣmaṇa from the snake-weapon?"

"None, Indra. No one can do anything."

"Ah, remember that Garuḍa is the enemy of the snakes as a result of a curse put on them by their mother, Kadru. She made a bet with her sister over the color of Indra's white horse: Kadru said that the horse was black, while her sister said white. They agreed that they would view the horse in the morning and that whoever lost would serve as the other's slave. That night Kadru called her snake-sons and told them to spit a little ball of poison on the horse and turn it black by morning, but the snakes refused, saying that they would not cheat their aunt. Furious, Kadru cursed them all to die, some by fire, some to be eaten by Garuḍa.

"Śiva knew about this curse when he received the snake-weapon from Brahmā. Eventually Indrajit won it, but while Śiva still held it, he issued a warning to the snake in his hair: 'Wander everywhere in the Fourteen Worlds, but do not visit the world of snakes.' Curiosity, however, drove the snake there, where the other snakes warned him, 'You are a special snake, from Śiva, but don't stay here because you'll be eaten by Garuḍa.' Still, the snake did not move, and soon Garuḍa came and drove him back to Śiva, who gave him refuge. Then Garuḍa also approached Śiva, received his blessings, and asked that the snake in his hair be given to him as food. Śiva hesitated, then agreed: 'During the *tretā yuga* you may eat this snake, too. Now go.'

"Because of Śiva's boon and Kadru's curse, Garuḍa can defeat this snake-weapon, but we gods must summon Garuḍa with meditation and praise-songs."[35]

[*The gods sing to Garuḍa, and soon his puppet appears on the far left of the screen.*]

"I've seen two miracles today."

"Indrajit's snake-weapon is one. What's the second, Indra?"

"Garuḍa's tears. You see, when he was born—no, that is a long story so we'll tell it tomorrow. Anyway, like many birds, he can see clearly for leagues and leagues, and he can fly so high that the world looks like a little black spot. Mt. Meru is thousands of *yojanas* away, but from its highest peak, Garuḍa spied Rāma in Lanka, and as soon as he saw him, he shed tears of pain and tears of joy at the same time!"

"We all cry tears of pain and tears of joy, but how can one do both at the same time? Explain, Indra."

"I don't understand it either, but that is all we can describe tonight. Tomorrow, when the sun sets, we will continue. Śiva's blessings be with you all; let Rāma and Nārāyaṇa protect you."

[*On the next night, the Brahmin puppets present their summary of the previous night.*]

"With the gods watching in amazement, Garuḍa flew to Rāma and tore apart the snakes that bound Lakṣmaṇa and the monkeys, reviving them all. Garuḍa then sang a series of songs celebrating the mystery of Rāma: 'You are the cause of all existence and also a human being who grieves over your brother's body.'[36] [*Garuḍa suddenly flew away, and Hanumān spoke*:][37]

"Rāma, we must take the initiative immediately. Consider Sītā, who is suffering from the news that the snake-weapon killed us, and consider Rāvaṇa and his generals, who are rejoicing inside the palace. If we raise a loud battle cry, Sītā will take heart and the demons will stiffen with fear. Give the word, Rāma."

"Hanumān, you are a genius. Monkeys, form ranks and advance on the palace with battle cries." [*They shout loudly.*]

[*Rāvaṇa*] "What? Their war cries again! But they're dead, fallen under the snake coils of the Indrajit's weapon. Still, that's the sound of Rāma's bow and that's Lakṣmaṇa's bowstring and Hanumān's roar!"

[*Rāvaṇa storms off to his son's bedroom and shouts at the sleeping Indrajit.*]

"Wake up!"

"Welcome, respected Raja and Lord of—"

"Forget those formalities and listen to that noise! Why are you still asleep?"

"Father, Lakṣmaṇa's arrows ripped holes in my body and drank my blood. Only my *māyā* kept me from death. I'm exhausted and need rest; that's why I'm lying down."

"What *māyā?*"

"I told you. I was losing, so I flew up into the sky and shot the snake-weapon. Lakṣmaṇa and all the monkeys were knocked dead."

"Dead? Listen to that noise outside the palace!"

[*Rāvaṇa orders his messengers to survey the battlefield; they return quickly and report that the monkeys are revived and ready for battle.*]

"Son, what shall we do? Quick, say something!"

"Rāvaṇa, I need a night's rest. Tomorrow morning I will shoulder the Brahmā-weapon and destroy our enemies."

"Sleep, Son, sleep. But we must keep the battle raging until morning. Generals, advance against the monkeys."

[*Rāvaṇa's bravest generals assemble their troops on the battlefield and advance against Rāma's army. As the battle begins, one of Rāvaṇa's generals shouts at the umbrella holder:*][38]

"Hey, *kuṭakkāraṉ*, hold up the standard!"

"Not without my pay."

"Pay? It's the middle of a battle. Hold up the umbrella!"

"I want my money from last time. No one paid me."

"False. We did pay you last time."

"Not *that* time. I mean the battle long ago, between the gods and demons when they churned the Milk Ocean. I'm owed money from that."

"You held the umbrella in that battle? Then you owe *us* money!"

"Me? Who says?"

"My wife. She keeps all the accounts."

"All right. I'll bear your banner in this battle, too. Pay me what you wish."

"Here. Now let's fight."

[*A strange cry is heard—"Kriyommmmmmmmmm"—and the umbrella holder addresses the speaker*:]

"Who are you?"

"I'm the *Veḷiccappāṭu*, the Light Crier."

"Then why don't you cry in the morning?"

"Not that 'light' stupid. Light as in 'clear.' I'm the oracle of Bhagavati. A priest, if you like."

"You serve Bhagavati?"

"Yes, and when she enters me, she calls out through my mouth, giving perpetual predictions, promises, and prognostications."

"Bhagavati enters you?"

"Yes, my whole body shakes—"

"It shakes for as long as Bhagavati possesses you?"

"Yes."

"But does your tongue shake, too?"

"Tongue shake? Never thought about it."

"Oh, well. What deities do you serve?"

"Kutichattan, Ciruchattan—"

"Which Bhagavatis?"

"Primarily one—the Money Maker Bhagavati."

"Sounds like the right idea."

"Yes. Worship the Money Maker and all the other Bhagavatis will follow."

"We'll see, smart alec. Ask that Money Maker Bhagavati to do something for me."

"Your wish is my—"

"But don't you have to get possessed first?"

"Right. Almost forgot. Let Bhagavati come on me and we'll see what she has to say. 'Kriyommmmm, kriyommmmm! *Kuṭakkāraṉ*! *Kuṭakkāraṉ*! Give a black chicken to the umbrella holder.'"

"That's timely. Let's hear from another Bhagavati."

"'Kriyommmmmm, kriyommmmm, split a coconut and gain two sons.'"

"Try another."

"'Kriyommmmmm. Twist four threads together and gain one hundred sons.'"

"A hundred kids!"

"Not what you want?"

"No. I've got a specific request."

"What?"

"My wife has been pregnant for eighteen months. Will the child be male or female? Born during the day or night?"

"'Kriyommmmmm, kriyommmmm! The child might be male, and it might be female. Or it might be a big-bellied goblin.'"

"What?"

"Well, anyone pregnant for eighteen months better expect some kind of monster."

"Useless, absolutely useless. Why are you here in the first place?"

"Going to war."

"A priest, a *Veḷiccappāṭu* to war? But if you insist, I'll hold the umbrella for you."

[*Loud screams and war drums are heard and then slowly recede until they stop altogether. When the messengers, Sangadi and his companion, report further losses to Rāvaṇa, the demon-raja again summons his only surviving son*:][39]

"Indrajit, do something fast, before we all are killed."

"My plan is this: we'll kill all the monkeys, then Lakṣmaṇa and Rāma, and show their corpses to Sītā."

[*Indrajit enters the field with sixty divisions, causing the monkeys to flee in panic, but Rāma and Lakṣmaṇa, riding on Hanumān, come to the front and destroy most of his army. Then Indrajit blows his victory conch and shouts:*]

"Lakṣmaṇa, think of this: the younger brother performs funeral rites for the older brother. If Rāma dies first, that's fine, but who will perform Rāma's rites when I kill the second-born first?"

"What about your own younger brother Atikāyaṉ, whom we slew? Will he perform your funeral rites, Indrajit?"

"Your deaths will repay me for the deaths of my brothers, Atikāyaṉ and Akṣakumāraṉ, and my uncles, Kumbhakarṇa and Kara."

"Do not worry, demon, all requisite funerary rites will be properly observed. Your grieving father will conduct your funeral, after which Vibhīṣaṇa will do the same for him."

[*In fierce fighting, Lakṣmaṇa destroys Indrajit's chariot and drives him back to Rāvaṇa's palace, where Rāvaṇa's minister, Mahōdara, devises a plan to take Lakṣmaṇa off guard: assuming the guise of Indra, he rides on Indra's white elephant and appears to Lakṣmaṇa, who puts down his bow and respectfully raises his hands to the king of the gods. Immediately, the demons inform Indrajit, who flies up into the sky to survey the scene.*][40]

"This is the time for the Brahmā-weapon: neither Rāma nor Vibhīṣaṇa is on the field, and Lakṣmaṇa is defenseless."

[*He releases the Brahmā-weapon, killing Lakṣmaṇa, Hanumān, Sugrīva, and all the other monkeys.*]

"Hey, *kuṭakkāraṉ*, witness my power this time!"

"Yours? You shot the Brahmā-weapon, true, but as they fell I came and stabbed each one of them with my staff."

"Is that right?"

"Who's that?"

"Naḷaṉ."

"Kalaṉ?"

"No. Na-ḷaṉ."

"Pa-laṉ?"

"Ah! You murder the language."

"Who died?"

"Forget it. Let him have it; he built the bridge to Lanka."

"Who's that?"

"Sugrīva."

"I know him well. One day myself and Rāvaṇa—"

"Wrong again. Say, 'Rāvaṇa and I.'"

"Sure. Rāvaṇa and I, and some women—"

"Not 'women,' 'ladies.'"

"All right. Rāvaṇa and I, and some ladies, and a missinger—"

"'Messenger,' stupid."

"Have it your way. Point is that we all were standing on the tower when that Sugrīva leapt up, knocked off Rāvaṇa's crown, and cuffed him."

"Who's that?"[41]

"Lakṣmaṇa."

"Rāma's brother?"

"Right, the one who mutilated my aunt, Śūrpaṇakhā."

"Hmmm. Better give him a few extra stabs."

"Wait. He's a great yogi. He's also a 'full quiver.'"

"Why does he quiver? Rheumatism?"

"No. 'Full quiver' means his weapons are powerful."

"Terrible to shiver so."

"Shut up and stab him hard."

"Who's this?"

"Hanumān."

"Ohhh . . . see you later—"

"Hey! Where you going?"

"Remember when this monkey secretly entered Lanka? As he was leaping from roof to roof, I stuck out my head to see who it was and—Wham! Bham!—he beat me with his tail."

"Kill him!"

"Right. He's dead now."

"Let these bodies lie here until the morning. We'll cut off their heads then."

"Oh, great idea! Just like last time, when you shot the snake-weapon and the eagle revived them all?"

"Don't worry. Garuḍa was able to release the snake-weapon because he is the sworn enemy of snakes, but he has no connection to the Brahmā-weapon."

"Maybe, but some other bird might come—"

"No bird is going to come."

"If you say so, but—"

"Let's report to Rāvaṇa." [*Indrajit returns to the palace.*]

"Enter, Son."

"Father, we have killed them all, all except Rāma and your brother Vibhīṣaṇa. I am exhausted and need rest. Tomorrow, you may enter the field and fight Rāma, all alone."

[*Rāma returns to the field and, seeing his allies again lying dead, cries out*:]

"As brave generals and wise ministers,
Seven armies they entered the field,
But no voice speaks to me now,
They have entered the heaven of ancient kings.[42]

"Sugrīva, speak to me! Speak as you spoke when you befriended me in the forest after I had lost Sītā. Rise up, friend, you who revived my courage when you knocked off Rāvaṇa's crown. Rise up and say something. Is that Aṅgada? I remember . . .

As he lay dying, your father's soft hands
Held mine and placed you in my care;
Now your hands are torn and bleeding—in my defense!
Who would not die of this shame?

"And Hanumān! You saved me from death when you found Sītā in Lanka. But now it is I who weep like a warrior's widow over your dead body.

Cruel Indrajit felled you on this bloody field,
Great son of the Wind God, Oh Hanumān!
I see you and I cry like a woman;
Is anyone on earth more miserable?

"No! Not you, Lakṣmaṇa! You are mother and father to me. All that is good, all that I have is you, yet now, Little Brother, you are no more!

Father and mother, and all my strength,
Son, brother, and all my wealth are you;

You have left me and worldly fame,
And I remain, with the greater grief.[43]

Wives may die, but we marry again;
Our children die, and others are born;
Lost wealth is regained, knowledge retrieved;
But, tell me, is a dead brother replaced?[44]

"Speak to me, Lakṣmaṇa, speak! No. He will not. He is dead, and so is dharma."

[*Rāma falls in a swoon on Lakṣmaṇa's body. Again, the gods gather overhead and Indra speaks*:]

"Once more Indrajit has felled Lakṣmaṇa and the monkey army, and Rāma, having lost all hope, lies unconscious on his brother's body. Seeing this scene, different people would describe it differently. Ordinary people, for instance, would see it this way:

Who will soften Rāma's grief?
Who will console him, speak kind words
Or move his hands from his brother's body?
Abandoned, alone, this is the evil of death.[45]

"This first interpretation of the scene is the common man's view. To him, Rāma was born of Kausalyā, married Sītā, and lived the life of a hermit in the forest until he was deceived by the golden deer and Sītā's desire for it. Disguised as a sage, Rāvaṇa captured Sītā and started the war, and now, overcome with grief at Lakṣmaṇa's death, Rāma is himself prepared to die. This is how most people would describe the scene. Moved by Rāma's grief, and with no one to console him, they would go to him and say, 'Rāma, everyone who is born must die. Do not lose heart. Do not think of suicide.' Their sympathy for Rāma as a man who married Sītā and then lost his little brother and allies would lead these people to support him.

"Other people, those with great bhakti, would react to the same scene with different emotions, as in this verse:

When we petitioned you, scion of great kings,
To annihilate the demons and end our suffering,
You showed compassion and took birth as Rāma;
Why present this magic show to us?[46]

"You see, these devotees would remember that we gods petitioned Viṣṇu to save us and that he agreed and was born as Rāma in Ayodhya. They know that Rāma went to the forest with Lakṣmaṇa and

Sītā, that she was stolen by Rāvaṇa, that Indrajit defeated Lakṣmaṇa, and that Rāma fell on his brother's body in grief. Nonetheless, they know also that all this is a sham, a show, since Rāma is Nārāyaṇa and Lakṣmaṇa is Ādiśeṣa, upon whom Rāma rests even now, on the battlefield. That's why these devotees would sing: 'Why present this magic show to us?' They realize that Viṣṇu's avatar has no little brother, no mother, and no father, because he is deathless.

"If the first group views Rāma as a human warrior and the second as Viṣṇu's avatar, the third group understands something more:

> Drawing in all worlds, all lives, insides and outsides,
> Emerging and growing, becoming everyone, everything,
> Like a spider spinning webs and threads from itself,
> You fashion past and present, yet remain unchanged.[47]

"These people realize that beyond our attachment to earth, beyond money, beyond pleasure, is the state of *brahman*. Nothing else is real! Nothing! This state of bliss encompasses the fourteen known worlds, the thousand and eight outer regions, the countless celestial realms—and all this is Śiva. Like thousands of ornaments shaped of gold, the life-forms in these worlds are but aspects of *brahman* or Śiva. Even Rāma, fallen over his little brother on the battlefield, is nothing but *brahman*. We see Rāma, but he is *brahman*. Like bubbles rising from water, Viṣṇu takes form in every eon—as a fish, as a child, and now as Rāma. And the Lakṣmaṇa whose death he seems to mourn is not dead, for he has no birth. People with this knowledge of *brahman* would say to Rāma, 'Do not mourn for that which was not born. Do not curse dharma, for there is neither dharma nor adharma.'

"These, oh gods, are the three ways of understanding Rāma's grief. And we must wait for Vibhīṣaṇa to return from the forest to see if he can lift the power of the Brahmā-weapon."

"Yes, Indra. But look, Rāvaṇa's messengers are returning to him."

[*Several demon women take Sītā above the battlefield to show her Rāma's corpse, but Trijata (Vibhīṣaṇa's sister) convinces Sītā that Rāma is not dead. Celestial dancers are summoned to Rāvaṇa's palace for another* nāṭakam. *Later, on the battlefield, Jāmbuvāṉ wakes up when he hears his name.*][48]

"Who's that? Sounds like Vibhīṣaṇa, but how could he be alive? Is it Rāma? Or maybe the demons have come because they know I am immune to the Brahmā-weapon. Or it might be the gods, come to ask me to help Rāma."

"Jāmbuvāṉ, it's me."

"Vibhīṣaṇa! Didn't the Brahmā-weapon hit you?"

"No. Rāma sent me into the forest for fruits."

"Please, get me some water; I'm dying of thirst."

"Here, Jāmbuvāṉ, drink slowly; your wounds are not yet healed."

"Ah! This water is wonderful. Where'd you get it?"

"The gods gave it to me when they saw that you had all been knocked down."

"It's like water from the Ganga. Actually, when I was born, my father gave some to me and that kept me alive for three days—ah, that's a long story and we must find Hanumān, since he, too, will have survived the Brahmā-weapon, and give him some of this water."

"He's already here."

"What! Everything's done before I ask."

"Hanumān, we depend on you for everything. If you live, we all live. If you revive Lakṣmaṇa, Rāma will live, and if he lives, then dharma, the Vedas, and everything, including these Fourteen Worlds, will continue. Only by thinking of you can we survive."

[*Hanuman, chuckling*] "How can that be, Jāmbuvāṉ?"

"What do you mean?"

"You say you live by thinking of me, but if you're not alive how can you think of me to live?"

"Well—don't confuse me. Anyway, thinking isn't enough. You must act."

"But I am alive and the armies are not, yet you said that if—"

"Listen, Hanumān, we have only three-quarters of an hour to revive Lakṣmaṇa and the others; then the sun rises and Indrajit will behead them. Before that, you must travel seventy-three thousand *yojanas* to the Medicine Mountain, find the longevity herb, and return."

"Are you joking?"

"Joking?"

"Seventy-three thousand *yojanas* in three-quarters of an hour? And return? It's . . . it's impossible."

"But, Hanumān, if you don't—"

"That far, that quickly, to locate a rare herb for an incurable disease? Ridiculous, that's all."

"But, Hanumān, listen:

In a drop of water from Brahmā's nose
In the seventh kalpa I was born, Hanumān;
Many miracles, many eons I have seen;
You shall revive them instantly.[49]

"Hanumān, I know what I'm talking about. Rāma's and Lakṣmaṇa's lives depend on you. Find this special herb and return in three-quarters of an hour."

"Jāmbuvāṉ, it's seventy-three thousand *yojanas*!"

"You won't need a quarter of an hour, not five minutes, not even one minute."

"But—"

"Don't question me, Hanumān. You can travel there in a flash."

"'Flash'?"

"Let me give you an analogy. Suppose you hold seven lotus flower stalks closely together and then pierce them in the center with a sharp needle. The time it takes the needle to leave one stalk and enter the next is the time you will need to travel to the Medicine Mountain and back."

"How do you know?"

"I've seen many miracles, including your three fathers and mothers—"

"What? Three fathers and mothers!"

"You've forgotten what I told you long ago—"[50]

"Tell me your own story, Jāmbuvāṉ."

"It's a long, long story, requiring more than an eon to recount and we've only got three-quarters of an hour. But, briefly, I am a child of Brahmā. Let me explain. Existence moves in cycles of creation and dissolution because everything that is born—from the Three Gods to an insect—also dies. These cycles are divided into days and nights of Brahmā: when he sleeps, there is an eon of dissolution; when he wakes, there is an eon of creation. Each eon contains one thousand smaller cycles of the four *yugas*, and when seventy-one of these cycles are completed, a *manumantra* is over. After fourteen *manumantras*, or nine hundred and ninety-four cycles of *yugas*, there is a twilight period, a final cycle of four *yugas*, before the new *manu* appears.[51]

"During all these cycles of four *yugas*, dharma appears in different forms. During the first *yuga*, when it takes the form of a holy cow and walks on four feet, dharma is everywhere, in every life-form; temples, icons, and worship are thus unnecessary. In the second *yuga*, however, when dharma appears in the form of an ass, those physical symbols of dharma are necessary. Finally, during the last *yuga*, the terrible Kali Yuga, the castes are mixed, demons multiply, and famine stalks. People live for only twenty-six years, girls have their first period at six, and we all shrink in size. In the first *yuga*, people are one thousand feet tall, four hundred feet in the second *yuga*, forty in the third, but only four feet tall in the last *yuga*. Of course, the *Devī Māhātmya* says that even in the Kali Yuga, the Great Goddess sends wise men to earth to help others, but I don't know whether this is true.

"Anyway, when Brahmā had finished an eon of creation, a hundred years of drought parched the earth, the sun multiplied into a thousand suns, and everything on earth burned. Unable to bear the heat, Ādiśeṣa spat out a poisonous fire that dried up the Seven Seas, and there was no water even to bless the ashes of dead men; but somehow good men found their way to Brahmā. After a hundred years of fire, Brahmā sent searing winds that beat the surface of the earth for another hundred years, and finally, a deluge covered everything, during which Brahmā slipped back into the lotus bud that receded into Viṣṇu's navel. Then another eon of dissolution, another night of Brahmā, began. During this night of water, when everything is Viṣṇu, Brahmā was not asleep (as he should be) but was already planning his next creation. Irked by Brahmā's pride, Viṣṇu created the demons Madhu and Kaitabha, who sprang from his ears and leapt into the waters. They were hungry until the Earth Goddess fed them and offered them a boon, for which they chose this: 'Let no enemy kill us; let us decide how we shall die.' Armed with this boon, they swam through the water, looking for enemies until they saw the lotus stalk growing from Viṣṇu's navel. They grabbed it and challenged Brahmā, who awoke shaking with fear.[52]

"Hanumān, that's when I was born. As Brahmā shook in fear, a drop of sweat rolled from his nose and rested in the cleft of his chin, and from that drop of sweat I was born, just three days before Brahmā created the world again. Born at night, the *cāma kāla*, I was named Cāmpavān̲. There's a *piramān̲am* that explains it this way: 'Born at the time [*campavam*] of night, Cāmpavān̲ is his name.' Because I protected Brahmā from Madhu and Kaitabha when he created the world three days later, Brahmā placed me as the firstborn on Rose Apple [*jambu*] Island, and so my name is Jāmbuvān̲."

"How old are you, then?"

"We are now in the *tretā yuga*, the second age when the Rāma-avatar appears, in the twenty-seventh *Mahāyuga*, during the seventh *Manu*, and in that sense, I am 'seven.' But how many human years, I can't say. Listen. The gods—Pārvatī, Viṣṇu, Śiva, Brahmā—each gave me a special seed and told me to plant them on Rose Apple Island.

'The joining herb, healing herb, soothing herb
And the incomparable longevity herb—
Plant these four on Rose Apple Island,'
The gods commanded me.[53]

"Those herbs grow now on Visvapatri mountain, near the northern slope of Mt. Meru. One of them revives the dead after the breath has left the body—that's the longevity herb; another joins parts of a severed body; a third revives people from an unconscious swoon; and the last is an herb that cures all diseases. But you must bring back the first, the longevity herb, the Sanjeevi."[54]

"Which direction do I go?"

"From here, from Lanka, you leap one hundred *yojanas* to the mainland, then nine thousand *yojanas* to the foothills of the Himalayas, which are two thousand *yojanas* wide and ten thousand high. Jump over them to reach Mt. Kinka [?] and Mt. Putkonam, which is fifteen thousand miles high. Cross it and you enter the Ancient Forest, nine thousand miles deep, and beyond it you'll enter another thick forest, after which you will see Mt. Meru. On the southern slope is Kailasa and a lake, but don't go that way because Pārvatī once cursed men there to be born as women. Instead, go west toward Vaikunta, past Alakapuri, until you reach Visvapatri to the north where the garden of special herbs is guarded by devotees of Viṣṇu. Tell them you were sent by Jāmbuvān̲ to get the longevity herb for Rāma. They'll give it to you."

"I'm off."

"First you must assume your true size; only then can you cover the distance in a flash."

[*Hanumān sails over the various landmarks, until he reaches the Medicine Mountain, where he chants Rāma's name.*]

"Who are you?"

"I'm Rāma's emissary, Hanumān, sent by Jāmbuvā<u>n</u> to get an herb to resuscitate Rāma and Lakṣmaṇa, who are lying helpless on the battlefield."

"The Rāma-avatar? Oh, is it the *tretā yuga* already?"

"Yes. Please hurry, you see—"

"Jāmbuvā<u>n</u> sent you? So he's still there?"

"Yes. Please—"

"All right. Specifically, which herb do you want?"

"Ah! I don't remember the name."

"Then you better go back and—"

"That's impossible. No time. I'll take the whole mountain with me!"

"Whole mountain?"

"There's no other way."

"Take it and bring it back without injury."

"This is a Rāma mission. There is only victory."

[*Hanumān uproots the Medicine Mountain and flies back to Lanka, where Jāmbuvā<u>n</u> and Vibhīṣaṇa marvel at his strength and devotion. The longevity herb is given to Rāma, Lakṣmaṇa, and the others, who awaken and ask Hanumān to lead them into battle. Marching to Rāvaṇa's palace, where victory celebrations continue, Hanumān shouts:*]

"Demons! Come out and fight us!"

"Rāvaṇa, did you hear that? They've been revived again!"

"What can we do now, Indrajit?"

"Here's my plan: we'll make a fake Sītā and kill her in front of Hanumān; then I'll say that I am leading an army against Ayodhya. That will demoralize Rāma, while I build a sacrificial fire to get new weapons."

[*Indrajit flies above and kills the fake Sītā in front of Hanumān, but Vibhīṣaṇa, using one of the coconut-shell lamps inside the drama-house, inspects the puppet slumped on the floor and reports to Rāma that it is a false Sītā. When he also reports that Indrajit is raising a sacrificial fire in order to gain a powerful bow, Lakṣmaṇa, Vibhīṣaṇa, Hanumān, and Aṅgada battle Indrajit at the fire. Hanumān and Aṅgada are driven back, but Lakṣmaṇa confronts Indrajit. Indrajit shoots a dozen special arrows, each one guided across the screen by the puppeteers, but they are blocked by Lakṣmaṇa and fall to the floor of the drama-house with a clatter. Lakṣmaṇa speaks*:]

"Indrajit, your body looks like a pin cushion!"

"Here's the Nārāyaṇa-weapon."

"Śrī Rāma, Rāma, Rāma—"

"What's that you're mumbling, Lakṣmaṇa?"

"Release your arrow; you'll see."

[*The Nārāyaṇa-weapon circles three times around Lakṣmaṇa and then settles at his feet. Shocked, Indrajit goes back to Rāvaṇa with new doubts.*]

"Lakṣmaṇa cannot be human; he is invincible. But could Rāma really be an avatar of Viṣṇu? That would be a *māyā* even greater than mine."

"What is this, Son? You're shaking like a snake cornered by Garuḍa. What happened to the sacrifice?"

"They put it out and then we fought, but my missiles were deflected by Lakṣmaṇa. Then I shot the Nārāyaṇa-weapon, but . . . but it worshiped him!"

"Impossible! The Nārāyaṇa-weapon worships no one but Nārāyaṇa."

"That's just it. I fought him from above, from below, with every kind of weapon and deceit, and still I could not defeat this Lakṣmaṇa. He's not human, Father, he's an aspect of Viṣṇu."

"Nonsense!"

"He will reduce the Three Worlds to fine powder if he wishes. If we continue to fight him, Lanka is doomed. That woman you stole is not human either, and the moment you release her, they will call off their attack."

"Don't speak to me of—"

"Do you wish to live, Father? I ask because I love you."

"Quiet!"

"Then you wish to kill me, yourself, and the rest of our race? Release Sītā or we will all find our fate on the points of Rāma's arrows."

"You talk like an slobbering idiot! When I first brought Sītā here, I heard no objection from you, but now, in the face of battle, you quake like a woman yourself. If you won't fight Lakṣmaṇa, I will! Stand aside and allow me to protect the name of Lanka.

> Prattling idiot! Not by releasing that woman in front of the gods,
> But by releasing this water-bubble body in battle
> Will twenty-armed Rāvaṇa earn a glory
> More permanent than these Three Worlds."[55]

"Father, I can't let you die—"

"Out of my way!"

"As long as I still live, I will not allow you to fight, Father. Stand back and let me pass to the battlefield."

"Go, my son, but take my chariot and my bow with you."

[*Indrajit mounts the huge chariot and commands the driver to find Lakṣmaṇa on the battlefield. On the way, he encounters a series of bad omens and then reaches Lakṣmaṇa, who speaks*:][56]

"Back again, Indrajit?"

"With your death certificate. Take this."

[*Lakṣmaṇa deflects all Indrajit's arrows while his own strike Indrajit's chariot and bow again and again but cause no harm.*]

"Vibhīṣaṇa, what can I do? I shatter his bow with my arrow, but it remains intact. I destroy his chariot, but it still moves."

"Lakṣmaṇa, shatter his jeweled ring and his bow will shatter; break the axle and the chariot will collapse."

[*Indrajit*] "Traitor! You're my uncle, Vibhīṣaṇa, but you've betrayed me by revealing these secrets."

"I've done nothing to match your crimes!"

[*As the gods watch overhead, Lakṣmaṇa shatters Indrajit's jeweled ring and his chariot axle and then cuts off his head. Red dye is thrown on Indrajit's puppet, which dangles lifelessly from the cloth screen, as the puppeteers sing the last verse of the performance*:]

> 'Rāma, Rāma' in my heart,
> 'Rāma, Rāma' in my deepest dreams

'Rāma, Hari-Rāma'
I call out every day.
When fear strikes,
or life is cruel
I simply call your name:
'Rāma, Hari-Rāma.'[57]

"Tonight we end the story here, and tomorrow we tell of the colossal battle between Rāma and Rāvaṇa."

Creating Conversations

In reading these translated performances and threading through their frequent digressions, readers may appreciate the point of the previous chapter that the puppeteers do not "tell" Kampaṉ's Rāma story as much as they explain it. In what follows, I expand that argument by analyzing the creation of conversations as the primary technique by which the puppeteers explicate and thereby gain control over Kampaṉ's text. My description of these conversations covers not only verbal exchanges between epic characters, who speak in voices either faint or heard not at all in the epic text, but also dialogic relations between the oral commentary and the chanted verses.[58] In discussing these mechanics and varieties of talk in the puppet play, I am guided by Bakhtin's concept of double-voiced or embedded speech, in which a second speaker imposes new intentions on another's speech, for this is the interpretive task of the puppeteers.[59]

Four different conversations are spoken inside the drama-house.[60]

1. The first conversation is spoken between the Brahmin puppets, Muttuppattar and Gangaiyati, who were introduced in chapter 3 as the narrators during the "Song of the Drama-House." I said there that their "master-of-ceremonies" repartee does not appear in Kampaṉ and is a product of the puppet play, but what is salient here is that they deliver it entirely in dialogue. This first conversation indicates the drive to dialogue in the puppet play because performances might have been framed by a single voice—of one of the famous puppeteers saluted in the introduction, for example.

2. Once the Brahmin puppets are removed from the screen (never to return), the role of narrator is largely ignored as the performance moves into the second conversation, that spoken between epic characters

pinned up on the screen. In this second dialogue, which is heard throughout performance, puppeteers link each verse and each segment of the commentary in a conversational chain: the verse is chanted as if spoken by one character to another and then followed by commentary either in the first speaker's voice or as a response from another speaker, which prompts another verse, and so on, until morning.

3. A third conversation is spoken whenever the puppeteers veer off into an auxiliary story (see previous chapter) that contains dialogue. Although descriptive passages in these auxiliary stories are not invariably in dialogue, they are nonetheless spoken as part of the conversation between epic characters (conversation 2) in which those stories are embedded.

4. A fourth and final conversation is heard between Indra and the gods, who act as detached narrators. After the Brahmin puppets (conversation 1) leave the screen, the role of narrator is only clumsily handled by the epic characters (in conversations 2 and 3), who must somehow double as actor and independent observer, for example, during Vibhīṣaṇa's long speech to Rāma with which the translation above begins. (Readers may want to reread that speech because it is adduced several times in this discussion.) Puppeteers sometimes slowly slide the identity of the speaker from epic actor to narrator, as in this speech to Rāma, for instance, when Vibhīṣaṇa says, "Rāma, notice that the poet here calls you *āriya*," and then provides an exegesis for that word. Small-scale explications of this nature are regularly achieved without a formal shift in conversational frame; however, if the puppeteers wish to comment on weighty events—to set right the meaning of Rāvaṇa's first defeat, disclose the full meaning of Indrajit's death, speculate on various interpretations of Rāma's grief, or tell the story of how Kampaṉ composed his epic—they shift to a dialogue between Indra and the gods pinned high up on the screen above the epic action.

Unlike the Brahmin narrators, this pair of speakers is not a folk innovation, although the puppet play does alter their role. In Kampaṉ, Indra and the gods appear seldom and nearly always as characters who speak directly to the epic characters in order to influence the epic action at crucial moments: advising Bharata to return to Ayodhya, reminding Rāma of his dharma mission, and sending Rāma a chariot in the final battle, for example. In the shadow puppet play, by contrast, Indra appears frequently, always with another puppet (who represents the other gods collectively) and always as a narrator who speaks with his fellow gods but not with epic characters.[61] Nevertheless, as an audience for the epic actors, Indra and the gods are not insignificant. In the last scene of the great battle, as we shall hear, Rāvaṇa urges Rāma to spare no effort to present a spectacle worthy of the gods, and Rāma addresses them before he kills the demon-raja: "Gods, I, Rāma, now kill Rāvaṇa."

In and of themselves, these four conversations are not unusual, but it is remarkable that the puppet play creates them by a systematic and deliberate conversion of Kampaṉ's text. Each Kampaṉ verse is changed to speech, which is then woven into a dialogue with speeches in the oral commentary; as a result, every word in performance (except the infrequent prose transitions [*avatārikai*] and some devotional songs) is spoken to a listener in an unbroken flow of conversation which ceases only when the puppets are taken down at five o'clock in the morning. Even the abrupt and frequent alternations between chanted verses and declaimed commentary do not break the conversational thread of performance. For example, consider again the example of the dialogue between Vibhīṣaṇa and Rāma at the beginning of the translation above. In the first verse, Rāma poses a question ("Who is this mighty warrior?"), which he expands upon in the commentary until Vibhīṣaṇa responds with the second verse ("Listen, Noble One"), after which Vibhīṣaṇa continues to ramble on in commentary for almost half an hour. However far Vibhīṣaṇa may wander—and when a puppeteer sails away with his favorite topic, the commentary sounds very much like a monologue—he is always hauled back into dialogue by a question put by himself or his partner. Every word in the verses and every word in commentary is spoken within one of these four conversations.[62]

The relationship between verses and commentary is itself dialogic and reveals how conversations enable the puppeteers to gain control of the epic story. I find it useful to think of commentary and text as a form of double-voiced speech, along the lines suggested by the Russian critic, M. M. Bakhtin, who identifies a variety of forms in which a second speaker overlays the first speaker's words with a second and contrasting meaning. Parody is a good example. As Bakhtin points out, not all quoted or embedded speech is double-voiced; only when the two voices convey two distinct intentions is the utterance double-voiced because only then is the speaker able "to impose a new intention on the utterance, which nevertheless retains its own proper referential intention."[63] When the puppeteers chant the verses, we hear two voices but not two intentions; when they repeat verse words in commentary, however, and, even more, when they abandon simple exegesis for their own discourse, two voices are audible. This distinction between the voice of the commentary and voice of the verses may be plotted along a continuum from lesser to greater discord: at one end, the voice of the puppet play imitates Kampaṉ; at the other, it speaks independently of and sometimes (as explained in the next chapter) against the poet's intention.

At the imitation end of the spectrum are the chanted verses, during which the performer's voice is least distinct from that of the medieval epic. Because the words of the verses are (in Bakhtin's term) "already occupied," chanting them is single-voiced, and the puppet play attempts to impersonate Kampaṉ's text. As Bakhtin explains, "If we hear another voice, then we hear something which did not figure in the imitator's plan."[64] Nonetheless, even at this "imitation end" of the continuum, the folk tradition asserts some control by converting the verses to speeches and then linking them in the uninterrupted chain of conversation spoken by epic characters throughout the night-long performance. Many of Kampaṉ's verses are already dialogues between epic characters, but they differ from the folk performance in the crucial aspect of voice. Speeches in Kampaṉ are encased within the poet's voice, which appends a finite verb ("he said", "she shouted," etc.) at the close of each verse or at the close of the last verse in a series, whereas speeches in the puppet play are spoken directly by the epic characters. To achieve this immediacy, the puppeteers systematically drop the finite verb—the quotation marks, so to speak—from Kampaṉ's verse; as a result, instead of reading (the line) " 'Who is that great warrior?' asked Rāma," we hear Rāma ask: "Who is that great warrior?"[65] (Although in written dialogue the finite verb is often necessary to indicate the speaker, in oral performance this is usually obvious by context.) This minor but consistent omission throughout performance alters the effect of the chanted verse; the textual intention still dominates, but now the puppeteers speak through the characters.

This conversion of Kampaṉ's dialogue verses to speech is not a conversion from reported speech to direct speech; both Kampaṉ's verses and the performed verses are direct speech, and such terms are inaccurate in any case since direct speech contains a "report" of who spoke and what the person said.[66] For a sharper distinction between Kampaṉ's dialogue and the puppeteer's dialogue, and perhaps between other forms of written literature and oral performance, I prefer the term "vocalization." Briefly defined, words spoken and heard are vocalized; words read silently, even in dialogue, are not. Although recent research has narrowed the once great divide between written and oral expression, especially in terms of shared formal features, such as parallelism, I am convinced that they remain radically different in effect, which we recognize whenever we read a play and then see it on stage. In other words, the contrast between the puppet play and Kampan̲'s poems is that between speaking and writing, or, in Albert Lord's apt phrase, between "words heard and words seen."[67] Kampan̲'s text, too, was probably orally recited, but even hearing dialogue written in the third person lacks the immediacy of hearing dialogue spoken in the first person. Truly direct speech is vocalized—spoken and heard in oral performances, or conversations, like those in the puppet play.

In addition to Kampan̲'s dialogue verses, his descriptive verses are also vocalized in first-person speech by the puppeteers. Although converting these verses to dialogue is more complex than the single-word omission used to convert dialogue verses, it is still relatively simple. One or two new lines are often required, but the most frequent method is to replace the finite verb at the end of a verse with a vocative or imperative or both. An example is the puppeteer's vocalization of Kampan̲'s famous opening verse of the Śūrpaṇakhā episode, which likens the beauty of the Godavari River to poetry. When chanting this verse, the puppeteers change Kampan̲'s final words "the heroes saw" (*vīrar kaṇṭār*) to "look, brother" (*tampi, kāṇāy*); rather than reading the poet's description of what Rāma saw, we hear Rāma describe it to Lakṣmaṇa:

> "Look, Brother, here is the Godavari,
>   lying as a necklace on the world
> Nourishing the rich soil
>   rushing over waterfalls
> Flowing through the five regions
>   in clear, cool streams
> Like a good poet's verse."

Alternatively, the puppeteers sometimes omit the descriptive verses altogether from the scenes sung in the puppet play; for instance, when Vibhīṣaṇa extols Kumbhakarṇa's prowess (in the opening scene above), a string of verses detailing the warrior's appearance, his chariot, his armor, and his armies is dropped, and only the dialogue verses are retained (and altered, as already described) by the puppet play. If we look back at the Śūrpaṇakhā and Vāli episodes in chapters 4 and 5, we will see that they, too, are presented almost entirely in dialogue, and this principle of omitting descriptive verses in favor of conversation governs the adaptation of episode after episode in the puppeteers' telling of the Rāma story.

In its continuous drive toward dialogue, the puppet play reaches deep into Kampaṉ's verses and converts even inner thoughts to speech. This conversion requires substantial alteration, and sometimes the whole Kampaṉ verse is replaced by a folk equivalent; in this case, emotions unspoken in Kampaṉ are vocalized by another character to herself or to an imagined interlocutor, as when Śūrpaṇakhā, burning with lovesickness, addresses the moon. A comparison of Kampaṉ's verse describing Śūrpaṇakhā's feelings with its vocalized adaptation sung by the puppeteers illustrates the difference:

Kampaṉ
Now as the warm wind from the Malayas entered her chest
Like Death's long spear, she who had thought herself
Able to consume the God of Love and the full moon
For a curry along with him was suffering and losing strength.[68]

Puppet Play
Waxing moon! I'll make a curry of you! and then eat Rāma, too.
But, no, the mountain wind, like harsh Death's spear,
Enters my seething breast,
And now I will sleep.

Although the puppeteers make revisions to Kampaṉ's verse (the God of Love is omitted from, and Rāma added to, Śūrpaṇakhā's intended curry of victims; "losing strength" becomes "I will sleep"), they omit nothing essential and retain the poet's central image of the mountain breeze piercing, as death's spear, Śūrpaṇakhā's chest. Despite this continuity of content, however, the verse sung in the puppet play is cast in a new psychological light because Śūrpaṇakhā's emotions are spoken in her voice rather than refracted through the poet's words. If Kampaṉ's verse is sorrowful, turning on the contrast between Śūrpaṇakhā's desire and her suffering, then the folk verse is pathetic, almost comical, exposing the foolhardy bravado of one who boasts to the moon in the first line and yet is laid low by love in the last line.

Silent thoughts in Kampaṉ are also voiced in the puppet play when the speaker addresses herself with a single word, commonly a vocative (*maṉacē*, "Oh, heart") which replaces the last phrase of a verse ("he thought", "she feared," etc.). To understand this contrast between emotions thought and emotions spoken, I again compare verses from the Śūrpaṇakhā episode, but instead of altering a Kampaṉ verse, this time the puppet play replaces it entirely with a folk verse. Having seen

Rāma on the banks of the river, Śūrpaṇakhā attempts to identify the handsome figure:

Kampan̲
"The God of Love," she thought, "who lives in the heart
Had his body destroyed and Indra has a thousand eyes.
Śiva has three eyes like lotus flowers and Brahmā
Who created the world from his navel has four arms."[69]

Puppet Play
Is he Kāma, visiting this earth with his love-bow?
Or Indra, king of gods, or some earthly raja?
Could he be Lakṣmī's consort, Viṣṇu?
Or Śiva glistening with garlands?
Or the Sun-god in his circling chariot?
Oh heart [*man̲acē*], who is this man?

This and all similar vocalizations of Kampan̲'s verses, I am arguing, increase the puppeteers' control over the epic in performance. Vocalizations appear to imitate the text, to speak in its voice, but they also open the door to a second intention; and once this dialogic wedge has been inserted between the text and its recitation, conversations created by the puppet play pry them further and further apart. This distinction between the text and the puppeteers' voice sharpens as the performance moves from Kampan̲ verses to their own commentary. After the imitative chanting of the four-line verse, the puppeteers repeat the first line and then provide a gloss which may unfold into tales and myths; the remaining three lines may also be repeated and glossed, but more common is the repetition and explication of single verse words (*āriya* and *aṭitalam* in the initial verse in the above translation). Such repetitions of verse lines and verse words push performance away from imitation and toward double-voiced speech, for now the poet's word is subject to the puppeteers' interpretation. Just as the poet embeds his characters' speech within his own, the puppeteers speak these verse fragments within their own commentary and thereby infuse them with new meaning. Rather than speaking as the poet (in a chanted verse), the puppeteers speak for him, and Kampan̲ becomes another voice, another character, like the many traditional sayings (*piramāṇam*) that the puppeteers manipulate for their own interpretive ends. Although the repeated verse words echo the epic poem, they also build small bridges to the more expansive commentary, within which the textual voice will eventually fade; the word *āriya*, for instance, leads into the theology of the body, a discourse on grammar, and a telling of the Mārkaṇḍeya story. Although a dialogic gap has been opened, the puppeteers' voice still supplements Kampa̲n, with only a minor difference in intention, and does not yet supplant the poet's words.

That difference becomes the distinction of doubled speech when the puppeteers elaborate their exegesis and spin out digressions. With the chanted verses steadily receding from the performative present, the resulting disjunction between epic action and oral commentary may itself become the topic of discussion, as is demonstrated by the now familiar example in the initial segment of commentary when Vibhīṣaṇa speaks to Rāma. While Kumbhakarṇa and his armies of elephants and horses charge toward them, Vibhīṣaṇa addresses Rāma, and when the giant warrior is nearly upon them and the earth quakes beneath them, still Vibhīṣaṇa speaks. For nearly two hours he speaks, slowly raising his right hand and carefully lowering it, two or three times, to dramatize a point. With no other movement visible on the screen, we understand Rāma's growing anxiety about the "giant warrior bearing down upon" him as Vibhīṣaṇa expatiates on the epithet "worthy one" (*āriya*), tells the story of Mahābali, and explains noun classifications, all the time ignoring his Lord's pleas, and finally concludes with a long account of the Mārkaṇḍeya story. Rāma, however, must show patience while the puppeteers tell their own stories.

At times, this incongruity between rambling commentary and imminent epic action is comical, as in another, later example from the translation in this chapter, when Jāmbuvā̲n speaks to Hanumān. The monkey devotee must travel to the Medicine Mountain seventy-three thousand *yojanas* away and return quickly with the magical herbs that will revive Lakṣmaṇa and the monkeys, but Jāmbuvā̲n leisurely describes his own birth:

> "It's a long, long story, requiring more than an eon to recount and we've only got three-quarters of an hour. But, in brief, I am a child of Brahmā. Let me explain. Existence moves in cycles of creation and dissolution, since everything born—from the Three Gods to an insect—also dies . . ." [and so forth, for several minutes].

If it could be said in 1935 that the puppets "often remain stationary, merely gesticulating with right or left hand, during long spells of cadenced chants," I can confirm that they have not picked up much speed over the past half century.[70] Given the commentarial nature of the puppet play, some tension between rapid plot and long-winded exposition is unavoidable, but the puppeteers flaunt this disparity rather than conceal it. Kumbakharṇa charges at Rāma, and Lakṣmaṇa and the monkey army lie unconscious, but the epic action must wait for the stories told in the commentary.

A less deliberate but more vivid illustration of the commentary's ability to invest the text with new intentions is the story of Kampaṉ's poem told by Natesan Pillai, which was mentioned in the previous chapter. The story is prompted by a verse: during the construction of the causeway to Lanka, the ambitious monkey Kumutaṉ throws an enormous boulder into the sea, sending water drops (*tumi*) to the gods in heaven, who believe that ambrosia will rise again, as it did when the gods and demons churned the Milk Ocean.[71] When chanting this verse, the puppeteers merge their voice with that of the text, but when they quote the verse and gloss the word *tumi* in the commentary, we hear their voice speaking. Once the verse is within their interpretive grasp, they crack it wide open to reveal the history of Kampaṉ's text, from the desire of a Chola king to hear a "Rāma story in the southern language" to the debate over *tumi*, from Kampaṉ's deceit and Bhagavati's assistance to the poet's triumph over his rival and the composition of the *Kamparāmāyaṇam*. Through this extraordinary story, the puppeteers also gain control of the text by historicizing it. Although the verse about Kumutaṉ appears halfway through the ten thousand verses of Kampaṉ's text, the commentary claims that is was the very first verse written by him, and Natesan Pillai's story closes by stamping the epic with the day and year when Kampaṉ first recited his composition. By creating these conversations in which the poet speaks, lies, worships, and eventually recites his own composition, the puppet play gives voice even to Kampaṉ himself.

Doubled speech, competing intentions, and the puppeteers' grip on performance is evident also in ordinary dialogue spoken by epic characters (conversation 2). To say that the puppeteers speak in their own voice is more than metaphor here, since the epic characters speak not in Kampaṉ's literary Tamil but in an idiomatic Tamil (*ceṭṭi bāsai*); unlike the converted verses and repeated verse-words, these dialogues are not "occupied" by the poet's meanings and are thus more susceptible to the intentions of the puppeteers. We do not hear this dialogue if, as in our favorite scene between Vibhīṣaṇa and Rāma, the speeches last for five or ten minutes, but when the speakers alternate more quickly, the puppeteers' voices are distinctly audible. An example from the above translation occurs when Rāvaṇa considers what to do after Kumbhakarṇa's death:

"First that monkey burned our city, and then my palace is put under siege. I've lost a battle to Rāma, Kumbhakarṇa has been killed, and now I've lost my son!"

[*His wife, Danyamālīṉi*:] "Kumbhakarṇa is gone, our beloved son is dead, and who is next? All this because you want to keep that Sītā as a concubine! [*To Indrajit*] Son, your brother is dead and now the fate of Lanka rests on your shoulders."

"Do not grieve, Mother. I will surely defeat our enemies. Father, send me to battle."

"Just seeing your strong hands, Son, gives me courage, but we have suffered another loss, a great loss.

"Now you tell me! Why did you send my little brother when I, conqueror of Indra, was here to fight? I humiliated that monkey Hanumān when he spied on us. Armed with special weapons, I leave for the battlefield this very minute."

"What weapons have you, Son?"

"Many. Śiva granted me the snake-weapon, the Brahmā-weapon, and the Nārāyaṇa-weapon, and many more. And they have not yet been used. Remember that I am your son and will enter the field chanting your name."

"Yes! Go! Go and kill them both, especially the younger one who has killed your brother."

"Lakṣmaṇa? I'll offer his head as a gift to the Earth Goddess."

The performed epic is loosened still further from its textual moorings when the dialogue accelerates into a rapid-fire argument between two characters, as in this excerpt from the translation in this chapter, in which Indrajit and Hanumān trade insults:

"Monkey-face! Stop jumping around and talk with me like a man."

"I'm not—"

"Shut up, monkey, and listen to me. Is this some kind of game you're playing? Attacking me not with bow or spear but with trees and stones? Are you mad? Will that spindly branch ward off my missiles?"

"With this stone—"

"Speak up, animal, speak up!"

"You think words will defeat me? Quit babbling and fight. Why should I stop to talk? Does lightning wait before it strikes? Or a lion before it leaps? Advance, brave Indrajit, or are you afraid?"

[*More battle noises*]

"Take this, runt!"

"I'll rip out that tongue of yours!"

Here the epic characters respond to each other and not to the long-forgotten verse that prompted this heated exchange. Performance moves even further outside the text and into the world created by the puppeteers when dialogue is spoken not between epic characters but within an auxiliary tale (conversation 3). In the story of Poor Brains, for instance, the words are trebly distanced from the verses: they are spoken by characters in a story told by the umbrella bearer to Indrajit within the oral commentary spoken by the puppeteers.

Although the skillful performer eventually joins his commentary, whatever its contents, to his explication of a verse, these conversations between epic characters and within auxiliary stories are spoken by equal, distinct voices. Throughout the night, the puppeteers will chant and explicate verses, but they lay their surest claim to the *Kamparāmāyaṇam* by creating conversations.

Behind the ventriloquism of the puppets is yet another conversation, one in which the puppeteers speak with each other. I save this for last because it contains that interaction between speakers and listeners I had expected to find between the puppeteers and an audience on the other side of the screen—that dialogue whose absence baffled me for so long and yet was present all along when I learned where to look. Like their puppets, Kerala puppeteers always speak in pairs: a lead man and his support. After the initial pair have performed for an hour or so, a third man, who has been sleeping or resting in the drama-house, relieves one of them, who then sleeps for some time until he spells his now exhausted original partner. This rotation of chanting and sleeping (one of the world's more bizarre work schedules) requires three men, and given the dwindling numbers of active puppeteers, seldom are more than three present in the drama-house. Seated together on a wooden bench or woven mats, the exchange between lead and support man assumes various forms but never abandons conversation. When a verse is recited, for example, the lead usually chants the first half of each line and his partner completes it; during the commentary, on the other hand, their interaction is reduced to a minimum when the lead puppeteer speaks uninterruptedly for several minutes.

As stated earlier, verse and commentary speak as voices within a continuous conversation, and when we realize that these are puppeteers speaking to each other, we can identify other dialogic devices. First, the conversational thread of the commentary is tenuously, if monotonously, sustained by the droning sound ("ahhhh . . .") muttered by the support man whenever his lead pauses for breath or thought and by questions from the support man (like the straight man in a comedy routine). Second, irrespective of length, speeches open and/or close with epithets employed as vocatives ("Rāma-god" for Rāma; "Young god" for Lakṣmaṇa; "Ruler of Lanka" for Vibhīṣaṇa). Ostensibly addressed to the epic characters, these epithets actually cue the exchange between puppeteers. If in the middle of an exchange between Rāma and Vibhīṣaṇa about the upcoming battle, to return to our well-worked example, the lead man inserts the long tale of the Churning of the Ocean and only returns to the epic narrative thirty minutes later with the question, "So what do you think . . . ?" his partner is likely to have forgotten who is speaking about what to whom; the panic on a young performer's face is painful but brief for he is rescued when the lead man appends to his question the epithet, "Ruler of Lanka?" With context thus restored, the support man is able to respond convincingly as Vibhīṣaṇa.

Contrary to the impression this book might give, the commentary is not merely a series of long-winded discourses by sleepy puppeteers. Everything changes, as seen above, when the lead man shortens his speeches or his partner interrupts in an attempt to wrest control for himself; and when the interaction inside the drama-house escalates into this rapid-fire exchange, it is obvious that underneath the puppets' conversations the puppeteers have been speaking to themselves all along. In the example referred to above, when Indrajit insulted Hanumān (with cries of "Take this, runt,"), the puppeteer speaking for Indrajit challenged his partner, jabbing his finger and shouting at him, and nearly knocked him off the bench, while Hanumān's speaker raised his eyebrows and responded with cool disdain for Indrajit's aggressive posturing. On another occasion later in the same performance, a puppeteer surprised his partner by asking an unexpected question and skillfully drew out the answer he (Aṅgada) needed in order to dismantle his partner's (Jāmbuvāṉ's) argument that fighting for Rāma was futile:

[*Aṅgada*] "Sure, sure, Jāmbuvāṉ, but who killed Madhu and Kaitabha?"

[*Jāmbuvāṉ*] "Er . . . Viṣṇu."

"And who killed Hiraṇya?"

"It was Viṣṇu . . . in his man-lion avatar."

"And who is going to kill these demons who face us now?"

"It will be Rāma . . . as Viṣṇu's avatar. I see what you mean, Aṅgada. But how can I face Rāma after this disgraceful retreat?"

When performance moves into this high-speed, unpredictable exchange, one forgets the puppets pinned motionless on the cloth screen. Their flickering shadows are still visible for more than a hundred yards outside, but the performance has become a conversation spoken by the men inside the drama-house.

Tactics of talk employed by the puppeteers to control their conversations range from ordinary jibes to special puppet-play rules. Locked in an argument about the etymology of one of Indrajit's names, for instance, a puppeteer will not hesitate to cry, "Perhaps, but you sleep too much to be trusted with mental matters!" Similarly, the inveterate tendency of some puppeteers to speak at length on issues of vital importance to themselves often tests the limits of collegial respect: "Let that be," a frustrated partner once interrupted his lead's relentless description of Rāvaṇa's palace and towers and chambers, "and explain how you got here, Vibhīṣaṇa." Certain senior puppeteers are notorious for their self-satisfying discourses and cavalier disregard for time, while others, fearful that the sun will in fact rise before Hanumān returns with the medicinal herbs, attempt to hasten the pace of the commentary in order to complete the night's action. One night, as a senior man was gliding languidly through Jāmbuvāṉ's account of the origin of the world, his partner cut him short: "I see, Jāmbuvāṉ, so that's how you were born; but what can we do about Lakṣmaṇa's death?" Of course, no one likes to be interrupted, and puppeteers not willing to relinquish control of the commentary will raise their voice, speak faster, or simply stonewall their partner. A cleverer trick for wresting verbal control, however, lies in the rules of the drama-house: if a puppeteer sails blissfully away on a digression, one need only recite a *piramāṇam* or quote a line from the verse under discussion (which everyone has forgotten), and suddenly, by force of professional habit, the puppeteer who was speaking will stop in mid-sentence and sing the line in unison with the man who has now wrested control of performance.

Despite this verbal jockeying for position, nights in the drama-house are not soured by antagonism. Frustration is common but not hostility. Looking back at the hundreds of performance hours I observed, and after making allowances for the odd egotist or disgruntled puppeteer brooding on some personal problem, I am struck by the cooperation and mutual respect displayed by the performers. The learned quotation and rapid retort, the skillful parody and display of logic are all calculated to please the little band of fellow puppeteers. Even when only two puppeteers are awake, they take pride in explaining how Rāvaṇa got his name or in exposing the tomfoolery of the messenger Sangadi. A measure of shame is likewise shared when someone hesitates, forgets the next verse, or begins with the wrong line. That is why neophyte performers clutch a crib sheet listing the first letter of each verse written in sequence in a tiny script, and why senior puppeteers also take into the drama-house a notebook containing the full verses (and sometimes *piramāṇam*), which they may refer to but not read. Only once did I see a junior puppeteer completely at a loss; the poor man suddenly went blank in mid-verse; "I don't know the verses here," he murmured to his partner and hung his head, while the senior man looked at him in a mixture of pity and contempt and carried on with the commentary.

Quality counts on the other side of the cloth screen, too, as I explained in chapter 1, but the puppeteers have little direct interaction with their patrons. Temple officials and influential men will eventually decide whether or not to invite the troupe back next year, and hundreds, sometimes thousands, of individuals will register their approval with one-rupee donations. However, the timing of these individual donations only points up the isolation of the puppeteers: whereas in most oral performances such donations are made *during* performance as a means of communicating with and influencing the performers with requests, in the puppet play those gifts are made *before* the performance begins, and the donors will not be present when their names are sung to secure blessings from the goddess Bhagavati. This absent audience of temple officials and one-rupee donors, like the goddess and the sleepy crowd in front of the drama-house, hear words and see shadows only on the outside of the white cloth screen, where certain details of the epic action are invisible (such as Vibhīṣaṇa's inspection of the false Sītā fallen on the floor of the drama-house, and a small *pūjā* when Sītā is about to enter the fire).[72] The puppet play's public audiences do not participate in the performance; at best, they overhear it.

To be sure, all forms of puppetry impede interaction with an audience because the performer is hidden, and performances depend on the ventriloquist's illusion. For the spectator, part of the pleasure of the performance is to allow oneself to be fooled by the deception and to see through it at the same time, to hear the hidden puppeteer's voice and to pretend it comes from the visible puppet.[73] Shadow puppetry, however, asks of spectators yet another degree of self-deception because (with rare exceptions) they do not even see the puppets clearly. In Kerala, the illusion is perhaps too successful. High up in the drama-house behind shadows, screen, and puppets, chanting medieval verses and a learned commentary, making few concessions to music or movement, these puppeteers have receded into their private world.

Puppeteers with whom I discussed the lack of an audience did not see it this way, however. They claimed a Golden Age once existed when they were patronized by local rajas and played to vast crowds who were later lured from the drama-house to the movie-house. Undoubtedly, large audiences did occasionally gather to see the puppet play, for they do so occasionally today—when the puppet play is presented concurrently with more popular events of the temple festival. I have also seen photographs of several hundred people gathered to see a performance on the final day of a festival held in the mid-1950s. All other evidence, on the other hand, suggests that these occasions are exceptions that prove the rule that the puppet play in Kerala is not performed for entertainment. For instance, the puppet play's absent audience was noted in 1935 by a foreign observer and again in 1943 by a local scholar who left no room for doubt: "It does not matter whether there is an audience or not."[74] Shortly thereafter, and still nearly two decades before movies reached villages in Kerala, another scholar made this recommendation:

> If the olapavakuthu [puppet play][75] is to survive (and it would be a great pity if it did not), it will apparently have to undergo considerable renovation in the reduction of exposition, a change that would have the desirable effect of quickening the movements of the figures on the screen

> and bringing the kuthu [puppet play] nearer the natural desire of people for rhythmic representation. (Cousins 1970 [1948]: 212)

Although scant, these pre-1950 descriptions of performance are enough to indicate that the puppet play's tortoise-like pace and lack of an audience are not recent losses in a media war with movies and television. Equally important, they remind us that the puppeteers are expounders, not tellers, a fact that the above recommendation, with its friendly advice for a "reduction of exposition" and a "quickening of movements," did not grasp.

What that advice also failed to understand is that, unlike other storytelling traditions that use marionettes, scrolls, cards, puppets, and other props, the aesthetic of the Kerala puppet play is not visual; it is verbal. Nowhere is this verbal orientation, and the primacy of the commentary, more apparent than in the battle scenes and death scenes of the War Book. These fast-moving, action-packed scenes, especially Garuḍa's rescue of Rāma, do attract some spectators to the drama-house, and such episodes are standard fare when the puppeteers perform at cultural festivals in New Delhi or elsewhere.[76] But even in the War Book, when leather weapons are hurled across the cloth screen and thrust into leather chests, the puppets are very often at rest, pinned motionless on the screen for thirty minutes or an hour while the commentary rolls on and on without interruption. It is significant that the Kerala puppets are *pinned* on the screen, whereas elsewhere in India they are temporarily held against it, and in Southeast Asia they are inserted in a banana-tree trunk, to be taken out and manipulated later. Even the manufacture of the Kerala puppets leaves little doubt as to their intended activity on the screen, for typically they are made with only one movable arm and one movable hand.[77] Behind this static tableau of pinned puppets, the puppeteers are less concerned with a visual presentation of events for an external audience than with creating conversations for those inside the drama-house. It would be difficult to improve on this description written more than fifty years ago:

> It is a privilege to listen to their discourses and the subtleties of their discussion, which are animated by competitive enthusiasm, and there is hardly any subject on which they have not something to say. (Achuyta Menon 1940: 17)

CHAPTER 8

Rāma's Coronation: The Limits of Restoration

This book has described two primary means by which the puppeteers recontextualize Kampan̲'s Rāmāyaṇa. While chapters 4 and 5 emphasized the narrative alterations that occur within the drama-house, chapters 6 and 7 argued that the oral commentary and conversations place performance even more firmly in the hands of the puppeteers. Such a separation of narrative content from performative technique is artificial, of course, and this final chapter brings them together in a discussion of the voices that challenge the bhakti text. These countervailing voices are particularly audible in the concluding episodes of the epic, and especially in the very last scene, Rāma's coronation (*paṭṭābiṣēkam*), where they test the limits of that restoration. With that scene, the puppet play, Kampan̲'s poem, and this book conclude.

The translation below covers the final two nights of performance—Rāvaṇa's death and Rāma's return to Ayodhya. I recorded them at Palappuram, a major site of the puppet tradition nearly twenty miles west of Palghat and a few miles north of the Bharatapuzha River. Palappuram is a prosperous town, boasting a private college and a complex of three Bhagavati temples, which sponsor an elaborate annual festival (*pūram*), complete with papier-mâché horses in mock combat and a series of special events (Kathakaḷi, modern drama, classical music) that rival the famous festival at Trichur, not far away. In a society that ranks festivals by the number of elephants, Palappuram need not be ashamed of its twenty-four pachyderms hired for the occasion. Mixing the sprawling chaos of an American county fair with the fervor of a

Hindu religious pageant, the Bhagavati festival attracts sprawling crowds who mill around the temple grounds and frequent the temporary stalls to purchase food, beverages, *pūjā* accessories, cassette tapes of "bhakti pop," and, what is truly indispensable, firecrackers. The Palappuram temple complex hosting this festival is the hub of a network of smaller temples located in surrounding villages that help underwrite seventeen nights of shadow puppetry—a measure of local wealth and the prestige of the tradition here. Even more impressive were the twelve puppeteers (three or four are the norm) who filled the spacious, two-storied drama-house on the opening night in 1989. Nevertheless, and as I had learned to expect, near midnight, when the performance formally began, the crowds evaporated and these puppeteers sang to themselves. During the two performances translated here, which presented the colossal events of Rāvaṇa's death and Rāma's coronation, the nights were so still that I could hear the wooden wheels of bullock carts creaking on the asphalt road behind the drama-house.

The puppeteers of Palappuram are Tamil-speaking Mutaliyars who have practiced the art of shadow puppetry since they migrated from Tamil Nadu three or four hundred years ago.[1] Today they live in a cluster of streets set back from the busy state highway that roars straight through Palappuram. Leaving that main road and turning into their neighborhood, one enters a tiny Tamil enclave. The visual effect is immediate—the Māriyamman̲ temple at the near end of the street and the Gaṇeśa temple at the far end rise up in sculpted stone towers (rather than slope down with the wooden roofs of Kerala temples). Walking down this narrow street, one also hears a curious slapping sound, for inside the houses men sit at their pit looms, pulling the wooden shuttle back and forth—the same men who sit on a wooden bench and chant the Rāma story in the drama-house. Every year at festival time these Tamil families pool their money and construct a large papier-mâché horse to compete with those constructed by other settlements and villages in the mock battles at the Bhagavati temple in Palappuram; they do not, however, hold puppet plays in their own temples.[2] This small cluster of Tamil families surrounded by Malayalis replicates the position of the puppet play in the Bhagavati festival.

Presiding over this little kingdom of puppeteers and weavers is Annamalai Pulavar, a wispy, frail man in his late sixties. He is president of the local weavers' cooperative society, he owns some land, he leads the performances inside the drama-house, and his ancestral house dominates the main street in the Tamil quarter. Climbing a few steps out of the hot street, one enters a front room where guests are received and business transacted, and it is there I sit in a battered metal folding chair whenever I come to interview the grand old man. Hospitality is never lacking—good coffee, ripe bananas and homemade sweets were plentiful—but talking with Annamalai Pulavar does not fill many pages in my notebook. Although courteous, he seems to take little pleasure in talking about the puppet play. People he does discuss, especially his rival puppeteers, who "knew next to nothing," and the German researcher who came ten years ago and bought two manuscripts "for five hundred rupees;" he raises his hand high and spreads his fingers wide to make sure I count them. Attempting to deflect the conversation away from this tiresome issue, I ask questions about last night's performance, why Vibhīṣaṇa said such and such to Rāma, but he quickly loses interest and glances out the window, preoccupied. In the drama-house, however, his enthusiasm is unbounded, as evidenced by the eighty-minute commentary he delivered at the outset of the translation that follows. Sitting ramrod straight on the wooden bench, the gold settings of his stud earrings gleaming in the lamp light, he fixes a determined stare on everyone and commands high standards from his associates. He is physically enfeebled now and appears to wander at times, but his absorption in the epic characters has never failed to produce a convincing performance.

The translation follows directly on the previous translation and covers the final two nights of performance. We pick up the action at the end of the "Song of the Drama-House" (after the Brahmin puppets have thanked the sponsors) when Indra (Annamalai Pulavar) explains his good fortune at Indrajit's death.

Rāma's Coronation

[*Brahmin puppets*] "Indrajit is dead and when Rāvaṇa hears this news, he certainly will not sit idly in his palace."

"Certainly not. Moved by grief for his last surviving son, he will rise to fight Rāma."

"And then we can watch the great battle between Rāma and Rāvaṇa, but exactly how it will end we can't say."

"True. We know what to expect in general, but not the details."

"So let's wait here and watch what happens on the battlefield."

[*The Brahmin puppets leave, and gods appear overhead. As they watch Aṅgada carry Indrajit's head in procession to Rāma, Indra begins to sing*:]

Like the blemish on the moon in the night sky,
My humiliation, I feared, would never fade away;
But this brave bowman has erased it forever,
Now no obstacle, no travail, mars my good fortune![3]

"Do you realize what has just happened?"

"Tell us, Indra Maharaja."

"This long struggle between Rāma and Rāvaṇa is now ending. Indrajit was Rāvaṇa's life [*uyir*], and once the life is gone the body will not live long. Rāvaṇa may have conquered the Three Worlds, but no one was a greater warrior than Indrajit. Twice he knocked Lakṣmaṇa unconscious; twice Rāma lost heart, cursed dharma, and almost killed himself. Only an eagle and then a monkey saved them from final defeat, and from death. Armed with Śiva mantras and *māyā,* Indrajit was invincible except against a person who had fasted in the forest for fourteen years. Remember, too, that this demon once defeated and imprisoned me, earning the name Conqueror of Indra. Ever since that day I have lived in unending fear, but now Lakṣmaṇa's arrow has removed its source.[4]

"To understand how much I feared Indrajit, think of the moon, for it, too, is a raja, a monarch of the night. Even the splendor of the full moon, however, is diminished by scars on its surface, and Indrajit's curse on my life seemed as indelible as those black marks."

"How did the moon get its marks, Indra?"

"It's a long story, more than one story in fact, but you should know them for they take us back to the original form of Śiva, the Pure Light, without physical shape or quality, the light of lights that illumines all the worlds."

"All the worlds?"

"There's a *piramāṇam* for that: 'The primordial man has ninety-six million locks of hair.[5] Each lock holds one thousand million worlds; within each world is a set of Śiva, Viṣṇu, Brahmā, sages, and Brahmins.' This explains how the original Śiva stretches through space: his head is the heavens; his feet the netherworlds; his eight limbs the eight directions; his two eyes the sun and the moon. And his moon eye was without blemish. It preceded even the gods."

"How is that?"

"One story is that the moon was born from the eye of a sage named Atri. It happened this way. Another sage, Nārada, wished to humble the three goddesses Sarasvatī, Lakṣmī, and Pārvatī, who thought no woman was more beautiful than they. Nārada had peanuts made from the purest gold, put them in a pot, and went to Sarasvatī. Bowing with respect, he said: 'I'm hungry. Can you fry these golden peanuts so that I can eat?' But she replied, 'I'm not able to accomplish that task. Ask Lakṣmī in Vaikunta.'

"In the end, none of the goddesses—not Sarasvatī, not Lakṣmī, not even Pārvatī in Kailasa—could cook the golden peanuts. So Nārada took the pot of peanuts in search for someone to feed him, and eventually he came to Atri's hermitage. The sage was lost in meditation, but his wife, Anasūyā, greeted Nārada; and when he asked her to feed him by frying the peanuts, she said, 'I will, by the powers of my chastity.' Taking the pot in her hand, she meditated for a few minutes and then served ordinary, hot peanuts. Rather than eat them, however, Nārada ran to the goddesses and showed them what Anasūyā had done. Immediately they went to their husbands, Brahmā, Viṣṇu, and Śiva, touched their feet in deference, and made a request: 'Please go to earth and test the chastity of Atri's wife, Anasūyā. She appears to be chaste, but who knows?'

"At first the goddesses' husbands refused: 'No thanks. She's powerful and might trick us. Besides, everyone knows she's pure. No need to test her.' Their wives persisted, and eventually the gods agreed. Disguised as wandering holy men, they marched up to Anasūyā, but she knew who they were and spoke innocently:

"'Welcome, sages. What do you require?'

"'Feed us, please. But you must do so without clothes.'

"'Bathe first, and I will feed you.'

"When the gods left to bathe, Anasūyā thought, 'If I am to serve them without any clothes, let them return as newborn babies.' And so Śiva, Viṣṇu, and Brahmā were transformed into little babies whom Anasūyā held in her lap and fed soft rice. Later she placed each baby in a cradle and sang them to sleep. When Nārada reported this to the three goddesses, they went quickly to Anasūyā, who received them graciously: 'To what do I owe the honor of your visit?' Sarasvatī spoke first, 'You have turned our husbands into babies; please return them to us.'

"'They are here,' said sweet-natured Anasūyā, 'in these cradles. Please find your husband and take him.' Sarasvatī stepped up and looked into each cradle again and again but she could not identify her husband Brahmā, for the babies had identical faces, like the six faces of Murukaṉ when he was born. Then Lakṣmī and Pārvatī tried to find their husbands, but they, too, were frustrated. Finally, the three goddesses begged Anasūyā to restore their husbands to their real forms; Anasūyā agreed and the three gods appeared as one! At that moment, her husband, Atri, arrived, saw what had happened, and spoke to the goddesses: 'Are you ignorant of the fact, of the reality, that your husbands, Brahmā, Viṣṇu, and Śiva, are one?' The goddesses lowered their heads in shame, and the three gods, through Anasūyā's powers, separated out from their united form and rejoined their wives individually.

"She bade them farewell for it was twilight, but as the humiliated goddesses walked back to their heavenly homes, they cursed her: 'If she is so pure, let her lose her husband and suffer as a widow when the sun rises.' Nārada told Anasūyā of the curse, and she began to worship Sūrya, the Sun God: 'Do not rise again. Do not rise or my husband will die and I will suffer as a widow.' On the next morning, the sun did not rise and the earth remained dark endlessly, day after day, until the gods shouted in anger, 'That woman has plunged the world into total darkness.' They marched to the earth where they begged Atri to forgive their wives' pettiness and restore light to the world. Listening intently, Atri spoke: 'Let the sun and moon be born from my eyes.'

"That's one story, but the moon has other origins, as this *piramāṇam* explains: 'From Atri's eyes; from Viṣṇu's navel; from Svaha's stomach; from the Milk Ocean; from Brahmā's creation.' The worlds are created and destroyed, created and destroyed, in endless cycles. Some myths say Śiva creates the worlds, some say Viṣṇu, some Brahmā, and some claim that the sages create the worlds. Once when Viṣṇu was creating the worlds, the moon is said to have sprung from his navel; he was beautiful like Kāma and women followed him with their eyes. Even Svaha, wife of Agni, the Fire God, fell in love with the moon and made love with him. Afraid that her husband would get angry, she swallowed her lover to protect him, and later he was born from her stomach.

"Yet another story describes how the moon was born with a halo of stars from the Milk Ocean and placed in Śiva's matted locks. Still another explains how Brahmā created the moon. You see, gods, the stories are legion, but the point is that the moon was without blemish from the very beginning."

"But what about the 'mark,' the dark spot on the moon? How did it get there?"

"That's another story. Using the serpent Vāsuki as a rope, Mt. Meru as the stick, and the moon to fasten it, the gods and demons churned the Milk Ocean. When the poison flew up, the demons dropped the snake's head, the gods dropped its tail, and they all fled. Mt. Meru would have crashed down if Viṣṇu had not taken his tortoise-avatar and balanced the mountain on his back. Well, in the chaos, Vāsuki spat out hot poison, which splattered both Viṣṇu and the moon, and from that day Viṣṇu's body has been dark-colored and the moon has been stained. A different story goes back to the moon's birth from Svaha, wife of Agni. They say that when the moon emerged from Svaha's stomach, Agni was so angry that he fried the moon's body like a *pappadam*, creating the bubbles that we see as spots.[6]

"But the best story is about Dakṣa and his twenty-seven daughters.[7] One day the handsome moon came and married them all so that he was surrounded by stars. Back in his palace, however, the moon gave attention to only one of his wives, and the other twenty-six were never called to his bed. When these daughters complained to their father, Dakṣa summoned the moon: 'You have failed to treat your wives equally and therefore I curse you to lose your light and become a mere shadow.' Gradually, the moon began to lose power and pass through its phases until last phase began and it was about to lose all its light. Desperate, the moon finally found the sage Agastya, who advised him to eat rabbit meat in order to regain his strength. Afraid that he might not find the meat when he wanted it, the moon grabbed several rabbits and held them close to his chest, and they are the dark spots we see on the pale moon today.

"Still another story takes us back to Kiṣkindha, when Rāma shot his arrow straight through the seven *sāl* trees to convince Sugrīva that he was a worthy ally in the fight against Vāli. Looking at the seven trees, Rāma said to Lakṣmaṇa: 'Are these trees or mountains? They stretch so far into the skies that I wonder if their branches have scraped against the surface of the moon and created its dark spots.' All these stories, you must understand, prove that the moon was originally without defect and that later it was scarred."

"But, Indra, there *are* spots on the moon, so how can it be perfect?"

"The *Bhāgavata Purāṇa* says, 'Comparable to the highest reality, the moon is without blemish; its dark spot is the earth's shadow.' You see, the primordial reality has no qualities. Whether it manifests as *brahman*, as eternal light, as Śiva, or anything else, it remains flawless. Just as any blemish we may see is a reflection of us, the earth casts its shadow on the moon: in reality, neither is intrinsically defiled. This is the truth, the absolute truth! And this is the point: I, too, was plagued by an illusory scar, by fear of Indrajit, until this moment when Lakṣmaṇa cut off his head. His beheading, you are to understand, fulfills the pledge Viṣṇu made long ago to the Earth Goddess to destroy the demons: Viṣṇu was born as Rāma, his conch as Bharata, his discus as Śatrughna, and Ādiśeṣa as Lakṣmaṇa, who has now destroyed Indrajit. Having lost his 'life,' his son Indrajit, Rāvaṇa is certain to die and then we can enjoy the fruits of piety, meditation, and sacrifices again. Let us shower Rāma with flowers and shout his victory cry when the final battle with Rāvaṇa begins."[8]

"Yes, look below. There's a procession of monkeys led by Aṅgada, who carries Indrajit's head to Rāma."

[*Rāma speaks to Lakṣmaṇa*:]

> "Welcome my mother, my brother, my life,
> Come savior, come guardian of Daśaratha-Rāma,
> Come my precious brother, who killed the terror
> While I lay in an ocean of misery.

"Lakṣmaṇa! Once again you have saved me from my own doubts and fears. I placed those arrows in your hands and sent you to fight Indrajit, but—"

"I have killed him, as you commanded."

"No, Lakṣmaṇa, not you alone."

"Not me? Then who?"

"Lakṣmaṇa, no one can match you as a warrior, but without Hanumān neither of us would now be alive. As I lay unconscious on your body, his strength propelled him millions of miles to bring back the Sanjeevi herb to revive us all. Remember also Garuḍa, who defeated Indrajit when he ripped apart the snake-weapon with his beak and talons, and remember Vibhīṣaṇa, who defeated Indrajit by teaching you how to counter his *māyā*. And the gods, above all else remember the gods, who defeated Indrajit, because everything we do is their act. Still, among men, you alone were able to face and kill Indrajit in battle. I only praise the others so that they do not feel slighted and accuse me of favoring you. Now return the arrows to me."

[*Rāvaṇa, who has not yet heard the news of Indrajit's death, summons his messengers*:][9]

"What has happened to my son in his battle with Lakṣmaṇa? Run quickly to the battlefield and report to me."

[*One messenger*] "Sangadi, what did the raja say?"

[*Sangadi*] "What? You were in front and still didn't listen?"

"I thought you were listening, so I kept quiet."

"Hmmm . . . how do we carry out instructions when we don't know what they are? Better go back and ask."

"He'll be furious."

"We'll tell a little white lie and find out what we need to know."

[*They return to the palace, where Rāvaṇa receives them expectantly*:]

"You're quick. What's the news?"

"News? The prices in the market are soaring."

"Not that news, you fools! My son went to war—"

"Listen. We had an accident."

"What's that?"

"You summoned us and spoke some words to us, right? Well, that fool Sangadi took all the words and tied them up in a bundle. We came to a field and had to jump across an irrigation channel. Sangadi jumped—"

"He's a good jumper."

"Yes, but when he jumped all the words fell out of his bundle and into the water."

"Did you find the words?"

"We tried to. We drank the water but only got sick!"

"Don't lie to me; this is a lot of bull."

"No, really, we wouldn't make fun of you, Rāvaṇa. We just lost your words."

"All right. I'll teach you how to remember my words. Repeat exactly what I say."

"We're ready."

"Go quickly to the battlefield . . ."

"Go quickly to the battlefield . . ."

". . . and find out whether Lakṣmaṇa or Indrajit has won the battle."

". . . and find out whether Lakṣmaṇa or Indrajit has won the battle."

"Get going!"

"Get going!"

"Hey, don't talk to me that way."

"Hey, don't talk to me that way."

"Take this, you fool."

"Take this, you fool."

"Enough, Sangadi. Let's go."

"We just took a beating . . . because we did what Rāvaṇa told us to do."

"But we forgot his words the first time. Anyway, we better go to the battlefield and report back quickly."

[*Reaching the battlefield, they survey the corpses.*][10]

"Here's the battlefield. Look, there's Indrajit's indestructible chariot and bow."

"Who's that, lying down over there?"

"Does it look like Indrajit?"

"Can't see."

"Does he have a *poṭṭu* on his forehead?"[11]

"I'll go have a look. Oh, god, he doesn't even have a head!"

"Check his right hand; he wore a jeweled ring."

"Can't see. Too bloody. Oh, it *is* Indrajit!"

"It is? That's terrible . . . for Rāvaṇa I mean. He's lost all his brothers, and now all his sons."

"We must somehow tell him of this loss and show proper grief when we do it."

"Why? What's the loss of Indrajit to us?"

"I agree, but if we don't want Rāvaṇa's fury unleashed on us, we'd best pretend."

"Right. It's monsoon time again, and I guess we can put some chilies in our eyes to make us cry."

"We'll manage somehow."

[*They sing a mock dirge, a parody of what Rāvaṇa will later sing*:]

> "Oh, Indrajit, our nation's son, you've gone forever!
> Sangadi, Sangadi.
> Oh, Indrajit, our local boy, we've lost you forever,
> Sangadi, Sangadi."

"Why are you calling 'Sangadi' and putting me into a funeral song?"

"Nothing special. When someone dies, everyone gathers and sings whatever comes into their heads. It's the same the whole world over. That's all."

[*When they reach the palace, Rāvaṇa speaks*:]

"What's all this crying about? I sent you to find out about my son, and you come back singing a funeral song."

"Sangadi's only son died just three days after receiving his college degree."

"Too bad, but it will pass. But what about my son?"

"Your son?"

"Yes! He went to war!"

"Oh, that. It's like this—"

"You mean he defeated his enemies, right?"

"No. It's just that—"

"What? He went to heaven?"

"Maharaja, Rāvaṇa, listen: your son has been killed by Lakṣmaṇa."

"No! Not him, too! [*Rāvaṇa moves toward Indrajit's body and cries out.*] This cannot be! Not long ago you seized Indra's throne as if it were a mere plaything, and fragrant garlands wreathed your body that now lies beheaded, to be eaten by vultures and dogs. Simply because I loved that woman Sītā, today I must perform for you the funeral rites that one day you should have performed for me.

"When you were a baby, I watched you grow stronger day by day, like the waxing moon. Every day I prayed hard that I would see you defeat the gods, but now I see only your headless body. We all must die some day, I know, but must it be this horrible? I remember, too, the games we played when you were a baby, and I still hear the jingle of silver bells on your tiny feet. One day you caught two lion cubs and tumbled with them in the grass while I watched and laughed. At night I used to hold you on my lap and feed you soft rice until the moon rose; I pointed to it and sang, 'Come down, little moon, come down and play with my little boy.' And you, when you saw that rabbit in the moon, you jumped up and down, trying to catch it! But, oh, my son, what pleasures can now be mine?"

[*After prayers to Śiva, Rāvaṇa and his wife bathe Indrajit's body and prepare it for cremation. Then Rāvaṇa shouts*:]

"I can't stand it anymore! I've lost my brothers and my sons, and it's she, it's Sītā, who's to blame. With one swing of this sword I'll cut her in two! [*He rushes toward the Ashoka grove and meets Mahōdara, his Prime Minister.*] Out of my way, step aside."

"What is your destination, Rāvaṇa?"

"Out of my way!"

"I am your Prime Minister and deserve to know your plans, sir."

"I'm going to the Ashoka grove."

"Going to talk with Sītā?"

"Not exactly."

"Then?"

"Did you know that Indrajit is dead?"

"No."

"Well, you know it now. All my brothers and sons are dead, and Rāma's wife has caused it all. She deserves to die. Out of my way!"

"Rāvaṇa, you are respected as a great raja and a brave warrior. Why bring disgrace upon yourself by killing an innocent woman?"

"Disgrace?"

"If you take up your sword in anger and kill a woman known for her purity, everyone will mock you. Śiva, Viṣṇu, and Brahmā, from whom you descend, will clap their hands and laugh: 'That Rāvaṇa is truly great! He kills innocent women!' "

"You are right . . . you are right. It would be wrong."

"Besides you have another duty."

"To go to battle."

"Yes, against Rāma, not Sītā. Think: If you kill Sītā and then defeat Rāma—and in this second battle you will be victorious—when you return to the throne, your love for her will torment you."

"Hmmm."

"You will live with her memory, but she won't be there. Without brothers, without sons, and without Sītā, suicide might be your only course. Therefore, first go to war against Rāma."

"What you say is correct, but there's a problem."

"What?"

"You, me, Māliyavān̲, and the messengers are the only ones left. Everyone else has died in battle."

[*Mahōdara reminds Rāvaṇa that a ferocious horde of demons, once attached to Kumbhakarṇa, live in the netherworld. They are summoned and advance to Lanka, creating a huge dust storm that blackens the sky. Having reached the palace, they address Rāvaṇa*:][12]

"Brother of Śūrpaṇakhā, Kumbhakarṇa, and Vibhīṣaṇa, master of the Sāma Veda, shaker of Mt. Kailasa, Conqueror of the Cosmic Elephants, Daśagrīva, we bow our humble heads at your lotus feet. Why have you called us here?"

"I've called you to help me accomplish a task. Two princes of the solar dynasty, Rāma and Lakṣmaṇa, and Rāma's wife, Sītā, built a hut in the forest at Pancavati. When my sister, Śūrpaṇakhā, passed the spot and saw Sītā's beauty, she attempted to bring her to Lanka as my wife, but Rāma's brother Lakṣmaṇa cut off her nose and breasts. When, in blood and tears, she told me this story, I resolved to avenge her humiliation. And so, with Mārīca's help, I went myself to Pancavati and brought Sītā back to Lanka."

[*Vaṉṉi, leader of the new armies*] "And you've invited us here for your marriage to Sītā?"

"No . . . we're not . . . married yet. I mean, certain circumstances have arisen . . ."

"Circumstances?"

"The trouble began when Hanumān, son of the Wind God, entered Lanka and found Sītā. He left, but not before he killed my son Akṣakumāraṉ and thousands of demons and set fire to the city. Then Rāma and his monkey armies set siege to the city, and the battles began. I lost the first battle and, then, one by one, I lost my brother Kumbhakarṇa and my sons Atikāyaṉ and Indrajit—all killed in battle. That is why I have called you: to face my enemies in battle tomorrow."

"Is that all?"

"What do you mean 'all'?"

"We thought you had summoned us to lift up the earth, or to pulverize the Seven Mountains, or to drink up the Seven Seas. And now you tell us it's only to fight a couple of humans and a troop of monkeys!"

"Do not dismiss lightly these humans and monkeys."

[*Māliyavāṉ*] "Wisely spoken. Rāvaṇa had the same attitude when Rāma and his army first set siege to Lanka. Besides, those puny humans, as you call them, vanquished Vāli."

"Vāli? Really?"

"And they killed your leader, Kumbhakarṇa."

"*They* killed Kumbhakarṇa?"

"Yes. As for the monkeys, one named Hanumān leaps over oceans, sets cities on fire, and makes widows by the thousands."

"I see. It's not a marriage we've been invited to—it's a real war!"

[*In the morning, after a* nāṭakam *of celestial dancers, Rāvaṇa and Vaṉṉi lead their armies to the battlefield; Indra, watching from above, addresses the gods*:]

"Look, Rāvaṇa and his armies have massed for another attack. They have a thousand divisions, but Rāma only—"

"Do not worry, Indra, even a million demons cannot kill Rāma."

"I know you are right. Still, let us chant for his victory as we watch the battle."

[*While the gods chant 'Victory to Rāma,' the limitless demon army takes the field. Seeing them, Jāmbuvāṉ loses heart and leads the monkeys in flight, but Rāma sends Aṅgada to stop them.*]

"Halt! Halt!"

"Aṅgada, come on, we're running for our lives. What can our seventy divisions do against their thousand? We'd only make a meal for them! I'm not ready to die yet."

"Jāmbuvāṉ! Don't say that. Once, at my father's death, you spoke brave words and now you talk of retreat!"

"You're a young boy, Aṅgada, and cannot understand what these demons can do in battle. Rāvaṇa has hordes, and this time Rāma will not defeat him."

"But, surely Lakṣmaṇa, Hanumān, and Sugrīva—"

"Don't be naive. Do you think we are anything more than bodyguards to them? Did anyone protect my son, Vacantaṉ, when Kumbhakarṇa mauled him? And no one will stop the pain when you die, either. Better to escape into the forest and drink pure water and eat fresh fruits. Let Rāma win or lose; what's it to us anyway? Why should we die for them?"

"Jāmbuvāṉ, do you think—"

"Listen, you just mentioned that I spoke to you at your father's death. What do you know of death if you've only seen one?"

"Well, what do *you* know of death?"

"Boy, I've seen death since the day I was born, since the third day of this era. Māli and Māliyavāṉ, Kāla Nēmi and Hiraṇya, Madhu and Kaitabha—where are they all now?"

"Sure, sure, Jāmbuvāṉ, but who killed Madhu and Kaitabha?"

"What?"

"Who killed Madhu and Kaitabha?"

"Er . . . Viṣṇu."

"And who killed Hiraṇya?"

"It was Viṣṇu . . . in his man-lion avatar."

"And who is going to kill these demons who face us now?"

"It will be Rāma . . . as Viṣṇu's avatar. I see what you mean, Aṅgada. But how can I face Rāma after this disgraceful retreat?"

"Don't worry, I'll make sure that Rāma knows nothing."[13]

[*Amid loud war drums and furious fighting, Rāvaṇa hurls a spear at Vibhīṣaṇa, but Lakṣmaṇa steps in front and receives it in his chest. Hanumān, sent again by Vibhīṣaṇa, brings medicinal herbs and revives the lifeless Lakṣmaṇa; Rāvaṇa's armies are annihilated.*[14] *From his palace tower Rāvaṇa sees the massive destruction and prepares to fight Rāma. As he mounts his chariot, he speaks to Maṇḍōdari, Mahōdara, and his private troops:*]

"This will be the final battle. From tomorrow, either Sītā or Maṇḍōdari will live as a widow. You soldiers who remain alive, fight beside me against Rāma."

[*As the war drums roll below, Śiva speaks to Indra:*]

"Rāvaṇa has finally ridden out to battle against Rāma in his flower-chariot. But, look, Rāma is on foot! Send him your chariot, Indra."

[*Indra sends his chariot to Rāma, who mounts it and arrives on the battlefield; Mahōdara enters first and Rāma kills him with many arrows, each severing a separate part of his body.*[15] *Suddenly a strange cry startles Rāma.*]

"Who are you?"

"I'm an umbrella holder."

"I can see that! What are you doing on this battlefield?"

"Look. You have killed everyone in sight. All that remains is Rāvaṇa himself."

"So?"

"When he comes to battle, you'll kill him, too."

"I will."

"Before you . . . er . . . do away with him, can you give me some lib'ation?"

"You're thirsty?"

"No. I want you to fight me so I can get lib'ation."

"You mean you want me to kill you and grant you 'liberation'?"

"Yes, but first I would like your blessings."

"What do you wish for?"

"Well, in this life I've had to scrape by, so in the next birth I want to be rich. Second, my body looks like a shrunken gourd, so next time I want to be handsome 'cause then women will wink at me instead of spitting betel juice in my direction."

"Wealth and beauty—what else does one need? Meditate on my name and they are yours. Now you must die."

[*Rāma raises his sword, but the umbrella holder cringes*:]

"Oooooouch!"

"You shouldn't fear death."

"I know, but I do . . . just a little."

[*Rāma kills him. The war drums announce Rāvaṇa's entrance on the battlefield.*]

"Prepare to meet your death, Rāma.

Listen here, human!
Do not think Rāvaṇa will lose this battle!
Fierce arrows will bathe your body in blood
And Yama will come for you today!"

[*Rāma responds*:][16]

"Compassion spared you in the first battle,
But don't count on that today, Mr. Rāvaṇa.
I offer your head as a gift to the gods.
Look quickly, behold my war dance!"

"Listen, Rāma. . . .

Down in Patala, in the skies, in Lanka,
On middle earth, on Wheel Mountain, upon Mt. Meru,
My flower-chariot flies, and you, poor human,
Cannot conquer my victory flag.

"Rāma! Look above you. Gods and humans have gathered to watch our majestic battle. You in Indra's chariot and I in my flower-chariot, we will fight on earth, in the netherworlds, and in the heavens—over the full length and breadth of the worlds. Let no one say this was an ordinary battle."

"Fly where you wish, Rāvaṇa. Choose the spot for your death."

"On earth!"

[*They battle everywhere, but as neither Rāma nor Rāvaṇa is able to gain an advantage, Rāvaṇa turns to his priest.*]

"Súkra, this Rāma seems invincible. Is there no way to defeat him?"

"Go to Patala Lanka, raise a sacrificial fire, and from it you will receive a special bow and arrow with which you can kill Rāma."

[*With Maṇḍōdari's help, Rāvaṇa chants mantras and raises a fire. Unable to find Rāvaṇa, Rāma is confused and complains to Vibhīṣaṇa, who finds Rāvaṇa raising the fire, assumes the form of a bee and stings the fire, a bad omen which Rāvaṇa curses. Vibhīṣaṇa resumes his normal form and reports to Rāma*:]

"Act quickly, Rāma! Rāvaṇa is building a huge fire in the netherworld to gain new weapons. Destroy that fire immediately!"

"Go, Vibhīṣaṇa, destroy the sacrifice! And if you fail, drag Rāvaṇa's wife by the hair to the sacrifice for that will surely disturb his concentration and his sacrifice."

[*On Rāma's orders, Vibhīṣaṇa flies on Hanumān's back, battles the demons, and scatters the fire.*[17] *Then Maṇḍōdari addresses Rāvaṇa*:]

"The sacrifice has been destroyed! Now I'll have to light a fire for your funeral!"

"No, Maṇḍōdari. Do not worry; no one can kill me, and my only sorrow is that I will outlive you."

[*On the battlefield, Rāma and Rāvaṇa counter each other's weapons until, finally, Rāma is able to cut off Rāvaṇa's heads and arms but not kill him. Rāma then speaks to a sage*:]

"Agastya, each time I sever one of Rāvaṇa's heads, another grows in its place."

"Pray to the Sun God and he will reveal a secret."

[*Rāma sings and Sūrya appears.*]

"Sūrya, is there no way to kill Rāvaṇa?"

"Rāma, listen carefully. Rāvaṇa's strength lies in a pot of ambrosia hidden in the left side of his chest. If you destroy it with your Brahmā-weapon, he will die and you will be absolved of the sin of killing a Brahmin."[18]

[*Rāma shoots his Brahmā-weapon, which pierces Rāvaṇa's chest and destroys the pot of ambrosia.*]

"Now I'll cut off nine of his heads. Done! And with this final arrow I'll sever his tenth and final head!"

[*When Rāma cuts off his last head, Rāvaṇa slowly chants a verse in praise of Rāma*:]

"Gōvinda! All-Knowing Viṣṇu! Rāmachandra! In my final moments, grant me your blessings."

"Whatever you wish, Rāvaṇa."

"You are destined to destroy me in three incarnations. In your man-lion incarnation you killed me as Hiraṇya, and now in your human form you kill me as Rāvaṇa. In your next incarnation, I ask that you kill me and take me to heaven with you.[19] Show compassion and grant me this request."

"Granted."

"My second request is that you show me your cosmic form."

"Granted, but first you must cover your eyes to protect them."

[*Rāma reveals his absolute form; Rāvaṇa chants Rāma's names and then speaks*:]

"Rāma, kill me as I meditate on your cosmic form."

"Gods, I, Rāma, now kill Rāvaṇa!"

[*An arrow is placed through the Rāvaṇa puppet, which is then splashed with red dye and left dangling from the cloth screen while the gods sing*:]

"'Rāma, Rāma' in my heart
 'Rāma, Rāma,' in my deepest dreams
'Rāma, Hari-Rāma,'
 I call out every day
When fear strikes
 or life is cruel,
I simply call your name,
 'Rāma, Hari-Rāma.'"

[*Vibhīṣaṇa tells Rāma that the monkeys are mutilating Rāvaṇa's corpse and that he cannot bear to watch. Rāma orders the monkeys to desist, and they answer*:]

"But, Rāma, he's evil."

"No longer. Leave him and let Vibhīṣaṇa perform the last rites for his brother."

[*Vibhīṣaṇa approaches Rāvaṇa's body and is overcome with grief*:]

"Poison does not kill if not swallowed,
 yet the fatal poison called Sītā
Struck you dead when you looked at her;
Destroyer of kings, Yama to gods,

mighty brother, dead on the field,
What do you think now of my words
that once you scorned?"[20]

[*Maṇḍōdari comes to her husband's body and wails:*]

"When Rāma's arrows ravaged and covered from head to toe
Your splendid body that shook Mt. Kailasa and white-flowered Śiva,
Did they enter looking for your life force?
Or for that secret chamber where you hid love
for sweet-haired Sītā?"[21]

[*Fireworks celebrate Rāvaṇa's death outside the drama-house.*]

[*Vibhīṣaṇa*] "Maṇḍōdari, grief is useless now. Our duty is to cremate his body properly."

"Yes. I will bathe, put on new white clothes, and prepare to burn with him on the pyre."

[*The fire lit, Maṇḍōdari burns with Rāvaṇa. Rāma then orders Lakṣmaṇa to conduct the coronation of Vibhīṣaṇa as Raja of Lanka. After circumambulating Vibhīṣaṇa, Lakṣmaṇa places the crown on his head. Rāma speaks:*]

"Vibhīṣaṇa, you must rule Lanka justly. Hanumān, bring Sītā here."

"And here we end the story for tonight. Tomorrow, come to Ayodhya and watch the coronation of Rāma!"

[*On the final night of performance, the Brahmin puppets speak:*]

"Last night we told of the great battle, the Rāma-Rāvaṇa battle, fought in the Three Worlds and eight directions. In Lanka, with Rāvaṇa dead and Vibhīṣaṇa crowned Raja of the city, Hanumān sang to Sītā."

"Good news, Sītā, good news! Rāma has killed that giant Rāvaṇa! Your perseverance, your endurance in this prison, is rewarded and your long, beautiful black hair may now join with Rāma. Like Síva and Pārvatī, like Atri and Anasūyā, Satyavān̲ and Sāvitrī, Hariścandra and Candramatī, you and Rāma will live united. By Rāma's order, Vibhīṣaṇa has been crowned Raja of Lanka, with Nīlan̲, Sampāti, and An̲n̲al as his ministers. Vibhīṣaṇa will rule justly because he is not touched with hate, and he will treat the descendants of Rāvaṇa as his own. All the soldiers have been killed—"

"But, Hanumān, their widows . . . what of them?"

"Vibhīṣaṇa will see to their welfare. Sītā, why are you silent? You are like a mother to me. Speak."

"Hanumān, you see—"

"What? Tell me, what is wrong? Do you think me an imposter? I am the same Hanumān who came to you in the Ashoka grove and predicted that Rāma would rescue you within a month. Rise up, Sītā, and come with me to Rāma."

"Hanumān, you are a true friend, and I remain silent not for the reasons that you imagine. You alone know what I suffered in Rāvaṇa's prison; abused, tormented, with no word from Rāma, I decided to kill myself . . . once I tied a vine to a tree . . . and at that moment you appeared. When you left, I vowed that I would kill myself if Rāma did not come within thirty days, and now you are here with this news! What does one say to a person who has twice saved one's life? I know no words and that is why I cannot speak. Even if I gave the earth, heaven, and the underworld, they would not suffice because everything in those Three Worlds is mutable, whereas you are eternal. So I have decided merely to bow my head at your feet; at least the respect you receive from me will never perish."[22]

"No, Sītā, do not bow to me. You are a goddess, a holy mother to me. Please respect my feelings. If you must offer something, give me a boon. That will be enough."

"Ask for anything you wish."

"There is only one boon that I could possibly desire—that you and Rāma will live together forever. I will be content to serve you, to bring you flowers, and keep you cool, like a deep pool of water."

"If that is your wish, it is granted."

[*Meanwhile Rāma addresses Vibhīṣaṇa*:]

> "Hanumān delays, Ruler of Lanka!
> Go to Sītā and console her
> And bring her here in full beauty
> That she may dazzle my eyes![23]

"Where is Hanumān? I told him to bring Sītā and still he has not returned. Vibhīṣaṇa, bring her dressed in jewels and a sari, as if she were entering the marriage hall."

[*Vibhīṣaṇa turns to face Sītā and Hanumān.*]

"Sītā, your fidelity has been rewarded. Rāma has entered Lanka, destroyed Rāvaṇa, and set you free. Your husband wishes to see you; even the gods are waiting to receive you. Take off your prison clothes, and dress in your finest sari and jewels so that they will be pleased."

"Vibhīṣaṇa, you are Rāma's messenger and I do not wish to oppose you or my husband. But consider this: everyone knows that I have been separated from Rāma for a year, imprisoned in Rāvaṇa's palace. What would those gods, sages, and royal women think if they see me appear in my wedding jewels? 'Where did she get them? She's looking pretty!' they will sneer. No, I will remain as I am, for if a woman is separated from her husband, she should remain in rags until she is reunited with him. To do otherwise would invite unkind suspicions about my conduct. Certainly, you do not wish to encourage that, and I doubt that it would give Rāma pleasure, either."

"Sītā! Sītā! There is no need for concern on that issue. No one doubts your fidelity to Rāma. We all know that since the day you were separated in Pancavati, you have refused clothes, food, even water. You are the very model of truthfulness, who never so much as thought of another man while separated from your husband. Wearing fine clothes will not tarnish your reputation. Go now and change, to please Rāma."

"Vibhīṣaṇa, I will accept your word as I would accept Hanumān's. Although I feel it is not proper to put on royal clothes before actually seeing Rāma, I will change and join you." [*She turns to Hanumān.*] Why are you silent? Is something wrong?"

"No—"

"Then lead me to Rāma."

[*A seated Sītā puppet, representing her imprisonment, is replaced by a standing Sītā puppet; all puppets turn to face Rāma, and Sītā speaks*:]

"Rāma, I bow to you as my husband, as protector of all living creatures. We are only 'bodies,' and you guide us through this sea of suffering called life. Do you know, can you possibly imagine, how I longed for you? Only yesterday, I had given up all hope of ever seeing you again, and now you are here. We must resume our married life. I swear to you, Rāma, that I have been faithful to you in mind, deed, and speech. If I have ever committed a minor oversight, a child's forgetfulness, you must forgive me. For one year I suffered in Rāvaṇa's captivity—even Hanumān cannot tell you all I suffered."

"I see no signs of suffering, Sītā. The only change is that your conduct has suffered."

"Rāma, what are you saying? If you reject me now, I—"

"You know very well that a woman separated from her husband must not wear new clothes or jewelry, nor loosen her hair, nor enjoy good food or drink. But I see no evidence of such deprivation in you. If you had fasted for this year, like ascetics who uphold virtue, you would be weak, emaciated. But, no, you are round and healthy. And look at your clothes! Those jewels!"

"Rāma, when Vibhīṣaṇa came to lead me here, I was not wearing these clothes. Since the day I was captured by Rāvaṇa, I did not change my clothes or wear jewelry, but Vibhīṣaṇa said you desired to see me in fine clothes. Inside I said 'No,' but Vibhīṣaṇa insisted that it was your order. I have preserved my fidelity, as a gift I would offer you when you rescued me. Accept me now as your wife."

"How can I after you've been in Rāvaṇa's palace? Obviously you enjoyed yourself in his court, and now that he is dead you ask me to take you back! And you say that this is what I 'desired'? A demon's wife?"

"Rāma! Believe me! I wore no other clothes until Vibhīṣaṇa ordered me to change into these. Then the maidservants continued to fasten on more jewels; I said, 'No more,' but they insisted that it would please you. I did fast in Lanka; my only subsistence was your name, which I chanted and meditated upon every day. Just as the sages in the forest grow healthy in the fiercest austerities, I, too, grew strong meditating on your name. Examine my body, if you wish; you will find no trace of food."

"Do not fall at my feet and cry that I should accept you. Cry only that your Rāvaṇa is dead!"

"How can you call me a courtesan! If you believe that, you must leave me since you know the custom that a man should enter the forest when he renounces his wife. Yes, you've done your duty—killed Rāvaṇa and crowned Vibhīṣaṇa—so what keeps you here in Lanka? Leave me and go into the forest as a wandering ascetic. Otherwise, why did you send for me?"

"Why? Listen.

> I crossed seas, overcame fierce enemies,
> Destroyed demons with lightning-fast weapons,
> And came to Lanka not to rescue you,
> But to rescue my own honor.[24]

"I did not come to Lanka to rescue you; Rāvaṇa stole my wife, and I came here to remove that disgrace from my name. The demons are destroyed and my honor restored. Now—"

"What! You came here to restore *your* honor? Killed Rāvaṇa so that you would remove the stain on *your* name?"

"I came here to exonerate myself."

"Wait! Who ordered Vibhīṣaṇa to bring me back dressed in fine clothes? Am I wrong to have considered him your emissary? Should he have disobeyed your command and not told me to change?"

"You repeat your claim that Vibhīṣaṇa made you change your clothes, but if a woman is touched by another man, if her chastity is compromised, any good woman would first ask forgiveness from her husband. Not you. From the beginning you have professed your innocence. As for what Vibhīṣaṇa said, will you obey whatever words escape from his lips? 'Will the planets stop just because Parameśvara [Śiva] says "Stop"?' One's sense of decency should guide one's actions. Yours has not. Therefore, either ask forgiveness or be gone!"

"Rāma! I am innocent! I have done nothing wrong. All my long and painful sacrifice in Lanka, unlike that of an ascetic, bears no fruit. How can you, who are learned and compassionate, order me to leave?"

"Who can understand women? Gods see into all things as clearly as they see into a *nelli* fruit, but they cannot penetrate a woman's mind.[25] Brahmā does not understand Sarasvatī; Viṣṇu lies in Lakṣmī's arms but does not comprehend her; even Śiva, who is himself half-woman, cannot make sense of Pārvatī."

"How can you speak like this, Rāma?

> The whole world knows my chastity,
> Even Brahmā cannot sway my woman's mind,
> But if you who protect us all refuse me,
> Can any god change your mind?[26]

"Look closely at me, at my actions, Rāma. There is only fidelity, nothing more. But if you will not believe me, there is one thing left for me to do. Lakṣmaṇa, gather wood for a fire."

[*Lakṣmaṇa turns to Rāma for permission, but Rāma is silent. Lakṣmaṇa stacks the wood, and Sītā invokes the Fire God as the puppeteers perform a small* pūjā *behind the screen*:]

"Come, Agni! Come to me! Long ago in Mithila, after Rāma broke my father's bow, I invoked you as a witness to my pledge never to leave my husband. Now, once again, I call on you to bear witness: If I have ever been unfaithful to my husband, in word, thought, or deed, then burn me with your flames. If I am innocent, return me to Rāma."

[*Chanting Rāma's name, Sītā leaps into the flames, and Agni speaks*:]

"Her fire is too hot! Sītā's chastity is burning me. Sītā, return to Rāma."

[*Rāma*] "What is this? One woman jumps into the flames, and another emerges unharmed? Who are you?"

"No, Rāma, I'm not a woman. I am Agni and she is your wife. When she entered my flames, she scorched me with her truth. She has done you no wrong.

> In mind, word, and body she knew only you;
> But do you harbor base thoughts,
> Or are you wise, Rāma?
> Accept her and end her long suffering."

"Because you, Agni, vouch for her, I will accept Sītā as my wife."

[*Sītā stands behind Rāma while the gods appear overhead and address Rāma*:]

"Rāma, have you forgotten that you are the avatar of Nārāyaṇa, the protector of dharma on earth, and that Sītā is Lakṣmī? How can you imagine that she would err? Look, above you. It's Daśaratha in his celestial form."

[*Rāma bows to his father, who speaks*:]

"The past is over, Son, and you must prepare for your coronation. Rāma, how I longed to see you. That fear—that I would never see you again—is what killed me. When I heard the words that sent you into exile and made Bharata king, they pierced my chest like sharp spears. Only now, by embracing you, have they been removed. Take this crown that I have brought from Brahmā's heaven. Take it and rule Ayodhya!"

"Father, I know full well how you suffered in granting those boons, and now I will return to Ayodhya for my coronation."

"Rāma, I offer you two boons."

"These are my requests:

> You gave boons to mother and brother,
> Then renounced them as unworthy 'wife' and 'son';
> I ask that you, my father,
> Return 'mother' and 'brother' to me."[27]

"Rāma, I only renounced Kaikeyī and Bharata because I thought they had wronged you. But I was mistaken; neither acted against you. Oh, the story of those treacherous boons began even before I offered them to Kaikeyī on the battlefield. [*His puppet moves upward and is removed.*][28]

[*Rāma*] "Vibhīṣaṇa, we must now prepare to leave for Ayodhya. But how? Is there some vehicle we can use?"

"Yes, Rāma. We will use Rāvaṇa's flower-chariot."

[*Lakṣmaṇa, Sītā, Vibhīṣaṇa, and Rāma settle in the chariot. In an abrupt shift, all the puppets turn from facing left, toward Lanka, and face right, toward Ayodhya.*]

"What's that, Vibhīṣaṇa?"

"Rāvaṇa's tower, where he slept before a battle. If you want it, we can rip it up and take it with us."

"No. I don't need it."

[*Jāmbuvāṉ enters and cries out:*][29]

> "I saw Māli and Māliyavāṉ,
> I saw Kāla Nēmi and Hiraṇya,
> But never have I seen
> A person revoke a gift he gave!"[30]

"Oh, I see what you mean, Jāmbuvāṉ. Vibhīṣaṇa, do you grant me permission to use Rāvaṇa's chariot?"

"Yes."

"Now, are we ready to depart?"

"Rāma, do not leave us monkeys behind. We also want to see your coronation in Ayodhya."

"All right. Climb aboard."

"Rāma, I will not set foot in that chariot."

"Jāmbuvāṉ! Why not?"

"I want to see my son, Vacantaṉ, who led the troops against Kumbhakarṇa and was killed. I will not leave without him."

"I understand. Lakṣmaṇa, write a message to Yama asking him to revive Vacantaṉ and his two regiments of soldiers."

[*Hanumān takes the message to Yama, who sends him to Brahmā's heaven, whence he is sent to Viṣṇu's heaven, where he retrieves the soul but not the body of Vacantaṉ. Finally, Brahmā recreates Vacantaṉ from his soul, and Hanumān leads him back to Rāma. With no further reason for delay, Rāma, Sītā, Lakṣmaṇa, Hanumān, and all the monkeys depart for Ayodhya in the chariot. Sītā speaks*:]

"Rāma, you came all the way from Pancavati to Lanka on foot; show me what happened along the way."

[*Rāma points out various landmarks of his journey to Lanka, until Sītā says*:][31]

"Tell me about this place, from which you built the bridge."[32]

"It's called Rāma's Lord [Ramesvaram] and it purifies all sins. As you know, one will suffer in hell for any of thirty thousand crimes; and if you commit one of the five heinous sins[33]—murdering a Brahmin, a cow, your guru, wife, or parents—then you never leave hell. However, if you bathe in the holy waters of Ramesvaram, even these terrible sins, even killing a parent, will be absolved. Everything—including the greatest sin of refusing food to mendicants when you hide behind closed doors and eat sumptuously—even that unforgivable sin will be washed away in these waters."

"Is there no sin that cannot be absolved there?"

"There is: ingratitude. All else will vanish, like dew drops before the sun, but not repaying a kindness done on your behalf—that's never excused. As the proverb says: 'To forget a small kindness is not a small error.' And now we need to build a Śiva temple here at Ramesvaram. Hanumān, go to Kaci and bring back a Śiva lingam."

[*When Hanumān does not return, Rāma grows impatient and orders Sītā to form a lingam from the sand, but just as Sītā completes her lingam, Hanumān appears with his.*]

"Hanumān . . . you were a little late, so Sītā has made a lingam with her own hands. We have just consecrated it, infusing it with life. This lingam might curse yours, so we must separate them. Curl your tail around ours, and move it over there."

[*Hanumān*] "Ugh! I can't budge it. Not an inch!"

"Leave it where it is. All who come here to Ramesvaram will worship your lingam first, and afterwards, this Rāma lingam. If anyone worships the Rāma lingam before your Śiva lingam, then their sins will not be absolved by bathing here. Now, we must continue our journey back to Ayodhya."

[*Flying in the chariot, Rāma points out landmarks of their adventures in exile, and Sītā recalls that Bharadwaj invited them to visit his ashram on their return, but Rāma recalls something else*:]

"Remember also what Bharata swore on the day we left him fourteen years ago: 'If you do not return by sunrise on the first day of the fifteenth year, I will immolate myself.' Hanumān, go quickly and tell Bharata that we are here in Bharadwaj's ashram."

[*Scene switches to Bharata and Śatrughna on the outskirts of Ayodhya, where they have lived in semi-exile since Rāma left.*]

[*Bharata*] "Śatrughna, Rāma has not yet returned and time is running out! We must determine the exact time; consult the Brahmins."

"They say it's exactly two hours until sunrise."[34]

"And still Rāma is not here. I gave my word to Rāma and I will keep it. Prepare the fire pit immediately."

"But Bharata! Let me talk with Kausalyā first."

[*Kausalyā arrives and speaks*:]

"Bharata—"

"I gave my promise to Rāma and I intend to fulfill it. That is all."

"Bharata, there may be a million Rāmas, but you are incomparable. Your death would leave the world without compassion. If Rāma does not come tonight, he will come tomorrow. Do not throw away your life uselessly."

"Mother, even you cannot sweep away my vow to Rāma. I have said that I will die on the first morning of the fifteenth year, and that time has come."

"Bharata, listen to me—"

"No. Śatrughna, is the fire ready?"

"Ready."

"Rāma, Rāma, Rāma—"

[*As Bharata jumps into the flames, Hanumān arrives disguised as a Brahmin and speaks*:]

"Stop! Stop! Rāma has come! He and Lakṣmaṇa are at Bharadwaj's ashram. Your death would have accomplished nothing. There! I've put out the fire."

"But who are you?"

"Hanumān, son of Vāyu and emissary of Rāma. [*Brahmin puppet removed; Hanumān puppet pinned up*] Here is Rāma's signet ring."

"His ring? Then, I accept you."

"Come, let's all go to greet Rāma. Climb in this chariot; later I'll tell you the long story of what happened." [*They fly back to Rāma.*]

"Rāma! Greetings to you, brother."

"Bharata, tell me about Ayodhya. How is everyone?"

"Since the day you left, Rāma, I have been engaged in austerities. You must ask Sumantra about the affairs of state since they were left to him."

"Tell us, Sumantra. What has transpired during these fourteen years?"

"Rāma, . . .

> Like women desiring ornaments of gold
> Like grain aching for fresh rain,
> Like mothers longing for their first son
> We waited and waited, for you.[35]

"This verse, better than anything I might say, describes Ayodhya since your departure; we have done nothing but think of your return: 'Is it today that he comes? Tomorrow?' No other words have been spoken in Ayodhya for fourteen years."

[*Bharata*] "Rāma, we must prepare for your coronation. First bathe in the Sarayu river, then take off that forest bark and put on your royal dress. The rest of you, decorate the palace. We need flower garlands everywhere! Hang them from every corner and every roof. Prepare the temple! Invite the fifty-six rajas!"

[*Conch shells sound, cymbals ring, and drums boom, as the puppeteers chant loudly*:]

"Rāma is Raja of Ayodhya!"

The Limits of Restoration

Rāvaṇa is dead, Rāma reigns, and the epic struggle is resolved, but behind the finality and tranquility of Rāma's coronation lie the tensions that this book has traced through the now completed series of overnight performances inside the drama-house. Discussing those tensions in the preceding chapters has led me to identify several distinct features of the puppet play and its adaptation of the *Kamparāmāyaṇam*. Let me summarize those findings as background before extending the analysis in this concluding chapter.

1. The Tamil Rāmāyaṇa composed by Kampa<u>n</u> (twelfth century?) in the Chola country was transmitted to the Palghat region of Kerala by Tamil weavers and merchants in the fifteenth or sixteenth century and was adapted by those groups to the art of shadow puppetry sometime before the mid-eighteenth century. Both the *Kamparāmāyaṇam* and the Rāma story told by the puppeteers are composite texts borrowed from diverse sources.
2. The linguistic and cultural admixture of the Kerala puppet play (Tamil text in a Malayali temple festival performed [primarily] by Tamils for Malayali patrons in a Tamil-Malayalam hybrid) is inseparable from the history of the Palghat region as a borderland and a nexus for trade.
3. The puppet play relies heavily on the *Kamparāmāyaṇam*: 70 percent of the verses are chanted verbatim with printed editions of that text or vary by no more than two words.
4. The puppet play, however, recontextualizes Kampa<u>n</u>. The puppeteers sing Kampa<u>n</u>'s composition in a context in which Rāma is not worshiped, demonstrating that a Rāma story is not the same as Rāma bhakti. The general principle of adaptation is additive; rather than rewrite Kampa<u>n</u>'s poem, the puppet play reorients it through innovations ("Song of the Drama-house," Brahmin narrators, *nāṭakam*, conversations, oral commentary, auxiliary stories, folk verses, altered Kampa<u>n</u> verses).

5. Narrative change is one major technique by which the puppeteers adapt the medieval epic to its new context: through limited but strategic alterations in content, bhakti ideals of isolation and perfection are tempered by folk principles of relation and balance; in particular, the puppet play narrows the moral distance between Rāma and the demons.
6. The puppeteers also recontextualize Kampa<u>n</u>'s poem through oral commentary and conversations. In their commentary the puppeteers reach beyond Kampa<u>n</u>'s text and tell stories from the wider Rāma tradition; through a set of four conversations, which comprise the whole of performance, the puppeteers weaken the voice of the poet and speak in their own voice.
7. These conversations create internal listeners, inside the text and inside the drama-house. The absent (external) audience is a consequence of several factors: the medium of shadow puppetry, a removed stage, difficult language, slow commentary, verbal (rather than visual) orientation, and the ritual role of performance.
8. Finally, however, the puppet play's adaptation of Kampa<u>n</u> is an accommodation. Rather than reject the bhakti ideals of Kampa<u>n</u>'s epic, the puppet play complicates them with a folk morality, and the result is a Rāma story more complex than either Kampa<u>n</u> or any single folk text.

Two of these conclusions are the core of the puppeteers' recontextualization of the *Kamparāmāyaṇam* in Kerala: the narrative and moral shift (5); and the commentary and conversations (6). These two primary means of adaptation—changes in content and changes of speaker—work together, especially in the countervailing voices of the puppet play. Skeptical, angry, comic—these are the voices that we heard when Śūrpaṇakhā mourned her son and when Vāli rebuked Rāma, and we hear them again during the coronation of Rāma when they deflate epic intent and tilt the story toward the ethical balance sought in those earlier episodes. These countervoices also complete the analysis of vocalization begun in the previous chapter for they speak in sharp opposition to the received text. Critical words are heard in Kampa<u>n</u>, too, but the puppet play amplifies them and creates new characters to express them, especially on the two final nights translated in this chapter when the puppet play tests the limits of Rāma's triumphant return to Ayodhya.

At the outset, we must understand both that Kampan̠'s conclusion is a restoration and that it is only one of three typical conclusions to a Rāma story. Folktales and songs, for example, often omit more than half of what is considered the plot and close with the marriage of Rāma and Sītā; auspicious and joyful, this first typical conclusion is not clouded by later events in the forest and in Lanka. Longer, "epic" texts of the Rāma story, like other epics in India, however, seldom settle for such a simple resolution and instead drive into tangled allegiances and dilemmas to reach, despite the temporary solutions achieved by victory and revenge, an uncertain end. In many oral epics, for example, the hero fades away, as a holy man or as a warrior lifted to heaven, and some go out of their way to deny the hero a marriage (conclusion 1) by dragging him from the wedding pavilion to the battlefield, where he will die.[36] Tragedy and ambiguity, the hallmarks of this second conclusion to Rāma texts, take the story far beyond the exile and into the Uttara Kāṇḍa, where Sītā is banished and finally received into the earth while Rāma ascends to heaven. A third conclusion, midway between the felicitous marriage and the fadeaway Uttara Kāṇḍa, is Rāma's coronation (*paṭṭābiṣēkam*) at Ayodhya, and this is the ending in many bhakti texts, including Kampan̠.[37] That event, occurring long after the marriage but before the final separation of Sītā from Rāma, is both auspicious and ambiguous: bhakti theology demands more than marriage—the avatar of Viṣṇu must confront evil and lust, and subdue them—but can Rāma remain untouched by that contact?

In the *Kamparāmāyaṇam*, Rāma's coronation is a triumphant restoration, a culmination of recuperative events set in motion by Rāma's conquest of Rāvaṇa. As I said earlier, Rāvaṇa's death, at the end of the penultimate performance, is not the puppet play's dramatic climax; but Rāvaṇa's puppet, splashed with red dye and dangling upside down on the screen, is the final image of the vanquished enemies of dharma. When the bloodied screen is taken down (some say to remove the evil of killing the Brahmin Rāvaṇa) and a new cloth tied up for the next night, the long war is at an end. An even more decisive shift is enacted on the final night when Sītā is vindicated in the trial by fire and stands by Rāma's side; at that point, the epic appears to have overturned the past, to have erased fourteen painful years that began with a mother's fear and led to exile, abduction, bloody war, and death. On the cloth screen, this turning point is unmistakable: from their very first appearance many nights ago, Rāma, Lakṣmaṇa, and their allies have faced left (viewed from inside), toward Lanka, until suddenly, after the trial by fire, all the puppets turn and face right, toward Ayodhya. Soon the long dead Daśaratha appears, deus ex machina, and declares to Rāma: "When I heard the words that sent you into exile . . . they pierced my chest like sharp spears. Only now . . . have they been removed." Restitution is complete when Rāma requests that his father restore Bharata and Kaikeyī to their former status as his brother and mother, and Daśaratha does so. These reconciliations achieved, the restoration of lost harmony is symbolized by Rāma's return to Ayodhya, an aerial journey that is an event-by-event retracing of the unhappy path to Lanka, a Rāmāyaṇa in reverse.

At the coronation in Ayodhya, after Rāvaṇa and his demon armies have been eradicated, Vibhīṣaṇa crowned king of Lanka, and Sītā reunited with Rāma, the whole earth rejoices in the restitution of Rāma's rule. The narrative of the puppet play does not deviate from the received text in this regard, and after twelve or twenty or forty nights of chanting, the puppeteers faithfully rest their telling with King Rāma, until this final moment represented by a standing puppet, now seated on the throne at Ayodhya. Much has been restored, but like Vālmīki and other texts that extend into the Uttara Kāṇḍa, the puppet play is only half convinced by this conclusion. The triumphant return of the exiles and Rāma's righteous rule are called into question by the puppeteers' commentary on the last nights of performance, specifically by Sītā and Jāmbuvāṉ, who remember what the epic has turned its back upon.

Scrupulously the puppeteers adhere to Kampaṉ's narration of Sītā's trial by fire—they do not alter a single verse nor omit a detail (that Sītā's purity burns the Fire God, for example), yet the scene seethes with a hostility only hinted at in the epic text. Sītā's reunion with Rāma is far from harmonious even in Kampaṉ, where the entire episode is off-kilter, shot through with a metaphysical "lunacy," as David Shulman remarked.[38] In the puppet play, the disorder in this abrupt return to normality erupts into discord, vocalized through Sītā, who now speaks with a sarcasm we do not hear from her in the epic text.[39] At issue is her fidelity. A woman separated from her husband is, by tradition, a widow; during her year in Lanka, Sītā therefore has refused to eat Rāvaṇa's food or to wear fine clothes and jewelry. But now that Rāvaṇa is dead, should she go to Rāma in rags or wear a beautiful sari? Sītā knows that this is a serious question, and Rāma will seize upon her improper vestiture as evidence that she has been unfaithful to him, yet on this critical point,

Kampan̲'s Sītā, though not silent, is acquiescent.[40] When she learns from Vibhīṣaṇa that Rāma desires her to come to him "dressed beautifully" (*cīrōṭum*), Sītā at first hesitates:

> To remain as I am is virtuous and pious,
> As the gods, my husband, the sages,
> And chaste women of high rank all know;
> To wear fine clothes is not proper now, Oh mighty Vibhīṣaṇa.[41]

But when Vibhīṣaṇa insists that this request is Rāma's order, Sītā agrees and does not protest again.

In the puppeteers' commentary, however, Sītā is far from silent and speaks from the first in a mocking voice to Vibhīṣaṇa. Not to go to Rāma in her torn clothes, she declares, "would invite unkind suspicions about my conduct. Certainly you do not wish to encourage that, and I doubt that it would give Rāma pleasure, either." Only after wisely securing these grounds for her innocence and only after Vibhīṣaṇa reassures her (as he does not in Kampan̲) that no one doubts her chastity, does Sītā accept Rāma's order. She is then dressed by servants and prepares to follow Vibhīṣaṇa, yet as she leaves, she turns to Hanumān and asks him the question that he asked her only a few minutes ago: "Why are you silent? Is something wrong?" "No," Hanumān replies, but plainly he and Sītā understand something that Vibhīṣaṇa and Rāma do not.

For a short moment, when first in Rāma's presence, Sītā believes that all her sorrows are lifted, until suddenly Rāma accuses her of infidelity, of growing fat on palace pleasures, and rejects her. In Kampan̲, Sītā responds by reminding Rāma that Hanumān himself must have informed him that she suffered terribly. Next she despairs that all her self-denial amounts to naught, that all the gods know she is innocent, yet her own husband does not comprehend a woman's mind; with no alternative, she decides to die and asks Lakṣmaṇa to prepare the fire. She is distraught, even angry, but Kampan̲'s Sītā does not openly contradict her husband or accuse him of cruelty; her voice is plaintive and confused, but never mocking or bitter. Confronted on the cloth screen, however, Sītā speaks fire in her defense and turns her scathing tongue against the patently weak arguments of her husband. For instance, when Rāma announces in a verse that he came to Lanka not to rescue her but to kill Rāvaṇa and regain his lost honor, the puppeteers' Sītā interrupts: "What! You came here to restore *your* honor? Killed Rāvaṇa so that you would remove the stain on *your* name?" Earlier, when Rāma accuses her of enjoying Rāvaṇa's bed, she shrewdly turns this argument against him:

> "How can you call me a courtesan [*vēsi*]? If you believe that, you must leave me since you know the custom that a man should enter the forest when he renounces his wife. Yes, you have done your duty—killed Rāvaṇa and crowned Vibhīṣaṇa—so what keeps you here in Lanka? Leave me and go into the forest as a wandering ascetic."

To appreciate Sītā's sarcasm we must know that in a previous verse Rāma condemned Sītā for not acting "like ascetics who uphold virtue"; now Rāma must himself return to the forest if he wishes to uphold his ascetic ideal. But Rāma, whose words are harsh enough in Kampaṉ, speaks with the heartlessness of a wounded lover in the puppet play: "Do not fall at my feet and cry that I should accept you. Cry only that your Rāvaṇa is dead!" In the end, and only on the strength of Agni's testimony of Sītā's purity, Rāma accepts his wife, yet it is difficult to imagine that their bitter, mutual recriminations have left no scars.

Precisely at this moment of reunion, the celebration is undercut by another voice, that of Jāmbuvāṉ, leader of Rāma's bear allies. With the puppets turned to face Ayodhya for the return journey, with Rāma, Sītā, Lakṣmaṇa, and all the monkeys seated in defeated Rāvaṇa's chariot, and with the past apparently erased, Jāmbuvāṉ enters in tears. Asked why, he explains in a folk adaptation of a Kampaṉ verse:

> I saw Māli and Māliyavāṉ,
> I saw Kāla Nēmi and Hiraṇya,
> But never have I seen
> A person take back what he gave.[42]

With this verse and the scene that follows, the puppet play presents an abbreviated form of "The Revival of Vacantaṉ." In this episode, considered a later addition to Kampaṉ manuscripts, Jāmbuvāṉ questions Rāma's character, but even those interpolated verses do not burn with the accusatory tone heard in the folk verses in the puppet play. In the verse above, Jāmbuvāṉ's allegation that Rāma is using Rāvaṇa's chariot, which he only minutes ago gave to Vibhīṣaṇa, may appear contrived, but the rancor it injects into the scene is not: Jāmbuvāṉ is angry at Rāma's indifference to the death of his son, Vacantaṉ, who died unnoticed by the poet in the ferocious battle with Kumbhakarṇa and now stands as symbol of those who lost their lives in defense of Rāma's cause. Rāma may celebrate that his brother and wife are alive, but what of the thousands who died that they should live? Are they to be forgotten amid the reconciliations and return to Ayodhya?

Wise, old Jāmbuvāṉ, never quite as pious as Hanumān or Sugrīva in the puppet play, has had misgivings about Rāma and his war all along.[43] Much earlier, when Aṅgada attempted to halt his retreat from battle, the old leader explained:

"What can our seventy divisions do against their thousand? We'd only make a meal for them! I'm not ready to die yet."

"Jāmbuvāṉ, don't say that! Once, at my father's death, you spoke to me with brave words and now you talk of retreat!"

"You're young, Aṅgada, and cannot understand what these demons can do in battle. Rāvaṇa has hordes, and this time Rāma will not defeat him."

"But, surely Lakṣmaṇa, Hanumān, and Sugrīva—"

"Don't be naive. Do you think we are anything more than bodyguards to them? Did anyone protect my son, Vacantaṉ, when Kumbhakarṇa mauled him? And no one will stop the pain when you die, either. Better to escape into the forest and drink pure water and eat fresh fruits. Let Rāma win or lose; what's it to us anyway? Why should we die for them?"

Jāmbuvāṉ questions Rāma's war in Kampaṉ, too, though his words are less caustic. In one Kampaṉ verse he asks, "If men rule or Rāvaṇa rules, what's the difference?" but this is a tepid and strategic revision of a proverb often quoted to express skepticism toward authority: "If Rāma rules or Rāvaṇa rules, what's the difference?" In the puppet play, Jāmbuvāṉ attacks Rāma's motives with the same skepticism as the proverb and other countervailing voices that refuse to accept the bhakti text's attempt at restoration.

Even Rāma is disgusted with war and loses heart in his campaign against the demons.[44] When we compare the treatment of his emotions in Kampaṉ with that in the puppet play, however, two related differences emerge which confirm earlier observations: (1) the emphasis is verbal in the puppet play but visual in Kampaṉ; and (2) the puppet play vocalizes emotions mute in the epic text. As a first example, consider the parallel verses given below, which describe Rāma's reactions when he sees Lakṣmaṇa felled by Indrajit's snake-weapon:

Puppet Play
No more war for me, and no more fame!
My victory bow, my wife, my kingdom
Even Śiva who gave me life—I renounce them all!
If you, Lakṣmaṇa, do not live.

Father and mother we left; Ayodhya we left;
Yet, like the Vedas, we were inseparable, Lakṣmaṇa;
Now you've left me and earth is not my home;
Let my soul leave, too, if Yama will receive it.

Kampaṉ
Strong-shouldered Rāma looked at his bow
  at the knots of the snake-weapon
Looked at the still dark night,
  at the gods in heaven and
Screamed, "I'll rip up this earth";
  then, biting his coral lips,
He considered what wise men had said,
  and remained calm.[45]

He rubbed Lakṣmaṇa's feet
  with his lotus hands
Opened Lakṣmaṇa's lotus eyes
  and peered inside;
Hearing his heartbeat, he rejoiced
  lifted him to his chest,
And lay him on earth;
Looking into the sky, he wondered,
  "Is that devious Indra around?"

Although Rāma's anger and frustration are evident in both sets of verses, those emotions are suggested in Kampaṉ by what he sees and expressed in the puppet play by what he says. For instance, the first Kampaṉ verse is structured by the recurrence of "looking" (*nōkku*): he looked at the useless bow, the knots of the snake-weapon, the night, the gods. Rāma does scream but bites off his feelings and retreats inside, remembering that calm befits a perfected being. In the first folk verse, by contrast, the recurring element is verbal; crying *vēṇṭē!* ("no more"), Rāma condemns war and its rewards in the first line and cries louder with each repetition of that word. Similarly, in the second Kampaṉ verse, Rāma remains mute and continues to look, into Lakṣmaṇa's eyes and again at the sky while contemplating revenge against Indrajit; in the second folk verse, however, we hear only Rāma's sad words. Rāma does not look at the source of his grief in the puppet play, he speaks of it.

Rāma's despair at death is expressed again in a later, parallel scene when he finds his armies felled again, this time by Indrajit's Brahmā-weapon, and again the puppet play replaces the Kampa<u>n</u> verses with others more verbal and emotive. Moving along the battlefield, Rāma stands over the body of Aṅgada, whom he has pledged to protect and whose father he has killed. This highly charged scene is sung in the puppet play with a string of folk verses, the first of which and its equivalent Kampa<u>n</u> verse read as follows:

Puppet Play
As he lay dying, your father's soft hands
Held mine and placed you in my care;
Now, your hands are torn and bleeding in my defense:
Who would not die of this shame?

Kampa<u>n</u>
Like a bull fallen among a noble herd,
He saw that strong elephant,
Aṅgada, his spear eyes blazing fire;
"This is the value of my protection," he cried,
"This shame, these battle wounds."[46]

Kampa<u>n</u>'s verse again works through visual imagery—we see fallen bulls, strong elephants, fiery eyes—and even when Rāma speaks of his shame (*pa<u>l</u>i*) in the last two lines, he draws us to its visible manifestation in Aṅgada's wounds. His feelings are also constrained by self-mockery when referring to his pledge of "protection." The folk verse, on the other hand, is almost entirely verbal; Rāma addresses Aṅgada directly, tenderly, and without the distance of self-reproach. When he refers to his failure to protect Aṅgada and then juxtaposes Vāli's "soft hands" with Aṅgada's bloody ones, there is no irony, only remorse. A similar verbalization of grief recurs throughout the puppet play, for instance, when Rāma, leaving Aṅgada's body, moves further along the battlefield and sees Lakṣmaṇa's body. Although Kampa<u>n</u>'s eight beautiful verses describe Rāma's emotions, the hero speaks in none of them, whereas in the puppet play he cries out:

Wives may die, but we marry again;
Our children die, and others are born;

Lost wealth is regained, knowledge retrieved;
But, tell me, is a dead brother replaced?

Rāma's sorrow, Sītā's sarcasm, and Jāmbuvān's cynicism do not share in the rejoicing that trumpets so loudly in the final scenes of the medieval text. They do not celebrate a future; they grieve. But the countervailing voices in the puppet play are not always grim, and some are comic, even farcical, especially when spoken by characters either absent or insignificant in Kampan. Among these clownish folk characters, the most talkative is the umbrella holder (*kuṭakkāran*), who is nowhere found in Kampan but is conspicuously stationed next to Rāvaṇa on the cloth screen. He first stirs from his silent pose when he unexpectedly meets Indrajit on the battlefield and they survey the litter of corpses felled by Indrajit's snake-weapon. Speaking to the mighty warrior, the umbrella holder mimics the sounds of war:

"Bing-bang! Wham-bang! Bing-bang, who are you?"

"Me? I just shot the snake-weapon, the whole point of this performance."

. . .

"Problem is your snake-weapon didn't kill them; only knocked 'em out. I'll finish them off by stabbing them with the tip of my staff."

This scene, repeated with minor differences when Rāma's army is knocked out by the Brahmā-weapon, contains compound deflations of the epic text. Pairing the umbrella holder, a lowly servant who washes his wife's saris and "just grabbed onto the chariot and came along for the ride" with Indrajit, the most powerful figure in the epic, is not intended to elevate the stature of the demon-warrior. The servant's umbrella staff turns out to be more potent than Indrajit's snake-weapon, the epic's most lethal armament; and war itself is mocked by the umbrella holder's first words, which playfully simulate the battle sounds produced by drums in the drama-house. Parody extends to a later scene, too, when the epic battle grinds to a halt because the umbrella holder refuses to hold the banner of Rāvaṇa's armies without receiving his pay. Like Jāmbuvān's intrusive demand for his son's life, but gentler and more absurd, his strike for wages (as Lysistrata's for peace) exposes the fragility of the noble cause. As if these blasphemies were not sufficient, we then watch the umbrella holder march down the line, condemn each of Rāma's captains (Naḷan̲ is a boss-man; Sugrīva a drunk; Aṅgada ill-mannered) and stab them one by one while they lie defenseless on the ground. In the end, this marginal and unrepentant figure appears fully converted to the bhakti ethos when he requests that Rāma grant him *mokṣa*; yet, just as Rāma is about to strike, he flinches.

The nameless umbrella holder also plays the wise fool. In his conversation with Indrajit, he appears stupid, thinks intelligence is a "thing," and mangles grammar, but only he has the foresight to warn Indrajit that his dead enemies may be revived. Similarly, although he cannot pronounce the word "liberation," he is smart enough to gain boons for beauty and wealth in the next life. He also admonishes Indrajit to discriminate between bravado and courage when he tells an edifying folktale about another apparent dimwit, Poor Brains the frog, who warns his own exalted friends about an impending disaster.[47] The frog's friends, Thousand Brains and the others, confident of their superior endowment, dismiss the threat and decide to remain in the doomed pond. Though skeptical, Poor Brains remains with them, and after the others die from their stupid pride, only he survives. Through the character of the umbrella holder, the puppet play recommends not cunning but prudence and common sense, which was taught also in the cautionary tale told in the "Song of the Drama-House" (chapter 3) about wisely giving money and brides.

The comic voice in Kerala is spoken as well by more respectable epic characters, including Hanumān, the ideal devotee. His journey to the Medicine Mountain in order to save Rāma and Lakṣmaṇa, indisputably one of the solemn moments in the War Book, is my favorite example of the puppet play laughing at epic inflation. Jāmbuvān̲ speaks excitedly:

"Listen, Hanumān, we have only three-quarters of an hour to revive Lakṣmaṇa and the others; then the sun rises and Indrajit will behead them. Before that, you must travel seventy-three thousand *yojanas* to the Medicine Mountain, find the longevity herb, and return."

"Are you joking?"

"Joking?"

"Seventy-three thousand *yojanas* in three-quarters of an hour? And return? It's . . . it's impossible."

"But, Hanumān, if you don't—"

"That far, that quickly, to locate a rare herb for an incurable disease? Ridiculous, that's all."

If Hanumān's critical mission to revive Rama and Lakṣmaṇa is not immune to the puppet play's parody, what is? Nothing held in high regard, it seems, and certainly not the oracle-priest of Bhagavati. As described in chapter 1, the *veḷiccappāṭu* is the ritual link between temple and drama-house when he leads the procession to the puppeteers and offers them the official cloth and rice on the first night of performance; and he, after becoming possessed by Bhagavati, blesses their performance on each succeeding night. The oracle-priest also appears as a character in the puppet play, but only once, on the night of Indrajit's death, when, paralleling the umbrella holder's sham battle sounds, he playfully imitates the temple oracle's cries during spirit possession: "Kriyommmmmmmm!" That the pronouncements of this possessed oracle turn out to be hocus-pocus is not surprising since his spiritual inspiration is a phoney Bhagavati called Money Maker.

Dismissing the temple oracle by debunking his prophecies is part of the puppeteers' broad satire of verbal authority, including their own. The oracle's gibberish and the umbrella holder's grammatical blunders ("Rāvaṇa and me went") are linguistic transgressions so obvious that they draw attention to the verbal rules governing performance itself. The puppeteers are wordsmiths who must memorize at least twelve hundred (and as many as two thousand) verses and hundreds of quotations, deliver a lengthy, learned commentary, and comment on derivations and usage. Against these high demands, the puppeteers' play on words may be a charm intended to defuse the power of words: "Sticks and stones may break my bones," they seem to say, "but names [words] will never hurt me." In any case, words play tricks on nearly every major figure in the story. Rāvaṇa's messengers, an insignificant pair in Kampa<u>n</u>, for instance, take a verbal beating on several occasions. Once, when neither has bothered to remember Rāvaṇa's orders, they attempt to avoid punishment by inventing a story: the words were tied up in a bundle, they say, but it fell into a river. Having lost the bundle of words, the messengers are then forced to relearn them, this time by repeating each phrase Rāvaṇa speaks, an exercise in tomfoolery that ends in a beating for the witless messengers when they duly restate Rāvaṇa's angry blast: "Don't talk to me like that, you dog!" Even Rāvaṇa is coaxed by Viṣṇu (disguised as a Brahmin) into using a word that "cancels" most of the future lives granted to him by Śiva. All this verbal chicanery, however, is not what it seems, and although the victims appear to be fools, the joke is on language itself. When the umbrella holder errs or Rāvaṇa is duped, it is not that they are stupid but that speech is deceptive, indeterminate, dangerous. After all, Kampaṉ began his epic by telling a lie.

Clowns and fools are prominent in the shadow puppet traditions elsewhere in south India (notably Andhra Pradesh and Karnataka), but the differences with the Kerala clown figures are revealing. In Andhra Pradesh, as Jonathan GoldbergBelle has shown, the clowns appear regularly in interludes or "skits" unconnected with the epic story and indulge in sexual slapstick complete with huge penises, aggressive homosexuality, and female promiscuity. Drawing on Don Handelman's work, GoldbergBelle concludes that these clowns represent "internal oscillation" and not role reversal; that is, rather than simply reversing norms, the clowns contain both social and asocial roles, between which they vacillate.[48] In Kerala, however, the umbrella holder and other humorous figures are jesters of a different order. Because performance serves as temple ritual and because the Kampaṉ text is considered close to scripture, the umbrella holder and his foolish friends display little overt, or even covert, sexuality, and their scenes are more tightly integrated into the epic story. Nor do these clowns contain contradictory states within themselves; instead, they represent one half of a complementary pair that juxtaposes authority with its caricature (Rāvaṇa and the messengers, Indrajit and the umbrella holder, the oracle-priest parodied by the sham oracle-priest). The comic characters in Kerala thus achieve, by deflation, the balance that the puppeteers pursue throughout the puppet play.

These deflating figures and their countervailing voices bring our study of the Kerala puppet play full circle for, although we hear them most frequently in the War Book, we have heard them before. Sītā's anger and Jāmbuvāṉ's mockery, like Śūrpaṇakhā's defense of *kāma* and Vāli's condemnation of Rāma, arise from a worldview that reveals hidden affinities and seeks to redress injustice. Under this watchful eye, the Rāma story told by the puppeteers cannot be a tale of triumph celebrating Rāma's victory and coronation. On the contrary, if one emotion pervades the puppet play, it is grief, a sentiment that runs deep in the wider Rāma tradition, especially the Uttara Kāṇḍa, from which the puppet play draws so much. A popular story explains that the *śloka* (a type of verse used by Vālmīki) arose from the poet's *cōkam* (grief) when he saw a lovebird cruelly killed by a hunter's arrow. Similarly, the goal of puppet-play performance in Malaysia, according to Amin Sweeney, is to induce weeping in Rāma and the audience.[49]

The puppet play also cries aloud and often. Beginning with Śūrpaṇakhā's wailing over her son's body and continuing on to Maṇḍōdari's mourning of Rāvaṇa, the Rāma story told by the puppeteers is a tale dominated by the pain and separation of death. Comedy is not missing, as we have seen, but humor often appears only in order to relieve the relentless sorrow that attends the war against Lanka. We know that countervailing voices grieve when others celebrate, as Jāmbuvāṉ does in the "Revival of Vacantaṉ," but they also laugh when others mourn. Twice Rāma weeps over his fallen comrades and brother, and twice his agony is preceded by the umbrella holder's and Indrajit's routine in which jokes are played and dirty laundry exposed. An even more explicit parody of grief occurs just before Rāvaṇa learns of Indrajit's death. Returning from the battlefield to report this sorrowful event, the messengers indulge in a mock dirge for Indrajit, inserting chilies into their eyes to cry crocodile tears. When they reach the palace and Rāvaṇa asks for news (of his son), they trifle with his sentiments, equating that news with gossip in the marketplace; anticipating Rāvaṇa's tears when he hears that his son is dead, they comment sarcastically, "It's monsoon time again." Nearly every major scene of mourning in the puppet play is similarly hedged with comedy, as an antidote, I think, to the intense sorrow that underlies the puppet play. The senior puppeteer Natesan Pillai once told me something that I duly wrote down but did not fully understand: "People like the Rāma story," he said, "because it has so much sorrow (*cōkam*); they hear it and they get some relief from their own problems; it makes them happy." At first I thought that his words merely explained why so many people donate a rupee to performance—to eradicate disease, mitigate misfortune, or stake a claim to future success—but now I realize that they say something more: the power of the Rāma tale told in the drama-house resides not in the divine status of its hero but in the soothing sadness of its stories.

No one grieves on the final day of performance. After the puppeteers declaimed the last words translated in this chapter, they left Rāma on the screen, put up the Brahmin puppets, and for nearly four hours they read the names of twelve hundred one-rupee donors and sang songs on their behalf. At seven o'clock in the morning, with the sun already warm, they took down those puppets, pinned them on the outer side of the white cloth screen, and departed by bus for their homes. Only then, with the puppeteers gone and the story over, was the Rāma puppet, seated on the throne at Ayodhya, fully visible to the public; and it remained on view throughout the last day of the festival. As the final scene of the Rāma story in both medieval poem and oral performance, this sight of the righteous king at rest is an auspicious resolution, an end to the epic conflict of betrayal, death, and mourning. But the puppet play in Kerala is a conversation, not a visual tableau, and there can be no complete restoration because other voices have spoken and the past is not so easily forgotten.

The puppeteers headed home, and next year they will return to tell their Rāma story, unresolved and incomplete, but how many years they will continue to perform is anyone's guess. Already, as of 1989, the tradition is losing ground, and the lamps are no longer lit in at least a dozen temples that sponsored puppet plays as recently as 1960; at several other temples, the number of nights has been reduced from sixteen to twelve or from twelve to eight. More important, when puppets become damaged, new ones are no longer manufactured because the skin (of deer and buffalo) has become too expensive and the skill of puppet making too rare; torn puppets are patched together or discarded, and a complete set of intact puppets is not to be found. In 1979, upon learning that the most well-endowed puppet troupes had only about half of the more than one hundred puppets required for a full set, the All-India Handicrafts Board initiated a scheme to revive the skill of producing puppets, but it failed for lack of funds; a minor success is that one young puppeteer completed a course in puppet making at Pinguli, Maharashtra, though since then, no one has asked him to make puppets.[50] Here and there, one sees drama-houses abandoned and in disrepair; I spent days looking for a particular drama-house outside Palghat and was eventually directed to a field, but it had vanished—its bricks and beams sold to a contractor.

Perhaps another two or three generations will pass before the Kerala shadow puppet play joins other folk performing arts in India's cultural museums. That end appears inevitable not because patronage will dry up—the personal problems which villagers seek to alleviate with one rupee are not likely to cease—but because there will be no puppeteers to receive patronage. The simple fact is that puppeteers are not being replaced by younger men. Forty puppeteers were reported to be active in 1982, of whom only twenty-five still performed in 1989, and many of them were too feeble to chant through the night.[51] Over the five-year span of my research, three puppeteers died and one retired from illness, but not a single new man entered the drama-house. The reason for this puppeteer drain, I believe, is that performing behind the cloth screen requires many years of training yet earns little income and prestige. While puppeteers are not treated with disrespect, neither are they shown the attention and courtesy accorded to higher caste performers. It is hard to imagine that conditions were dissimilar in the "good old days," but the art of shadow puppetry apparently holds even less attraction for young men today. Will the puppet play adapt and become more entertaining in order to survive? I see no sign of any change in the puppeteers' ritual recitation, but predictions of an early demise often prove to be notoriously shortsighted. An inexperienced but perceptive American observer of the Kerala puppet play wrote this:

> The life of a puppet is said to average the life of a man. But in all probability, these puppets will not wear out, for the traveling days of the shadow play will no doubt soon be over. When the twenty-seater busses bring the sound and shadow-play of our own day, sound on film, within easy reach of the jungle, then these shadows of a remote age will fade out. The puppets will lie all year in the palm-frond case or stand shadowless behind glass in some museum.[52]

That was written in 1935, and although the cinema has overtaken Palghat district, as it has all of India, the puppets still throw shadows in more than eighty drama-houses.[53] One reason for such persistence is the prestige of the text, but more influential is the belief that donations, in whatever amount, will benefit the donor; this belief, shared by the tens of thousands of individuals who donate one rupee and the dozens of families who give hundreds or thousands of rupees each year, supplies lifeblood to the tradition. The possibility of personal relief also explains both how the puppet play has withstood the onslaught of the cinema and why it requires no public audience: it is not popular entertainment; it is temple ritual. The *Kamparāmāyaṇam* is respected, but presenting it with shadow puppets is considered by most to be a common man's *pūjā,* a medium through which everyone may address their problems to Bhagavati, though attendance is not required. Others may concur with those observers who have faulted the Kerala tradition for its remote puppeteers, and I cannot disagree that insulating them from audience interaction has denied the puppet play popularity, both locally and nationally, or that such isolation may well prevent the tradition from adapting and, ultimately, from surviving in a world of electronic entertainment.[54] Yet weaknesses are sometimes strengths, and I believe that the Kerala puppeteers' anonymity and absent audience have stimulated them to create conversations inside the drama-house. Whatever its future, the shadow puppet play in Kerala shows us that stories and their audiences are not always what or even where we think they are.

APPENDIX A

Three Samples of the Puppeteers' Commentary in Transliteration

Note: Malayalam words and suffixes are printed in italic. Breaks in the commentary are indicated by a slash mark (/).

Sample 1: Formal Exegesis of a Verse

arakkaṉ cēṉaiyai nekuṭiya cilai Rāmaṉ tōḷ vali kūṟuvōrkku naṟṭiya poruḷ naṟpalaṉ uṇṭākum./ arakka cēṉai iḻantatu coṉṉāl rāvaṇāti rākṣasātikaḷ āṉa tuṣṭaṉmārkaḷ/ inta cēṉaikaḷai ellām taṉ karittiṉ iṭattil uṇṭākiya kōtaṇṭam ākiya villai vaḷaittu/ cakavanti villāṉ inta astiraṅkaḷ eṭuttu maḻai poḻivatāṉa taṉmai pōla poḻintu/ taṉ *nikkirakattu* ceyyakūṭiya *carvēccuramāṉa* Rāmacuvāmiyiṉuṭaiya tōḷ vali kūṟuvōrkku puja pala parākkiramamāy viḷaṅkum inta veṟṟiyai/ eṭuttu kūṟappaṭṭa pērkaḷum, aṉpōṭu kūṭi kēṭkappaṭṭa pērkaḷum/ aṉupavikka kūṭiya palaṉākiya pirayōjaṉum eṉṉavākilum eṉṟu pārkkiṟa pōtu/ 'Nāṭiya poruḷ. . . . ' [Here the puppeteer returns to the verse.]

Sample 2: Conversation Between Epic Characters

(Jāmbuvāṉ:) "Atu *māttram* illai. Rāmaṉukku iḷaiya tampiyākiya cōbika inta iḷaiyacuvāmi, inta iḷaiyacuvāmi āṉavar inta brahmāstiram ēvuntu ujīvikapōṉa kālam ākilum. 'Muḻu mati ulakum mūṉṟum nalaram mūrtti tāṉum.' Ālōcikum*āy* iruntāl, antaram, mattiyam, pātāḷam, eṉṟu coṉṉāl inta mūṉṟu lōkaṅkaḷ iruntu piḻaiccatu; atāvatu, cuvāmiyāṉavar piḻaikka vēṇṇum*āy* iruntāl, iḷaiyacuvāmi piḻaikkavēṇṇum, iḻaiyacuvāmi piḻaikka vēṇṇum vantāl, cuvāmiyiṉuṭaiya *muharasiyum* tīrum. Cuvāmi ujīvacca eṉṟu vantāl, inta mūṉṟu lōkaṅkaḷ ujīviccatu eṉṟu tāṉ colla vēṇṇum . . . inta vastukaḷ piḻaikka vēṇṇum*āy* iruntāl, Hanumāṉāṉa nī oruvaṉ *vijāriccāl* pōtum.

(Hanumān:) "Ah ha."

"Ellā pērkaḷum piḻaikkum."

"Eṉṉa aiyā, Jāmbuvāṉ Mahārāja, niṉ-tiru-aṭi collukiṟ*atu?*"

"Eṉṉa?"

"Aṭiyēṉ *vijāriccāl,* ellā pērkaḷum piḻaikkum eṉṟu coṉṉāl, aṭiyēṉ *vijāriccāmalō?* Aṭiyēṉ *vijāriccāl,* eppaṭi piḻaiccavatu?

"Nī ippoḻutu *vijāriccāl* piḻaiccu kāṇukiṟatu illai. *Allaiyō?*

"Ah."

"Āṉāl appaṭi maṉaciṉālē *vijāriccāl māttram* pōrātu."

Sample 3: Rapid Dialogue Between Rāvaṇa and Messengers

(Messengers:) "Ceyti ellā terintatu."

(Rāvaṇa:) "Eṉṉa?"

"Cantaile ellā cātaṉaṅkaḷukkum ellā vilai jāsti ākum."

"Eṭā! Keti keṭṭa pērkaḷē! Atu illai nāṉ coṉṉ*atu*. Eṉ makaṉ pōrukku pōṉa ceyti . . ."

"*Allai* . . . oru āputam nērittatu eṅkaḷukku."

"Atu eṉṉa?"

"Vēṟu oṉṟum illai. Niṉ-tiru-aṭi eṅkaḷai aḻaiccatu, *illaiyō?* Aḻaiccatu etu etō vārtaikaḷ coṉṉiyē. Anta vārtaikaḷ ellām eṉakku piṟaku nikkiṟavaṉ, Sangadi, atu ellām avaṉ oru *bantamāka* koṇṭu kaṭṭiṉ*atu* . . ."

"Kaṭṭi . . ."

"Kaṭṭi, atu oru reṇṭam muṇṭil kaṭṭi, cumai ēttiṉ*atu*."

"*Antaramō?*"

"*Antaram,* nāṅkaḷ appaṭi vaḻi natantu pōkiṟatu pōtu oru vayal mārkkamāka pōṉ*atu*."

APPENDIX B

Sample Commentary in Tamil Script

Source: Appendix A, sample 1: formal exegesis of a verse.

அரக்கன் சேனையை நெகுடிய சிலை ராமன் தோள் வலி கூறுவோர்க்கு நாடிய பொருள் நற்பலன் உண்டாகும். அரக்க சேனை இழந்தது சொன்னால், ராவணாதி ராக்ஷஸாதிகள் ஆன துஷ்டன்மார்கள், இந்த சேனைகளை எல்லாம் தன் கரத்தினிடத்தில் உண்டாகிய கோதண்டம் ஆகிய வில்லை வளைத்து, சகவந்தி வில்லான் இந்த அஸ்திரங்கள் எடுத்து, மழை பொழிவதான தன்மை போல பொழிந்து தன் நிக்கிரகத்து செய்யக்கூடிய சர்வேச்சரமான ராமசவாமியினுடைய தோள் வலி கூறுவோர்க்கு புஜ பல பராக்கிரமமாய் விளங்கும் இந்த வெற்றியை எடுத்து கூறப்பட்ட பேர்களும், அன்போடு கூடி கேட்கப்பட்ட பேர்களும், அனுபவிக்க கூடிய பலனாகிய பிரயோஜனம் என்னவாகிலும் என்று பார்க்கிற போது -- நாடிய பொருள் ...

Literal translation:

Those who tell of the strong shoulders of the bowman Rāma, who destroyed the demon army, will realize their desires. To say "the demon army was destroyed" means that the discus-bearing bowman [Rāma] took up his hard bow, fitted many arrows, and poured them down like a torrential rain upon Rāvaṇa and all his *rākṣasas*, all those cruel beings and their armies. To know what benefits accrue to those who tell of the powerful shoulders of Lord Rāma, the compassionate all-god, and of his fruitful, magnanimous victory, and what benefits those who kindly hear [the story] will enjoy . . . desired things [repeat line of verse].

APPENDIX C

Main Characters in the Puppeteers' Rāma Story

Rāma's Family

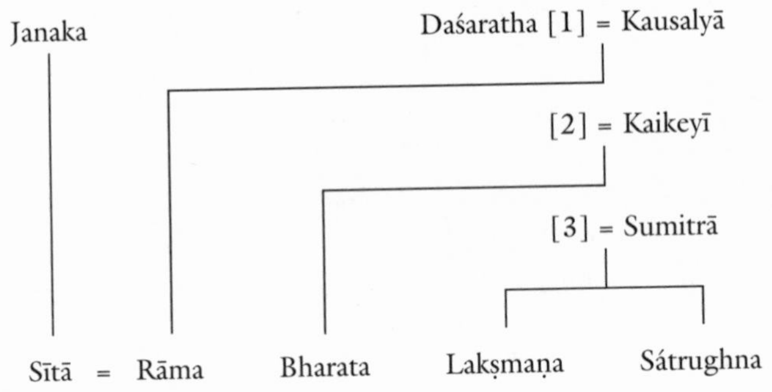

Rāvaṇa's Family

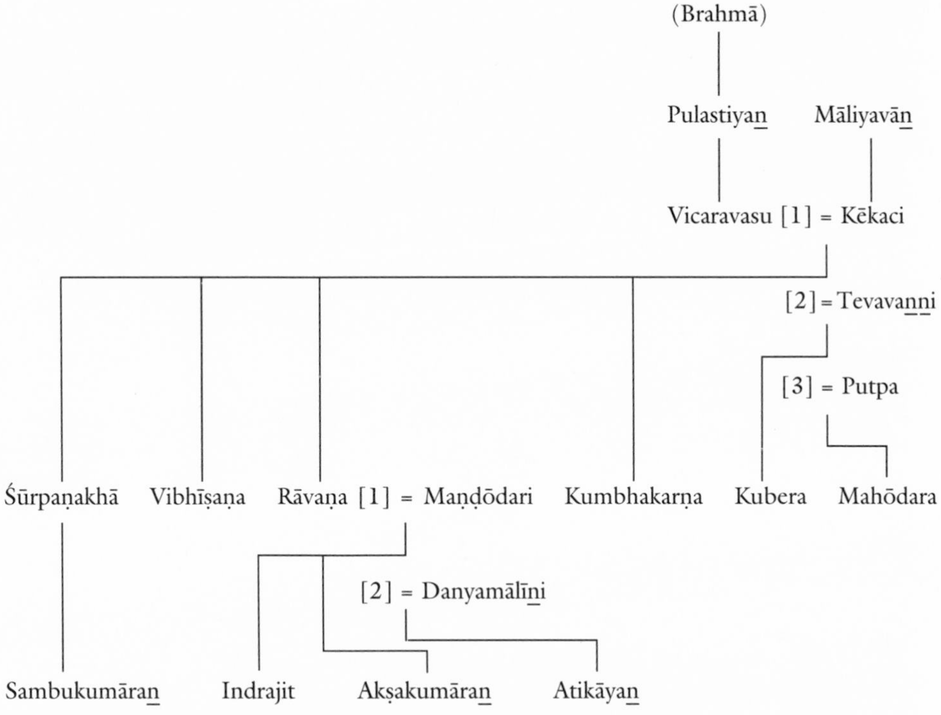
(Brahmā)
Pulastiyaṉ
Māliyavāṉ
Vicaravasu [1] = Kēkaci
[2] = Tevavaṉṉi
[3] = Putpa
Śūrpaṇakhā
Vibhīṣaṇa
Rāvaṇa [1] = Maṇḍōdari
Kumbhakarṇa
Kubera
Mahōdara
[2] = Danyamālīṉi
Sambukumāraṉ
Indrajit
Akṣakumāraṉ
Atikāyaṉ

Monkeys and Bears

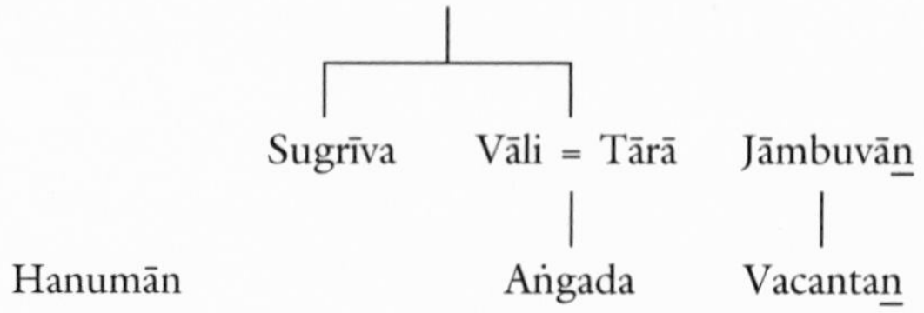

Notes

Chapter 1. An Absent Audience

1. The title of Kampaṉ's poem is *Irāmāvatāram*, "The Descent [avatar] of Rāma," but it is commonly known as *Kamparāmāyaṇam*, the "Rāmāyaṇa of Kampaṉ."

2. On this debate, see Stache-Rosen 1984; Mair 1988, chapter 1.

3. See chapter 7.

4. These invocations on behalf of the one-rupee patrons are sung during a *nāṭakam*, or "dance" of celestial women who are summoned to entertain Rāvaṇa (infrequently Rāma) at various points during the puppet play. With the dancer puppets pinned on the screen, the puppeteers sing songs in praise of Bhagavati, Rāma, Murukaṉ, and other deities. See, for example, chapter 6.

5. A *vēsti* (*vētti*) is a sarong-like garment worn by men in south India.

6. Despite his ritual office and spirit possession, the oracle is not highly respected; to the puppeteers, he is a temple servant and an easy target for caricature (see chapter 6).

7. The details and scope of this opening *pūjā* varied greatly from troupe to troupe; some worship only the Rāma puppet, while others worshiped all the major puppets together.

8. These puppets are perforated and opaque, not translucent. For details on the manufacture and iconography of puppets in Kerala, see Seltmann 1986; UCLA Museum of Cultural History 1976.

9. One drum, *paṟa*, is a double-headed barrel drum played with one or two sticks; the other, *mattalam*, is also double-headed but oblong in shape and played with the hands. They are often accompanied by a pair of heavy brass cymbals (*ilattāḷam*), and occasionally by an oboe-like curved horn (*kuḻal*). All these instruments are played by the puppeteers themselves or by their associates, who receive a fraction of the puppeteers' pay and form part of the overnight, catnapping audience inside the drama-house.

10. Cash is usually distributed to the puppeteers only on the final day.

11. *Kabadi* is a popular game played by young men, in which players cross a line and attempt to tag members of the opposing team without being tagged themselves, all the time repeating "kabadi, kabadi." If they are tagged or tackled or fail to repeat the word, they are out.

12. The text versus context dichotomy has been questioned on many fronts; see Ben-Amos 1993.

13. Jakobson 1960.

14. A good example of these early studies is Abrahams 1976. For India, see Lutgendorf 1991; Kapur 1990; Qureshi 1983; Hess 1983; Flueckiger 1988. For an analysis of audience-performer relations in New Mexico, see Briggs 1988. Finnegan (1977:214–35) discusses types of audience, while Bauman and Briggs (1990) provide an overview of research on audience.

15. Hymes 1975:18–19.

16. Hobart (1987:30) explains that this Balinese performance is "given primarily to an invisible audience, i.e., the gods, the human spectators being essentially irrelevant"; although performances adhere closely to texts, the story presented has "little or no conflict" and is "hardly audible" (pp. 162–63, 178).

17. Keeler 1987:15.

18. Zurbuchen (1987:238), for example, describes the active "evaluation" and "feedback" by audiences for ordinary night performances in Bali.

19. Proschan's claim that "[e]very traditional puppetry performance is a collaboration between puppeteer and audience" requires qualification (Proschan 1987:30). See also Proschan 1983:18–19.

20. Keeler 1987:17.

21. Keeler 1987:219.

22. Handelman 1990:41–48.

23. See Lutgendorf 1991:115–19.

24. Flueckiger 1991.

25. Narayana Rao 1991.

26. Foley 1991.

27. Kapur 1990:23.

28. Some temples divide the rupee donations between the puppeteers (60 percent), musicians (20 percent) and temple (20 percent). Inflation had raised the standard donation to 1.25 rupees at a few sites by 1989.

29. Family-sponsored performances are known as *nērccai kūttu* (drama [as offering in fulfillment] of a vow); village-sponsored performances are *dēsam kūttu* (village-[sponsored] drama).

30. Narayan 1989.

31. Mills 1991.

Chapter 2. Rāma Stories and Puppet Plays

1. The proverb in Telugu (courtesy of V. Narayana Rao) is "*kaṭṭe, koṭṭe, tecche.*"

2. This *Campū Rāmyaṇa* might also be the twelfth-century Sanskrit text attributed to Bhoja, which is based on the southern recension of the Vālmīki and

includes several incidents found in the puppet play. On the debate over the *Mahānāṭaka*, see S. K. De 1931.

3. Rāvaṇa's death is one example; see chapter 8, note 18.

4. For this conversation, see chapter 6.

5. Jesudasan and Jesudasan 1961:183. Perhaps the best known adaptation of Kampan̲ is the *Rāma Nāṭakam*, an early eighteenth-century composition in a popular song genre (*kīrttan̲a*) by Aruṇācalakkavirāyar.

6. For Kampan̲'s influence in Southeast Asia, especially Thailand, see Singaravelu 1968.

7. See Sanford 1974:12–18, passim; Champakalaksmi 1981; Cēturāman̲ 1985; Pollock 1993:271.

8. Sanford 1974:17–18; Champakalakshmi 1981:118–23. Two eighth-century Pallava Rajas were also compared to Rāma, but the evidence is not quite as impressive as one might think: in one case the king is compared to everyone from Arjuna to Manu, while in another the Rāma comparison is merely an inference (*South Indian Inscriptions*, vol. 1, no. 25; vol. 3, no. 206).

9. See Shulman 1985:25–26.

10. For the publication history of the *Kamparāmāyaṇam*, see Civakāmi 1978.

11. On the politics of Tamil nationalism, see Irschick 1969 and Arooran 1980; on the various ideological strands of the Dravidian movement, see the 1992 dissertation by Sumathi Ramaswamy.

12. Cuppiramaṇiya Pārati (1882–1921), for example, celebrated Kampan̲ as a symbol of pure Tamil in his poem "Cen̲ Tamil̲ Nāṭu" ("Pure Tamil Land").

13. In 1924 Sir John Marshall regarded the Dravidian hypothesis as the most valid, and further evidence has confirmed his opinion (Parpola 1994:59, passim).

14. For another interpretation of the construction of this Dravidian identity, see Washbrook 1989.

15. Periyār 1972a:15.

16. Purnalingam Pillai 1985:223–24.

17. See, for example, Ponnambalam Pillai 1910:60.

18. Vedachalam Pillai (Mar̲aimalai Aṭikaḷ) 1939:66.

19. Aṇṇāturai 1961.

20. Tēcikavināyakam Piḷḷai 1953. On E. V. R.'s revision of the Rāmāyaṇa, see Richman 1991. For others in defense of Kampan̲, see Collamutam 1966; Naccumur̲i 1952.

21. For the Chola inscriptions, see Nilakantha Sastri 1975:468 and Cēturāman̲ 1985:52; for the Pandiya inscription, see Banerjee 1986, 1:216. The Kannada inscription, from Hassan District, is given in Rice 1902, no. 77, p. 53, verse 25), but Emeneau (1985) doubts that the Kannada *kamba* is the Tamil poet.

22. Nadar 1957:33.

23. In 1926 scholars at Alvar Tirunakari obtained a manuscript of the *Kamparāmāyaṇam* containing the information that it was "completed in M.E. 970 [A.D. 1792] by Tiruvenkatam Tacar," who is said to have consulted forty-nine manuscripts and labored for thirty-five years before issuing his definitive manu-

script (Kampan̲ 1942, 1:3). See also Vaiyāpuri Piḷḷai 1962:69; Srinivasan 1984, 1:172; Hikosaka and Samuel 1990:238.

24. The debate on authentic and spurious verses during the first decades of the twentieth century was carried on primarily in the scholarly journal *Cen̲ Tamil̲*.

25. These four are: (a) An edition by Vai Mu. Kōpālakiruṣṇamācāriyar, a learned, Vaiṣṇava scholar. (b) A critical edition with full apparatus compiled at Annamalai University. (c) The Kampan̲ Kaḻakam edition, which includes *mikai pāṭal* (extra verses) but no variant readings. (d) The Alvar Tirunakari edition, compiled at this Śrī Vaiṣṇava temple center in southern Tamil Nadu.

Hereafter, in notes, Kampan̲ verses are identified by their number in the Kōpālakiruṣṇamācāriyar edition.

26. Buchanan 1807, 2:347.

27. This historical sketch is drawn from Logan 1887 and Krishna Iyer 1973.

28. The southern portion was called *nāladēsam* or "four-villages," namely Chittur, Tattamangalam, Nallepilly, and Pattancheri, where Tamil influence remains strong.

29. Fullarton 1787:167.

30. In the early nineteenth century, a British official noted that the Palghat Rajas were poverty-stricken from the ravages of half a century of war (Buchanan 1807, 2:347).

31. Krishna Iyer 1973:44–46.

32. Interview with V. S. Mani Iyer, Palghat, February 1989.

33. Mahalingam 1972:312–13.

34. Govindakutty 1981. The *Āścaryacūḍāmaṇi*, a play text, begins with Rāma's and Śūrpaṇakhā's meeting, as does the puppet play (Jones 1984).

35. I have extrapolated this figure from census records for the several parts of the Palghat region (*Census of India*, 1901:120; *Census of India* 1941:89; *Census of India*, 1951:23–25).

36. Until recently, it appears that the puppet play comprised a Tamil and a Malayalam branch; see chapter 5, note 3.

37. On the importance of the trade route through the Palghat Gap, see Subrahmanyam 1989:78–79. On Tamil weavers and merchants in premodern Kerala, see Nayar and Mahalingam 1952:7, 21; Duarte Barbosa 1866:144–45; Vijaya Ramaswamy 1985:28, 150, 169.

38. The Kalpathy temple was built in 1425, bringing a sizable contingent of Tamil Brahmins and probably artisans and weavers, too, since temples are commercial as well as religious centers (Innis 1951:473; Logan 1887:cxxx).

39. Oral tradition among local Tamil Brahmins is that ancestors established eighteen (or ninety-six) Brahmin villages (*agraharams*) where the Vedas were taught. Today this Tamil Vedic culture is undergoing a minor revival; see *The Hindu*, 24 June 1988; *The Indian Express*, 20 June 1988.

40. At Kuttala, near Kunicheri, and at Punkunam, near Trichur, and at Tekkegramam, near Chittur. The last site also contains a memorial to El̲uttaccan̲, author of a celebrated Rāmāyaṇa in Malayalam. At two large Rāma temples in the puppet play area (Tiruvilyamala and Triprayar), episodes from the Rāma story are presented in Kathakaḷi and Cākkyār Kūttu, but not in shadow puppetry.

41. "Chettiyar" and "Mutaliyar" are labels often used by upwardly mobile groups; the Kerala puppeteers who use these terms appear to be Sengunthars (Kaikolars).

42. In the *Vinōtaracamañcari* (Vīracāmi Ceṭṭiyār 1891). On Kampan̲'s patron as a Mutaliyar, see Kampan̲ 1926–71, 1:5.

43. Even allowing for the fact that "Mutaliyar" is commonly added to names, the continuity between scholars and puppeteers is clear.

44. Kurup 1984:52, 116; Kurup 1988:49–50.

45. The reference appears in Nambiyar's "Gōsha Yātra" (Śivasaṅkara Piḷḷai 1970:81); I am indebted to Rich Freeman for his translation of the relevant lines.

46. The Telugu and Kannada data are given in Krishnaiah 1988; Goldberg-Belle 1984; and M. N. Sarma 1985; a Ceylonese tradition is noted in Coomaraswamy 1930. The Tamil literary evidence is summarized in M. Rāmacuvāmi 1978:21–24.

47. Mair 1988, chapter 4. To this list of visual storytelling props used in the northern Deccan, we may add painted figurines and painted tents (Thangavelu 1992).

48. For the Maratha influence on south Indian shadow puppetry, see GoldbergBelle 1984; Raventiran̲ 1982.

49. On these Maratha picturemen, see Stache-Rosen 1984; Ray 1978. Morab (1977:42–43) found that itinerant families of leather puppeteers in northern Karnataka wandered hundreds of miles every year before returning to their home village.

50. GoldbergBelle 1984:183–90; Krishnaiah 1988:21.

51. A permanent building (*kūttu māṭam*) constructed solely for shadow puppet performance appears to be unique to Kerala, although a photograph of "an old performance" in China shows what looks like a permanent stage (Jilin 1986:92).

52. On this verse, see chapter 6, note 20.

53. Although I was unable to compare handwritten texts used by different troupes, I discovered a close correspondence between a 1916 printed pamphlet of the verses and two recent books (Krishnan Kutty 1983 and 1987). The pamphlet contained many more verses than did the books, but verses common to them all rarely differed by more than a few words.

54. These "extra verses" (*mikai pāṭal*) the editors consider to be unauthentic, later additions to the text.

55. Three folk verses sung by the puppeteers are found in a Tamil folk Rāmāyaṇa manuscript (published as Naṭarācan̲ 1989) and a fourth in a *Kuyil Rāmāyaṇa* (Venugopal 1993:105). For a curious parallel with an Oriya and a Hindi text, see chapter 6, note 31.

Chapter 3. Ambivalent Accommodations: Bhakti and Folk Hinduism

1. On the development of Rāma bhakti and devotional Rāma texts, see Brockington 1985; Whaling 1980.

2. Durgā *pūjā* precedes Daśara in north India, but the celebration of Daśara as Rāma's victory is not at all common in the deep south, especially in local temple festivals. See Fuller 1992:108–19.

3. Goldman 1984:47.

4. See Balasubrahmanyam 1971:xx–xxxii; Sanford 1974:9–13; Champakalakshmi 1981:42–44, 120–25. Relief panels of the Rāma story appear in north India (at Deogarh) and the Deccan (Chalukyan sites) several centuries before the Chola period, however. Pollock (1993) remarks on the "scanty" evidence for a Rāma cult anywhere in India, except the Tamil country, before the twelfth century A.D.

5. Sanford 1974, especially 263–66. Historians studying Chola inscriptions have also found evidence of a royal Śiva cult (Stein 1994:323–38).

6. On these inscriptions, see chapter 2, note 21. A temple inscription at Ettamannur in central Kerala is also said to record endowments for the study of the *Kamparāmāyaṇam*, but I have found no further details (Nayar and Mahalingam 1952:x); see also V. Raghavan (1956).

7. Champakalakshmi 1981:116–24.

8. Caṭācivan̲ 1969; "hero" (*vīrar*) occurs nearly two hundred times, followed by "generous one" (*vaḷḷal*) approximately one hundred times.

9. On Cinna Tampi, legendary founder of the *tōl pāva kūttu*, see the discussion following this translation.

10. Appar and Cuntarar are major poets of early Śaiva bhakti in Tamil.

11. "Fifty-one letters" is reckoned (somewhat arbitrarily) as thirty-six in Tamil plus fifteen in Malayalam, which are used for sounds borrowed from Sanskrit.

12. Laksmana (Chettiyar) Pulavar is the late father of Krishnan Kutty Pulavar.

13. The unusually large number of Nayars (Malayalis) in this list of past puppeteers is accounted for by the fact that the performer is himself a Nayar.

14. This reference to the Raja of Guruvayur, a small but important Kṛṣṇa temple center on the western boundry of the tradition, is a rare mention of royal patronage in the puppet play; puppeteers in the Ponani area told me that they also include a mention of a Calicut king ("Camudira Raja") in their "Song of the Drama-House."

15. Here, and throughout this book, songs (*kavi*, or *pāṭṭu*) are indented.

16. The four poetic gifts (*nāl kavi celvam*) are: *maturam* (sweetness), *cittiram* (singing in accordance with metric conditions), *ācu* (ability to extemporize a composition), and *vittāra* (ability to compose a long poem on a single theme).

17. A comparison of this paragraph with its literal translation (Appendix A, sample 1) will indicate some of the condensation I have used in editing performances for this book.

18. A Tamil proverb: *Pāttiram ar̲aintu piccai iṭu; puttakam ar̲aintu peṇṇai koṭu.*

19. *Kātal iruvar karuttottu ātaravu paṭṭatu in̲pam.*

20. The verse to Kampan̲ (*campa*, invocation, 7), considered to be an interpolation in modern editions, is this:

We place on our head the feet of Kampan̲,
Who composed a story that spread and pleased all,

The story of the husband of flower-like Sītā,
The story of Rāma, whose name Śiva proclaimed to Pārvatī long ago.

21. A possible exception is a procession from a Bhagavati temple to a Viṣṇu temple in a nearby Brahmin settlement, although Brahmins do not participate in the festival, procession, or puppet play. Harding (1935:234) mentions that Brahmins were part of a procession from the Bhagavati temple to the drama-house on the final night of performance, but I suspect that his "Brahmins" are the non-Brahmin oracle and priests who lead the procession.

22. Most of these stories are recounted in Vīracāmi Ceṭṭiyār 1891 (*Vinōtaracamañcari*); Turaicāmipiḷḷai 1949 (*Tamiḻ Nāvalar Caritai*); Cārma 1922 (*Kampar Carittiram*); Purnalingam Pillai 1985:215 ff. See also Zvelebil 1973: 207–8.

23. See chapter 6.

24. Nilakanta Sastri 1975:2, pt. 2:524–28; Purnalingam Pillai 1985: 218.

25. Brahmin origins are often claimed for folk heroes in Tamil folklore, for example, the stories of Āṉantāci and Muttuppaṭṭaṉ (Blackburn 1988).

26. This last service is performed by Kaṇṇaki, the goddess of Madurai, who comes to Tanjore to aid the poet in the *Tiruvoṟṟiyūr Stalapurāṇam* (David Shulman, 1993, personal communication).

27. *Bhagavatikku nāṭakam*. In several Bengali texts, too, the goddess assists Rāma's victory; see W. L. Smith 1988:133.

28. On Śiva's prominence in Kampaṉ, see Maturai Palkalai Kaḻakam 1969.

29. As told to me by a puppeteer in 1989. Śiva's birth as Kampaṉ is sometimes left out of tellings. A shorter version explains that Bhagavati missed the original killing of Rāvaṇa by Rāma because she was herself involved in killing the demon Dāruka; when she complained, the puppet play began so that she could witness this spectacle every year. Vālmīki's story that Brahmā's door guardians, Jāya and Vijāya, were reborn as Rāvaṇa and Kumbhakarṇa is also told, with some variation, by the Kerala puppeteers.

30. Kōpālakiruṣṇamācāriyar (Kampaṉ 1926–71, 1:26) accepts this verse as "composed by Kampaṉ," but other editions indicate that it is missing from several manuscripts and hence consider it a *mikai pāṭal*, or added verse.

31. Thus "desired things" = *artha* and *kāma*; "wisdom and fame" = dharma; "liberation" = *mokṣa* (Kampaṉ 1926–71, 1:27).

32. As Ramanujan has observed, karma is a minor key in the explanation of events in Indian folktales (Ramanujan 1991b).

33. On the paradox of "giving" in Tamil culture, see Hart 1979. A similar lesson about the dharma of donations is taught by Rāma to Vibhīṣaṇa in the War Book.

34. For more discussion of dharma, and in particular the proper exercise of generosity, see the performance in chapter 7.

35. On the varieties of Kṛṣṇa bhakti, for example, see Hardy 1983.

36. O'Flaherty (Doniger) 1976:93.

37. On Rāma's ambiguity in Kampaṉ, see Shulman 1987; for the same in Vālmīki, see Pollock 1991:15–21.

38. See Hart and Heifetz 1988:26–30.

39. Hart and Heifetz 1988:29.

40. For Śrī Vaiṣṇava use of the Rāma story, see Carman and Narayanan 1989; Mumme 1991.

41. C. J. Fuller (1992:253) argues that one of the "fundamental objectives" of popular Hinduism is "to achieve identity between worshipper and deity." I agree that narrowing the distance between humans and gods is central to folk/popular religion, but only because the objective is access to power not identity with it.

42. An example of the Śrī Vaiṣṇava influence on the puppeteers' commentary is seen on pp. 139–40; for a sample of Saiva Siddhanta discourse, see pp. 101–2.

Chapter 4. The Death of Sambukumāraṉ: Kāma and Its Defense

1. Ramanujan has pointed out that opening scenes in Rāma stories often allude to their underlying themes (Ramanujan 1991a).

2. This verse, the first "narrative" verse in Rāma story told by the puppeteers, is well known because it has a double meaning (*cilēṭai*): all the qualities attributed to the river are equally attributable to poetry.

3. From this point forward, the performance continues as a conversation between epic characters. See chapter 7 for a description of conversations in the puppet play.

4. Here the puppeteers borrow a concept from classical Tamil poetry, *aintiṇai* (five-landscapes), to explain the place name, *pañca-vati* (five-lands).

5. Scrambling to find the tree puppet, which was not at hand, a puppeteer eventually settled on the tower puppet as a substitute and earned grimaces of disapproval from the others in the drama-house.

6. This verse (*māyam nīṅki*, 2.8.51) and the next (*mevu kāṇam*, 2.8.52) are borrowed from Kampaṉ's description of building another hut, at Chitrakuta.

7. *Viṇ-kaṇṭēṉ* (heaven-I saw) is a folk etymology for *vaikuṇṭam*.

8. Another Kampaṉ verse; see note 6 above.

9. The god of love, and of mischief, is Kāma, from *kāma* (sexual desire).

10. Other versions of Hindu cosmology are given by other puppeteers (for example, Mt. Chakravala is in the east, Mt. Astamana in the west).

11. The folk etymology here is that Pulastiyaṉ (the wise one) was born from Brahmā's *pulam* (wisdom).

12. This name for Śūrpaṇakhā is a combination of *kāma* (sexual desire) and *vaḷḷi* (creeper), a common epithet for women.

13. Kubera's mother was Tevavaṉṉi, Vicaravasu's first wife; Rāvaṇa and Śūrpaṇakhā were born from another wife, Kēkaci.

14. "Savapavam" replaces the usual "Carvapaumam"; the puppeteer forgot the eighth elephant's name.

15. *Muṭi vaṇaṅkāta maṉṉaṉ.*

16. "Disposition" translates *guṇa*.

17. Here the performer uses a *piramāṇam* from the twelfth section of the *Cutāmaṇi Nikantu*, a medieval Tamil grammar.

18. Śūrpaṇakhā cleverly substitutes the word *kāma* (with its intimations of passion and lust) for the usual *kātal* (romantic love) in this widely used proverb.

19. In Tamil: *mukattil maṉacu teriyum.*

20. Rāma's sarcasm in recommending Lakṣmaṇa as a possible spouse follows Vālmīki, not Kampaṉ.

21. Here Sītā speaks what Rāma thinks in Kampaṉ; in this scene in Kampaṉ, Sītā is voiceless and runs away when confronted by Śūrpaṇakhā. See discussion of vocalization in chapter 7.

22. At this point, a long *piramāṇam* (omitted here) from a Saiva Siddhanta text signals a shift from epic character to narrator, who delivers the discourse on the healing powers of the southern breeze (*teṉṟal*).

23. See Erndl 1991.

24. Malay manuscripts of the Rāma story (*Hikāyat Serī Rāma*) include the Sambukumāraṉ story, but only one of the many Malay shadow play performances recorded by Sweeney included it (Zieseniss 1963:40; Sweeney 1972: 229). At least three Jain texts include the episode, but another thirty do not (Kulkarni 1990:31n. 43, passim). References to other Rāmāyaṇa texts are from Gopalakrishna Rao 1984, passim; Brockington 1985:287; W. L. Smith 1988: 56–57. The episode in the *chitrakathi* tradition was confirmed by S. A. Krishnaiah (personal communication, 1988).

25. A frieze panel (in a series of Rāmāyaṇa panels) on the Hazara Rāma temple at Hampi (c. 1500 A.D.) in north Karnataka depicts another unusual variant in which Lakṣmaṇa appears to behead two ascetics. (Information and photograph of the frieze courtesy of Dr. Anna L. Dallapiccola).

26. From "The Ayōtti Katai," a manuscript collected from Kanya Kumari District, Tamil Nadu (author's collection); see its recent publication as Naṭarācaṉ 1987.

27. Rāmacuvāmi Pulavar 1956, 2:429–30. As commented upon later, the Uttara Kāṇḍa is often not included in editions of the Tamil Rāmāyaṇa; see Ce. Vēṅkaṭarāma Ceṭṭiyār, 1986.

28. See Bulcke's analysis of versions of the Śambūka story in north Indian literature (Bulcke 1962:616–20). I am indebted to John D. Smith for his patience in translating these passages for me.

29. Lakṣmaṇa kills Śambūka in the Jain *Paumacariya* (Bulcke 1962:619); the text in which Śambūka is cursed to be a tree is identified as "A. S. I." with no further explanation (p. 617). In many folk texts, Lakṣmaṇa does Rāma's work for him by killing Rāvaṇa as well.

30. A brief summary of this story is found in Father Bouchet's letter from the Coromandel, written in the seventeenth century (*Lettres Edifiantes et Curieuses*, 1718:172–73). Bulcke (1962:616–20) suggests that the Śambūka and Sambukumāraṉ stories are related, whereas Brockington (1985:267n. 19) appears to conflate or confuse Śambūka with Sambukumāraṉ.

31. Although Pollock (1991:3) notes the dramatic shift from the Ayodhya Book to the Forest Book, he debunks the two-separate-stories-theory on the basis of "what generations of performers and audiences have felt" (p. 5). One

wonders what evidence of those feelings is available to us; in Kerala, at least, the split between the two halves of the story is so apparent that the puppeteers begin their story at Pancavati.

32. Kampa<u>n</u> verse, *nīlamā* (3.5.8).

33. Padre Fenicio, a Portuguese missionary who lived on the Malabar coast from the late sixteenth to the early seventeenth century, summarizes this story in his journal, as edited by Jarl Charpentier (Fenicio 1933:80–83). I am indebted to Naomi Katz for translating this passage for me.

34. Narayana Rao (1991) summarizes a representative version of Śūrpaṇakhā's revenge as well as other women-centered tellings of the Rāma story. The revenge is more explicit in shadow puppet plays in northern Karnataka. In one version, Śūrpaṇakhā goes to heaven, gets ambrosia, revives her dead son's body, replaces his limbs, and asks him who killed him; he replies, "A man with an axe and Vaiṣṇava marks. You must get revenge, otherwise I'll become a *preta* ['hungry ghost']" (S. A. Krishnaiah 1988, personal communication). In some Tamil folk texts, Lakṣmaṇa, not Śūrpaṇakhā, is supplied with a motive for revenge: his mutilation of her is a response to her accusation that he slept with Viśvāmitra's mother (Parijātam 1987:140); and in E. V. Ramasami Naicker's retelling of the Rāma story, both Rāma and Lakṣmaṇa fall in love with Śūrpaṇakhā, who jilts them and is thus mutilated (Parijātam 1987:287).

35. On this Kampa<u>n</u> verse, see above, note 6.

36. Hart and Heifetz 1988:86.

37. On the pious demon, see O'Flaherty (Doniger) 1976:63–138; Shulman 1980:317–34.

38. Kampa<u>n</u> verse, *tītil* (3.5.38); Kampa<u>n</u> 1926–71, 3:179.

39. In Kampa<u>n</u>, Rāma remarks (to himself) on the "limitless beauty" of Śūrpaṇakhā/Mohinī, but his desire, fully revealed in the puppet play, is intimated in the southern recension of Vālmīki when he says, "For with your charming body, you do not look like a *rākṣasa* woman to me." Note that this line is excised from the critical edition of Vālmīki (Pollock 1991:274n. 16).

40. I am not suggesting that this alteration was deliberate, although that seems no more implausible than the alternative—that the change was inadvertent.

41. Kampa<u>n</u> verse, *aruttiyal* (3.5.51).

42. Kampa<u>n</u> verse, *tām u<u>r</u>u* (3.5.45).

43. See Pollock's useful commentary on this topic (1991:68 ff).

44. Śūrpaṇakhā marries Lakṣmaṇa, in their next births, in the Pābūjī epic (Smith 1991:93). In other folk texts, Sītā is teased about her relations with Rāvaṇa and asked to draw her captor's picture on her toe, or on a palm leaf, which then comes to life in her bedroom.

45. Goldman 1984:52–59.

46. The *Adhyātma Rāmāyaṇa* is one notable example.

Chapter 5. Killing Vāli: Rāma's Confession

1. The only major difference between the puppet play and Kampa<u>n</u>'s treatment of the missing episodes is a string of five folk verses in which Lakṣmaṇa cries out his anxiety while searching for Rāma in the forest.

2. Expenses for the Vāli episode are nearly twice that for ordinary nights; on this occasion, a family paid 2,001 rupees. The death of Indrajit and Garuḍa's rescue of Rāma also receive special ritual elaboration.

3. Some puppeteers in Palghat are Malayalis (principally Nayar, Nedungadi, and Panicker), who have learned the art from the Tamils and alongside whom they often perform, but the backbone of the tradition are Tamils. A Malayali performer told me that he sings the following verse in their "Song of the Drama-House" (although I did not record it): "We salute Kannappan Nayar and Ponnaccan Nayar, who belonged to the old and best Velur tradition and long ago established this Kampaṉ-drama."

4. On this special night, the sponsoring family hired a special musical group (*pañcavādhyam*) to lead the procession.

5. Kampaṉ verse, *maṇamum* (4.7.113).

6. Compare the folk verse with its Kampaṉ (*aiyā nuṅkaḷ* 4.7.104) equivalent below:

> The feelings of love with which Brahmā endowed
> The faultless, faithful women of your noble clan,
> Oh Rāma, he did not give to us;
> We enjoy what we can—that's how he made us.

7. Rāma's narration of the Gajendra story is omitted.

8. "Life-force" translates *uyir*.

9. This exchange between Jaṭāyu and Rāvaṇa, revealing the location of the life-index, is not found in Kampaṉ.

10. Rāvaṇa later mocks Hanumān as the servant of a "coward" (Aṅgada) who worships his father's killer (Rāma). See chapter 6.

11. Later, when Rāma sees Aṅgada bloody on the field, he recalls with pain this scene (see chapter 7).

12. This folk verse, in which Rāma admits his error, has no equivalent in Kampaṉ.

13. I truncate the translation at this point, after which Rāma instructs Sugrīva in statesmanship, Rāma pines for Sītā in the rainy season, and Lakṣmaṇa arrives in Kiṣkindha to summon the monkey army.

14. See W. L. Smith 1988:80–81.

15. Kulkarni 1990:33, 124–25; Brockington 1985:267–68, 273.

16. Vāli's boon is a gift from Śiva; see Kampaṉ verse, *kiṭṭuvār* (4.3.40).

17. Rācamāṇikkam 1965:6.

18. David Shulman (1979) provides a close reading of the theological issues in Kampaṉ's telling of the Vāli episode.

19. From the interpolated Vālmīki (W. L. Smith 1988:80).

20. A good example is the Bengali Rāmāyaṇa, *Meghanādavadha Kāvya*, by Michael Madhusudan Dutt; see Seely 1991.

21. See Richman 1991:184.

22. Achyuta Menon 1940:97–101.

23. See note 5, this chapter.

24. However contrived Lakṣmaṇa's explanation appears, it convinced one scholar, who wrote an exhaustive textual study of the Vāli episode in Kampaṉ (Srinivasan 1984, 1:217).

25. In a Malay text (*Hikāyat Serī Rāma*), Vāli catches Rāma's arrow before it reaches its mark and then convinces Rāma that he has done wrong; Rāma offers to grant Vāli his life, but his arrow must find its mark, and Vāli dies (Zieseniss 1963:56). Rāma also makes the offer in an Oriya text attributed to Bikrama Narendra (W. L. Smith 1988:83).

26. As Shulman (1987) points out, Kampan̲'s Rāma also is subject to the old Tamil code of shame and honor; cf. Hart and Heifetz (1988:28–30).

27. Although not included in the performance translated here, this prediction is often part of the puppeteers' commentary. It occurs in a Malayalam prose narrative of the puppet play (Karumaṅgurukkaḷ 1937) and in the Sanskrit *Mahānāṭaka*, in which Rāma instructs Vāli to kill him in his (Rāma's) sleep. In other texts (e.g., the Eastern recension of Vālmīki), Tārā curses Rāma to be killed by Vāli in a later birth (W. L. Smith 1988:94–95). On the pattern of violation-death-revenge in folk Hinduism, see Blackburn 1988.

28. Arunachalam 1981:112. Note also that in the reconstructed text, Rāma's admission comes *before* Vāli entrusts Aṅgada to him.

29. Even the puppet play is not immune from such pressures. In manuscripts and performances, Rāma's admission is made in the initial line of the folk verse: "Oh, listen, Vāli, I have done a great wrong (*pil̲ai ceytēn̲*)!" However, in a puppeteer's handwritten manuscript one letter is changed and the verse reads: "Oh, listen, Vāli, who have done a great wrong (*pil̲ai ceyta*)!" Blame is thus shifted from Rāma back to Vāli.

30. The eighteenth-century Bengali text is *Biṣṇupuri Rāmāyaṇa*; the two Tamil folk texts are "Vāli Mōṭca Nāṭakam" (Periya El̲uttu [chapbook] edition) and "Rāmāyaṇa Katai," a palm-leaf manuscript from Kanya Kumari (author's collection). In Kṛttibāsa's Rāmāyaṇa, Rāma confesses to Lakṣmaṇa that he is "filled with shame" for his killing of Vāli (W. L. Smith 1988:83).

31. Vīracāmi Ceṭṭiyār 1891:190–91.

Chapter 6. Rāvaṇa's First Defeat: The Puppeteers' Oral Commentary

1. See, for example, the folk texts in Kannada and Telugu described by Gopalakrishna Rao (1984:88, passim).

2. See Hatch 1934. The War Book is popular also in the shadow puppet play in Andhra Pradesh (C. R. Sarma 1973:44) and in the Chengam mural paintings in Tamil Nadu (Nagaswamy 1980:421).

3. Kampan̲ 1926–71, 6, pt. 1:iv. He also comments on the extraordinary number and variety of interpolations in Kampan̲'s War Book.

4. See Kampan̲ 1926–71, 6, pt. 2:ix. These episodes are accepted by some editors as part of Kampan̲'s original text.

5. The temple here is dedicated to Kaṇṇaki (not Bhagavati), the deified heroine of the *Cilappatikāram*, an epic composed by the brother of a Kerala king several centuries before Kampan̲; as in Kaṇṇaki temples in Tamil Nadu, the goddess here is imaged by a mirror and patronized by Chettiyars.

6. This privilege is called *māṭa pulavar aṭimai*, or "right of the [drama]-house puppeteer."

7. The *Kanta Purāṇam* is often thought to be a Tamil translation of the Sanskrit *Skanda Purāṇa*, but is, in fact, a very different text (Shulman 1980:30–31). The influence of this Tamil text on Kampan̲'s poem, which is acknowledged by the puppeteers, led the Dravidian movement leader E. V. Ramaswami Naicker to call the Rāma story a "stolen story" (Periyār 1972b: 59–64).

8. Kampan̲ verse, *kōnakar* (6.2.75).

9. *Tāy kon̲r̲ālum tūtan̲ kon̲r̲ātē.*

10. The puppeteers use *curuti* (Skt. *śruti*) as a synonym for the "Veda," including the Upanishads; *mūrtti* they explicate as "meaning" (*poruḷ*).

11. *Tīrtta* or "holy bathing place," "ford."

12. Omitted here is a description of the monkey army at work, including a conversation between Jāmbuvān̲ and Hanumān.

13. Kampan̲ verse, *kumutan̲* (6.7.42). Notice that this important verse is the only one in the translations not converted to dialogue by the puppeteers; also see note 15 below.

14. The Kiṣkindha Kāṇḍa has been omitted in this list.

15. In its second recitation, the verse, although unaltered, becomes dialogue because it is spoken by Kampan̲ himself.

16. Kampan̲'s text is seldom printed with the Uttara Kāṇḍa, however; see the discussion in chapter 8.

17. In the *Nāka pācam* episode (see chapter 7), Garuḍa rescues Rāma and his army from Indrajit's snake(*nāka*)-weapon.

18. The singer either forgot or simply omitted the third and fourth miracles.

19. Kampan̲ verse, *eṇṇiya* (invocation, 12). I follow Kōpālakiruṣṇamācāriyar's reading of this verse, which includes the famously disputed date of Kampan̲'s composition. See note 20 below.

20. Saka Era, after the Shaka kings in northern India, began in 78 A.D.; Saka 807 is thus 885 A.D. Most scholars consider this ninth-century date too early for the *Kamparāmāyaṇam* and, on largely literary evidence, date the poem from the late twelfth century. See Kampan̲ 1926–71, 1:xii–xiii; Zvelebil 1973b: 208.

21. Omitted here is a description of building the causeway, a long conversation between Rāma and Vibhīṣaṇa about Lanka, and a humorous scene in which Rāvaṇa's spies are caught by the monkeys and released by Rāma.

22. I have been unable to trace the source of this quotation.

23. Here I have truncated the puppeteer's commentary, which runs on at length and without eloquence, concerning the nature of Śiva.

24. This iconoclasm is not uncommon in south Indian Śaivism.

25. Compare this explanation with Rāma's terse answer in Kampan̲: *ayarttilēn̲*; *muṭivu atē* ("I have not forgotten; the result will be that [Rāvaṇa's death]").

26. I have omitted an argument between Aṅgada and Rāvaṇa about the power of Rāma.

27. This is one of numerous points where the lead puppeteer (speaking for Aṅgada) was cut short by another puppeteer in order to keep the narrative on track.

28. Kampan̲ verse, *vāraṇam* (6.15.1).

29. Another version of this story is told in the *Tiruvarañcuram Talapurā-ṇam*, a Tamil temple myth, in which the Brahmin form is assumed by Gaṇeśa, who tricks Rāvaṇa out of his boon from Śiva (in this case, a powerful lingam). The inverted bush also appears later in the same myth when Viṣṇu deceives Rāvaṇa and wins back Pārvatī (Shulman 1980:323–26).

30. At this point, Natesan Pillai jumped up from his catnap and entered the conversation. His explication of this verse has no parallel in the printed commentaries.

31. A folk verse. The same dialogue between Rāma's hands is recorded (with a minor difference—the right asks Rāma if it's proper to kill Rāvaṇa, a Brahmin) in an Oriya folk text (Misra 1983:75) and in Tulsīdās (Philip Lutgendorf 1991, personal communication).

32. Twenty-four minutes (*nāl̠ikai*), one-sixtieth of a day, is a traditional unit of time in Tamil.

33. Here the puppeteer draws on his knowledge of Tamil Siddha medicine; see Zvelebil 1973b:224.

34. The Kampan̠ verse, *vān̠aku maṇṇu* (6.15.11) compares Sītā's eyes to a spear (*vēl*).

35. Kampan̠ verse, *muḷaiyamai* (6.15.16). The puppeteers regularly gloss *puvan̠a mūn̠r̠um* as "gods of the Three Worlds," whereas other commentators read it as "He [Śiva] of the Three Worlds."

36. Foley 1991:6–7.

37. From the Sanskrit *pramāṇa* (citation).

38. On the independent status of the Tamil Uttara Kāṇḍa, see Vēṅkaṭarāma Ceṭṭiyār 1986, 2:iii–v.

39. The story of Vedavatī is found in the Sanskrit and Tamil Uttara Kāṇḍa, to which the puppeteers add Sītā's birth from Vedavatī's ashes in a vina played by Rāvaṇa; their version thus belongs to a cycle of folk stories that hint at a sexual relation between Sītā and Rāvaṇa.

40. This is an example of what I have termed the "backward-building" tendency in traditional Indian literature (Blackburn 1989).

41. On Vālmīki's curse of the bird hunter, which motivates his composition, see Shulman 1991b.

42. A more elaborate version of this story occurs in the *Vinōtaracamañcari*. Although that version follows the puppet play in nearly every detail, two major differences illustrate the theological shift from Vaiṣṇava bhakti to folk religion, discussed in chapter 3. First, in the printed account Kampan̠ is aided by Viṣṇu, whereas the Goddess plays that role in the puppet play. Second, in the printed account it is again Viṣṇu (carved on a stone pillar in the Srirangam temple) who confirms the authenticity of Kampan̠'s composition, whereas in the puppet play his poem is validated by a common woman's words.

Chapter 7. The Death of Indrajit: Creating Conversations

1. In Vālmīki's War Book, too, Indrajit's death is more important than Rāvaṇa's; see W. L. Smith 1988:123.

2. This scene has been considerably abbreviated in the translation.

3. The belief that only someone who has fasted in the forest for fourteen years (that is, only Lakṣmaṇa) is able to kill Indrajit is found in many folk texts.

4. On the truncated lives of Tamil folk heroes, see Blackburn 1988:34, 217–19.

5. On the pairing of king and renouncer, see Heesterman 1985. Notice, too, that Daśaratha, Rāma, and, to a lesser extent, Rāvaṇa exemplify the south Indian motif of an impotent monarch (Dirks 1987; Shulman 1985).

6. Krishnan Kutty Pulavar 1983, 1987. These books consist of the verses sung in performance and their formal exegesis.

7. Here ends the *akaval*, or prose summary that introduces each performance; this *akaval* is unusual in that it is spoken by Indra to the gods.

8. Kampaṉ verse, *tōḷoṭu tōḷ* (6.15.111).

9. On this subtle equivalence of *pūjyam* (cipher) and *pūjyaṉ* (noble one), the *Tamil Lexicon* offers both meanings for *pūcciyam*.

10. The three bodies are *sthūla, sūkkum*, and *kāraṇa*.

11. This is a Tamil version of the story of Śiva as Nīlakaṇṭaṉ, Dark-Throat, which appears also in Vālmīki's Rāmāyaṇa. The ascetic in this story is Cuntarar, an early Śaiva bhakti poet.

12. The Pankuni new moon is *amāvāci*; the three mantras are: *pañcāṭ-saram, māyā-mantra, saṭ-mantra.*

13. Thus concludes a skillful commentary: the puppeteer has digressed into several stories and yet, at the end, covers all the details in the verse under discussion.

14. Kampaṉ verse, *cūlamuṇṭatu* (6.15.122).

15. "Demonic disposition" translates *rākṣasa guṇa.*

16. Kampaṉ verse, *kālaṉār uyir* (6.15.117). Except for the initial words in their version (*kālaṉukku kālaṉ* instead of *kālaṉār uyir*), the puppeteers sing this verse verbatim with the Kampaṉ text. Their exegesis, however, takes the first two lines to refer to Śiva and not to Kumbhakarṇa as printed commentaries do.

17. From the Malayalam *kocca*; the Tamil word is *kokku.*

18. He requests, in other words, a girl who cannot possibly exist.

19. Recalling the discussion in chapter 4 on the concept of balance, note here the metaphorical "balance of this earth."

20. Kumbhakarṇa's victory over Viṣṇu (the puppeteers' reading of this verse) may refer to the former's earlier birth as Madhu, who battled Viṣṇu to a draw. The puppeteers' telling of this version of the story is omitted from the translation.

21. Vibhīṣaṇa's long speech is omitted.

22. A folk verse, *antaratti.*

23. *Kāppukku muṉ eṭukkum kaṭavuḷ tāṉ māl ākum.*

24. I have omitted a prosaic folk verse here because the commentary repeats its sense in more interesting language.

25. The feet of gods hover slightly above the ground.

26. See note 3, this chapter.

27. Omitted here is Vibhīṣaṇa's description of the "lotus formation" used by Indrajit in battle and the "swan formation" that Rāma's army must utilize to defeat it.

28. "Battle house" translates *pōr vīṭu.*

29. "Eat grass" is metaphorically what a defeated enemy must do.

30. A humorous interlude with the celestial dancers (*strī*), not found in Kampaṉ, is omitted in the translation.

31. Kampaṉ mentions that Indrajit visited women of pleasure after leaving the battlefield and before entering the palace.

32. This scene is abbreviated.

33. In Kampaṉ, too, Indra and the gods appear at this point.

34. Omitted here is a recapitulation of the entire Rāma story to this point, which the lead puppeteer spun out for half an hour.

35. In Kampaṉ, Garuḍa takes it upon himself to help Rāma.

36. According to popular legend (see chapter 6), Kampaṉ sang these songs in order to revive a dead boy in Chidambaram.

37. A description of Garuḍa's destruction of the snake-weapon is omitted.

38. Omitted here is a scene in which the two generals, Dhumrākṣa and Mahāpārsha, are ordered to be mutilated and exiled after they are caught stealing home to sleep with their wives. Māliyavāṉ intervenes and convinces Rāvaṇa that, given mounting losses, he cannot afford to kill any of his troops.

39. Omitted here is a scene is which Mahārakkaṉ, Kara's son, confronts Rāma and is dispatched by him.

40. Several battle scenes have been omitted.

41. I have omitted part of the dialogue in this scene, which is a formulaic repetition of the earlier scene when the umbrella holder and Indrajit surveyed the field after the snake-weapon had been released.

42. Here begins a string of three folk verses.

43. Kampaṉ verse, *tāyō* (6.21.207).

44. Folk verse, *oru maṉaivi.*

45. Kampaṉ verse, *tāṅkuvār* (6.21.201).

46. Kampaṉ verse, *arakkar kulattai* (6.21.224).

47. Kampaṉ verse, *aṇṭam* (6.21.226).

48. In Kampaṉ, Vibhīṣaṇa wakes Hanumān and together they find Jāmbuvāṉ, whereas the performance focuses on Jāmbuvāṉ, in accordance with his enlarged role in the puppet play.

49. Folk verse *aṟpa.*

50. Hanumān's three fathers are Śiva, Keśarī, and Vāyu; his mothers are Sambavī, Sadañjanī and Añjanī. His Saivite parentage is common in Rāma texts; one story, alluded to in the puppet play and told elsewhere, is that Śiva spilled his seed and Vāyu transferred it to an ape woman Añjanī, the wife of Keśarī (see W. L. Smith 1988:130).

51. I have abbreviated this account.

52. This version of the Madhu and Kaitabha story is foreshortened and highlights Jāmbuvāṉ's birth.

53. A folk verse, *cantaṉa.*

54. These herbs are described in Kampaṉ, but the puppeteers give them specific names: *cantaṉa karaṇi*; *calliya karaṇi*; *vacalliya karaṇi*; *amuta karaṇi.*

55. Kampan verse, *pētaimai* (6.27.9).

56. The omens are a single Brahmin, a widow, and a firewood seller (evidence of cremation?).

57. This verse is also sung both after Rāvaṇa's death and in the "Song of the Drama-House."

58. Bakhtin 1978; Volosinov 1978. See Trawick 1988 for an application of Bakhtin's ideas to Tamil folk songs.

59. Bakhtin 1978.

60. Coincidentally, recitation of the Hindi *Rāmcaritmānas* is also organized by four conversations, but they are more distant frames surrounding the text, whereas in the puppet play they vocalize action within the text. See Lutgendorf 1991:22–26.

61. The only exception to this rule (that I found) is the gods' rebuke of Rāma when he reluctantly accepts Sītā after the trial by fire.

62. The two segments of performance not in dialogue are (1) songs sung in the "Song of the Drama-House" and in the *nāṭakam*; and (2) the *avatārikai* prose transitions between scenes.

63. Bakhtin 1978:180.

64. Bakhtin 1978:181.

65. *Vīrar yār eṉṟār* becomes *Vīrar yār.*

66. For a critique of "direct" and "indirect" speech, see Coulmas 1986.

67. Lord 1991:16.

68. The translation is by Hart and Heifetz 1988:100.

69. The translation is by Hart and Heifetz 1988:86.

70. Harding 1935:234.

71. This verse is not adapted to dialogue because it is quoted like a *piramāṇam* rather than spoken by a character.

72. The puppets are seen by the public only once—after the final performance when Rāma is pinned up on the outside of the cloth screen. See chapter 8.

73. See Bogatyrev 1983:60.

74. Iyer 1943:4; Harding 1935.

75. One explanation for the term used here (*ola-pava-kuthu*) is that puppets were once made from *ōla* (palm leaf) not leather; another is that deer skin is as fine as a palm leaf (M. D. Raghavan 1947:39).

76. A senior puppeteer once explained to me that when his troupe went to Moscow, they adapted their performance to fit their new audience: "Those people [Russians] didn't know the language, so we did a lot of fight scenes and played the drums louder."

77. The majority of Kerala puppets have "one movable arm and hand, some have even two movable arms and hands, and very few have other movable parts" (Seltmann 1986:88).

Chapter 8. Rāma's Coronation: The Limits of Restoration

1. As mentioned in chapter 2, note 41, these Mutaliyars are also known as Sengunthars or Kaikolars.

2. The only exception, to my knowledge, is that a group of Tamils in Chittur (near Palghat) did sponsor puppet plays until in-fighting split the community and prevented further sponsorship.

3. Kampaṉ verse, *ellivāṉ* (6.27.61).

4. This section of the commentary has been abbreviated.

5. "Million" translates *kōṭi* ("crore," ten million).

6. A *pappadam* is a thin, crispy snack fried in oil.

7. Compare the earlier version of this story in chapter 6.

8. Thus ends Annamalai Pulavar's energetic eighty-minute commentary on a single verse. Several sections, which restate philosophical points already repetitiously explained, have been omitted.

9. The dim-witted messengers also appear in Kampaṉ, but their conversation here is an innovation of the puppet play.

10. A slapstick conversation between the messengers is omitted.

11. A *poṭṭu* is a dab of vermillion or ash (or both) in the middle of the forehead, often placed there after worship.

12. This summary in the brackets is itself highly condensed; these events consumed most of an hour.

13. Minor scenes of battle and tactical planning are omitted.

14. Here I have summarized a quick flurry of events (nearly the whole of the *Vēlēṟṟu paṭalam*) that require complicated movements of puppets on the screen.

15. Here the puppeteers show again that they know well Kampaṉ's verses, each of which they have reduced to a single line: "Indra-weapon, wham!" "X-weapon, wham!" etc.

16. Here follows a series of four folk verses: *maṉitā kēḷ, cavari, pātālattil, āṭā.*

17. The destruction of Rāvaṇa's sacrifice duplicates the earlier destruction of Indrajit's sacrifice; many of these events, including dragging Maṇḍōdari by the hair, are common in folk Rāmāyaṇas (W. L. Smith 1988:74–75) and are depicted in sixteenth-century temple paintings at Chengam, Tamil Nadu (Nagaswamy 1980:421–22).

18. The puppeteers' treatment of Rāvaṇa's death differs significantly from Kampaṉ's, in which Rāma himself realizes that he must shoot the Brahmā-weapon to kill Rāvaṇa. The puppet-play motif of disclosing Rāvaṇa's life-index in a pot of ambrosia is found in the *Rāmcaritmānas*, the *Adhyātma Rāmāyaṇa*, and several folk Rāmāyaṇas in south India (Gopalakrishna Rao 1984:103). However, whereas in all those texts Vibhīṣaṇa reveals the secret, in Kerala Agastya advises Rāma to call on Sūrya, who reveals the secret. Agastya appears in Vālmīki, too, but only to advise Rāma to meditate on Sūrya Deva, who confers his blessings on him without divulging the pot of ambrosia hidden in Rāvaṇa's chest.

19. That is, as Kṛṣṇa, who slays Kaṃsa.

20. Kampaṉ verse, *uṇṇātē* (6.36.220).

21. Kampaṉ verse, *veḷḷerukka* (6.36.239).

22. This point, not obvious in the verse, is also made by Kōpālakiruṣṇamācāriyar (Kampaṉ, 6, pt. 2:171), who adds parallels from the *Tirukkuṟaḷ* and Āṇṭāḷ's poetry.

23. This folk verse is very close in meaning to the equivalent verse in Kampa<u>n</u>, *e<u>nr</u>a pōti<u>n</u>* (6.37.37).

24. Kampa<u>n</u> verse, *u<u>nn</u>ai mīṭpā<u>n</u>* (6.37.63).

25. The *nelli* fruit, with its nearly translucent skin, is a folk metaphor for clarity; see also chapter 6.

26. Kampa<u>n</u> verse, *pārkkelām* (6.37.75).

27. This folk verse (*tampiyum*) borrows two lines from a Kampa<u>n</u> verse, *āyi<u>n</u>um* (6.37.129), and renders a similar meaning.

28. Daśaratha here tells the story of his promise to Kaikeyī's father that her son, not Kausalyā's, would inherit the throne.

29. Here the folk performance presents a condensed version of the "Revival of Vacanta<u>n</u>" episode (*Vacanta<u>n</u> uyir varu paṭalam*), sometimes called "Yama Episode" (*Iyama Paṭalam*); see chapter 8.

30. This hybrid verse illustrates well the puppeteers' use of Kampa<u>n</u>. The first two lines are a formula used both by Kampa<u>n</u> (*māliyai kaṇṭē<u>n</u>*, 6.30.52) and the puppeteers (chapter 8). The final two lines, not in Kampa<u>n</u>, make Jāmbuvā<u>n</u>'s point: that Rāma, having crowned Vibhīṣaṇa king of Lanka, has taken Rāvaṇa's chariot for his own use. In other Tamil folk Rāmāyaṇas, Jāmbuvā<u>n</u> speaks a variant of this hybrid verse to chide Sītā when she desires to remove a beautiful grinding stone from Lanka (C. R. Sarma 1973:66–67; Venugopal 1993:105–6).

31. The return journey to Ayodhya in Kampa<u>n</u> differs from that in the puppet play in the following details of the Kiṣkindha visit: (1) Sītā does not take the initiative to ask Rāma to visit Kiṣkindha; (2) Tārā first gives Sītā a garland; and (3) Sītā offers condolences for Vāli's death.

32. Here the puppeteers tell a truncated version of the story of Śiva's lingam at Ramesvaram, considered an interpolated episode ("The Pūjā," *pūcai paṭalam*). The Kerala version follows closely accounts in other folk texts and Tamil myths (*Kanta Purāṇam* and *Cētu Purāṇam*).

33. "Sins" translates *pāvaṅkaḷ*.

34. "Two hours" translates *aintu nā<u>l</u>ikai*.

35. Folk verse, *pūṇṇai nōkki*.

36. For this conclusion to Indian oral epics (especially Pābūjī, Ālhā, Lorik and Candā, Gūgā, Muttuppaṭṭa<u>n</u>), see Blackburn et al. 1989. Gopi Chand is yet another example (Gold 1992).

37. The Hindi Rāmāyaṇa by Tulsīdās extends into the Uttara Kāṇḍa, but holds out "the promise of a new kind of transcendent, personal *Rāmrāj*" (Lutgendorf 1991:373).

38. Shulman 1991a:95. See Shulman on these themes of restoration in Kampa<u>n</u>'s episode of Sītā's test by fire, although he finds more ferocity in Kampa<u>n</u>'s Sītā than I do.

39. In Kampa<u>n</u> and the puppet play, Sītā does speak sharply to Rāma in an earlier scene when he proposes that she should not accompany him into exile; in Vālmīki, she insults him (Sutherland 1989:74).

40. A medieval Śrī Vaiṣṇava commentator on Vālmīki justified Rāma's anger when Sītā carried out his command by explaining that both she and Vibhīṣaṇa should have divined his true intention (Mumme 1991:209). In a Kuṭiyāṭṭam

drama from Kerala, Sītā's appearance in fine clothes is explained away as a consequence of a boon from Anasūyā (Jones 1984:18).

41. Kampan̲ verse, *yān̲ ivaṇi* (6.37.40).

42. On this verse, see note 30, chapter 8.

43. In a south Indian Sanskrit text, the *Tattvasaṃgraharāmāyaṇa*, Jāmbuvān̲ challenges Rāma to a duel, but it is deferred until the Kṛṣṇa avatar (V. Raghavan 1952/53).

44. In Kampan̲, Rāma threatens suicide when he grieves over Jaṭāyu's body.

45. Kampan̲ verse, *villin̲ai* (6.18.224), followed by *tāmarai* (6.18.223).

46. Kampan̲ verse, *viṭaikkulaṅka* (6.21.197).

47. The puppeteers' telling is similar to one version in the *Pañcatantra* ("Hundred Wit, Thousand Wit, and Single Wit"; Ryder 1972:444–46). Both versions, for example, include the motif of the fish overhearing the fishermen the day before, which updates W. N. Brown's claim (1919:34) that this motif is found in literary but not popular versions. Another oral variant, in which a mongoose, cobra, and tortoise prevaricate about a fire in their haystack home, while a jackal flees and lives, is recorded in Beck and Claus 1987:235–36. See also tales 497 and 498 in Bødker 1957.

48. GoldbergBelle 1989. Handelman later refined his analysis of oscillating clowns (Handelman 1990:240–45).

49. Personal communication, 1992.

50. This information was gathered in 1990 from written records and interviews at the All-India Handicrafts Centre, Trichur, Kerala.

51. The 1982 figure is from Seltmann (1986:16–17); the 1989 figure is from my fieldwork.

52. Harding 1935:234.

53. My list of drama-houses, compiled from interviews with puppeteers, contains seventy-nine sites, to which I have added others from a list compiled by Venu (1990:65). Seltmann (1986), who completed his fieldwork in 1982, lists thirty-five sites.

54. I refer to Cousins (1970) and Harding (1935), as quoted above, chapters 7 and 8.

Glossary

Note: For main characters in the puppeteers' Rāma story, see Appendix C.

ĀDIŚEṢA (ŚEṢA): snake, coiled on the waters, upon which Viṣṇu sleeps
AGASTYA: sage who assists Rāma
AKAVAL: prose summary of previous night's action that introduces each performance
AVATAR: lit. "descent" of Viṣṇu, as Rāma and other figures
AVATĀRIKAI: prose narration used as transition between scenes
BHAGAVATI: important goddess in Kerala, in whose festival the puppet play is performed
BHAKTI: religious devotion, of several varieties
BRAHMAN: underlying unity of existence; monism
DHARMA: morally correct, prescribed action
GAṆEŚA: elephant-headed son of Śiva and Pārvatī, invoked in each performance as remover of obstacles
INDRA: king of gods; a narrator in the puppet play
KALPA: an eon in Indian mythology
KĀMA/KĀMA: sexual desire, lust/god of love
KATHĀ [HINDI]: a performance mode of *Rāmcaritmānas*
KAVI: verse (in Kampa<u>n</u>'s epic); *pāṭṭu*
KUṬAKKĀRA<u>N</u>: umbrella (parasol) holder; low-status servant in temples and courts, and puppet play
KŪTTU MĀṬAM: playhouse; stage for the puppet play
LAKH: 100,000
LAKṢMĪ: goddess of prosperity and wealth; wife of Viṣṇu

LINGAM: icon for Śiva

MAHĀBALI: king from whom Viṣṇu as Vāmana (dwarf-avatar) receives a boon of three steps of land

MĀYĀ: illusion, deceit

MIKAI PĀṬAL: "extra song/verse"; interpolated verse in manuscripts of Kampaṉ's epic

MOKṢA: spiritual liberation

MURUKAṈ: younger son of Śiva (cf. Skanda); important Tamil god

NĀRĀYAṆA: a name for Viṣṇu

NĀṬAKAM: "dance"; interruption in puppet play during which dancers entertain Rāvaṇa and puppeteers sing verses invoking blessings for their one-rupee donors

OṬṬAKKŪTTAṈ: poet of Tamil Uttara Kāṇḍa; Kampaṉ's rival

PĀRVATĪ: wife of Śiva

PAṬṬA PĀVA (I): Brahmin puppets who act as narrators during the "Song of the Drama-House," with which each performance begins

PĀṬṬU: song, verse, *kavi*

PIRAMĀṆAM: explication, quotation, rule (Skt. *pramāṇa*)

POṬṬU: ash mark placed on forehead, usually after *pūjā*

PŪJĀ: ceremony of worship

PULAVAR: learned man, scholar, puppeteer

PURĀṆA: myth or legend; "old story"

RĀKṢASA: demon; enemy of the gods

RĀMCARITMĀNAS: Hindi Rāmāyaṇa, composed by Tulsīdās in the sixteenth century

SARASVATĪ: goddess of learning and arts; wife of Brahmā

ŚĀSTRAS: books of codified rules and regulations

ŚEṢA: see Ādiśeṣa

SUDRA: lowest caste in normative caste system

TAPAS: religious austerities

TŌL PĀVA (I) KŪTTU: "leather puppet play"

TRETĀ YUGA: second of four eons in Hindu mythology, when Rāma appears

UTTARA KĀṆḌA: sequel to Rāma story included in many texts, such as Vālmīki, but not in Kampaṉ

VAIKUNTA: Viṣṇu's heavenly home

VAḶḶAL: benefactor, generous one

VĀLMĪKI: legendary poet of early Rāma text in Sanskrit

VEḶICCAPPĀṬU: oracle-priest in Bhagavati temples

VĒSTI (*VĒTTI*): man's lower garment in Tamil Nadu

VINA (*VIṆAI*): south Indian musical instrument, lute; cf. north Indian sitar

VYĀS (HINDI): Brahmin singers of *Rāmcaritmānas*

YŌJAṈA: traditional unit of distance; cf. "league"

YUGA: eon; age in Hindu mythology

Bibliography

Works in Western Languages

Abrahams, Roger D.
1976. The complex relations of simple forms. In Dan Ben-Amos, ed., *Folklore Genres*, pp. 193–214. Austin: University of Texas Press.

Achyuta Menon, C.
1911. *Cochin State Manual*. Ernakulam: Cochin State Press.
1940. *Ezhuthachan and His Age*. Madras: University of Madras.

Arooran, K. Nambi.
1980. *Tamil Renaissance and Dravidian Nationalism, 1905–1944*. Madurai: Koodal.

Arunachalam, M.
1981. T. K. C.'s interpretation of the Vali-vadham. In M. Arunachalam, ed., *Proceedings of the Fifth International Conference-Seminar of Tamil Studies, Madurai*, vol. 2, pp. 107–25. Madras: International Institute of Tamil Studies.

Bakhtin, M. M.
1978 (1929). Discourse typology in prose. In Ladislav Matejka and Krystyna Pomorska, eds., *Readings in Russian Poetics: Formalist and Structuralist Views*, pp. 176–96. Michigan Slavic Publications, no. 8. University of Michigan: Ann Arbor.

Balasubrahmanyam, S. R.
1971. *Early Chola Temples: Parantaka I to Rajaraja I*. New Delhi: Orient Longman.

Bannerjee, P.
1986. *Rāma in Indian Literature, Art, and Thought*. 2 vols. Delhi: Sundeep Prakashan.

Bauman, Richard, and Charles L. Briggs.
1990. Poetics and performance as critical perspectives on language and social life. *Annual Review of Anthropology* 19:59–88.

Beck, Brenda, et al., eds.
1987. *Folktales of India*. Chicago: University of Chicago Press.
Ben-Amos, Dan.
1993. "Context" in context. *Western Folklore* 52:209–26 (Special issue: *Theorizing Folklore*, Charles Briggs and Amy Shulman, eds.)
Blackburn, Stuart.
1985. Death and deification: Folk cults in Hinduism. *History of Religions* 24,3:255–74.
1988. *Singing of Birth and Death: Texts in Performance*. Philadelphia: University of Pennsylvania Press.
1989. Patterns of development for Indian oral epics. In Stuart Blackburn et al., eds., *Oral Epics in India*, pp. 15–32. Berkeley: University of California Press.
Blackburn, Stuart, Peter J. Claus, Joyce B. Flueckiger, and Susan S. Wadley, eds.
1989. *Oral Epics in India*. Berkeley: University of California Press.
Blackburn, Stuart, and Joyce Flueckiger.
1989. Introduction. In Stuart Blackburn et al., eds., *Oral Epics in India*, pp. 1–11. Berkeley: University of California Press.
Blackburn, Stuart, and A. K. Ramanujan, eds.
1986. *Another Harmony: New Essays on the Folklore of India*. Berkeley: University of California Press.
Bødker, Laurits.
1957. *Indian Animal Tales*. FF Communications No. 170. Helsinki: Suomalainen Tiedeakatemia.
Bogatyrev, Petr.
1983. The interconnection of two similar semiotic systems: The puppet theater and the theatre of living actors. *Semiotica* 48:47–68.
Briggs, Charles.
1988. *Competence in Performance: The Creativity of Tradition in Mexicano Verbal Art*. Philadelphia: University of Pennsylvania Press.
Brockington, John.
1985. *Righteous Rāma: The Evolution of an Epic*. New Delhi: Oxford University Press.
Brown, W. N.
1919. The *Pañcatantra* in modern Indian folklore. *Journal of the American Oriental Society* 39, 1:1–54.
Buchanan, Francis.
1807. *A Journey from Madras, through the Countries of Mysore, Canara, and Malabar*. 3 vols. London: T. Cadell and W. Davies.
Carman, John B.
1974. *The Theology of Ramanuja: An Essay in Interreligious Understanding*. New Haven: Yale University Press.

Carman, John B., and Vasudha Narayanan.
1989. *The Tamil Veda: Piḷḷāṉ's Interpretation of the Tiruvāymoḻi.* Chicago: University of Chicago Press.

Census of India
1901. Vol. 20, *Cochin*, pt. 1, Report. Ernakulam: Cochin Government Press.
1931. Vol. 21, *Cochin*, pt. 1, Report. Ernakulam: Cochin Government Press.
1941. Vol. 19, *Cochin*, pt. 1, Report. Ernakulam: Cochin Government Press.
1951. Vol. 15, *Madras. Village-Wise Mother-Tongue Data for Bilingual or Multi-lingual Taluks.* Madras: Government Press.
1961. *Kerala, Village Monographs*, pt. 6-B.

Chaitanya, Krishna.
1971. *A History of Malayalam Literature.* New Delhi: Orient Longman.

Champakalakshmi, R.
1981. *Vaiṣṇava Iconography in the Tamil Country.* New Delhi: Orient Longman.

Coomaraswamy, A. K.
1930. The shadow-play in Ceylon. *Journal of the Royal Asiatic Society of Great Britain and Ireland* 3 (July): 627.

Coulmas, Florian, ed.
1986. *Trends in Linguistics.* Vol. 31, *Direct and Indirect Speech.* Berlin: Mouton.

Cousins, J. H.
1970 (1948). Dance drama and shadow play. In Stella Kramrisch, J. H. Cousins, and R. Vasudevan Poduval, eds., *The Arts and Crafts of Kerala,* pp. 161–78. Cochin: Paico.

Daniel, Valentine.
1984. *Fluid Signs: Being a Person the Tamil Way.* Berkeley: University of California Press.

De, S. K.
1931. The problem of Mahanataka. *Indian Historical Quarterly* 7:537–74, 629–43.

Dirks, Nicholas.
1987. *The Hollow Crown: Ethnohistory of an Indian Kingdom.* Cambridge: Cambridge University Press.

Duarte Barbosa,
1866. *A Description of the Coasts of East Africa and Malabar, In the Beginning of the Sixteenth Century.* Translated by Henry E. J. Stanley. London: Hakluyt Society.

Emeneau, M. B.
1985. Kannaḍa Kampa, Tamil Kampaṉ: Two proper names. *Journal of the American Oriental Society,* 105:401–4.

Erndl, Kathleen.

1991. The mutilation of Śūrpaṇakhā. In Paula Richman, ed., *Many Rāmāyaṇas: The Diversity of a Narrative Tradition in South Asia*, pp. 67–88. Berkeley: University of California Press.

Fenicio, Father Jacobo.

1933. *Livro da Seita Dos Indios Orientais.* Edited by Jarl Charpentier. Uppsala: Almqvist and Wiksells.

Finnegan, Ruth.

1977. *Oral Poetry: Its Nature, Significance and Social Context.* Cambridge: Cambridge University Press.

Flueckiger, Joyce Burkhalter.

1988. He should have worn a sari. A failed performance of a central Indian oral epic. *The Drama Review* 32, 1:159–69.

1991. Literacy and the changing concept of text: Women's Rāmāyaṇ maṇḍali in central India. In Joyce Flueckiger and Laurie Sears, eds., *Boundaries of the Text: Epic Performances in South and Southeast Asia,* pp. 43–60. Ann Arbor: University of Michigan Center for South and Southeast Asian Studies.

Foley, John Miles.

1991. *Immanent Art: From Structure to Meaning.* Bloomington: Indiana University Press.

Fullarton, Colonel William.

1787. *A View of the English Interests in India.* London, Edinburgh: T. Cadell.

Fuller, C. J.

1992. *The Camphor Flame: Popular Hinduism and Society in India.* Princeton: Princeton University Press.

George, K. M.

1966. *Ramacaritam and the Study of Early Malayalam.* Kottayam: National Book Stall.

Gold, Ann Grodzins.

1992. *A Carnival of Parting: The Tales of King Bharthari and King Gopi Chand as Sung and Told by Madhu Natisar Nath of Ghatiyali, Rajasthan.* Berkeley: University of California Press.

GoldbergBelle, Jonathan.

1984. Tolubommalāṭa: The Andhra shadow puppet theatre. Ph.D. diss., University of Wisconsin, Madison.

1989. Clowns in control: Performances in a shadow puppet tradition in south India. In Stuart Blackburn et al., eds., *Oral Epics in India*, pp. 118–39. Berkeley: University of California Press.

Goldman, Robert., ed. and trans.

1984. *The Rāmāyaṇa of Vālmīki: An Epic of Ancient India.* Vol. 1, *Bālakāṇḍa.* Princeton: Princeton University Press.

Gopalakrishna Rao, T.
1984. *Folk Ramayanas in Telugu and Kannada*. Nellore: Saroja Publications.
Gore, A. N.
1943. *Bibliography of the Ramayana*. Poona: N.p.
Govindakutty, A.
1981. Tamil literary traditions and the oldest Malayalam Raamaayana. In M. Arunachalam, ed., *Proceedings, 5th International Conference-Seminar on Tamil Studies, Madurai*, vol 1., pp. 20–32. Madras: International Institute of Tamil Studies.
Handelman, Don.
1990. *Models and Mirrors: Toward an Anthropology of Public Events*. Cambridge: Cambridge University Press.
Harding, Stan.
1935. The Ramayana shadow-play in Malabar. *Asia* (April): 234–35.
Hardy, Friedhelm.
1983. *Viraha-Bhakti: The Early History of Kṛṣṇa Devotion in South India*. New Delhi: Oxford University Press.
Hart, George L.
1979. The nature of Tamil devotion. In Madhav M. Deshpande and Peter Erwin Hook, eds., *Aryan and Non-Aryan in India*, pp. 11–33. Michigan Papers on South and Southeast Asia. Ann Arbor: University of Michigan.
Hart, George L., and Hank Heifetz, trans.
1988. *The Forest Book of the Rāmāyaṇa of Kampaṉ*. Berkeley: University of California Press.
Hatch, Emily Gilchriest.
1934. Kathakali: The indigenous drama of Malabar. Ph.D. diss., Cornell University.
Heesterman, J. C.
1985. *The Inner Conflict of Tradition: Essays in Indian Ritual, Kingship, and Society*. Chicago: University of Chicago Press.
Hess, Linda.
1983. Rām Līlā: The audience experience. In Monika Thiel-Horstmann, ed., *Bhakti in Current Research, 1979–1982*, pp. 171–94. Berlin: Dietrich Reimar.
Hiltebeitel, Alf.
1988. *The Cult of Draupadī*. Vol. 1, *Mythologies: From Gingee to Kurukṣetra*. Chicago: University of Chicago Press.
Hobart, Angela.
1987. *Dancing Shadows of Bali: Theatre and Myth*. London: KPI.
Hymes, Dell.
1975. Breakthrough into performance. In Dan Ben-Amos and Kenneth Goldstein, eds., *Folklore: Performance and Communication*, pp. 11–75. The Hague: Mouton.

Innis, C. A.

1951. *Malabar*. Rev. ed. Madras District Gazetteers. Madras: Government Press.

Irschick, Eugene.

1969. *Politics and Social Conflict in South India: The Non-Brahman Movement and Tamil Separatism*. Berkeley: University of California Press.

Iyengar, K. R. Srinivasan, ed.

1983. *Asian Variations in Ramayana*. New Delhi: Sahitya Akademi.

Iyer, K. B.

1943. The shadow play in Malabar. *Bulletin of the Rama Varma Research Institute* 11, 1:3–12.

Jakobson, Roman.

1960. Concluding statement. Linguistics and poetics. In T. A. Sebeok, ed., *Style in Language*, pp. 350–73. Cambridge: MIT Press.

Jesudasan, C., and H. Jesudasan.

1961. *A History of Tamil Literature*. The Heritage of India Series. Calcutta: YMCA Publishing House.

Jilin, Liu.

1986. *Chinese Shadow Puppet Play*. Beijing: Morning Glory Press.

Jones, Clifford Reis.

1984. *The Wondrous Crest-Jewel in Performance*. Delhi: Oxford University Press.

Kali-Krishna, Maharaja.

1840. *Mahā-nāṭaka: A Dramatic History of King Rama*. Calcutta: N. Robertson.

Kapur, Anuradha.

1990. *Actors, Pilgrims, Kings, and Gods: The Rāmlīlā at Rāmnagar*. Calcutta: Seagull.

Kareem, C. K.

1976. *Kerala Gazeteers, Palghat District*. Ernakulam: Government Press.

Keeler, Ward.

1987. *Javanese Shadow Plays, Javanese Selves*. Princeton: Princeton University Press.

Krishnaiah, S. A.

1988. *Karnataka Puppetry*. Udipi (India): Regional Resources Centre for Folk Performing Arts.

Krishna Iyer, K. V.

1973 (1942). The Venganad Nambitis. *Bulletin of the Rama Varma Research Institute*. 10, pt. 1:41–56; pt. 2:92–106.

Kulkarni, M. V.

1990. *The Rāma Story in Jain Literature*. Saraswati Pustak Bhandar: Ahmedabad.

Kurup, K. K. N., ed.

1984. *The Kavalapara Papers*. Calicut: Calicut University.

1988. The Kavalapara family. In K. K. N. Kurup, ed., *Modern Kerala: Studies in Social and Agrarian Relations*, pp. 13–60. Delhi: Muttal.

Lettres Edifiantes et Curieuses Ecrites des Missions Etrangères par quelques Missionaries de la Compagnie de Jésus. 1718. Vol. 13. Paris.

Logan, William.

1887. *Malabar.* Vol. 2. Madras: Government of Madras.

Lord, Albert Bates.

1987. The *Kalevala*, the south Slav epics, and Homer. In Bo Almqvist et al., eds., *The Heroic Process: Form, Function and Fantasy in Folk Epic*, pp. 293–324. Dublin: Glendale Press.

1991. *Epic Singers and Oral Tradition.* Ithaca, N.Y.: Cornell University Press.

Lutgendorf, Philip.

1991. *The Life of a Text: Performing The Rāmcaritmānas of Tulsidas.* Berkeley: University of California Press.

Mahalingam, T. V., ed.

1972. *Mackenzie Manuscripts.* Vol. 1. Madras: Madras University.

Maharajan, S.

1972. *Kampan.* New Delhi: Sahitya Akademi.

Mair, Victor H.

1988. *Painting and Performance: Chinese Picture Recitation and Its Indian Genesis.* Honolulu: University of Hawaii Press.

Mills, Margaret.

1991. *Rhetorics and Politics in Afghan Traditional Storytelling.* Philadelphia: University of Pennsylvania Press.

Misra, Narendra Nath.

1983. Folk-elements in Jagamohan Ramayana. In Asit K. Banerjee, ed., *The Ramayana in Eastern India*, pp. 74–79. Calcutta: Prajna.

Morab, S. G.

1977. *The Killekyatha: Nomadic Folk Artists of Northern Mysore.* Calcutta: Anthropological Survey of India.

Mumme, Patricia Y.

1991. *Rāmāyaṇa* exegesis in Teṉkalai Śrīvaiṣṇavism. In Paula Richman, ed., *Many Rāmāyaṇas: The Diversity of a Narrative Tradition in South Asia*, pp. 202–16. Berkeley: University of California Press.

Nadar, A. C. Paul.

1957. The problem of the life and age of Kampan. *Tamil Culture* 6:31–49.

Nagaswamy, R.

1980. Sri Ramayana in Tamilnadu, in art, literature, and thought. In V. Raghavan, ed., *The Ramayana Tradition in Asia*, pp. 409–29. New Delhi: Sahitya Akademi.

Naidu, S. Shankar Raju.
1971. *A Comparative Study of Kampa Ramayanam and Tulasi Ramayan*. Madras: Madras University.
Nanu Pillai, P. V.
1910. The Ramayana-an historical study. *The Tamil Antiquary* 1, 7:11–26. Reprint, Asian Educational Services, New Delhi, 1986.
Narayan, Kirin.
1989. *Storytellers, Saints, and Scoundrels: Folk Narrative in Hindu Religious Teaching*. Philadelphia: University of Pennsylvania Press.
Narayana Rao, Velcheru.
1991. A Rāmāyaṇa of their own: Women's oral tradition in Telugu. In Paula Richman, ed., *Many Rāmāyaṇas: The Diversity of a Narrative Tradition in South Asia*, pp. 114–36. Berkeley: University of California Press.
Nayar, S. K., and T. V. Mahalingam, eds.
1952. *Selected Malayalam Inscriptions*. Madras: University of Madras.
Nilakanta Sastri, K. A.
1975 *The Cōḻas*. Rev. ed. 2 vols. Madras: Madras University.
O'Flaherty (Doniger), Wendy.
1976. *The Origins of Evil in Hindu Mythology*. Berkeley: University of California Press.
Pandurangan, A.
1982. Rāmāyaṇa versions in Tamil. *Tamil Culture* 21:58–67.
Pani, Jiwan.
N.d. *Ravana Chhaya*. New Delhi: Sangeet Natak Akademi.
Parpola, Asko.
1994. *Deciphering the Indus Script*. Cambridge: Cambridge University Press.
Pisharoti, M. A.
1933/34. Kerala theatre. *Journal of the Annamalai University* 1,2:91–113; 3,2:137–59.
Pollock, Sheldon.
1986. (Trans.) *The Rāmāyaṇa of Vālmīki: An Epic of Ancient India*. Vol 2, *Ayodhyā Kāṇḍa*. Princeton: Princeton University Press.
1991. (Trans.) *The Rāmāyaṇa of Vālmīki: An Epic of Ancient India*. Vol. 3, *Araṇya Kāṇḍa*. Princeton: Princeton University Press.
1993. Rāmāyaṇa and political imagination in India. *Journal of Asian Studies* 52:261–97.
Ponnambalam Pillai, T.
1910. The morality of the Ramayana-a rejoinder. *The Tamil Antiquary*, 1,7:53–82. Reprint, Asian Educational Services, New Delhi, 1986.
Proschan, Frank.
1981. Puppet voices and interlocutors: Language in folk puppetry. *Journal of American Folklore* 94:527–55.

1983. The semiotic study of puppets, masks, and performing objects. In Frank Proschan, ed., *Semiotica* 47 (special issue "Puppets, Masks, and Performing Objects from Semiotic Perspectives"): 3–44.

1987. Co-creation of the comic in puppetry. In Dina Sherzer and Joel Sherzer, eds., *Humor and Comedy in Puppetry: A Celebration of Popular Culture*, pp. 30–46. Bowling Green, Ohio: Bowling Green State University Popular Press.

Purnalingam Pillai, M. S.

1985. *Tamil Literature*. Rev. ed. Thanjavur (India): Tamil University.

Qureshi, Regula Burckhardt.

1983. *Qawwālī*: Making the music happen in the Sufi assembly. In Bonnie C. Wade, ed., *Performing Arts in India: Essays on Music, Dance, and Drama*, pp. 118–57. Berkeley: Center for South and Southeast Asia Studies, University of California, Berkeley.

Raghavan, M. D.

1947. *Folk Plays and Dances of Kerala*. Trichur: Rama Varma Archaeological Society.

Raghavan, V.

1952/53. *Tattvasamgraha-Rāmāyaṇa* of Rāma Brahmananaṇḍa. *Annals of Oriental Research*, 10,1:1–55. Madras: University of Madras.

1956. Methods of popular religious instruction in south India. In Haridas Bhattacharyya, ed., *The Cultural Heritage of India*, vol. 4, pp. 503–6. Calcutta: Ramakrishna Institute of Culture.

1975. *The Ramayana in Greater India*. Surat: South Gujarat University.

1975. (Ed.) *The Ramayana Tradition in Asia*. New Delhi: Sahitya Akademi.

Ramanujan, A. K.

1989. Where mirrors are windows: Toward an anthology of reflections. *History of Religions* 29:188–216.

1991a. Three hundred Rāmāyaṇas: Five examples and three thoughts on translation. In Paula Richman, ed., *Many Rāmāyaṇas: The Diversity of a Narrative Tradition in South Asia*, pp. 3–21. Berkeley: University of California Press.

1991b. Toward a counter-system: Women's tales. In Arjun Appadurai et al., eds., *Gender, Genre, and Power in South Asian Expressive Systems*, pp. 33–55. Philadelphia: University of Pennsylvania Press.

Ramaswamy, Sumathi.

1992. En/gendering language: The poetics and politics of Tamil identity, 1891–1970. Ph.D. diss., University of California, Berkeley.

Ramaswamy, Vijaya.

1985. *Textiles and Weavers in Medieval South India*. New Delhi: Oxford University Press.

Ray, Eva.
1978. Documentation for Paithan painting. *Artibus Asiae* 40,4:239–82.
Rice, Lewis, ed.
1902. *Epigraphia Carnatica*. Vol. 5. Hassan District. Mangalore: Mysore Archaeological Survey.
Richman, Paula.
1991. E. V. Ramaswami's reading of the *Rāmāyaṇa*. In Paula Richman, ed., *Many Rāmāyaṇas: The Diversity of a Narrative Tradition in South Asia*, pp. 175–201. Berkeley: University of California Press.
1991. (Ed.) *Many Rāmāyaṇas: The Diversity of a Narrative Tradition in South Asia*. Berkeley: University of California Press.
Ryder, Arthur. trans.
1972 (1925). *The Panchatantra*. Chicago: University of Chicago Press.
Sanford, David Theron.
1974. Early temples bearing Ramayana relief cycles in the Chola area: A comparative study. Ph.D. diss., University of California, Los Angeles.
Sarma, C. R.
1973. *The Ramayana in Telugu and Tamil: A Comparative Study*. Madras: Lakshminarayana Granthamala.
Sarma, M. N.
1985. *Tolu Bommalata: The Shadow Puppet Theatre of Andhra Pradesh*. New Delhi: Sangeet Natak Akademi.
Seely, Clinton.
1991. The Raja's new clothes: Redressing Rāvaṇa in *Meghanādavadha Kāvya*. In Paula Richman, ed., *Many Rāmāyaṇas: The Diversity of a Narrative Tradition in South Asia*, pp. 137–55. Berkeley: University of California Press.
Seltmann, Friedrich.
1986. *Schattenspiel in Kerala*. Wiesbaden: Franz Steiner.
Sen, D. C.
1920. *The Bengali Ramayanas*. Calcutta: Calcutta University.
Shulman, David.
1979. Divine order and divine evil in the Tamil tale of Rāma. *Journal of Asian Studies* 38:651–69.
1980. *Tamil Temple Myths*. Princeton: Princeton University Press.
1985. *The King and the Clown in South Indian Myth and Poetry*. Princeton: Princeton University Press.
1987. The anthropology of the avatar in Kampaṉ's *Irāmāvatāram*. In S. Shaked, D. Shulman, and G. G. Stroumsa, eds., *Gilgul, Essays on Transformation, Revolution, and Permanence in the History of Religions*, pp. 270–87. Leiden: E. J. Brill.
1991a. Fire and flood: The testing of Sītā in Kampaṉ's *Irāmāvatāram*. In Paula Richman, ed., *Many Rāmāyaṇas: The Diversity of a

Narrative Tradition in South Asia, pp. 89–113. Berkeley: University of California Press.

1991b. Towards a historical poetics of the Sanskrit epics. *International Folklore Review*, 9–17.

1993. From author to non-author in Tamil literary legend. *Journal of the Institute of Asian Studies* 10,2:1–23.

Singaravelu, S.

1968. A comparative study of the story of Rama in south India and south-east Asia. In S. Thani Nayagam, ed., *Proceedings of the First International Conference-Seminar of Tamil Studies, Kuala Lumpur*, vol. 1, pp. 89–140. Kuala Lumpur: International Association of Tamil Research.

Smith, J. D.

1991. *The Epic of Pābūjī: A Study, Transcription and Translation.* Cambridge: Cambridge University Press.

Smith, W. L.

1988. *Rāmāyaṇa Traditions in Eastern India.* Stockholm Studies in Indian Languages and Culture, no. 2. Stockholm: Department of Indology, University of Stockholm.

South Indian Inscriptions.

1890. Vol. 1. Madras: Government Press.

1929. Vol. 3. Madras: Government Press.

Srinivasan, S. A.

1984. *Studies in the Rāma Story.* 2 vols. Alt- und Neu-Indische Studien, Universität Hamburg, no. 25. Wiesbaden: Franz Steiner.

Stache-Rosen, V.

1976. On the shadow-theatre in India. In *German Scholars on India*, vol. 2., pp. 276–85. Cultural Department of the Embassy of the Federal Republic of Germany. Bombay: Nachiketa Publications.

1984. Story-telling in Pinguli paintings. *Artibus Asiae* 45,4:253–86.

Stein, Burton.

1994 (1980). *Peasant State and Society in Medieval South India.* Delhi: Oxford University Press.

Subrahmanyam, Sanjay.

1989. *Political Economy of Commerce, South India 1500–1650.* Cambridge: Cambridge University Press.

Sutherland, Sally J.

1989. Sītā and Draupadī: Aggressive behavior and female role-models in the Sanskrit epics. *Journal of the American Oriental Society* 109,1:63–79.

Sweeney, Amin P. L.

1972. *The Ramayana and the Malay Shadow-Play.* Kuala Lumpur: National University of Malaysia Press.

Thangavelu, Kirtana.

1992. Picture story-telling. Manuscript.

Trawick, Margaret.

1988. Spirits and voices in Tamil songs. *American Ethnologist* 15, 2:193–215.

1990. *Notes on Love in a Tamil Family.* Berkeley: University of California Press.

UCLA Museum of Cultural History.

1976. *Asian Puppets, Wall of the World.* Los Angeles: University of California, Los Angeles.

Vedachalam Pillai, Swami (Maṟaimalai Aṭikaḷ).

1939. *Ancient and Modern Tamil Poets.* Pallavaram: T. M. Press.

Venu, G.

1981. Tolpava koothu. *Quarterly Journal of the National Centre for the Performing Arts* 10,4:25–36.

1990. *Tolpava Koothu: Shadow Puppets of Kerala.* New Delhi: Sangeet Natak Akademi.

Venugopal, S.

1993. Ramayana episodes in south Indian folk-literature. In K. S. Singh and B. Datta, eds. *Rama-Katha in Tribal and Folk Traditions of India.* Calcutta: Seagull Books.

Volosinov, V. N.

1978 (1929). Reported speech. In Ladislav Matejka and Krystyna Pomorska, eds., *Readings in Russian Poetics: Formalist and Structuralist Views,* pp. 149–75. Ann Arbor: Michigan Slavic Publications, no. 8. University of Michigan.

Washbrook, David.

1989. Caste, class and dominance in modern Tamil Nadu: Non-Brahminism, Dravidianism, and Tamil Nationalism. In F. R. Frankel and M. S. A. Rao, eds., *Dominance and State Power in Modern India,* vol. 1, pp. 204–65. Delhi: Oxford University Press.

Whaling, Frank.

1980. *The Rise of the Religious Significance of Rāma.* New Delhi: Motilal Banarsidass.

Zieseniss, Alexander.

1963. Translated by P. W. Burch. *The Rama Saga in Malaysia, Its Origin and Development.* Singapore: Malaysian Sociological Research Institute.

Zurbuchen, Mary Sabina.

1987. *The Language of Balinese Shadow Theater.* Princeton: Princeton University Press.

Zvelebil, Kamil.

1970. From proto-South Dravidian to Malayalam. *Archiv Orientalni* 38,1:45–67.

1973a. *The Poets of Powers.* London: Rider.

1973b. *The Smile of Murugan.* Leiden: E. J. Brill.

Works in Tamil, Malayalam, and Hindi

Aṇṇāturai, C. N.
1961. *Kamparacam*. Madras: Tuyamalar Patippakam.
Appucuvāmi Aiyar, Pe. Na.
1942. Ćūrpaṇakai makaṉ. In Raghava Aiyangar, ed., *Āṟupatāṇṭu Niṟaivu viḻāmālai*, 161–65. Madras: n.p.
Aruṇācala Kavirāyar.
1844. *Rāma Nāṭakam*. Madras: n.p.
Bulcke, Camille.
1962. *Rāmakathā: Utpatti aur Vikās*. Prayāg: Pariṣad Prakāśan. (In Hindi.)
Cārma, Ne. Ra. Cuppiramaṇiya.
1922. *Kampar Carittiram*. Maturai: Minalocani Press.
Caṭācivaṉ, Mu.
1969. *Kampar Tārum Irāmaṉ Aruṭ Celvam (Dictionary of Epithets and Names of Śrī Rāma as found in Kamparāmāyaṇam)*. Madras: Pari Nilayam.
Cēturāmaṉ, N.
1985. Irāmar kōyilkaḷum kalveṭṭucceytikaḷum. In S. V. Subramaniam and G. Rajendran, eds., *Heritage of the Tamils: Temple Arts*, pp. 51–80. Madras: International Institute of Tamil Studies.
Chandrasekharan, T., ed.
1960. *Uttara-Rāmāyaṇa-Nāṭakam*. Madras Oriental Manuscript Series no. 69. Madras: Government of Madras.
Civakāmi, C. Ci.
1978. *Kampaṉ Āyvataṅkaḷ*. International Institute of Tamil Studies. Madras: Tamil Patikkam.
Collamutam (Kuṉṟakkuṭi Aṭikaḷār).
1966. *Kampaṉ Vēṇṭāmā?* Madras: Tamil Paṇṇai.
Hikosaka, Shu, and John Samuel.
1990. *A Descriptive Catalogue of Palm-Leaf Manuscripts in Tamil*. Vol. 1, pt. 1. Madras: Institute of Asian Studies.
Kampaṉ.
1861. *Balakandam of Camban's Ramayana*. Edited by S. Krishnaswamy Moodeliar. Madras: Adelphi Press.
1926–71. *Śrī Kamparāmāyaṇam*. Commentary by Vai Mu. Kōpālakiruṣṇamācāriyar. 6 vols. Madras: Kuvai.
1942–68. *Kamparāmāyaṇam*. 7 vols. Āḻvār Tirunakari: Ve. Na. Śrīnivācayyaṅkar.
1955–70. *Irāmāyaṇam*. 6 vols. Aṇṇāmalai: Aṇṇāmalai University.
1976. *Kamparāmāyaṇam*. Madras: Kampaṉ Kaḻakam.
Karumaṅgurukkaḷ, K. V.
1937. *Navīṉa Rāmāyaṇam*. Ovalakōṭṭu: Śrīrāmakṛṣṇōdayar Press.

Krishnan Kutty Pulavar, K. L.

1983.   *Ayodhyakanda of Tolpava Koothu.* New Delhi: Sangeet Natak Akademi.

1987.   *Tōlpāvakūttu: Kēralattinṟe Pārampryanilal Nāṭakasaili: Bālakāṇḍam.* Koonathara (India): the author.

Maturai Palkalai Kaḷakam.

1969.   *Kamparāmāyaṇam-Taṉi Vaiṇava Kāppiyamā?* Maturai: Maturai Palkalai Kaḷakam.

Meenakshisundaram Pillai, T. P.

1973.   *Tamiḻum Piṟa Paṇpāṭum.* Madras: New Century Book House.

Naccumuṟi.

1952.   *Kampaṉ Keṭuttā Kāviyum?* Madras: Kaṉṉi Veliyīṭu.

Narayana Pillai, P. K.

1970.   *Rāma Katha Pāṭṭu.* Kottayam: National Book Stall.

Naṭarācaṉ, Vai. T.

1987.   *Ayōtti Katai.* Nākarkōvil: Irājecvari.

Nayar, S. K., trans.

1967.   *Kamparāmāyaṇam* (Malayalam). Vol 1, *Bāla Kāṇḍam.* Madras: Madras University.

Parijātam, S.

1987.   Tamiḻ Irāmāyaṇa nūlkaḷ: Tiraṉāyvu. Ph.D. diss., Madurai-Kamaraj University, Madurai.

Periyār, I. Vē. Ra.

1972a (1930).   *Irāmāyaṇappāttiraṅkaḷ.* Tirucci: Periyār Cuyamariyātai Piracāra Niruvaṉam.

1972b (1964).   *Irāmāyaṇa Kuṟippukaḷ.* Tirucci: Periyār Cuyamariyātai Piracāra Niruvaṉam.

Rācamāṇikkam, M., ed.

1965.   *Kamparāmāyaṇam, Kiṭkinta Kāṇṭam.* Tirunelveli: South India Saiva Siddhanta Society.

Rākava Aiyaṅkār, M.

1964.   Irāmāyaṇamum Tamiḻ vaḷakkukaḷum. In Rākava Aiyaṅkār, ed., *Ārāycci Tokuti.* Madras: Pari Nilayam.

Rāmacuvāmi, M.

1978.   Tamiḻaka tōlpāvaniḷal kūttu. Ph.D. diss., Madurai-Kamaraj University, Madurai.

Rāmacuvāmi Pulavar, S. A.

1956.   *Kamparāmāyaṇa Vacaṉam.* 2 vols. Tirunelveli: South India Saiva Siddhanta Society.

Rāmaṉ Piḷḷai, A.

1924.   *Kamparāmāyaṇa Caritam.* Calicut: n.p.

Raventiraṉ, Ce.

1982.   Kiruṣṇaṉ Kuṭṭi Pulavar. *Yātra* 37:8–20.

Śivasaṅkara Piḷḷai, P. K., ed.

1970.   *Kuñcaṉṉampiyārute Thuḷḷalkathakaḷ.* Kottayam: National Book Stall.

Tēcikavināyakam Piḷḷai, Ci.
1953. *Kaviccakkaravartti Kampaṉ*. Madras: Pari Nilayam.
Turaicāmipiḷḷai, Cu.
1949. *Tamiḻ Nāvalar Caritai*. Madras: South India Saiva Siddhantha Society.
Vaiyāpuri Piḷḷai, S.
1962 (1955). *Kampaṉ Kāviyam*. Madras: Tamil Puttakālayam.
Vēṅkaṭarāma Ceṭṭiyār, Ce.
1986. *Uttara Kāṇṭam*. 2 vols. Aṇṇāmalai: Aṇṇāmalai University Press.
Vīracāmi Ceṭṭiyār, V.
1891 (1876). *Vinōtaracamañcari*. Madras: K. R. Press.

Index

accommodation 45–54, 92–3, 224; in the "Song of the Drama-House" 40–5
Achuyta Menon, C. 193
Agni (god) 218, 228
Anasūyā 198–9
Andhra Pradesh, puppet plays of 2, 35, 36, 37, 71, 235
Aṅgada (character) 87, 91, 99, 115, 116, 208, 229, 231
Annamalai Pulavar 195–6
Annaturai, C. N. 29
anti-Brahmin dramas 23
Arjuna 125
Arunachalam, M. 93
Atikāyaṉ (character) 132
Atri (sage) 198, 199
audience, absent 9–15, 191–2, 224
Auvaiyār 113, 129
avatar 54
Ayodhya Book 23–4, 96, 130, 136

Bakhtin, M. M. 178, 180, 181
balance, in folk Rāmāyaṇas 78, 224
Balinese shadow puppetry 10
Beautiful Book 25
"benefit of the text" (*nūl payaṉ*) 51–2
Bhagavati (goddess) 1, 4, 6, 8, 134; blessings from 15, 16; and Cinna Tampi 50; oracle-priest of 234; as ritual audience 12; temple 4, 5–6
bhakti and folk religion 39, 51–4, 78, 94, 224; and Rāma's killing of Vāli 89, 91, 92, 94; Śaiva poems 29
Bharata (character) 218, 219, 221–3, 226
Bhūmi Dēvi 119
Birth Book 23, 73, 96, 106, 129, 136
Brahmā (god) 116, 120, 123, 125, 126, 130, 131, 132, 173–4
Brahmin puppets (*paṭṭa pāva*) 5, 7, 46–7, 196–7, 213
Brahmins: and Cinna Tampi 46, 49; and *Kamparāmāyaṇam* 49

Cākkyār Kūthu 6
Caṭaiyappaṉ 35, 103–4, 106
Chidambaram Mudaliar, T. K. 93
Chola empire 1, 27–8, 103; and the Rāma cult 40
Cinna Tampi 45–6, 49–51, 97
comedy, in the Kerala puppet play 235, 236
commentaries: oral 1, 19, 21, 95, 127–33, 180, 185–6, 223, 224; printed 52
conversations, created by puppeteers 134, 178–93
Cosmic Elephants 116, 130, 131
Cousins, J. H. 193
cultural meaning, and performance 11

Dakṣa 124, 200
Daśagrīva (character) 130

Daśaratha (character) 108, 218–19, 226
dialogue, puppeteers' use of 134, 179–82, 186–90
Doniger, Wendy 53
drama-house. See *kūttu māṭam*
Dravidian movement 28–9; anti-Rāma campaign 90

family sponsorship 10, 15–16, 17
Flueckiger, Joyce 11
Foley, John Miles 14–15, 128, 153
folk Rāmāyaṇas 14, 78, 135, 181
folk religion, and bhakti 39, 51–4, 78, 94, 224
Forest Book 24, 73, 79

Gaṇeśa puppet 5, 7, 23, 47
Godavari River 59, 60–1, 182
GoldbergBelle, Jonathan 36, 235
Goldman, Bob 78
grief, in the Kerala puppet play 235–6

Handelman, D. 12, 235
Hanumān (character) 82, 87, 131, 187–8, 207; and Bharata 221, 222; and the death of Indrajit 155–6, 162–3, 167; and the defeat of Rāvaṇa 114–15, 116, 122, 126, 131; finding of Sītā 98, 99, 101; journey to the Medicine Mountain 171–5, 202, 233–4; and Sītā's return to Ayodhya 213–14, 220–1; and Sītā's trial by fire 227;
Hart, George 54
Hinduism, Four Goals of 52
Hyder Ali 32
Hymes, Dell 10

Indra (god) 103, 116–20, 126, 130, 131, 132, 156–7, 169–70, 197–201, 207; as narrator 179
Indrajit (character) 4, 25, 187–8, 233; death of 134–5, 149–78, 196–7, 202–5, 234, 236

Jain texts, and Rāma's killing of Vāli 89
Jakobson, R. 9
Jāmbūvan̲ (character) 158–9, 185, 208–9, 226, 228–9, 236; and Hanumān's journey to the Medicine Mountain 170–5, 233–4; and Rāma's return to Ayodhya 219–20
Javanese shadow puppetry 10, 11, 12

Kalaikottu Muni 108
kāma (love), and Rāma's meeting with Śūrpaṇakhā 67–8, 77–8
Kampan̲ 1, 2, 23; and the death of Sambukumāran̲ 72; dialogue verses 181–2; and the killing of Vāli 89, 91, 93; legends about 47–51, 104–9; and the puppeteers' oral commentary 132–3; and Rāma's meeting with Śūrpaṇakhā 71, 73, 75, 76, 77; Rāmāyaṇa 26–30, 106–9;
Kamparāmāyaṇam 1, 27–30; and the Chola period 40; and Cinna Tampi 46; in Kerala 30–1, 34–5; and the Kerala puppet play 223–34, 238–9; and the killing of Vāli 93; and the puppeteers 37–8, 132; and the Uttara Kāṇḍa 130
Kapur, Anuradha 15
Karnataka, puppet plays of 2, 35, 36, 37, 71, 235
kathā 13
Kathakaḷi plays 6, 96
Keeler, Ward, *Javanese Shadow Plays, Javanese Selves* 11, 12
Kerala 3; and the *Kamparāmāyaṇam* 30–1, 34–5, 54, 71; Palghat 1, 30–7, 46; puppets 36–7; shadow puppetry 1, 2, 10–12, 14, 192
Kiskindha Book 25, 79
Krishnan Kutty, K. L. 2–3, 4–5, 6, 7, 23, 37, 135–7
Kubera 116, 131
Kumbhakarṇa (character) 132, 137–45, 148–9, 182, 185, 229
kūttu māṭam (drama house) 3–5, 37; at Elakatu 137; at Kerala 11; at Mannur 80–2; at Palghat 97; at Suhavaram 3–9

Lakṣmaṇa (character) 5, 22, 23, 24, 25, 87; and the coronation of Vibhīṣaṇa 213; and the death of Indrajit 135, 150–7, 159, 165–6, 167, 168–9, 177, 201–2; and the defeat of Rāvaṇa 110, 113, 115, 118, 123–4, 125; and Indrajit's snake-weapon 230–1; and

the killing of Vāli 86, 89; killing of Sambukumāraṉ 61–2, 71–3, 74, 88; mutilation of Śūrpaṇakhā 70–1, 73, 88
Laksmana Pulavar 136
Lakṣmī (goddess) 198, 199
Lanka, defeat of 4, 99, 100, 131
legends: of Kampaṉ 47–51; of Madhu and Kaitabha 132; of Mārkaṇḍeya 145–8, 185; of the moon 124, 198–201
Lord, Albert 182

Mahābali, King 102, 140, 141–3
Mahābhārata 89, 93
Maharashtra 2
Mahōdara (character) 205–6
Mair, Victor 35–6
Malayalam language 3, 33–4, 128, 129
Malayali puppeteers 80
Māliyavāṉ (character) 99, 110, 120–7, 131
Maṇḍōdari (character) 134, 152, 213, 236
Mannur, drama-house at 80–2
Marathas 35–6
Mārīca (character) 126
Mārkaṇḍeya, legend of 145–8, 185
Menon, Achyuta 90
Mills, Margaret 17
"mirror events" 12
Mutaliyars 35, 195

Naicker, E. V. Ramaswami 29, 90
Nambiyar, Kuncan 35, 37
Nandi 116–17, 131
Nārada (sage) 14, 118, 198, 199
Narayan, Kirin 17
Narayan, R. K. 23
Nārāyaṇa (god) 124, 140, 141
narrators, gods as 179
nāṭakam (dance) 15, 223
Nayar, Narayana 3, 5
Nayar, Sankara 3

oral commentary 1, 19, 21, 95, 127–33, 180, 185–6, 223, 224
oral literary formalism 9
oral performance, and audience 9, 10, 12–15
Orissa 2

Oṭṭakkūttaṉ 28, 35, 49, 72, 104, 105, 106; and the Uttara Kāṇḍa 130
Ōṭṭan Tuḷḷal 3, 4, 6

Palappuram 16, 194–6
Palghat 1, 30–7, 46, 54, 80
Pārvatī (goddess) 14, 141, 152, 198, 199
patronage 10, 12, 15–18, 136, 137, 191, 237, 238; and payment of performers 17–18
paṭṭa pāva (Brahmin puppets) 5, 7, 46–7, 196–7
performance studies 10
Pillai, Natesan 18, 98, 132, 186, 236
piramāṇam (explanation or rule) 129, 133, 184
pulavars (poet-scholars) 45
puppeteers 1–2; and "benefit of the text" (*nūl payaṉ*) 51–2; creating conversations 134, 178–93; dialogue 179–82, 186–90, 314; earnings 15; foreign tours 136; and the Kampaṉ text 37–8; lack of new 237–8; legendary first puppeteer (Cinna Tampi) 45–6, 49–51; Malayalis 80; Marathi-speaking 36, 37; memorizing verses 37–8, 80; oral commentary 21, 127–33, 223, 224; of Palappuram 195–6; publication of texts 136; sung verses 38; Tamil-speaking 1, 34, 37
puppets: Kerala 36–7; making 237
Purnalingam Pillai, M. S. 29

Rāma 1, 2, 5; anti-Rāma campaign 90; and bhakti 53; confession 88–94; coronation of 16, 24, 26, 194, 196–223, 224, 225–9; and the death of Indrajit 135, 168–70; killing of Rāvaṇa 22, 26, 27, 53, 73, 210–13; killing of Vāli 59, 82–94; marriage to Sītā 23, 225; meeting with Śūrpaṇakhā 38, 59, 60, 64–71, 73–8, 183–4; and Rāvaṇa's first defeat 99–127; rejection of Sītā 59, 88, 227–8; return to Ayodhya 194, 213–23; stories 3, 22–6; and the Uttara Kāṇḍa 130; war 229–32
Rāma-Viṣṇu (god) 78, 132
Rāmāyaṇa; Kampaṉ's 26–30, 106–9
Rāmāyaṇas, folk 14, 78, 135, 181
Rāmcaritmānas 12–13

Rām Līlā drama 13
Rao, V. Narayana 14
Rāvaṇa (character) 22, 24–5, 87; abduction of Sītā 24–5, 73, 83, 85, 114, 169–70; death 134, 194, 225; and the death of Indrajit 135, 138–49, 163, 196, 201–5, 236; first defeat 99–127; and the puppeteers' commentary 131; Rāma's killing of 22, 26, 27, 53, 73, 210–13; and the Uttara Kāṇḍa 130; War Council 95
referentiality, traditional 14, 128, 133

Sambukumāraṉ (character), death of 59, 60–75, 88
Sangam poems 28, 29
Sarasvatī (goddess) 198, 199
Seltmann, F. 2
shadow puppeteers. See puppeteers
Shulman, David 226
Singer, Milton 10
Sītā (character) 5, 14, 22, 98; and the death of Indrajit 205–6; and the defeat of Rāvaṇa 122, 123, 126–7, 135; and the fall of Lanka 100, 101, 131; Hanumān's finding of 98, 99; killing of fake 175–6; marriage of Rāma and 23, 225; Rāma's rejection of 59, 88, 213–18; Rāvaṇa's abduction of 24–5, 73, 74, 83, 85, 114, 118, 169–70; return to Ayodhya 219, 220–1; trial by fire 218, 225, 226–8
Śiva (god) 14, 110, 111–12, 124, 130, 131, 197–8; and the defeat of Rāvaṇa 117, 118, 125, 126; and Kampaṉ 50; and Kumbhakarṇa 144–5; legend of "Poison Throat" 141
"Song of the Drama-House" 7, 40–5, 46, 47, 51, 82, 178, 223, 233
Śrī Vaiṣṇavism 53–4
Sugrīva (character) 82, 83, 84, 85, 86–7, 88, 89, 91, 92, 99; and the death of Indrajit 167, 168; and the defeat of Rāvaṇa 114–15
Suhavaram village, Kerala 2–9
Śukra 141–2, 143
Śūrpaṇakhā (character) 5, 23, 24, 92, 224, 236; Lakṣmaṇa's mutilation of 70–1, 73, 88, 94; Rāma's meeting with 38, 59, 60, 64–71, 73–8, 183–4
Svaha (goddess) 199–200
Swami, Ramalinga 29
Sweeney, Amin 236

Tamil 3
Tamil Brahmins (Pattars) 33, 34; and Cinna Tampi 46, 47
Tamil folklore, balance in 78
Tamil language 18, 33–4; and oral commentary 128; and the puppeteers 1, 34, 37; Tamil-Malayalam patois 34, 128, 223
Tamil movement, and the *Kamparāmāyaṇam* 28–9
Tamil Nadu 2, 3, 35, 36, 37
Tamil Uttara Kāṇḍa 72
Tārā (character) 82
temple patronage 16–17
Tirunakari Alvar 30
tōl pāva kūttu ("leather puppet play") 2, 12, 35
"traditional referentiality" 14, 128, 133
Tulsīdās 12–13, 14, 92

umbrella holder (character) 157–9, 163–4, 188, 209–10, 232–3, 234, 235
Uttara Kāṇḍa 129–30, 131, 225, 226, 235

Vacantaṉ (character) 220, 228–9, 236
Vāli (character), Rāma's killing of 59, 82–94, 99
Vālmīki 22, 27 29, 27, 35, 60, 104, 235; and Rāma's coronation 226; and Rāma's killing of Vāli 89; *Rāmāyaṇa* 46; Uttara Kāṇḍa 72
Vāmana (character) 142–3
Vaṉṉi (character) 207
Varuṇa (character) 101–3, 105, 116
Vedavatī 100, 101, 130, 131
veḷiccappāṭu (oracle-priest) 234
Velli Tampiran 30
Vibhīṣaṇa (character) 98–9, 100, 101, 111–13, 114, 131, 132, 226; and the death of Indrajit 137–8, 150–5; and Rāma's return to Ayodhya 217, 219; and Rāvaṇa's death 211, 212–13; and Sītā's trial by fire 227
village committees 12
village sponsorship 16, 17

Viṣṇu (god) 78, 85, 87, 102, 110, 117, 120, 125, 132, 173, 234

War Book 25–6, 38, 95–7, 130, 131, 193, 235; death of Indrajit 134, 138–78; Rāvaṇa's first defeat 99–127
women's singing groups 11–12

Yama (king of the dead) 78, 148

Composition:	Braun-Brumfield
Text:	10/13 Galliard
Display:	Galliard
Printing and binding:	Braun-Brumfield